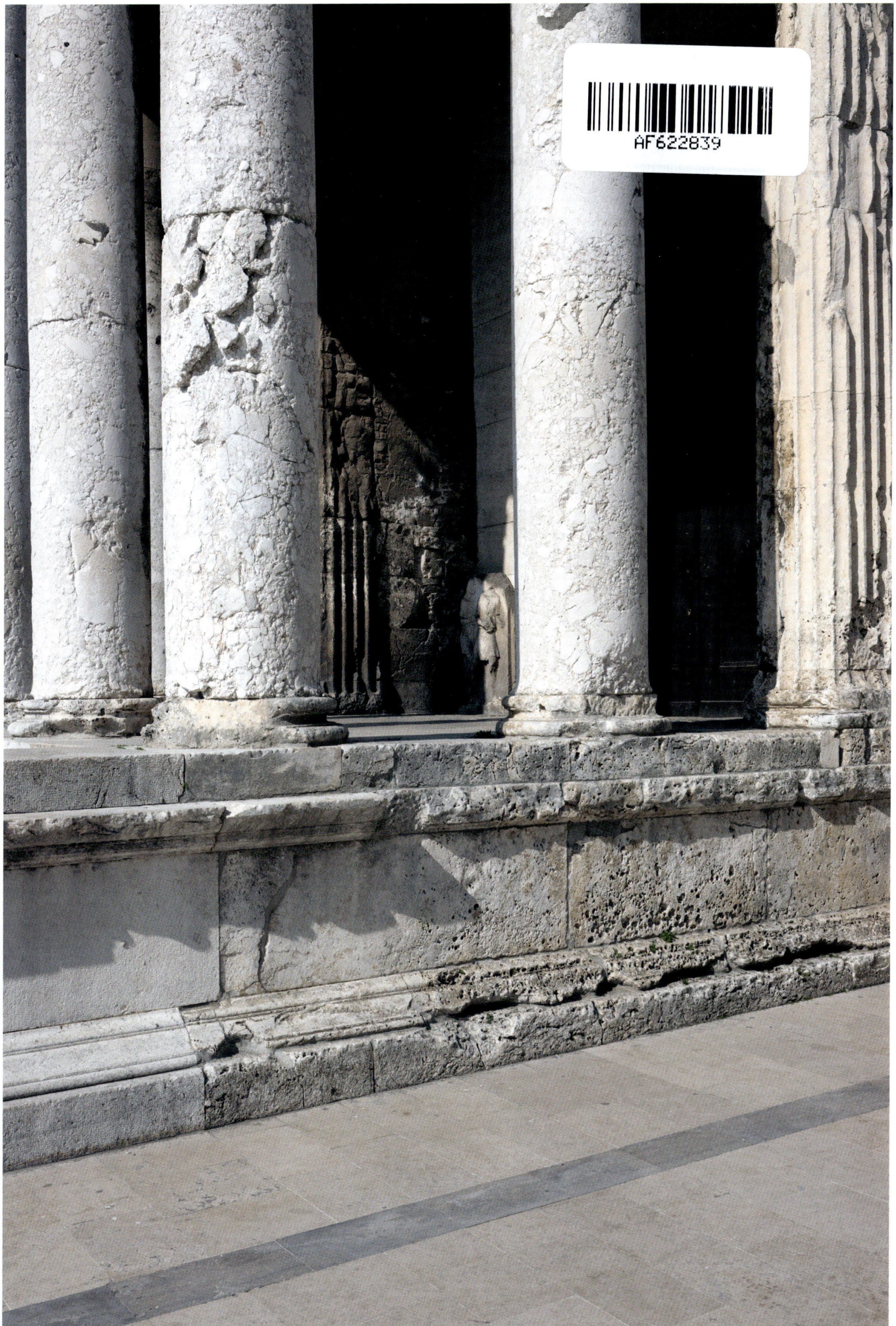

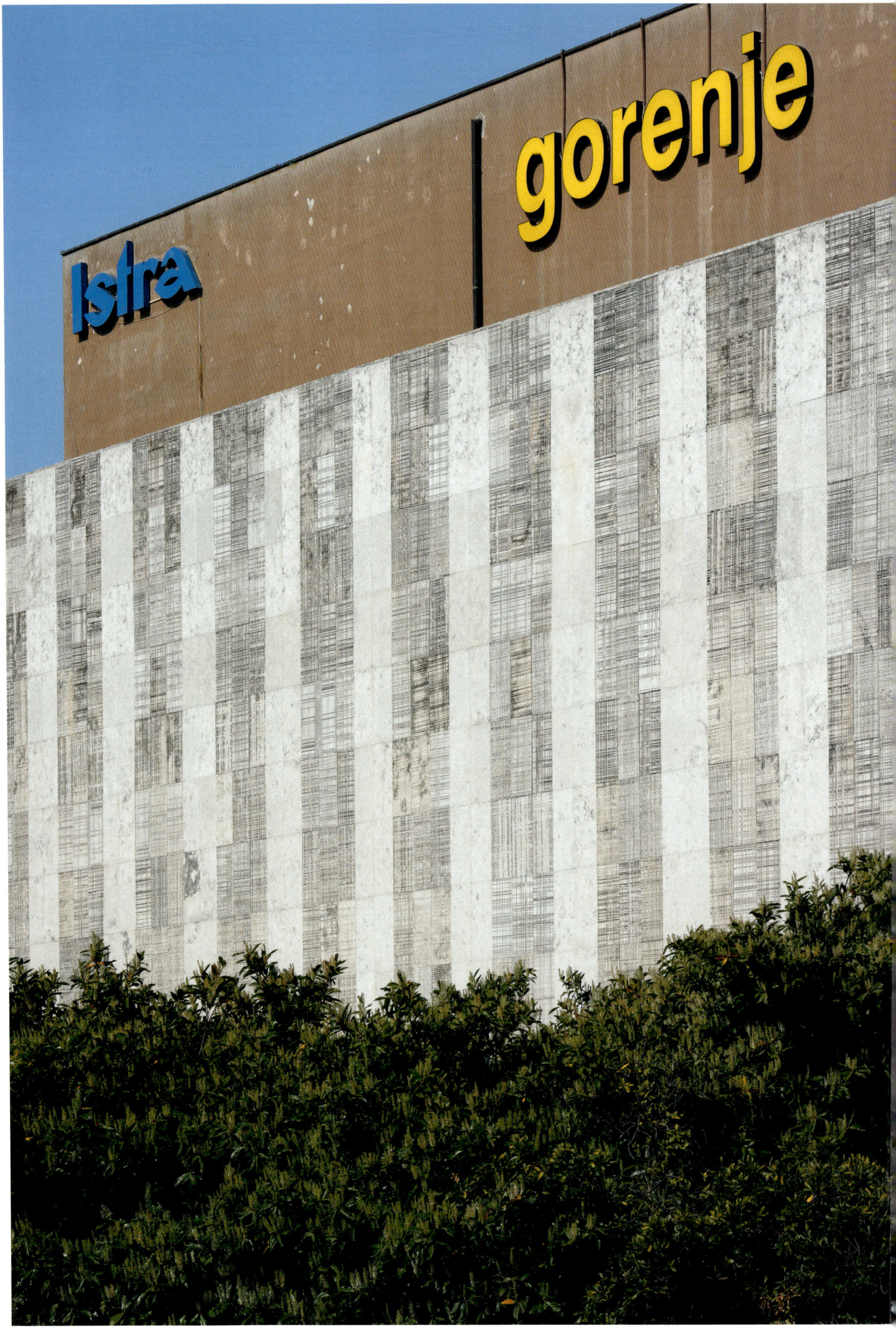
Istra
gorenje

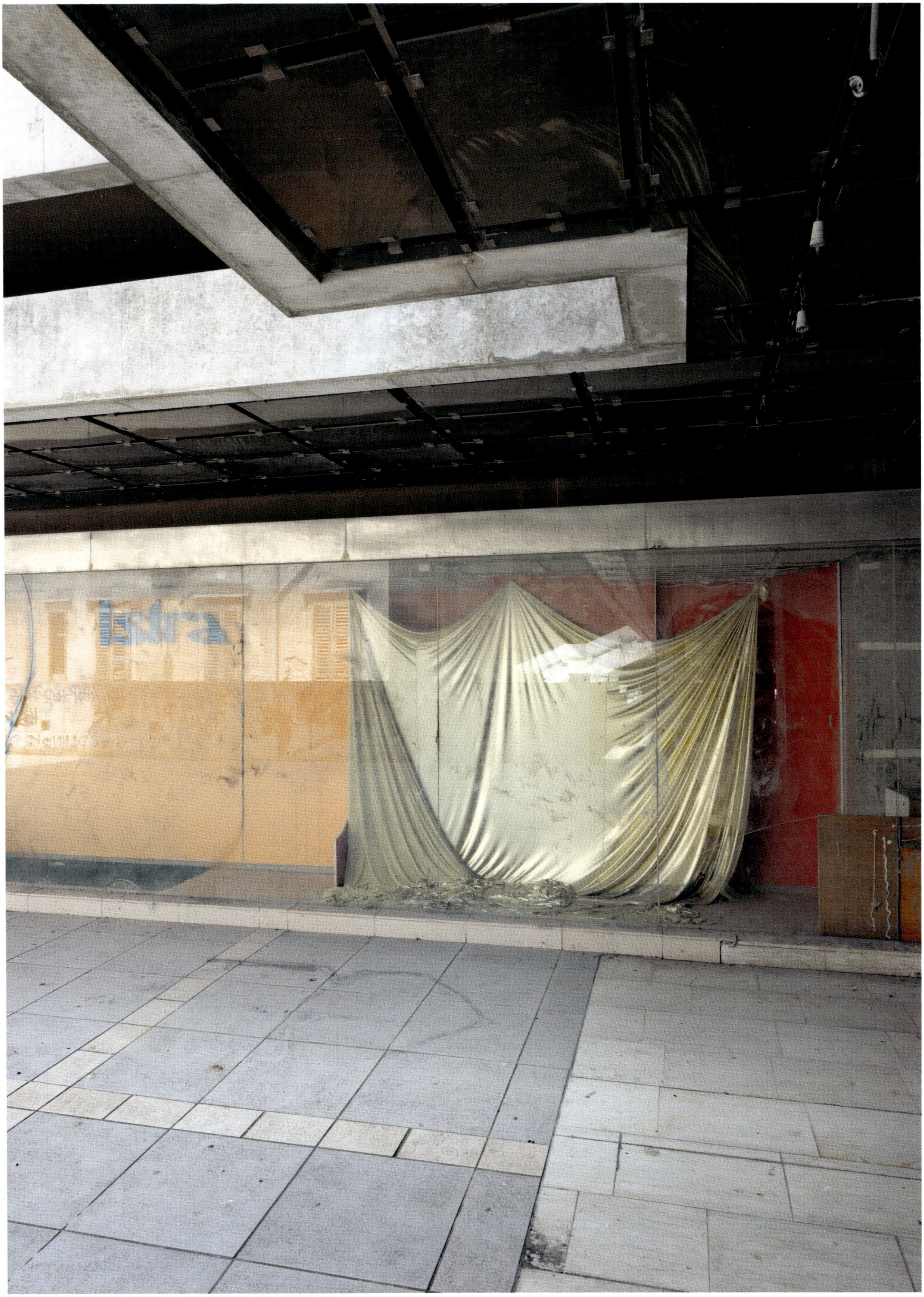
Istra

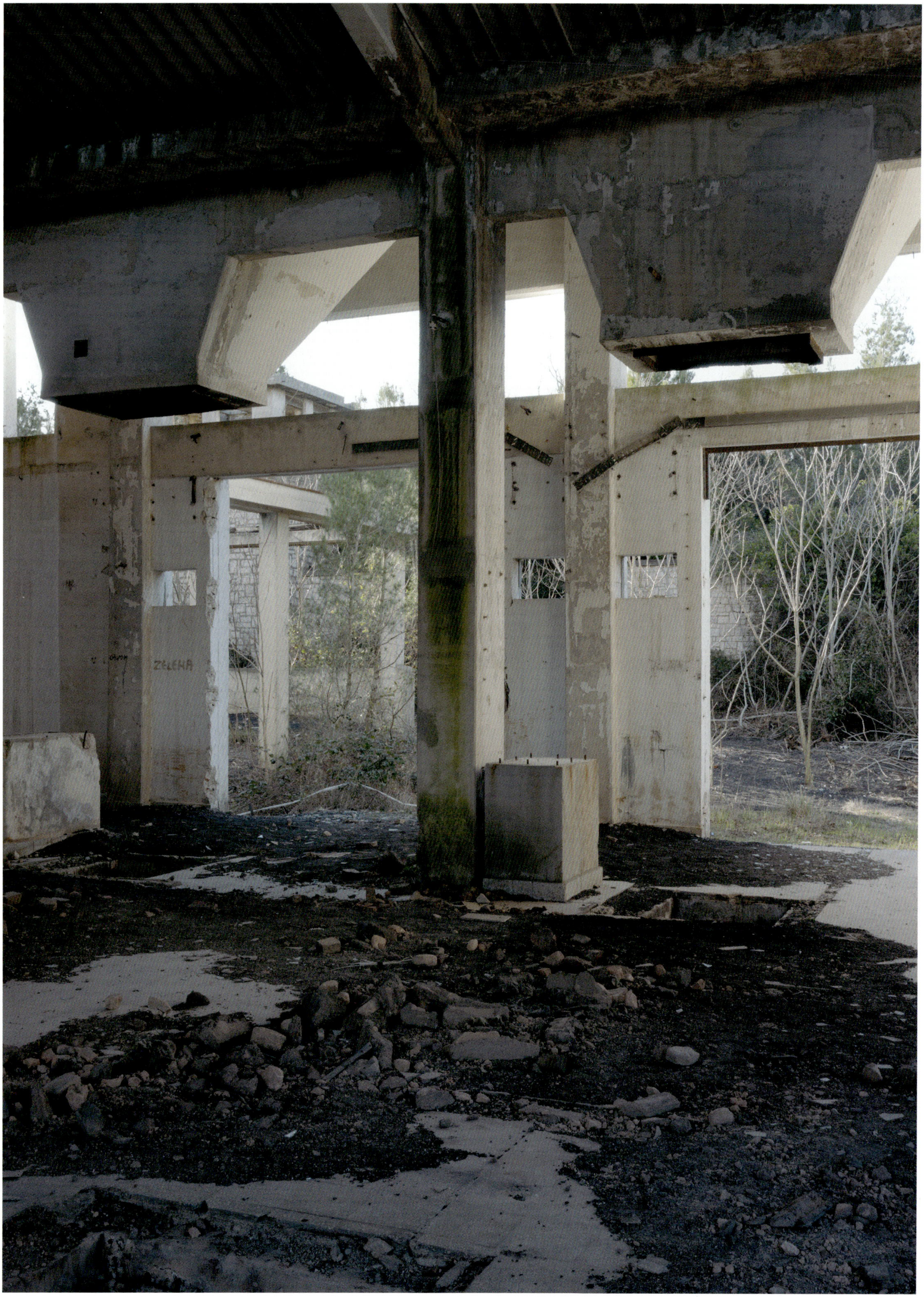
ZELENA

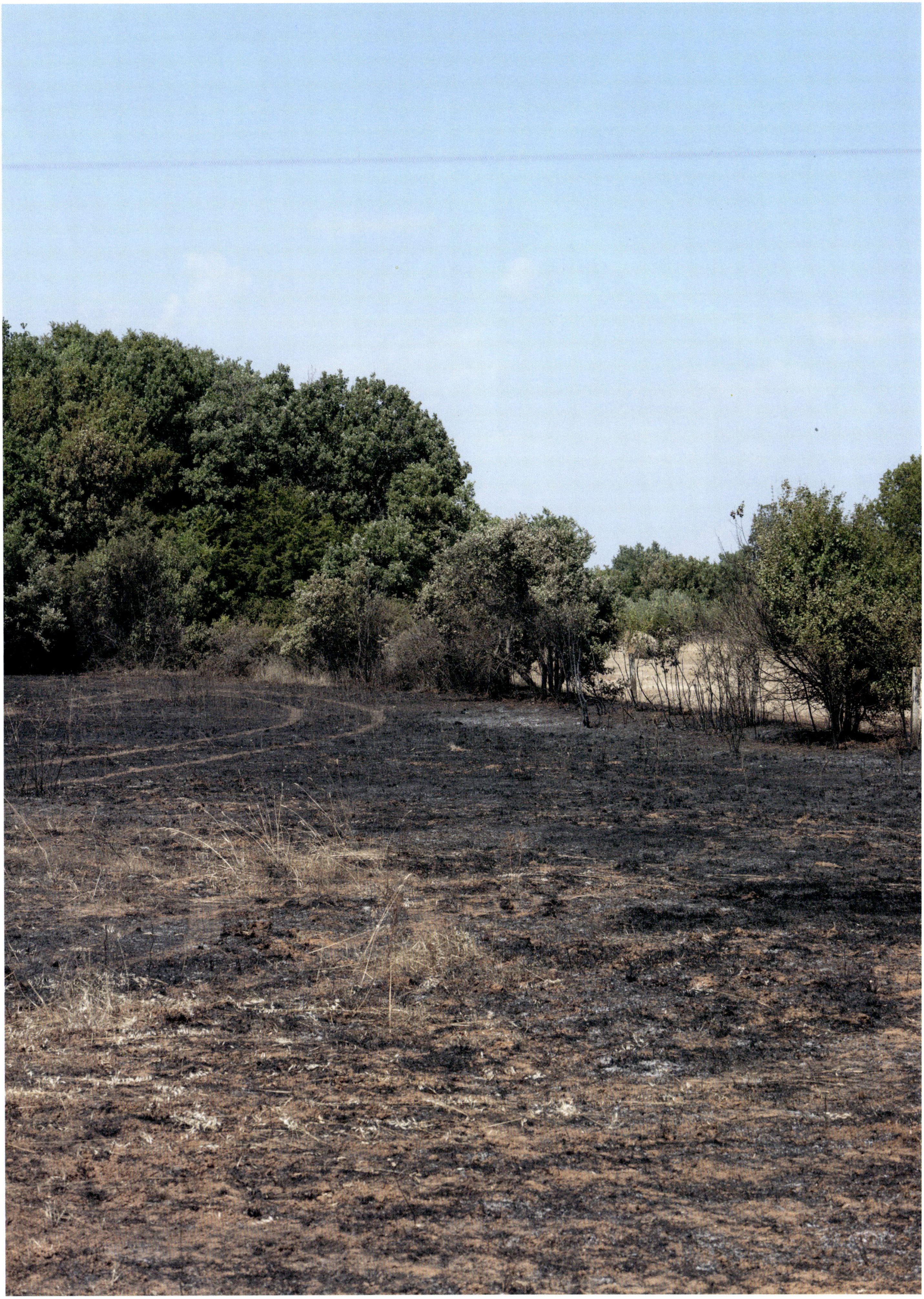

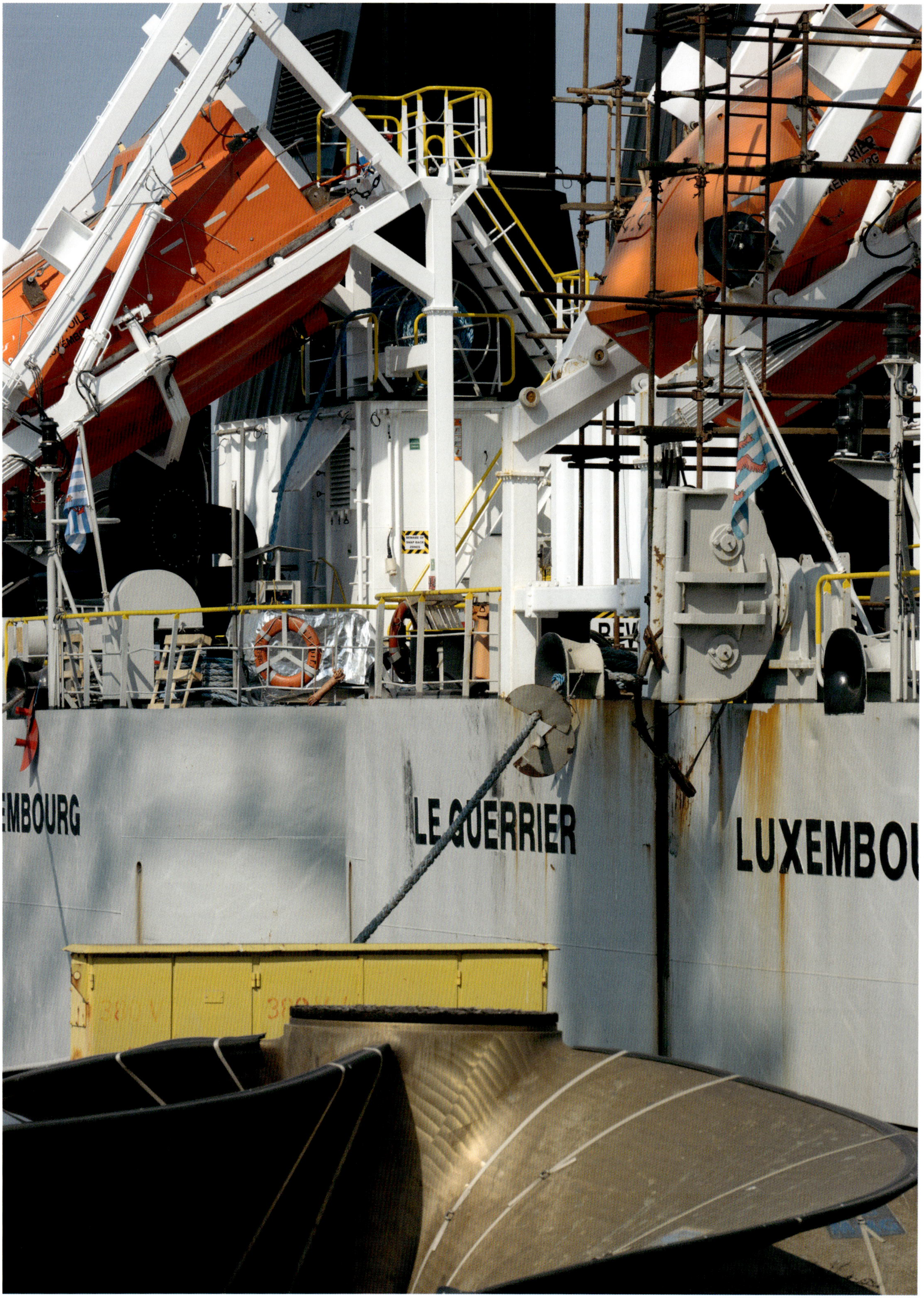
EMBOURG
LE GUERRIER
LUXEMBOU

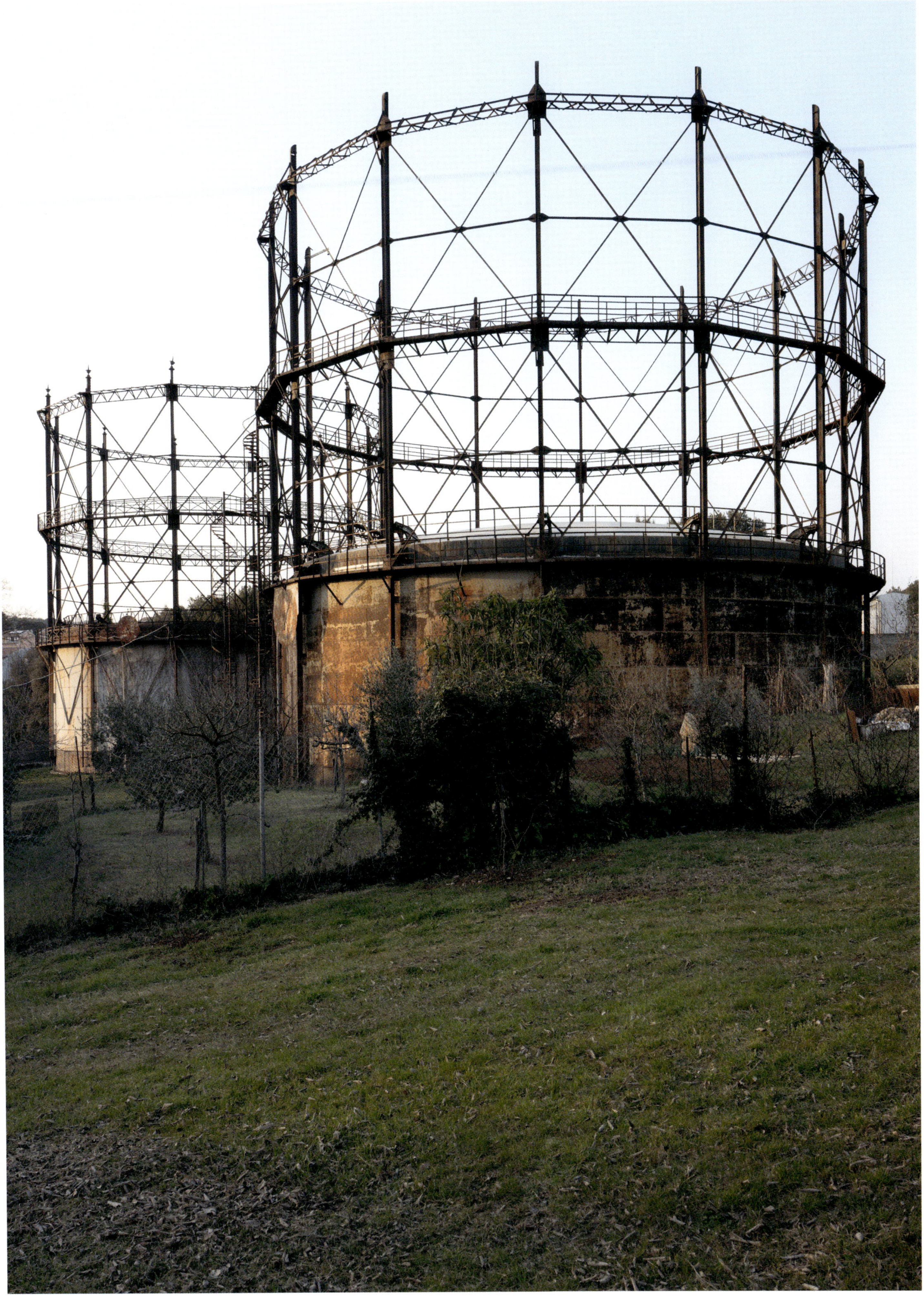

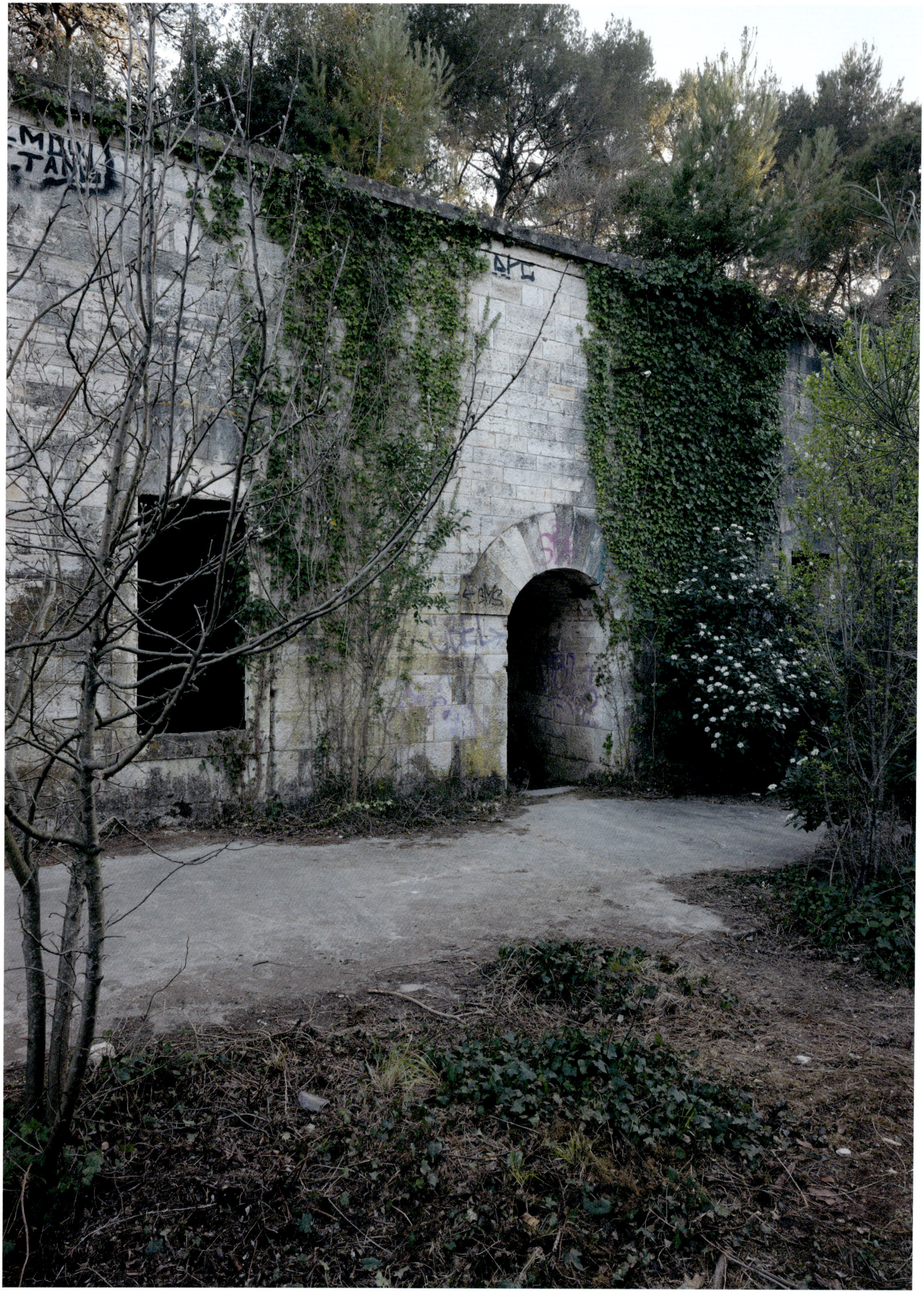

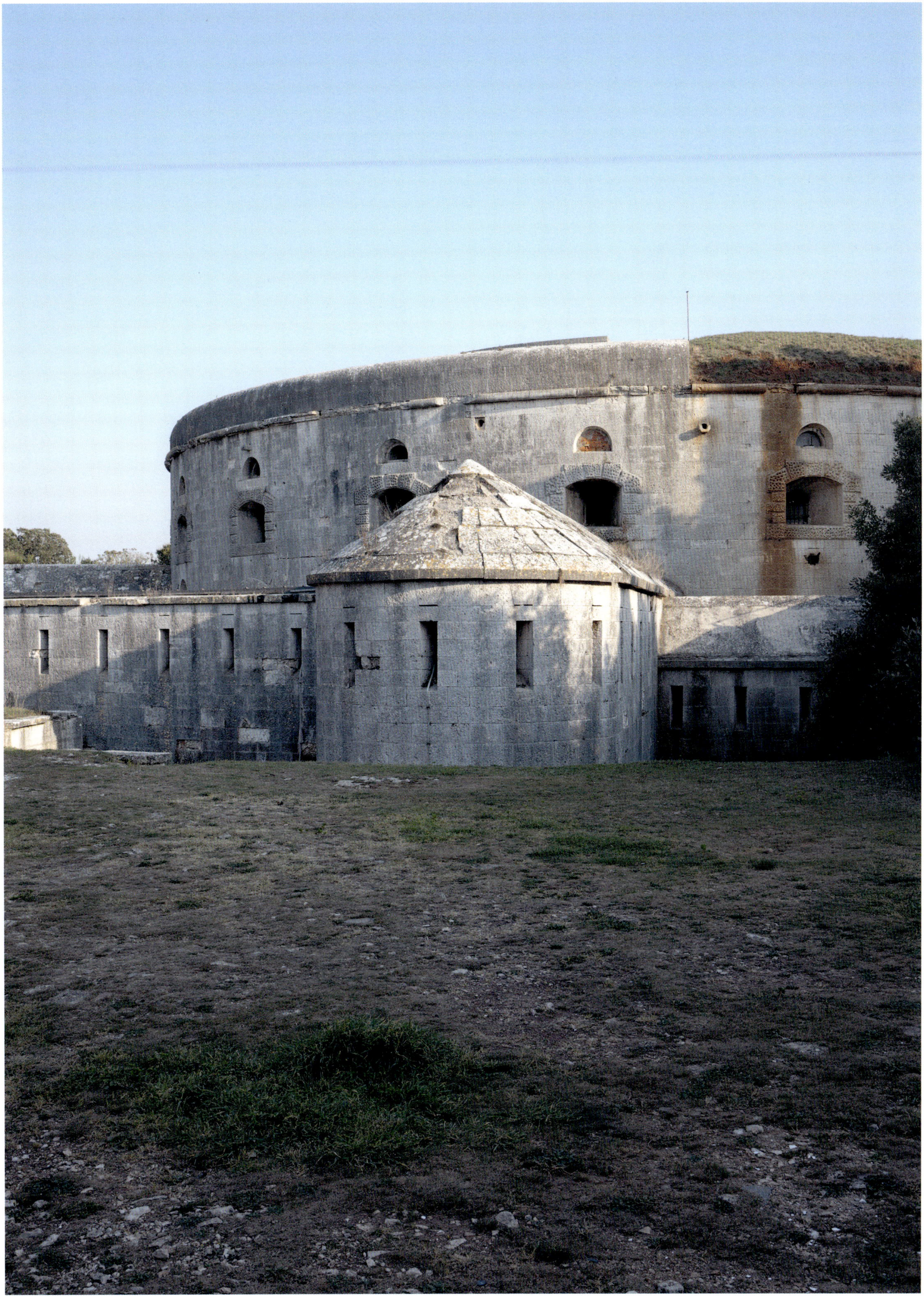

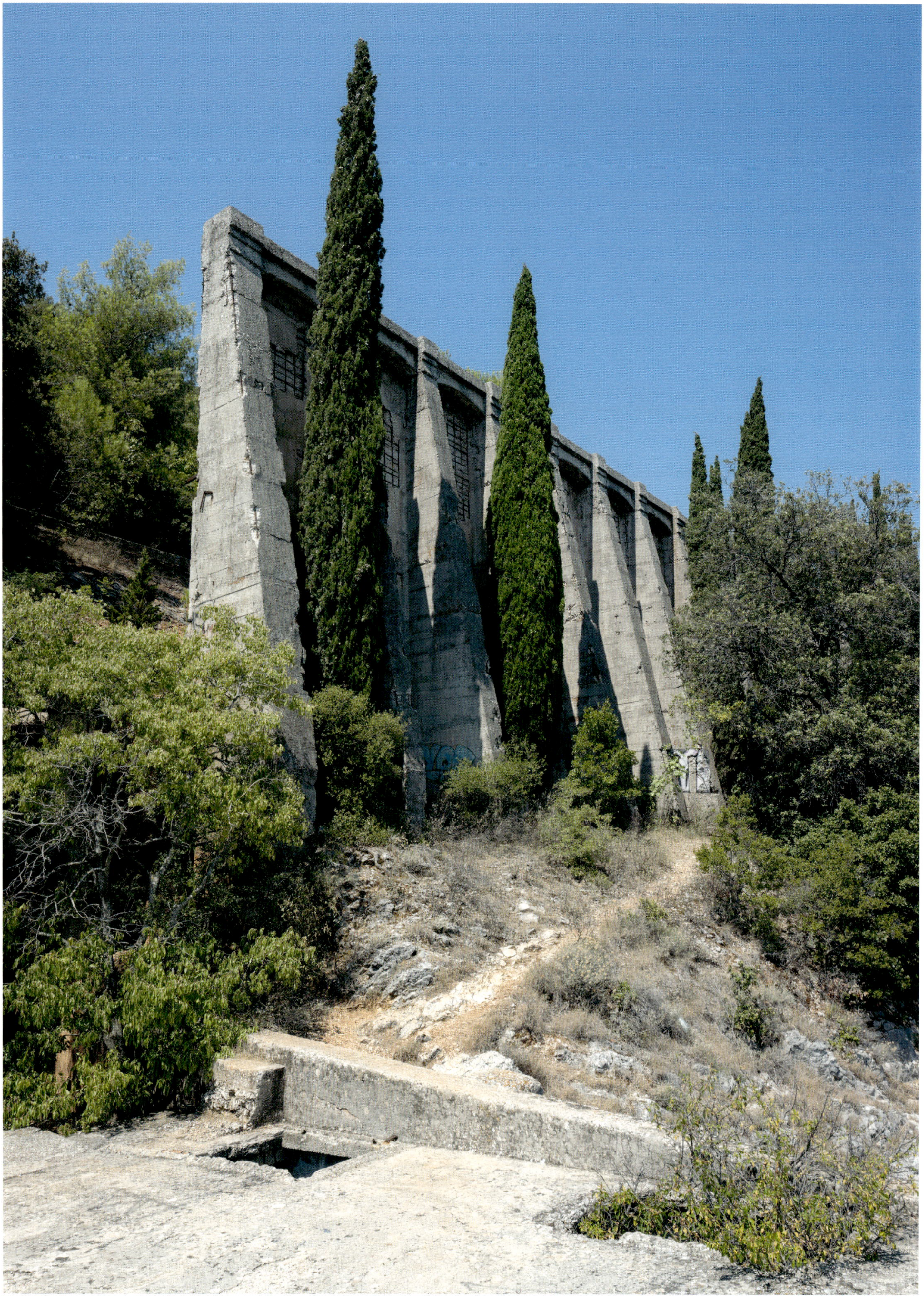

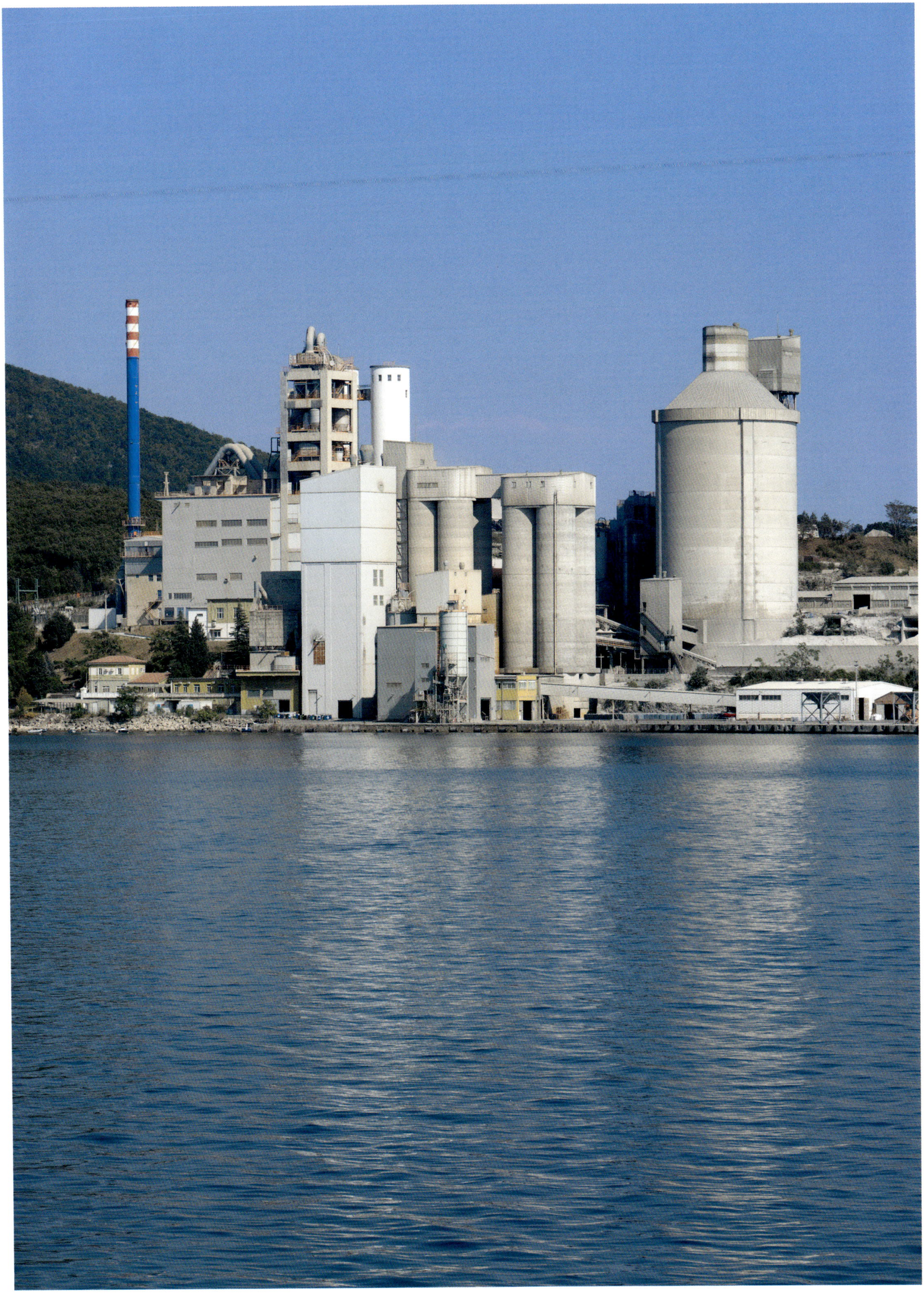

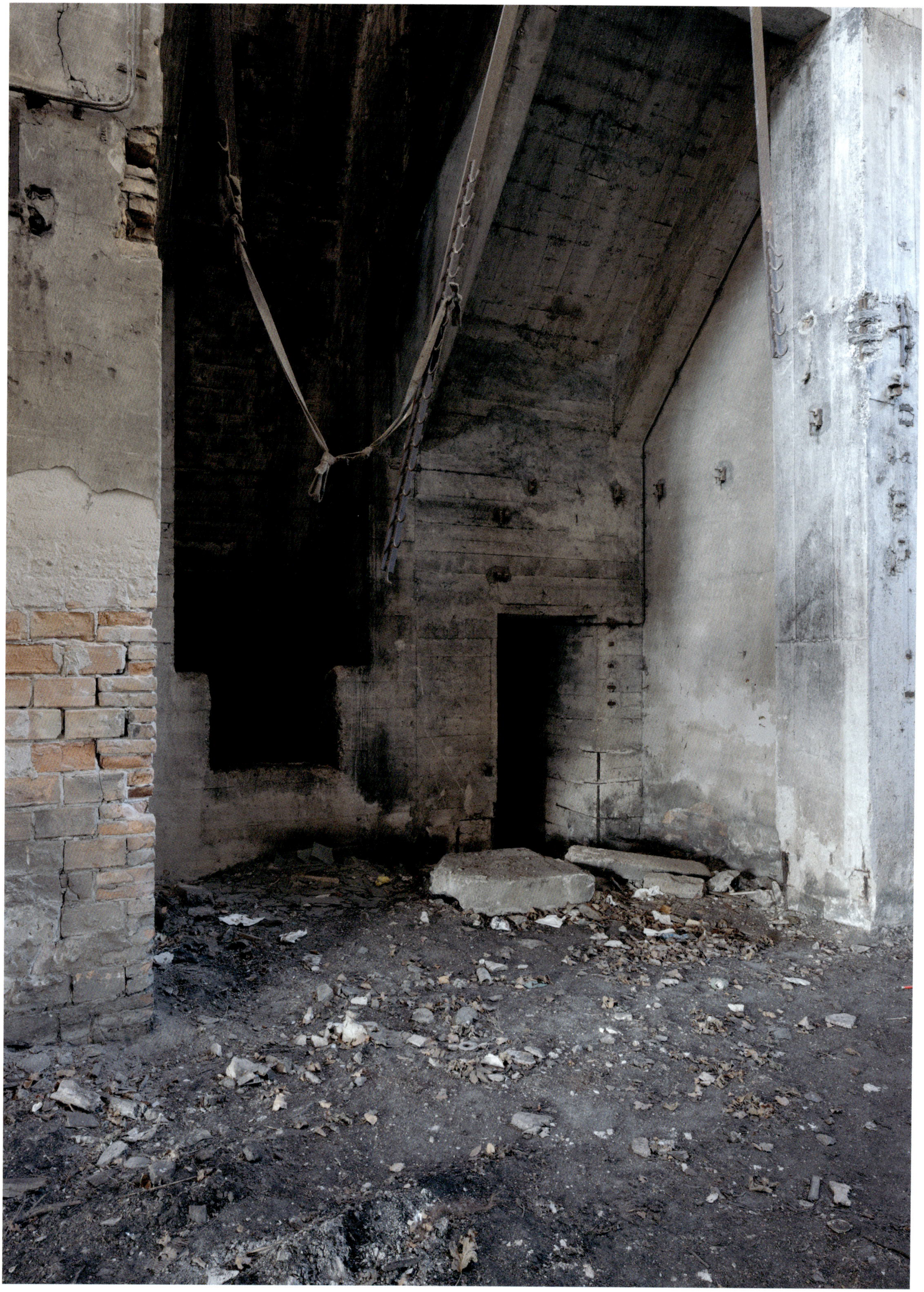

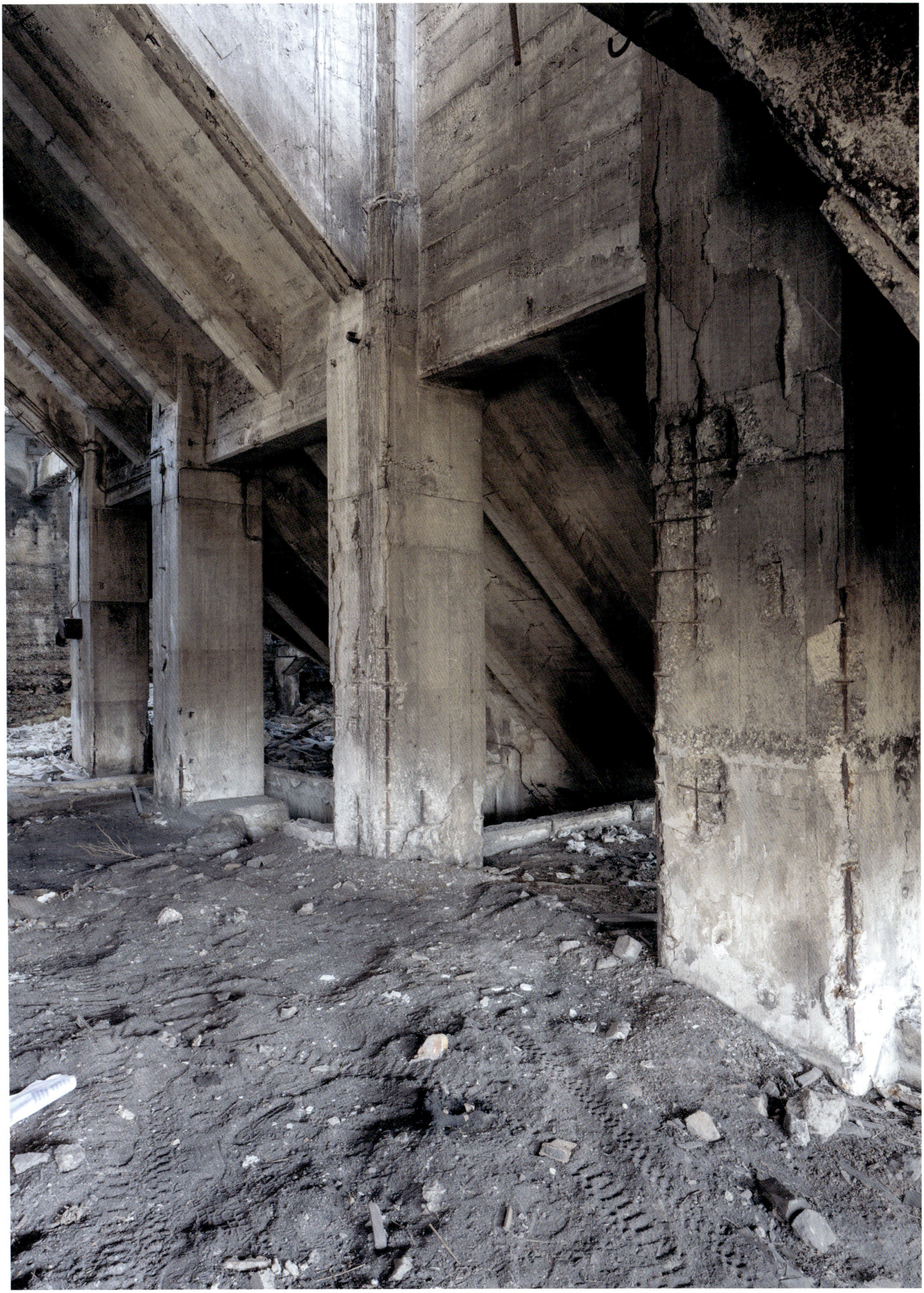

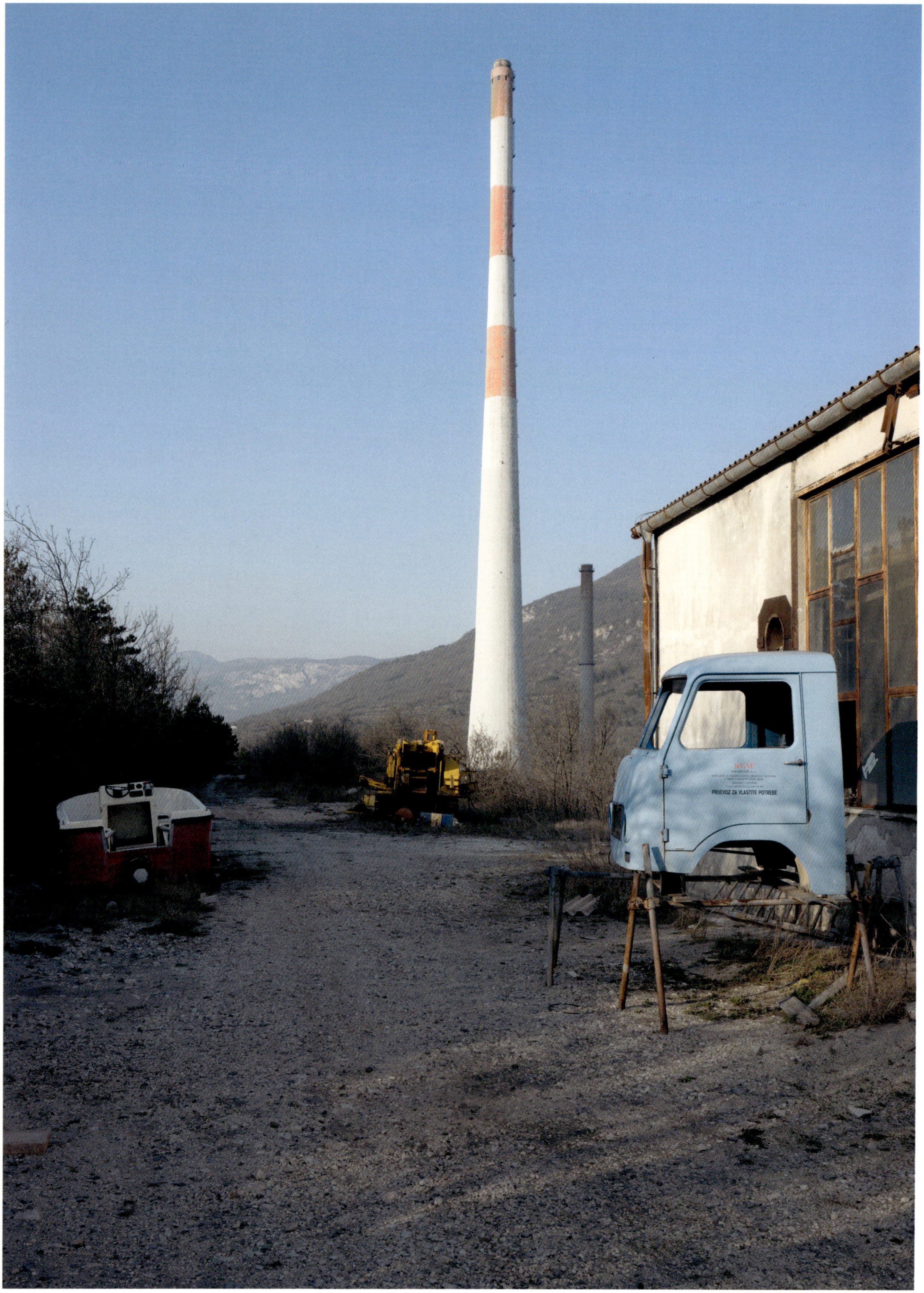
KGM
PRIJEVOZ ZA VLASTITE POTREBE

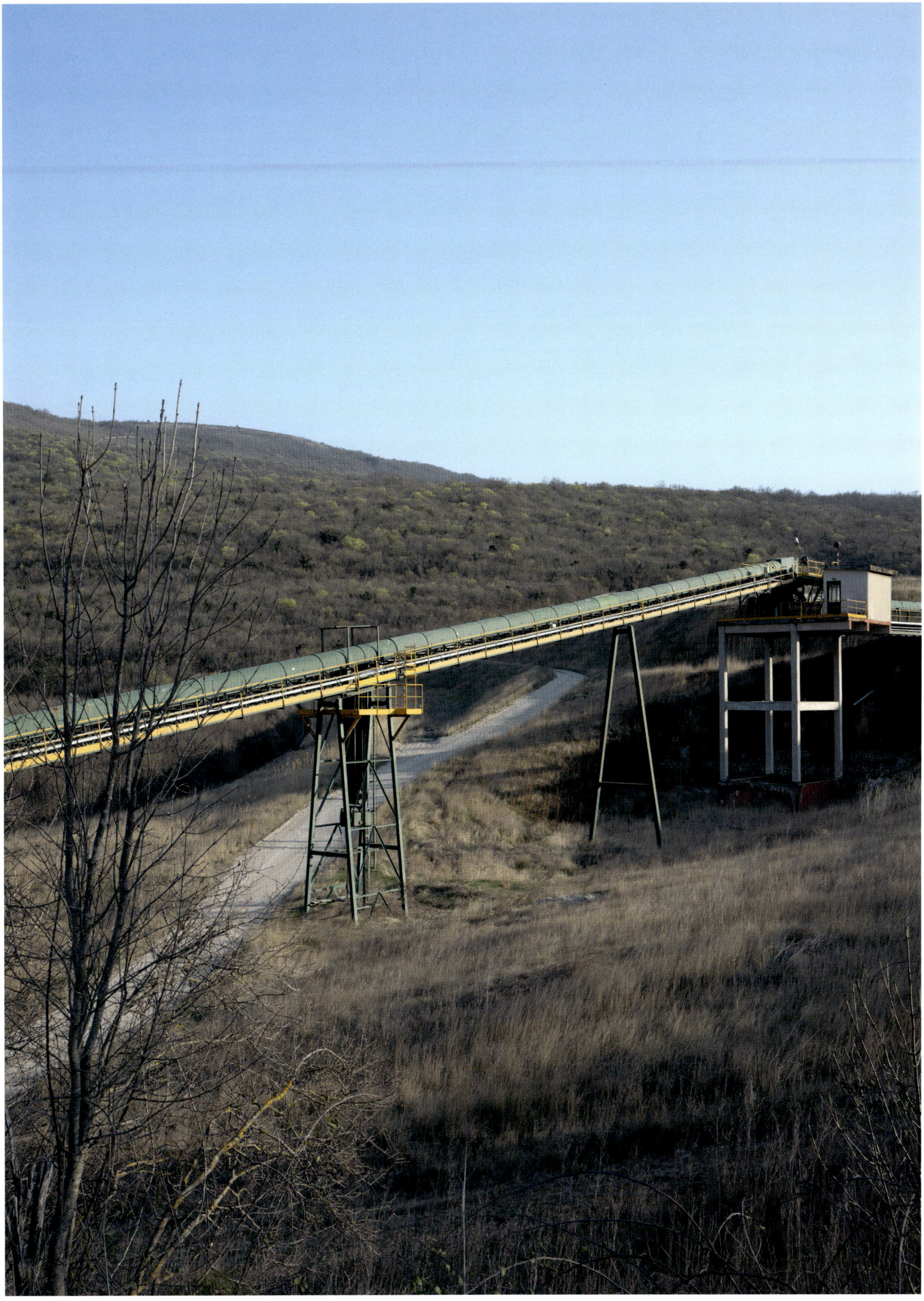

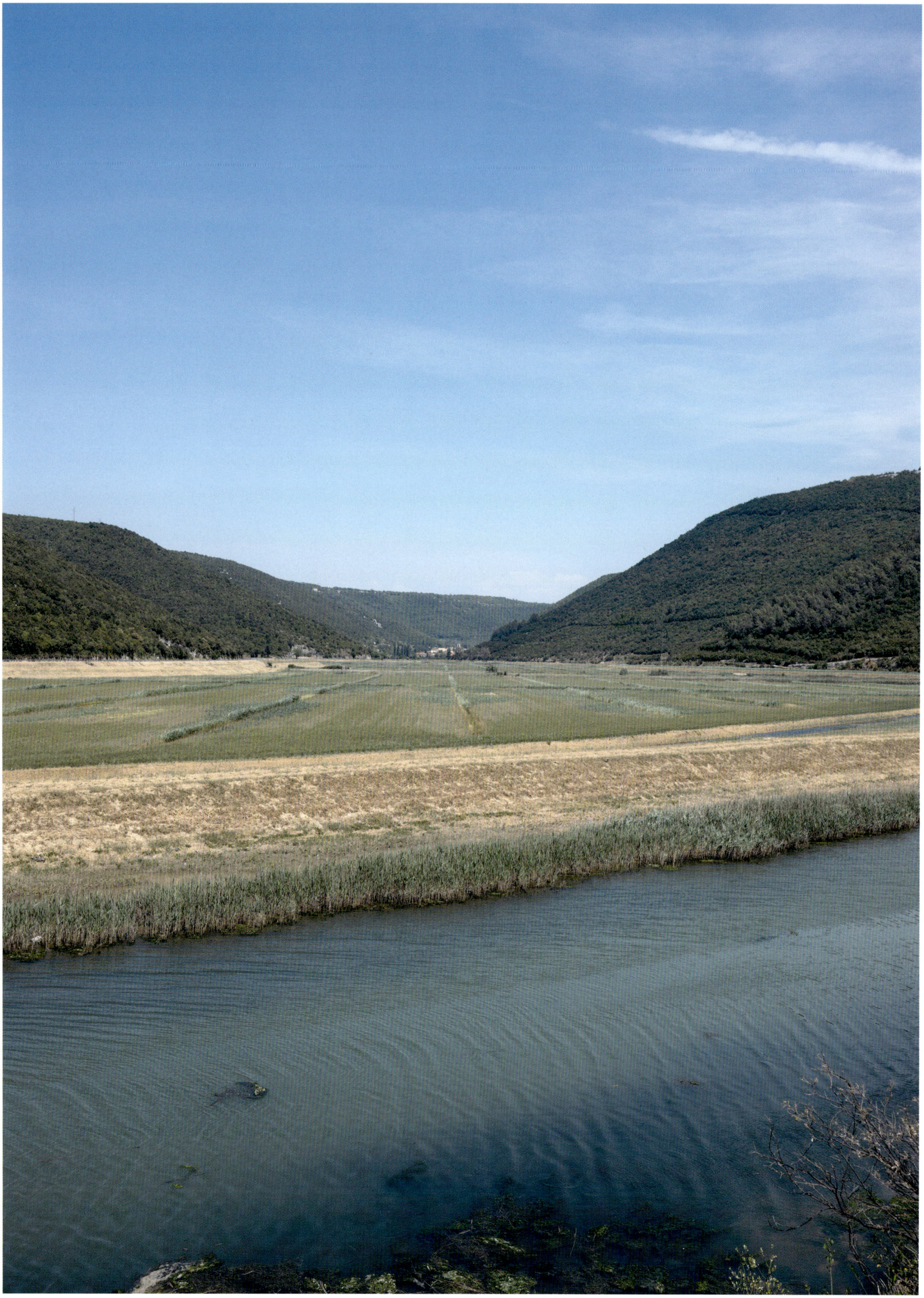

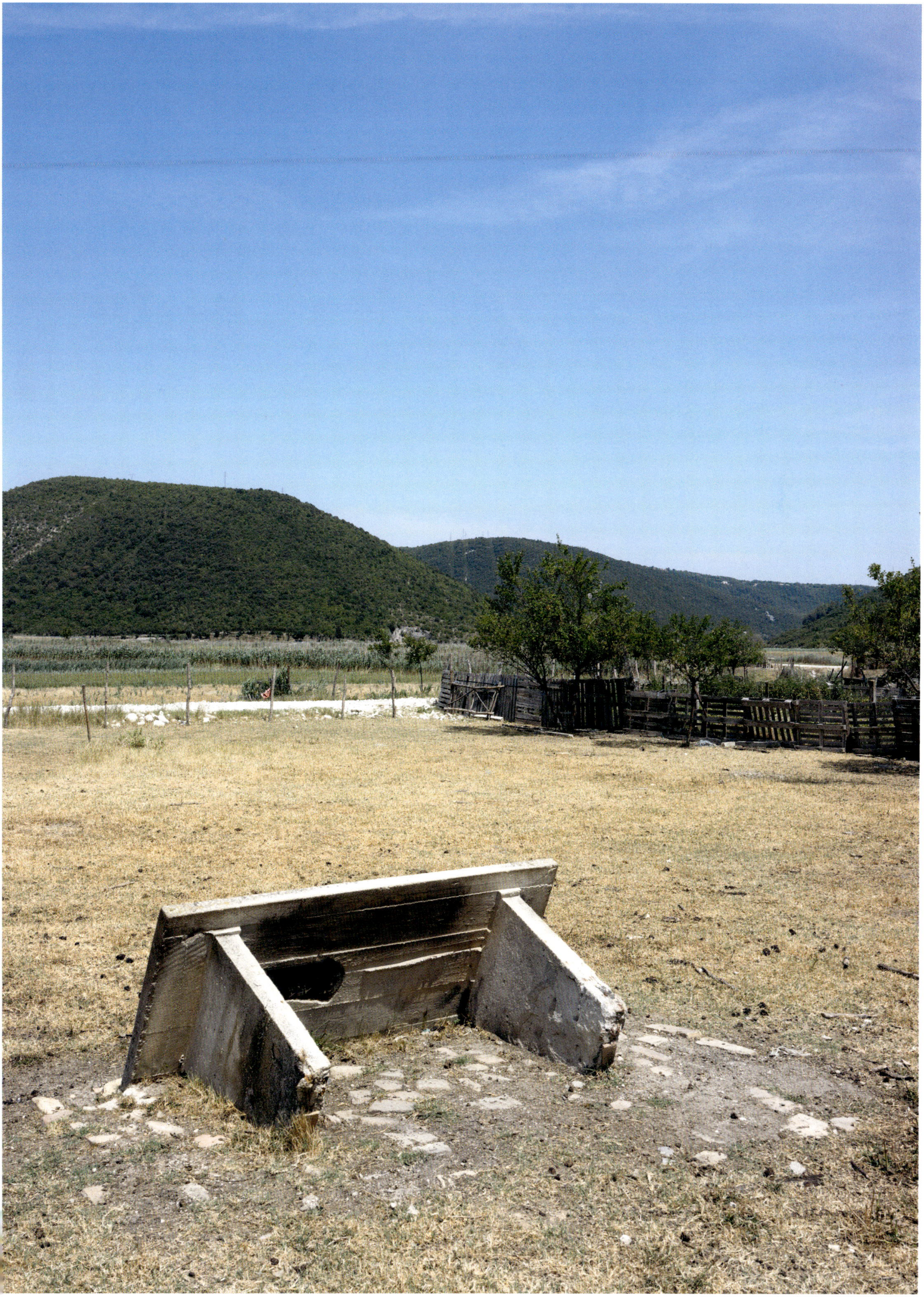

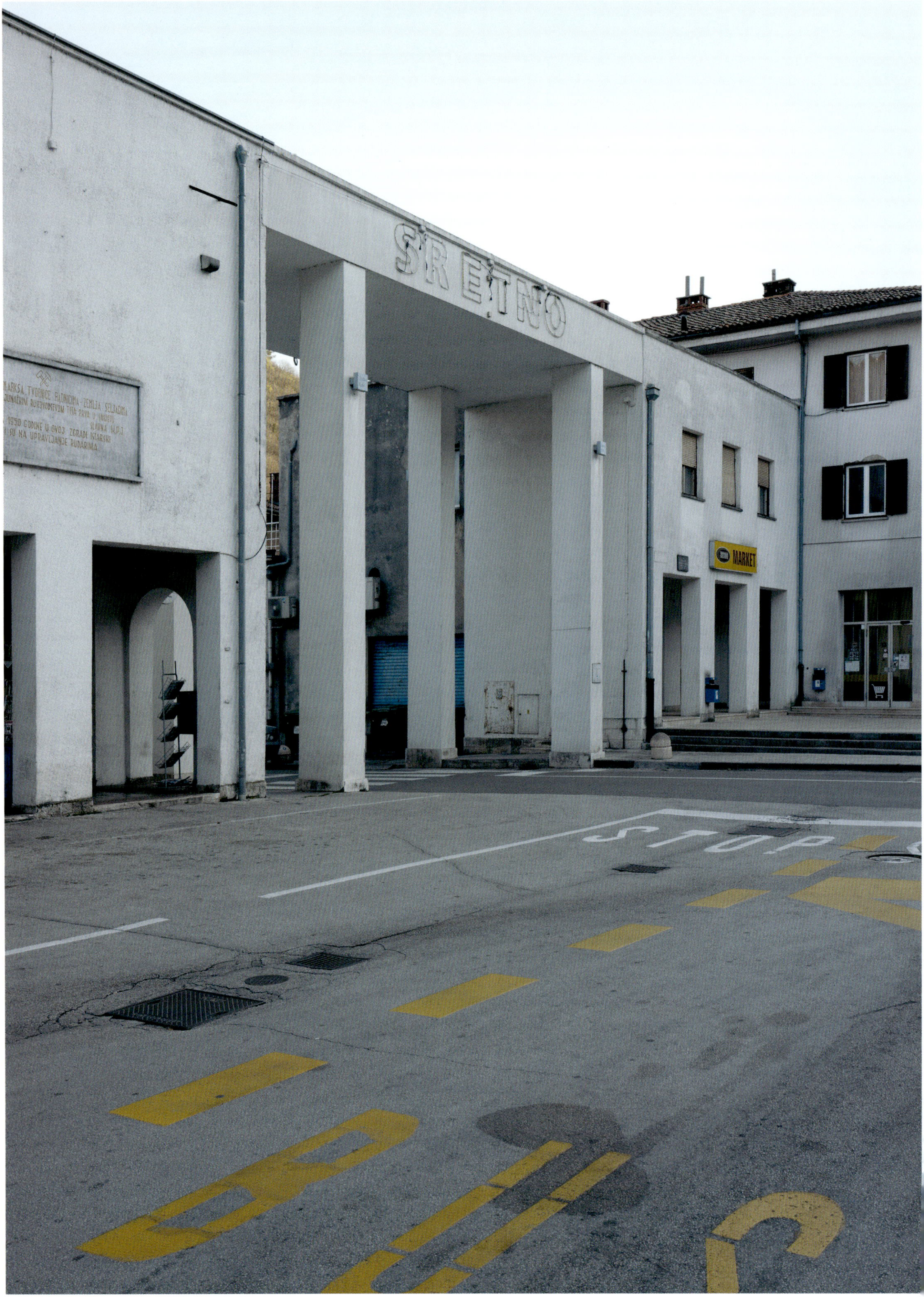
SRETNO
MARKET

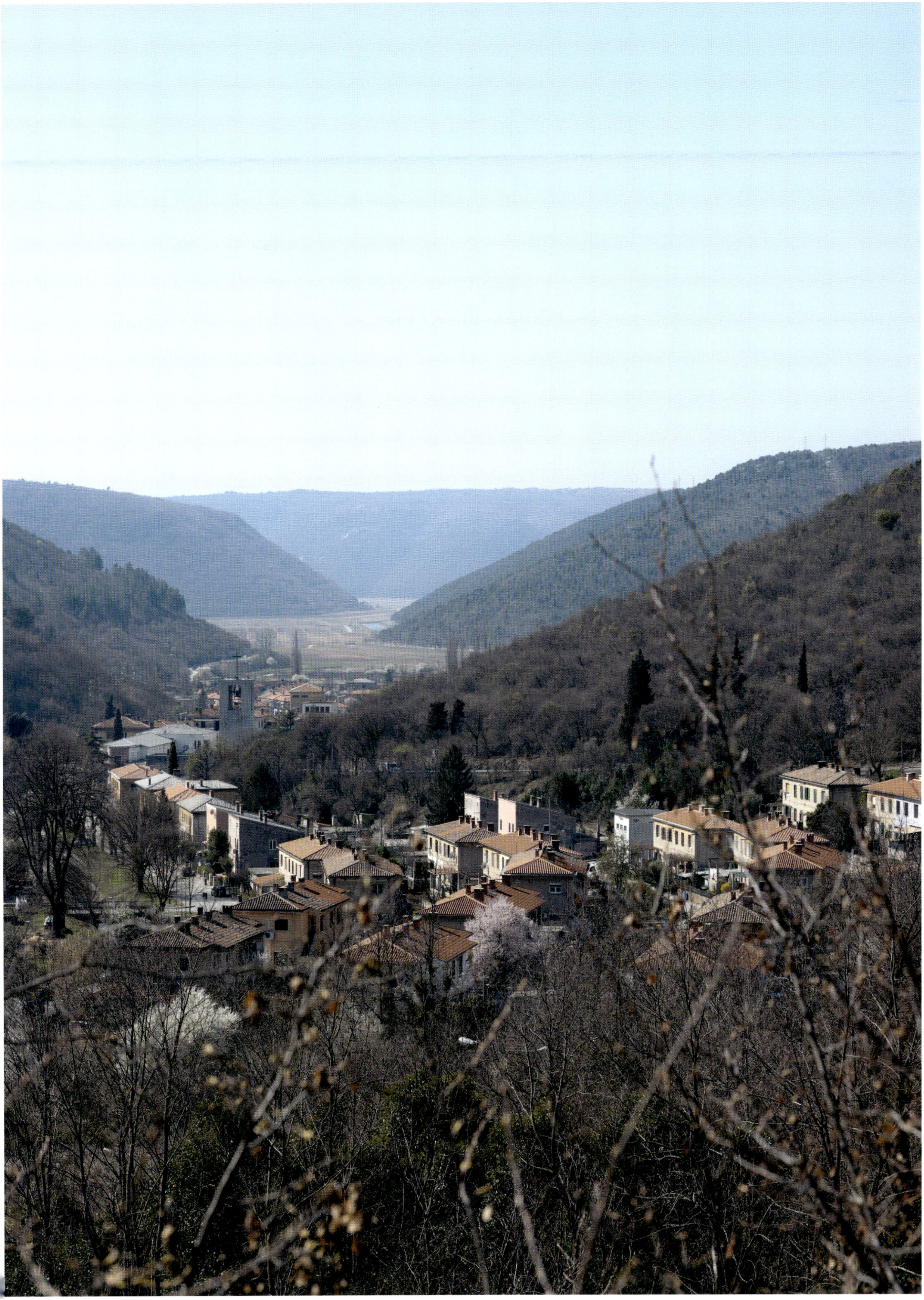

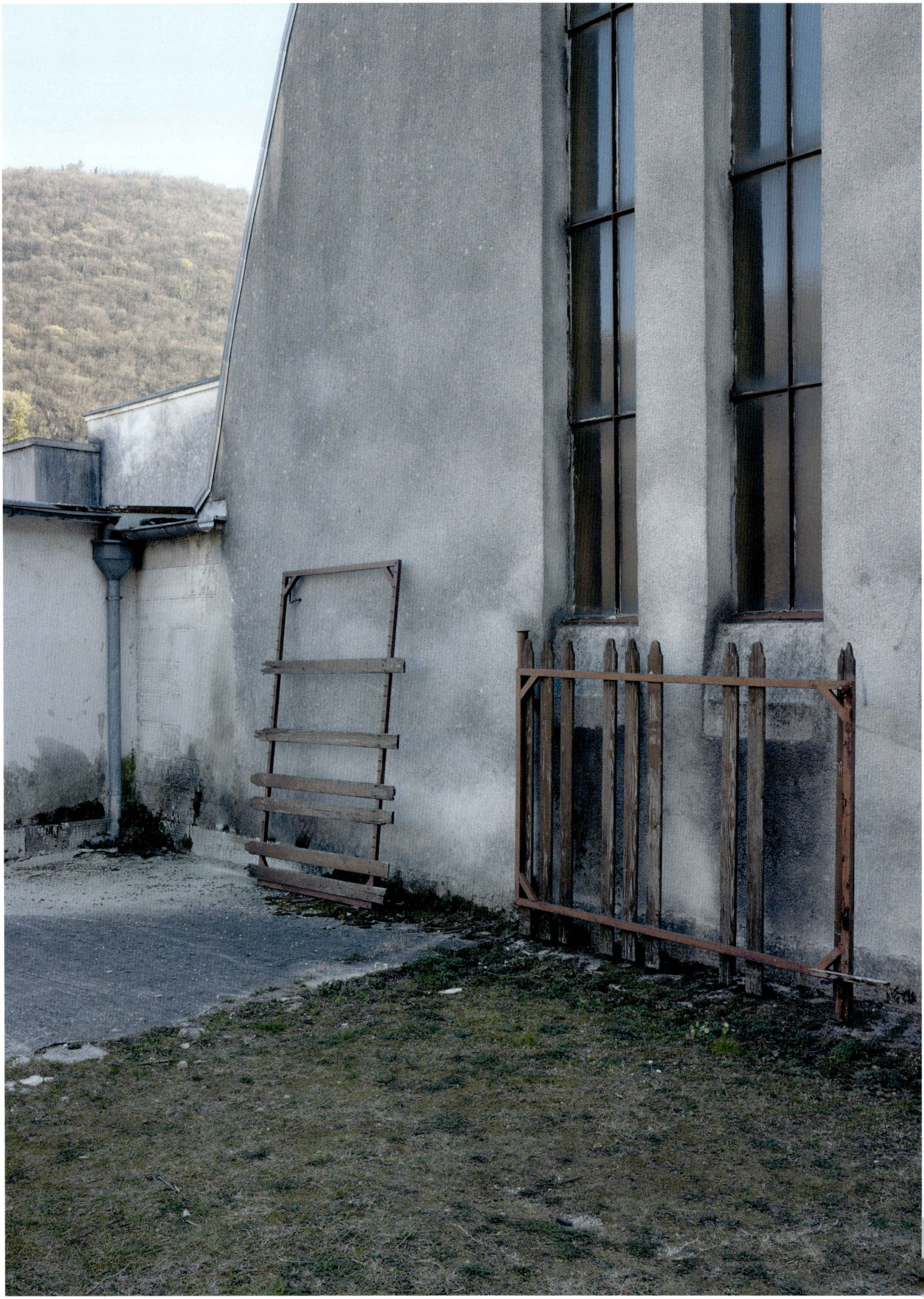

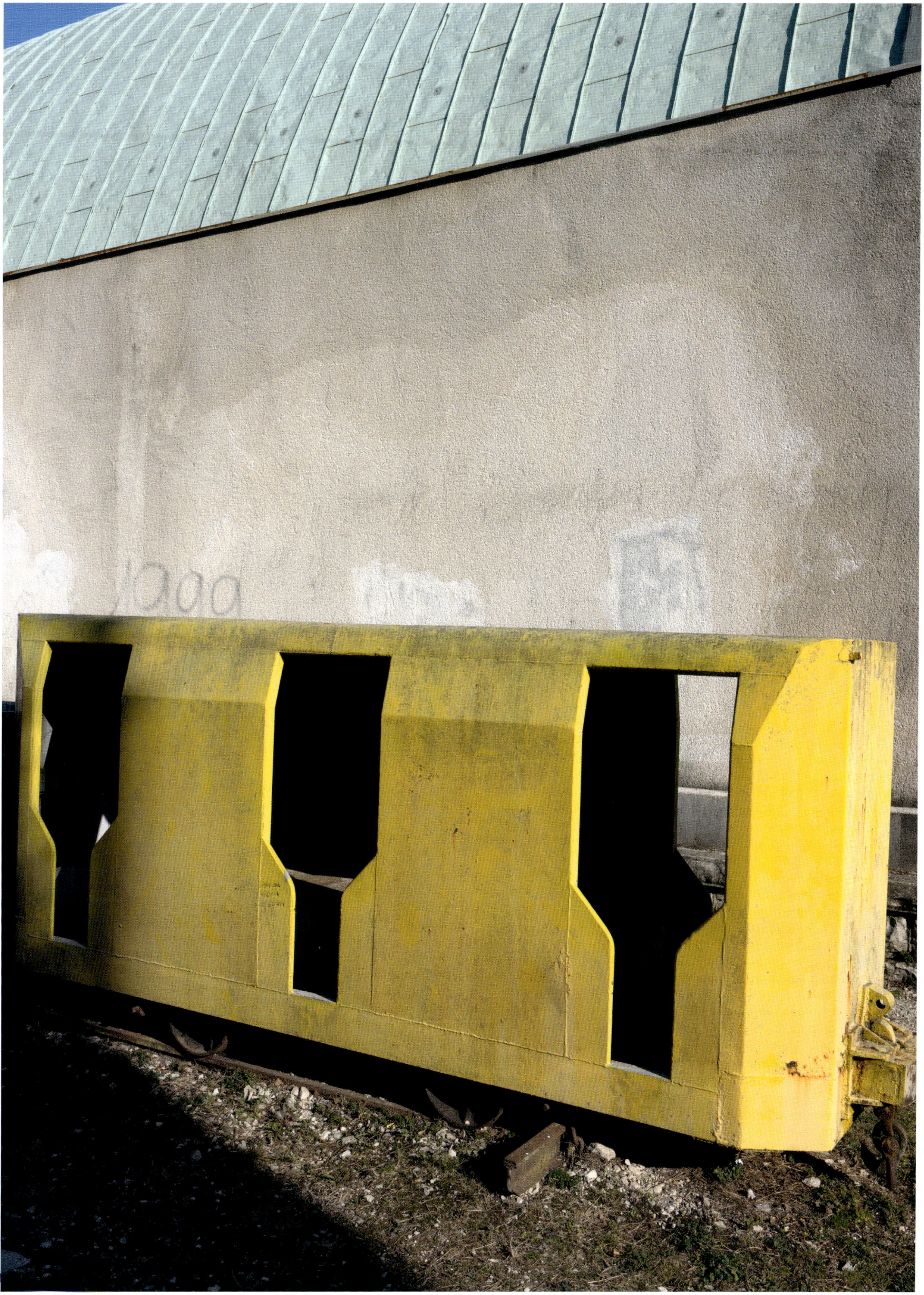

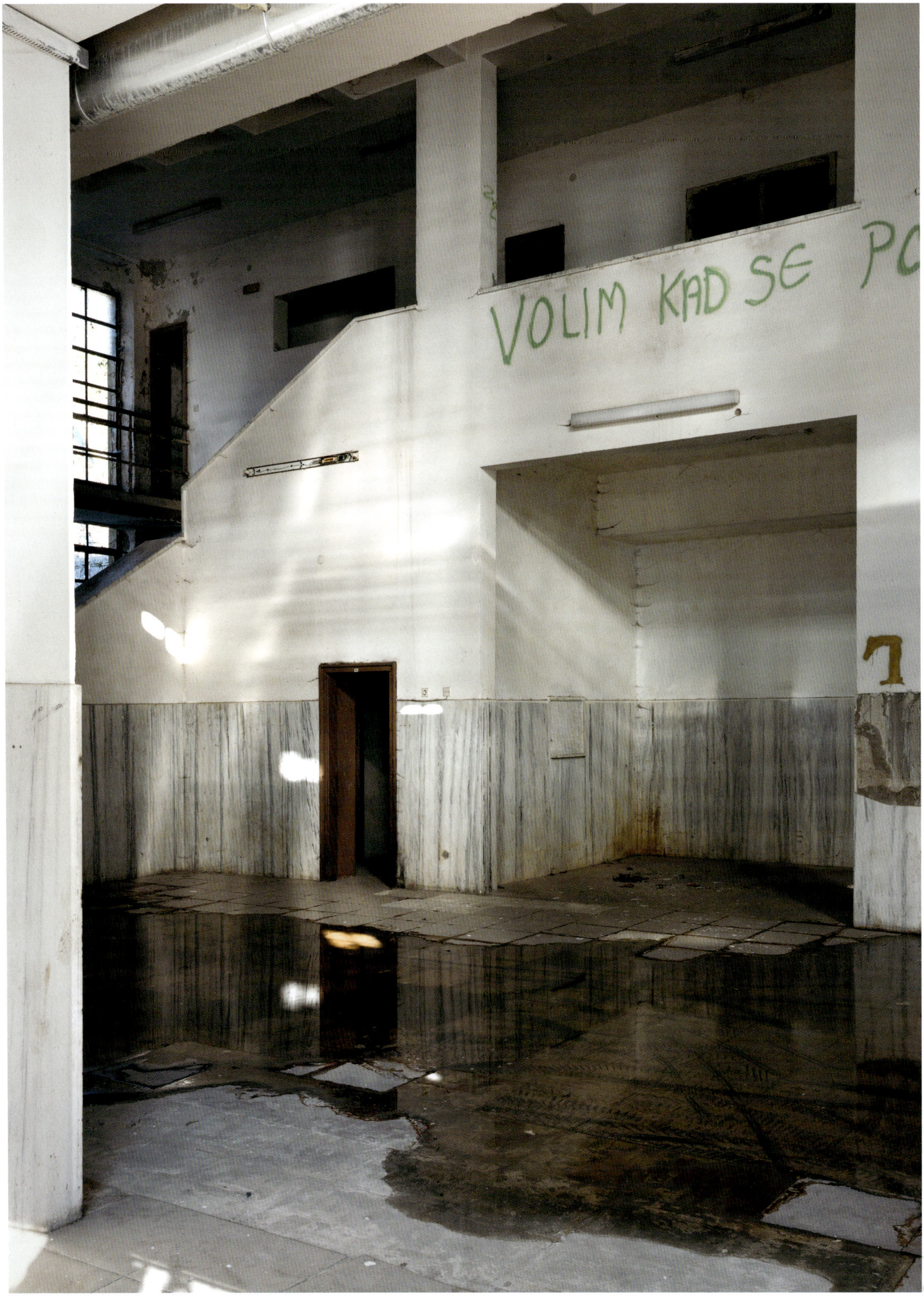
VOLIM KAD SE

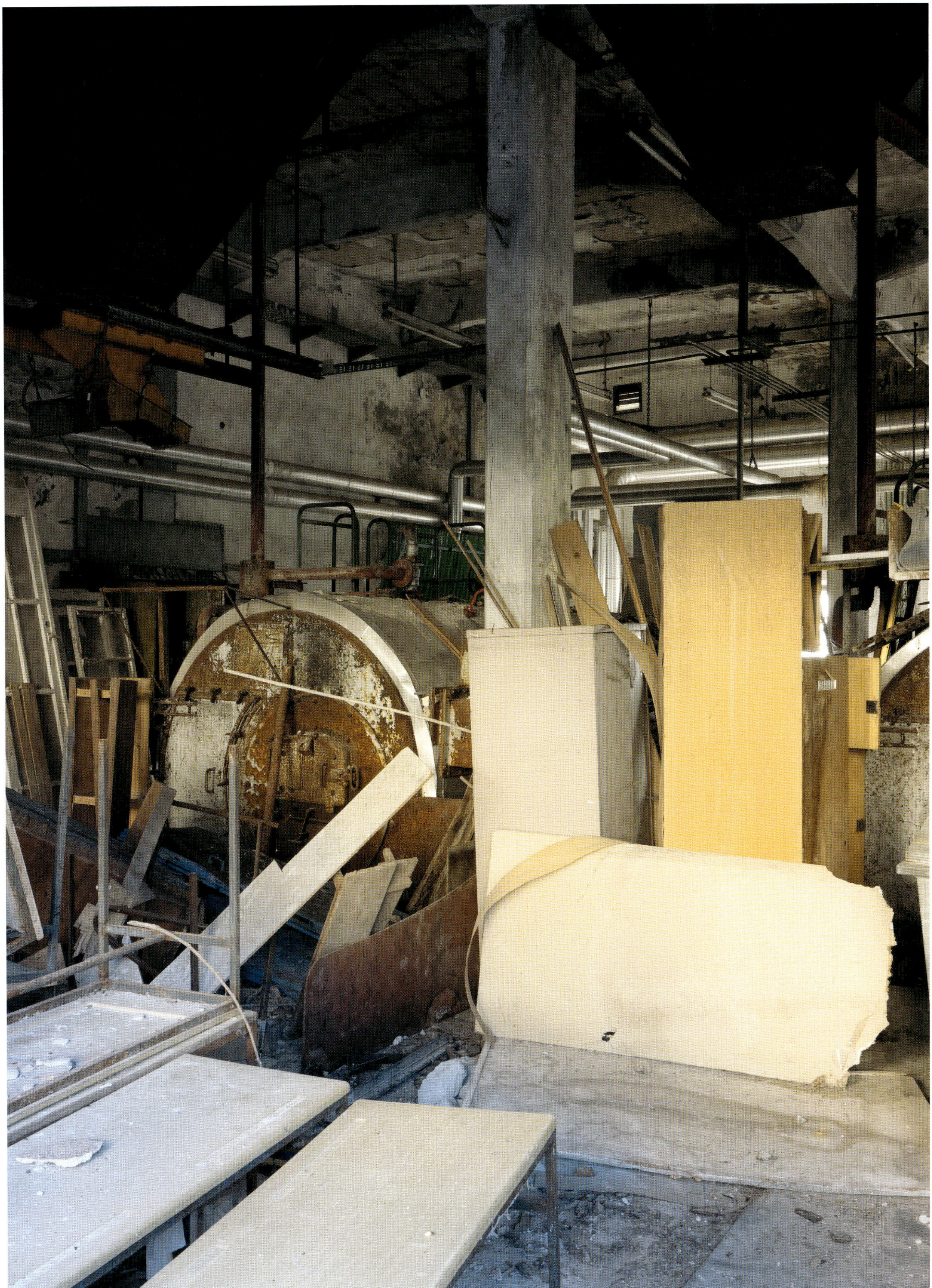

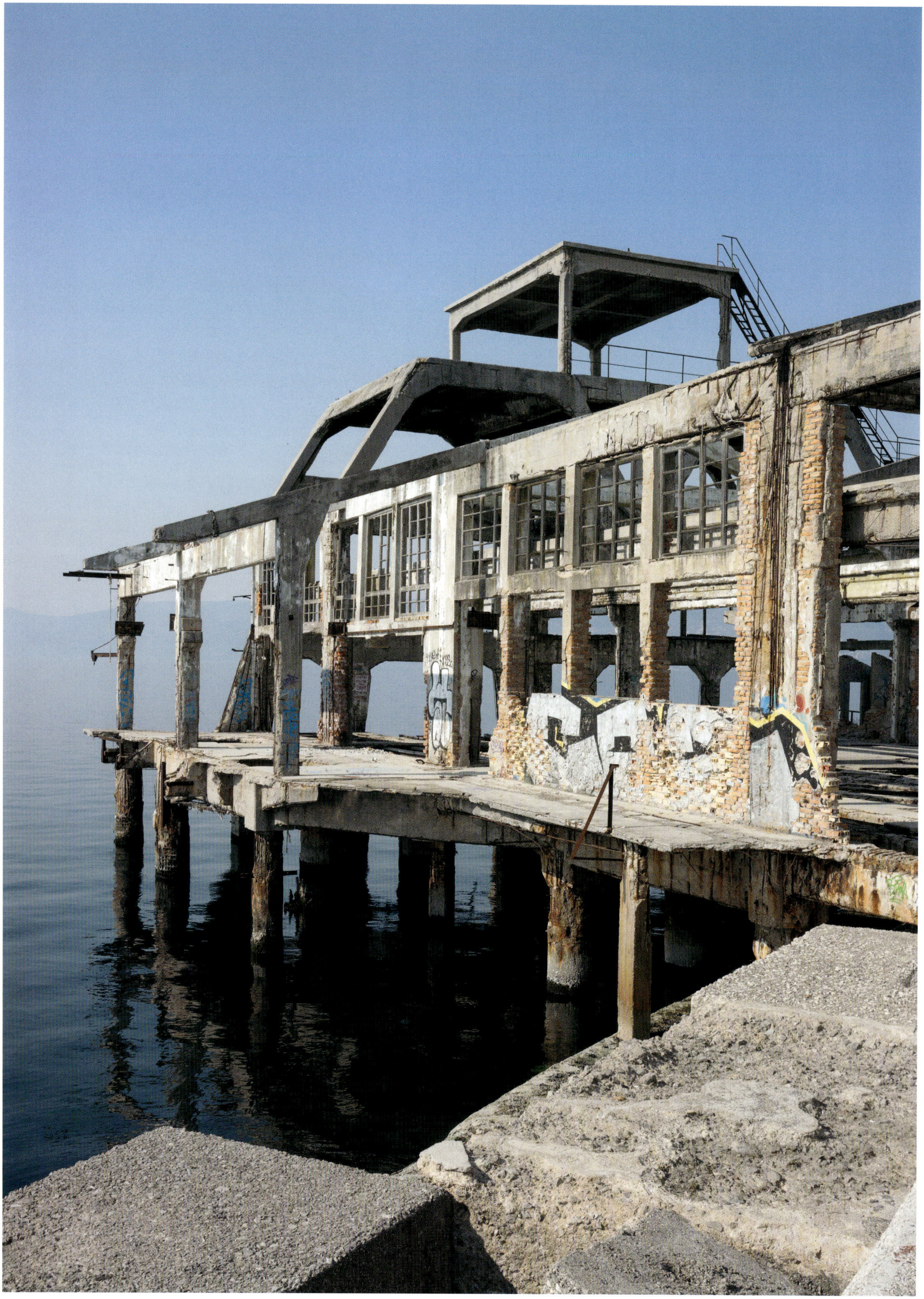

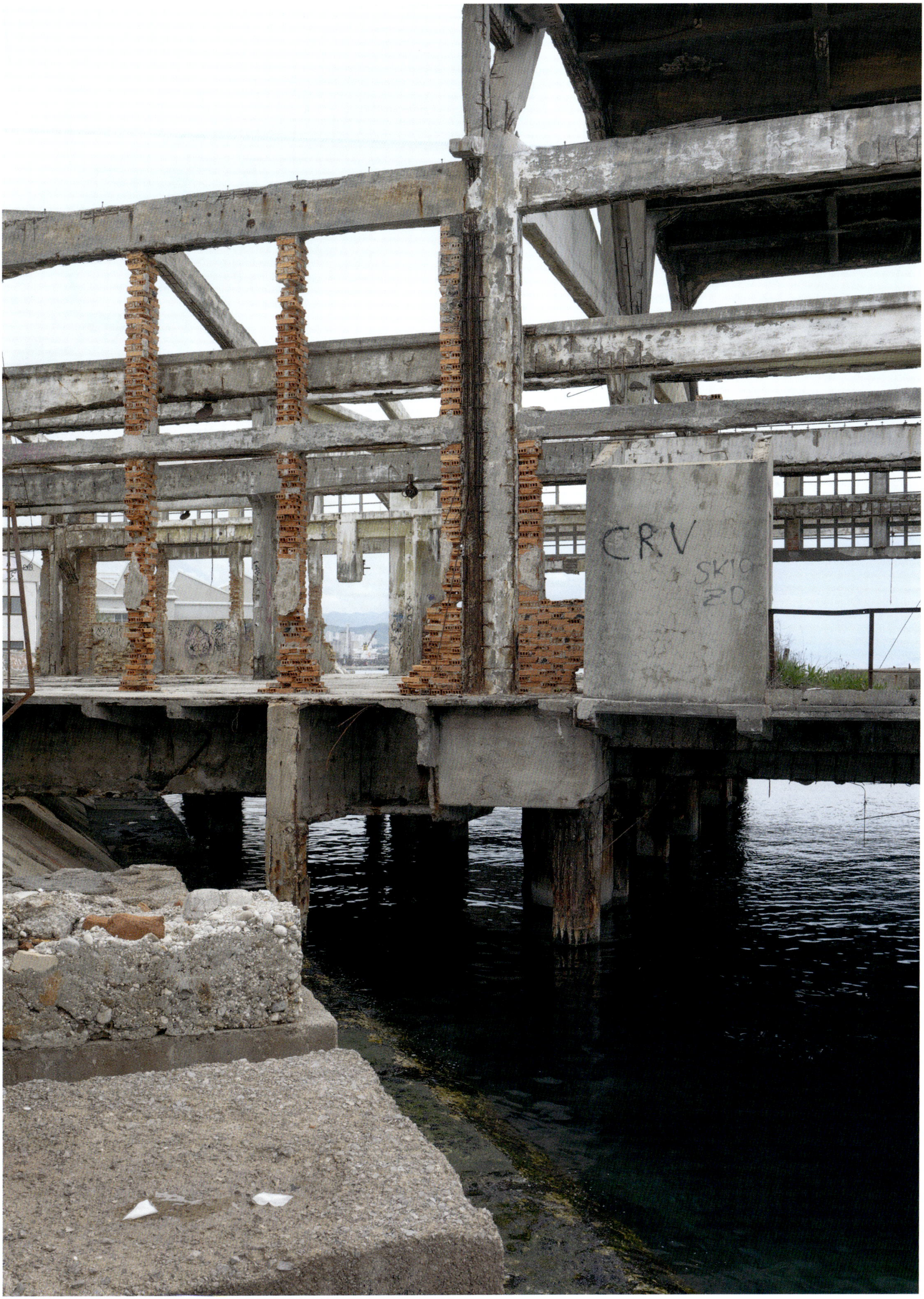
CRV

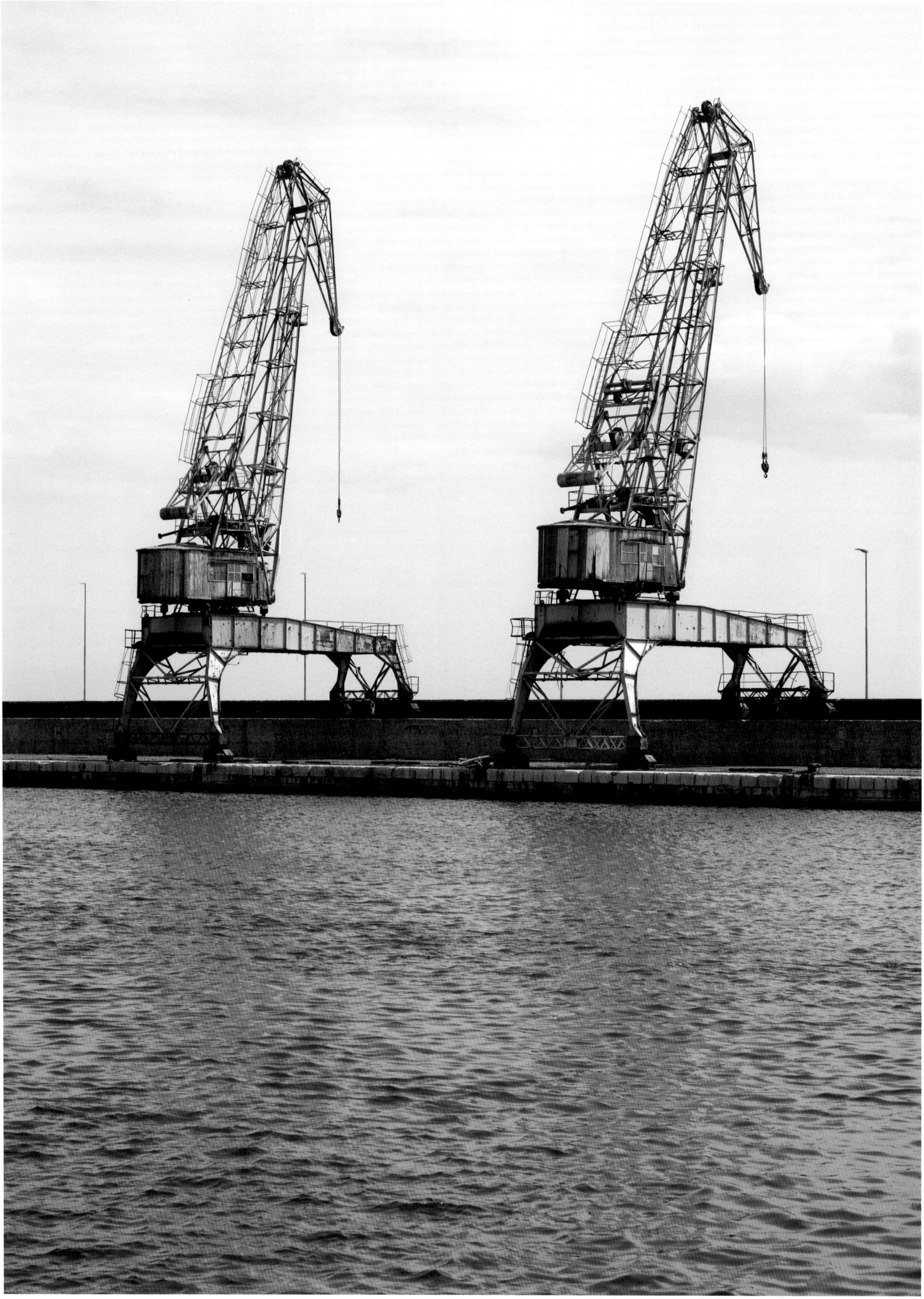

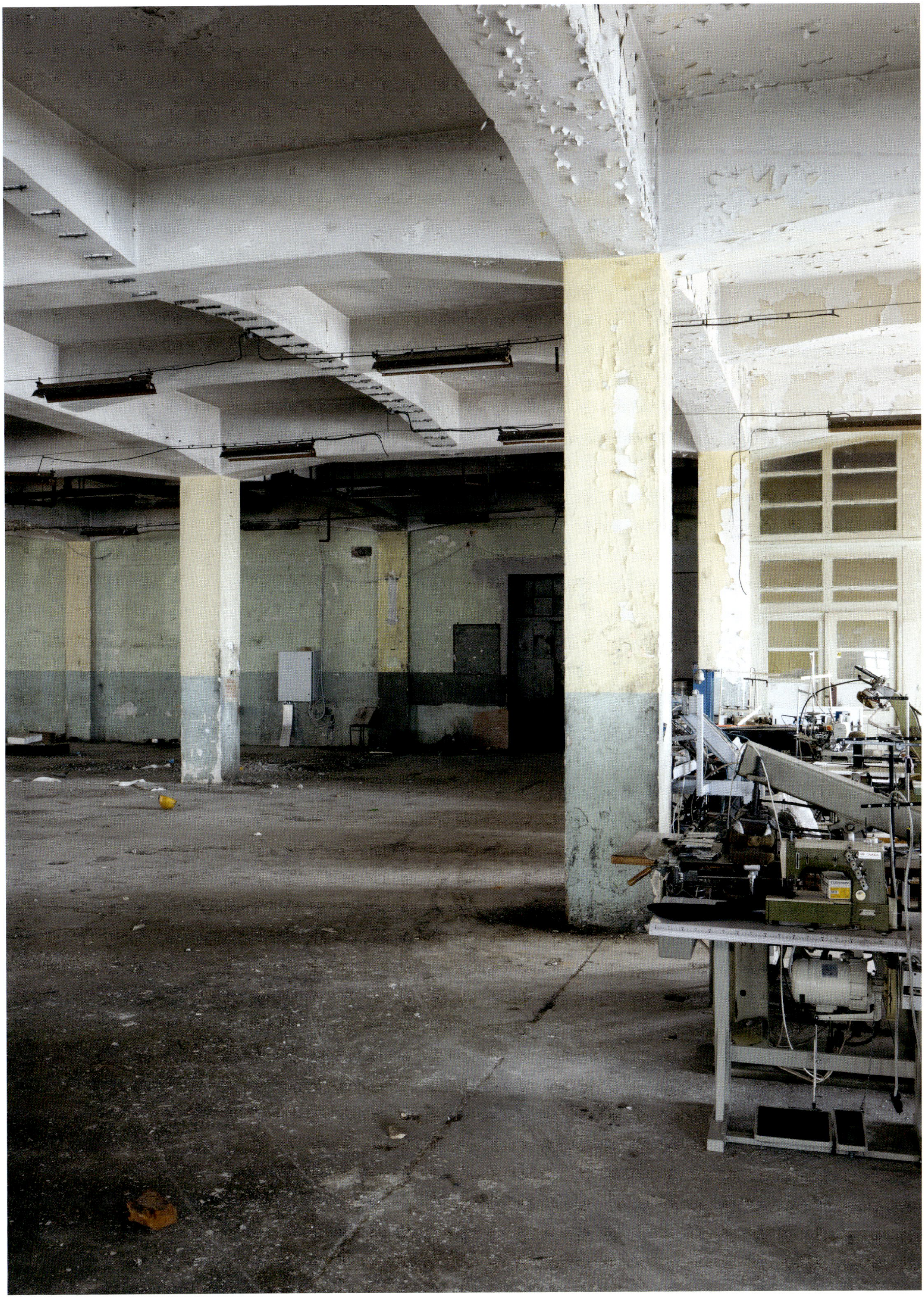

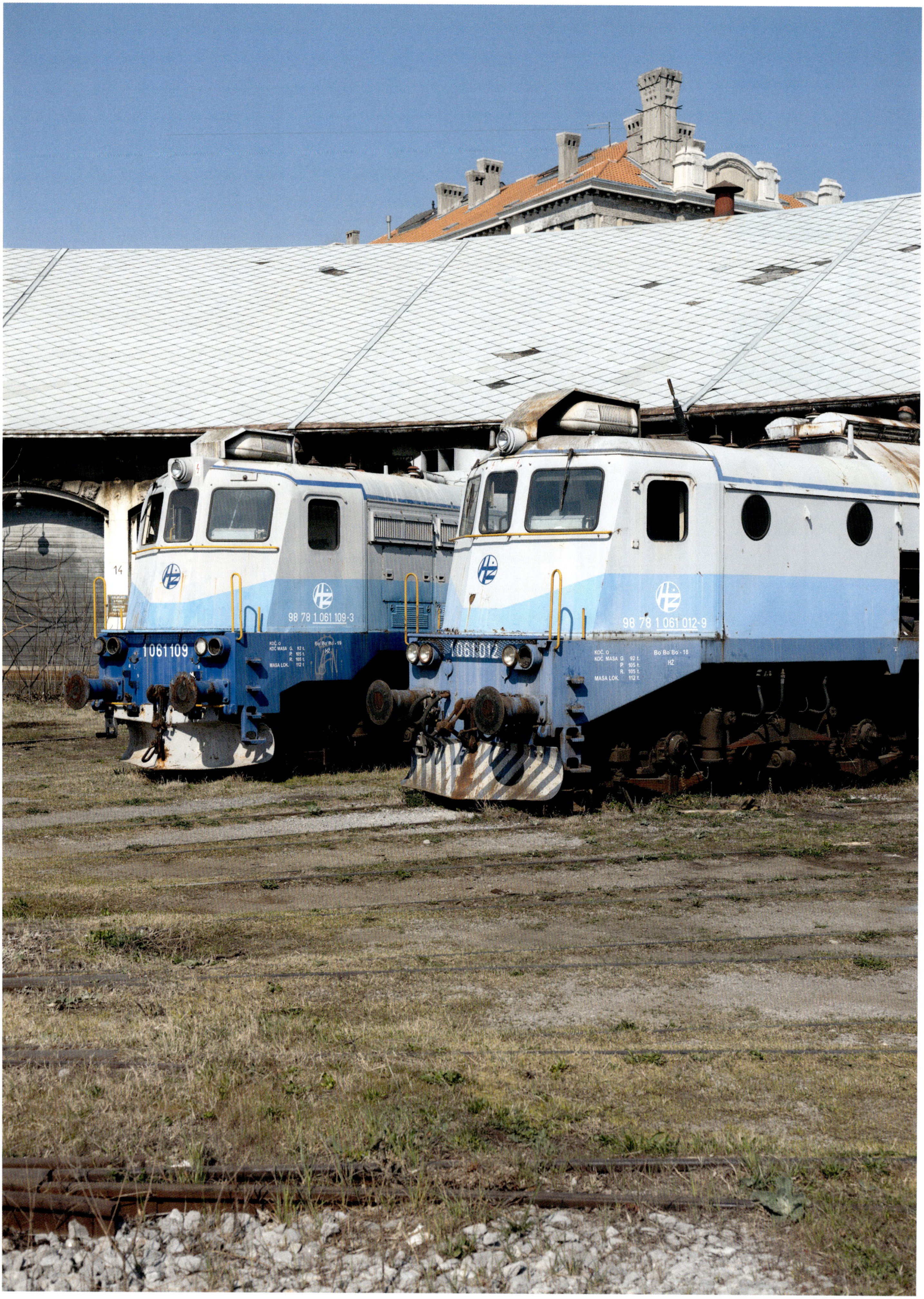
1061109
98 78 1 061 109-3
1061 012
98 78 1 061 012-9

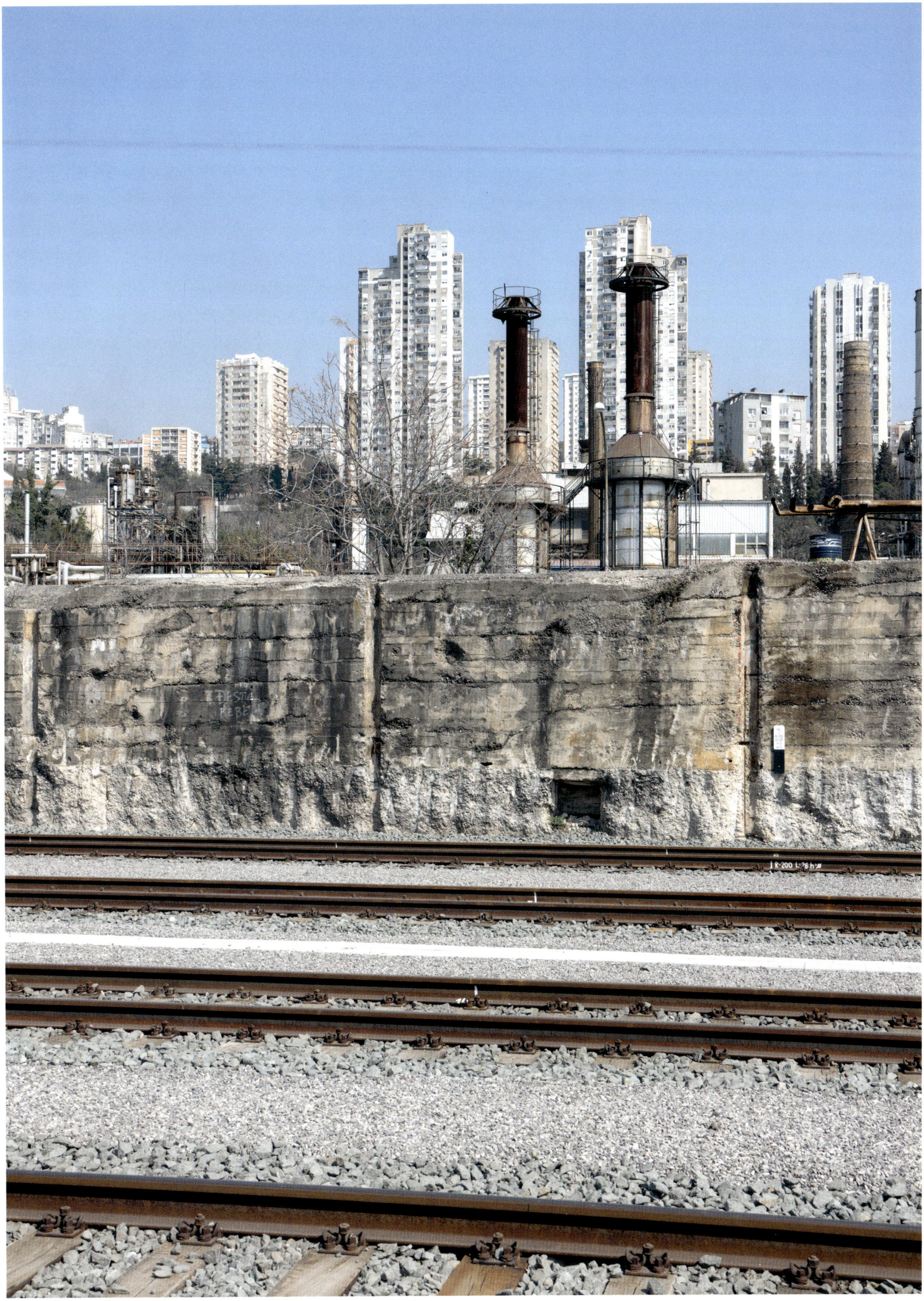

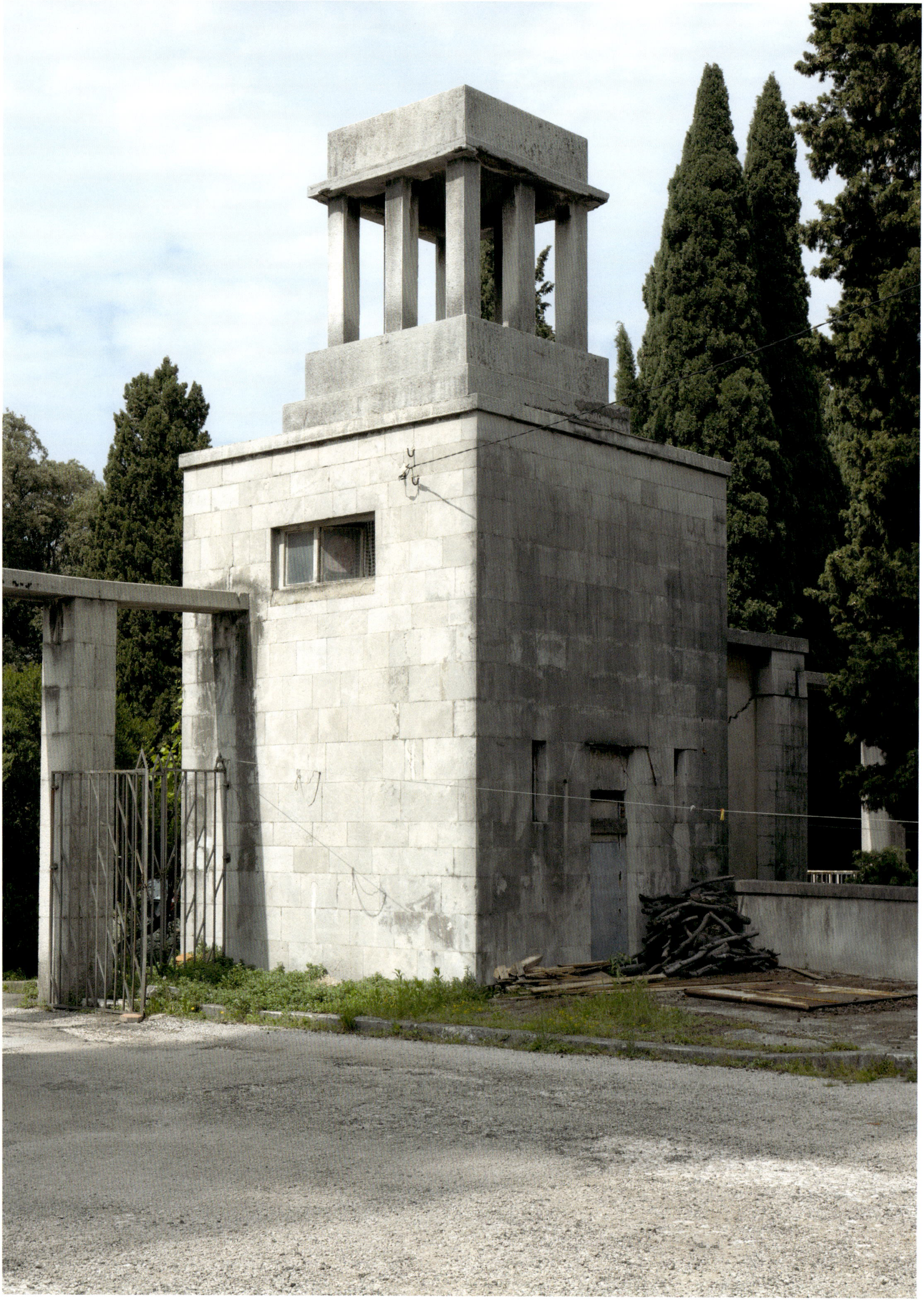

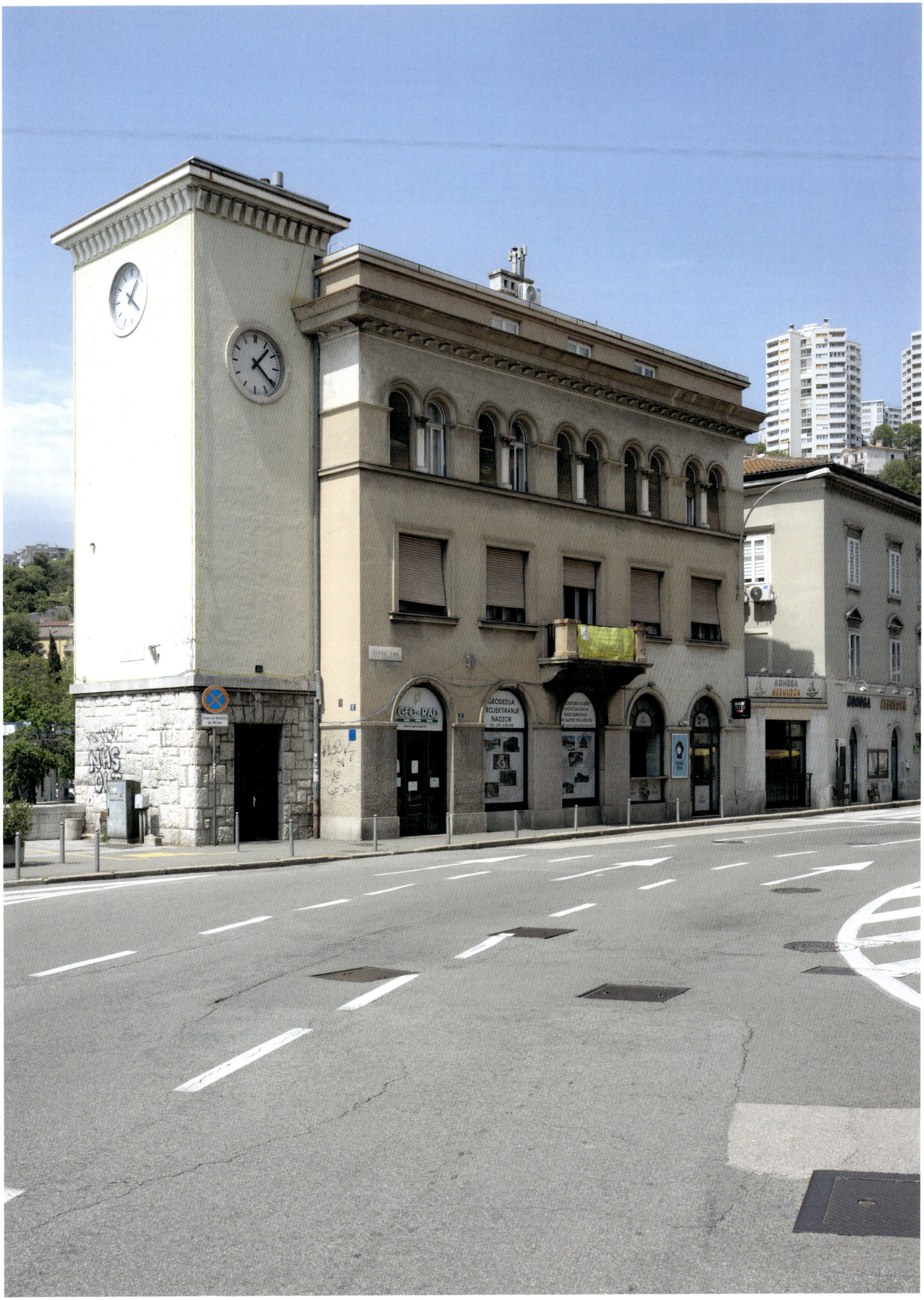
GEO-RAD
GEODEZIJA
NADZOR
KONOBA

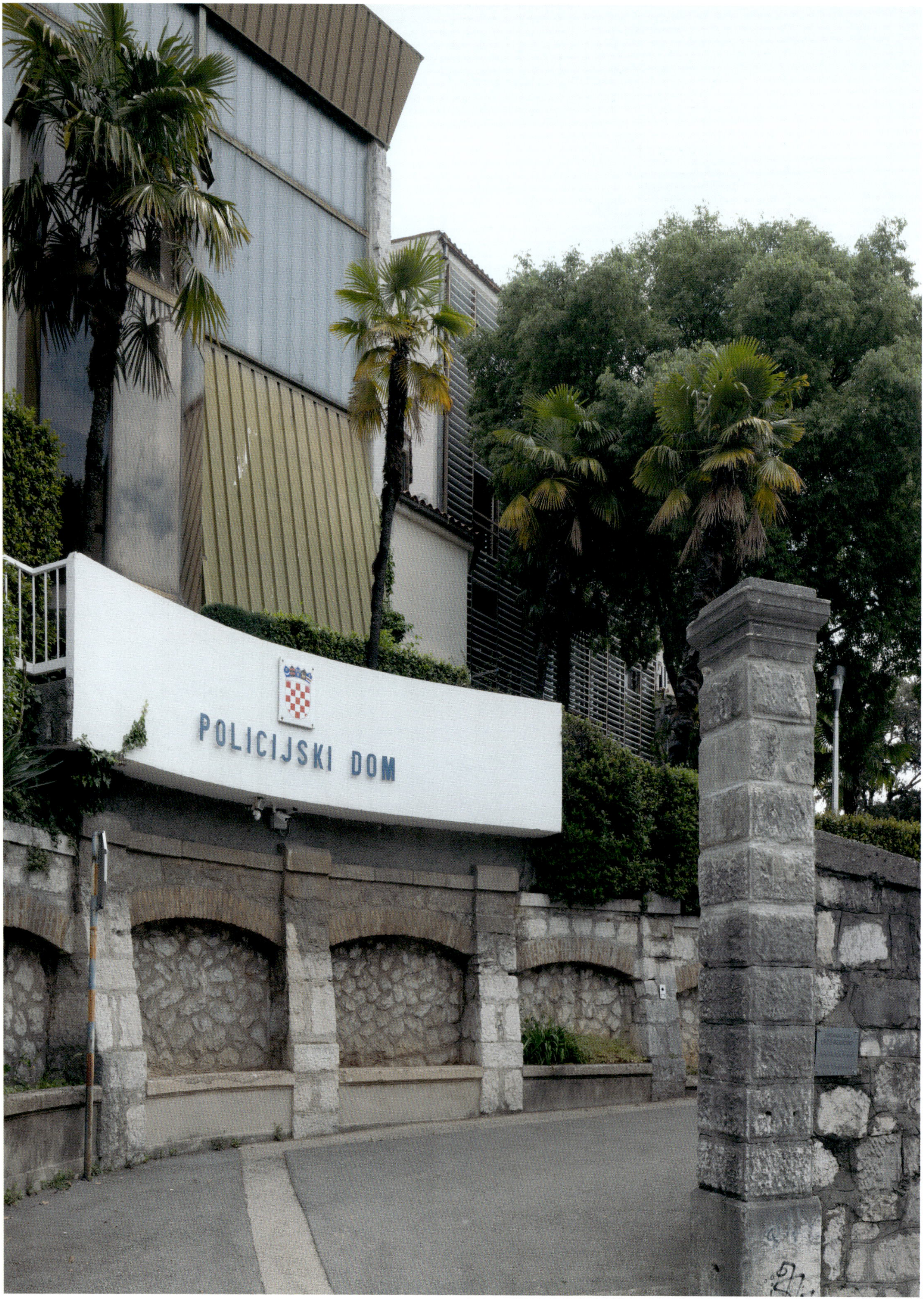
POLICIJSKI DOM

Landscapes of Desire

4th Industrial Art Biennial, Istria

Paolo Bianchi
Christoph Doswald

Verlag für moderne Kunst

Labin art express

Landscapes of Desire

4th Industrial Art Biennial, Istria

Curated by Paolo Bianchi and
Christoph Doswald

With works by Lara Almarcegui, Cristian Andersen, Charlie Billingham, Vanessa Billy, Werner Feiersinger, Fernanda Figueiredo, Clare Goodwin, Tatjana Gromača, Igor Grubić, Manaf Halbouni, Raphael Hefti, Gregor Hildebrandt, Christian Jankowski, Nikita Kadan, Sandra Knecht, Joseph Kosuth, Lena Lapschina, Sonia Leimer, Olaf Nicolai, Seçkin Pirim, Anna Piva, Marko Pogačnik, Tanja Helena Roscic, Karin Sander, Arcangelo Sassolino, Talaya Schmid, Natalia Stachon, Stefanos Tsivopoulos, Viktor Zahtila

Installation views by Jules Spinatsch

Text contributions by Paolo Bianchi, Marie-Janine Calic, Christoph Doswald, Isabella Flego and Tatjana Gromača

Verlag für moderne Kunst

Table of Contents

Catalogue of the Exhibition

Appendix

Introductory Greeting

Minister of Culture and Media Nina Obuljen Koržinek

Ever since its launch and the first edition in 2014 until today, the Biennial of Industrial Arts has developed into a unique artistic event, recognized as an innovative manifestation, significant because of its continuity in action and reflection, as well as opening of new topics and positions from which to problematize the current artistic and social context.

At the same time internationally relevant and strongly rooted in its origins and linked to the local community and the industrial heritage of the Labin area, the Biennial positions its own heritage in the international environment, ensuring a transdisciplinary and socially engaged approach to art with its program range. By repurposing industrial heritage buildings, which abound in this wider geographical area, for cultural uses, new polyvalent cultural centers and indispensable cultural points are created that contribute to the further development of the region. Culture is thus affirmed as a generator and activator of social development, and cultural spaces as zones of social contact, places of lively dialogue on all issues important to the life of the community, and spaces for artistic creation and the creation of new values.

Under the name *Landscapes of Desire*, this year's 4th edition of the Biennial expanded its geographical scope, taking place along the lines of the towns and cities of Labin, Raša, Pula and Rijeka, but also the scope of its artistic reflection, bringing together 29 international artists under the curatorial baton of Paolo Bianchi and Christoph Doswald, who required the "artistic (re)thinking for a sustainable world".

With the range and high quality of the exhibited works, putting an emphasis on spatial installations, the Biennial ambitiously connects geographically separate, but thematically interconnected exhibition units, bringing together associations and institutions, industrial spaces and galleries. At the same time, Istria and the region are becoming an experimental artistic laboratory for new artistic ideas and reflections on alternative approaches to the social, political, economic, ecological and every other context of the contemporary world.

Achieving local partnerships and networking in the field of culture and art is always important, especially in the context of creating manifestations of this scope. Their quality significantly affects not only the reach of the Biennial itself, but creates spaces where art is strongly networked with the local community that, far from being just an observer, becomes an active participant in the artistic process, interpreting and shaping the context of their region.

The goals of the 4th Biennial of Industrial Art have been achieved through a strong partnership led by the organizers of Labin Art Express XXI (L.A.E. XXI) and co-organizer Lamparna j.d.o.o., joined by the Archaeological Museum of Istria, the Historical and Maritime Museum of Istria, the Cvajner Gallery from Pula and the Museum of Modern and Contemporary Art in Rijeka. The synergy of all these stakeholders along with the artistic reflections of 29 artists will undoubtedly result in new interpretations, as well as new visions of the future of the Istrian region and its rich heritage.

Landscapes of the Possible. Arcadian Transmutation of Territories

Damir Stojnić
President of the Biennial

Dean Zahtila
Director of the Biennial

Taking into account all previous editions of the Industrial Art Biennial (IAB) – the pilot edition IAB 00 in 2014, IAB 01 in 2016, IAB 02 in 2018 and IAB 03 in 2020 – featuring a total of over 220 international participating artists – we can confidently say that this 4th edition is the most industrial so far. We have used 100 ton cranes, 20 ton excavators, more than 200 tonnes of Istrian stone, construction engineering, and many other local industrial resources. Moreover, according to the curatorial concept and the artists invited by Christoph Doswald and Paolo Bianchi, it is also the most poetic edition, since many of the specifically developed works refer, both conceptually and formally, to Istria as a "terra magica, terra incognita". While previous curatorial teams focused more on the socio-political issues and economic turbulence that shaped the lives of the inhabitants of Istria, the inspiration of IAB 04 curators was the actual Istrian peninsula which, because of its characteristics, is ideal material for a utopian reading, inspiring us to process it according to our desires.

For the last 30 years Labin Art Express (L.A.E.), the organizer of the Industrial Art Biennial, has treated the Istrian "genius loci" as a constantly flowing source of artistic visions and ideas which aspire to transform society, not only socio-politically, but also culturally and spiritually. For instance, through the re-contextualisation of the territorial phenomenon of the former Istrian coal mines in the area of Labin (Albona) and Raša (Arsia). As soon as we saw the enormous sprawling network of tunnels and halls, 150 m below the ground, connecting Labin and a few neighbouring towns with the Adriatic Sea in Rabac (Porto di Albona), we envisioned it as a futuristic Underground City of the 21st century, constitutively and constitutionally grounded in art and culture. We are still working on the constitution for this independent city-republic of the future, which was envisioned as a monolithic emblem in the main square in Pula for the 3rd Industrial Art Biennial in 2020. A year later, for the 100th anniversary of the revolutionary Labin Republic (1921), we moved it to Podlabin (Lower Labin), inaugurated in 1942 by its Italian builders as Pozzo Littorio. For this Biennial it will journey to Rijeka, a city which had the only known state constitution in history that mentions music (the arts) as the foundation of the state, written a century ago during D'Annunzio's occupation of the city, then known as Fiume. Our mobile symbol of two 4 m high monumental crossed miners' hammers will not rest there. It will complete its journey at the 5th edition of the Biennial in 2025, where, like Cerberus, it will be installed to guard the entrance to the future Underground City XXI.

This edition of the Biennial is unique, since it does not present artists as creative diagnosticians of socio-political, local-global pathologies, but as active participants in the Arcadian transmutation of territories, the population that inhabits them, and also themselves. This is the duty of art in today's society, which is dominated by technological progress that creates a new technological dependence, while being governed by destructive and extremely exploitative political-corporate forces that not only threaten the survival of human civilisation, but all beings and the planet Earth as a whole.

The obsession with unlimited economic growth and materialistic progress results in a culture that, adapting to such conditions, denies its own humanistic foundations. Since the time of the Industrial Revolution, contemporary art has been confronting a predatory capitalistic economy, which treats people as disposable consumables, just like Putin's soldiers in Ukraine. Therefore, the 4th Industrial Art Biennial presents the latest contemporary artistic practices which capture the complexity of Istria, in both the local-regional and global context. These *Landscapes of Desire* offer hope for the possibility of preserving the social and natural landscape, not only of our region but of the entire world. The possibility of major social changes towards a more just, moral, and sustainable society lies precisely in art, and that is what this Biennial clearly demonstrates. 29 artists explore new dimensions of post-industrial society, but they also open up space for its most suppressed element: human emotions. Artists, consciously or unconsciously, provide solutions to many problems of our increasingly chaotic everyday life, creating a new emotional superstructure that turns utopia into reality. During this process artists transform from passive commentators on the current state of things into worker-warriors. Warriors and workers for a world where miracles are possible, where landscapes of desire become landscapes of the possible. And today, faced with another possible landscape of our desires – Underground City XXI – we, the descendants of the revolutionary Istrian miners, say: GOOD LUCK!

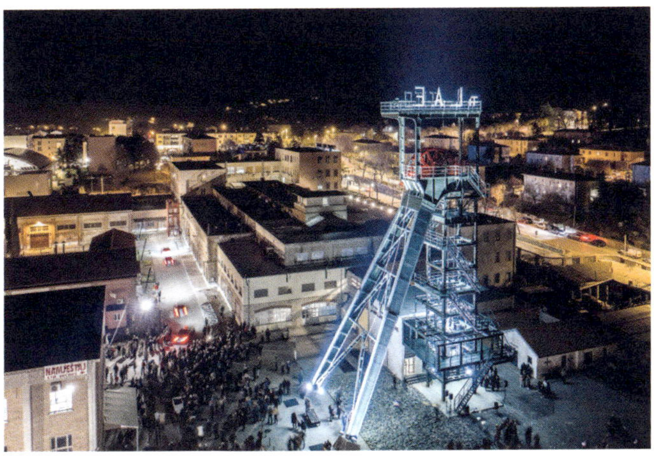

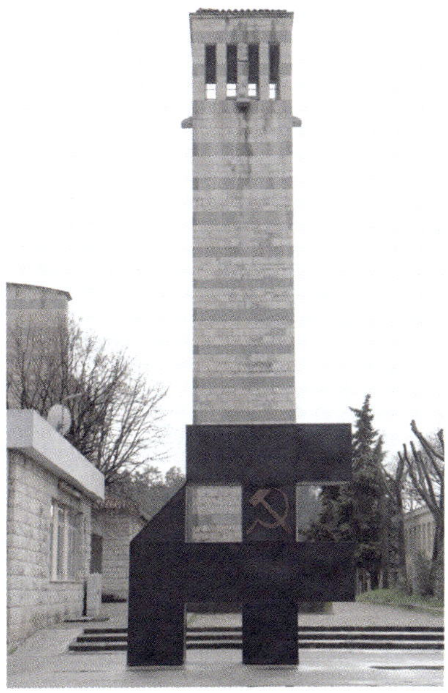

Pijacal with Lamparna, 2021

Landscapes of Desire

Christoph Doswald
Paolo Bianchi

The Industrial Revolution was not only followed by profound economic and social changes. It also led to a radical change in our understanding of art: Modernism, Futurism, Expressionism, and Impressionism are artistic reactions to the mechanisation of the world. New modes of expression were needed to understand the radical transformation of society. The 4th IAB reflects how the Istrian peninsula, including the cities of Rijeka, Pula, Labin, and Raša, was particularly influenced in many ways by these processes and was home to an impressive number of pioneering personalities and initiatives – attempting to turn utopian ideas into reality.

Artful thinking

Even today, many testimonies of visionary projects are visible and tangible in Istria. The civilizing achievement of the Pax Augusta (from 27 BC) manifests itself in the almost completely preserved Temple of Augustus in Pula, which is also described by Andrea Palladio in his architectural textbooks (*I quattro libri dell'architettura*) as an ideal, perfect building. The mining town of Raša (Arsia), designed by the Jewish architect Gustavo Pulitzer Finali on behalf of the Italian fascists, is a unique urbanistic ensemble from the period of Italian Rationalism. In the neighbouring mining town of Labin (Pozzo Littorio), also rich in industrial-historical buildings, the Republic of Labin was proclaimed from March 2 to April 8, 1921 – a republic self-governed by miners and peasants during a strike, a participative project avant-la-lettre.

The occupation of Rijeka (Fiume) by the Italian writer Gabriele D'Annunzio heralded a turbulent period of diverse political and nationalist visions after World War I, which manifested itself in a wild succession of government models in the Free City of Fiume. With the leading feminist and reform pedagogue Giuseppina Martinuzzi (1844–1925) and the pioneer of space exploration Herman Potočnik Noordung (1892–1929), Istria has produced two other personalities whose visionary viewpoints and researches still impress today.

Visionary viewpoints

The 4th IAB focuses on the exploration of those *Landscapes of Desire*, in Istria and beyond. With this narrative in mind, artists with different backgrounds were invited to develop on-site interventions, to undertake intensive field studies, and to research on specific utopian sources in a beautiful and rich territory. The exhibition-project is an innovative tribute to the utopian energy of the Istrian peninsula, with a focus on today's social, cultural, climate and economical challenges.

Post-Industrialisation plays a particularly important role in the current period of upheaval in the Antropocene: the artists of the Biennial are addressing issues of economic sustainability, cultural diversity, climate change, and are relying on the power of networking to overcome the boundaries of political and social borders. Artworks are sensory tools and methods to successfully challenge thought patterns. We need more artful thinking for a sustainable world. *Landscapes of Desire* has therefore a strong focus on interventions in public space. A large number of site specific interventions and new artworks was commissioned. With 29 participants this Biennial is conceived as an experimental laboratory, re-shaping the rich social, economical and cultural topography of Istria.

Wishful places

Landscapes of Desire is showing art works and projects in which – whether in fantasy or in reality – wishes, dreams, hopes and utopias always flow into the idea and experience of a landscape. Landscapes are, therefore, never pure and pristine, but have always been experienced as objects of enchantment and fear. Landscapes seduce, alienate, seize or arouse shivers in us. The German writer Jean Paul (1763–1825) wrote: "In Arcadia we would pine for utopias". This means that even in a blissful land, a utopian consciousness is at work. So even in paradise on earth, in the place of perfect fulfilment of all needs, a longing, wishing and hoping would accompany us, a belief that another, better life would be possible elsewhere. This leads us to the insight that both imagined topographies – such as Arcadia, Atlantis, Eldorado, Eden, Dreamland – and real found landscapes – such as meadows, steppes, forests, lakes, deserts, oases, seas, beaches, volcanoes, glaciers, mountains, waterfalls, clouds and other views of nature, of urban and industrial landscapes – can be regarded as wishful spaces, wishful places and wishful landscapes.

Aesthetical empathy

No doubt: The present and the future are related to the past. In Istria, this past is particularly present, and traces of Istrian history can also be found in the family biographies of the two curators. Based on these biographical references, discourses emerged that reach far beyond the personal and have exemplary validity for the issues of a European society. Back to the future with art and life. The photographic documentation of the 4th Industrial Art Biennial, realized by the well-known photo artist Jules Spinatsch, is also characterized by this approach. His images are not simply a documentation of the artworks; the photos embed the art-interventions in the context of the Istrian landscapes with aesthetic empathy, expertise and formal skill. The photographs of Spinatsch trace the curatorial dialogue of art and context.

Differentiated relationship

Thanks to the pioneering initiative of Labin Art Express – an artists' collective that, like the curatorial duo, has its formative roots in the anarchic 1980s – the important examination of Istria's valuable industrial as well as cultural-historical heritage has not been extinguished. For the perception of one's own history and for the confrontation with the European environment, it will be decisive how the relationship of Istria to this heritage develops, whether it succeeds in cultivating and utilizing the qualities of its cultural capital. The writer Tatjana Gromača relies on this, the poet Isabella Flego refers to it in her *Galleria della Memoria*. And the essay by Marie-Janine Calic also builds on this, emphasizing in her analysis the constructive significance of European networking and integration against the backdrop of historical legacies.

We are convinced, that artistic examination of the depths of Istrian history with the curious eyes of today will prevent revisionism and lay the foundation for a differentiated relationship to the heritage of this rich cultural landscape. Sretno!

The Where From, the Where To and the In-Between

Christoph Doswald

My story begins in Vienna. Sometime in the late 19th century. When the city was a melting pot of European cultures – a linguistic and colourful coexistence of people that was later immortalised in literature by Robert Musil under the term "Kakania" in *The Man Without Qualities*. The city of two million people was the political, cultural and industrial centre of the Austro-Hungarian Empire – the Dual Monarchy – which encompassed large parts of Eastern Europe. After Russia, Austria-Hungary was the second largest European state by area, and with more than 52 million inhabitants, it was also a huge market. Trade/commerce was the livelihood of my ancestors, who ran a "fittings and metal goods factory" at Buchengasse 15.

It must have been an extremely lucrative activity, as can be concluded from my grandmother's descriptions, from her ownership of a villa in the city and a hunting ground in Tyrol, as well as from the few printed testimonies that have survived the vagaries of the last 100 years. The company Pongracz & Bock included buildings that stretched around an entire street block in the 10th district. The owners of the company – my great-grandfather Othmar Bock (1871–1933) and his companion, a certain Mr. Pongracz – visited world fairs, among others Chicago (1893) and Paris (1900), where they gained an understanding of the latest production techniques, acquired the newest machines and were also inspired by the aesthetics of the Wild West. Even today, I still own a specially engraved Winchester rifle that my great-grandfather brought back as a souvenir from this business trip to America, which was significant for him.

The carefully designed catalogues of goods, published annually "to advertise the strong demand for our widely used and universally adopted special products", were linen-bound books of several hundred pages in an Art Nouveau aesthetic. Pongracz & Bock produced all the prestigious sanitary objects of the civilisational progress of the Wilhelmine era – water and gas pipes, bathroom fixtures, toilet facilities or steam pipes for hot water heating systems and much more. By means of rapid rail connections, the products of the Viennese manufacturers could be delivered throughout the Empire: from the Polish West Galicia to the Romanian Banat to the Carpathian Ukraine and other, even today exotic sounding, destinations. Who knows? Perhaps there were also customers in Rijeka, Pula, Opatija or Labin; the southern railway line to Rijeka was opened as early as 1873. "Delivery dates", it says in the Pongracz & Bock catalogue of 1912, "are kept to as far as possible". But: "In case of breakdowns,

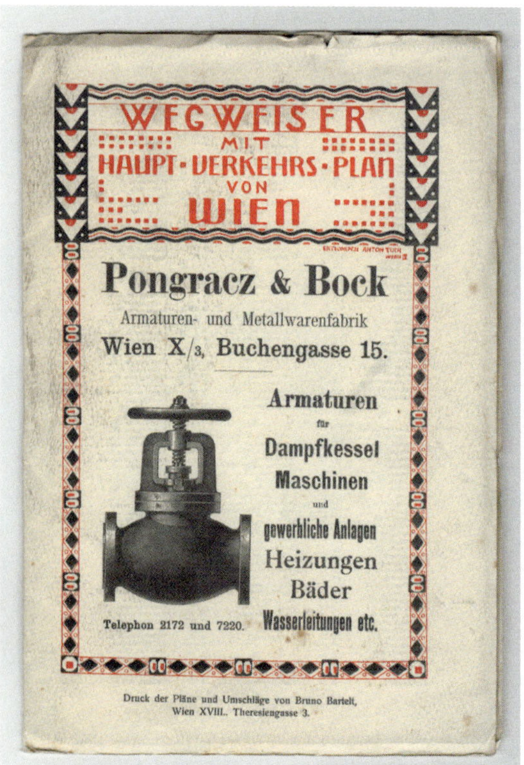

Pongracz & Bock promotional gift: Folding map with the Main Traffic Map of Vienna, 1908

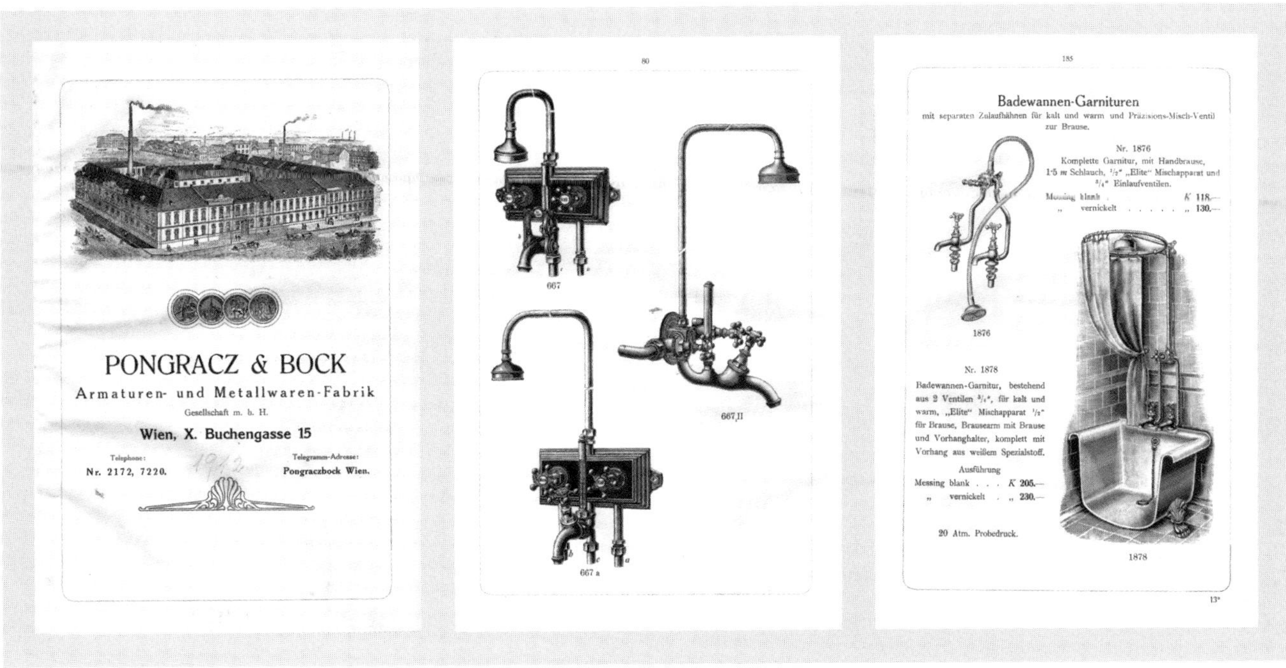

Pongracz & Bock products catalogue, 1912

strikes and lockouts, mobilisation, war, coal shortages [...] as well as force majeure, we are exempt from compliance".

Every summer, my grandmother told me, the whole family went south to the Austrian Riviera. They travelled according to their status, in an eight-seater open automobile with driver, maid and nanny via the Semmering pass road to Opatija, which the nobility and upper middle class frequented and where – favoured by the Mediterranean atmosphere of the Kvarner Bay – new business could probably also be arranged. The fashionable seaside resort functioned as an ideal stage for business, politics and society during the Belle Epoque, much like Nice, Brighton or Deauville. The legendary English historian Eric Hobsbawm pointed to this symbiotic intertwining of state and industrial capitalism on the basis of the English system in his study *Industry and Empire*. When the "long 19th century" (Hobsbawm) came to an end with World War I, the influence of imperial capitalism in Eastern Europe also waned. By this time, Othmar Bock had already left Vienna with his wife and three children, emigrating to Switzerland to spare his sons military service and to avoid having to manufacture weapons in the company. In Winterthur they entered the booming entertainment business, bought, built and ran cinemas. There, at the box office, my grandfather Adolf Doswald, an engineering student at the Technikum, met his future wife Mizzi, supposedly the most beautiful girl in Winterthur. But that's another story.

Why am I telling all this? Because this prehistory of boom, optimism, prosperity, tourism, war, migration and inter-culturality has provided me with important keywords for the exhibition *Landscapes of Desire*. Because such distortions are characteristic of the questions associated with the Industrial Art Biennial – with the context of a territory that shows the traces of migration, industrialisation, nationalism, war and globalisation in many ways. The Istrian peninsula consists of the most diverse, historical sediments that reach far back into antiquity. Starting from these points of reference, and along a curatorial practice of permanent self-assessment and self-reflection, *Landscapes of Desire* attempts to penetrate the stratifications of these histories with artistic means.

Anyone moving around Pula, Rijeka, Labin, Raša or Opatija encounters traces of the past at every turn: Roman, Venetian, Austro-Hungarian, Italo-Fascist, Yugo-Socialist, to give just a few examples. This sentimental feeling for the past, the loss of a supposedly better time, shapes the

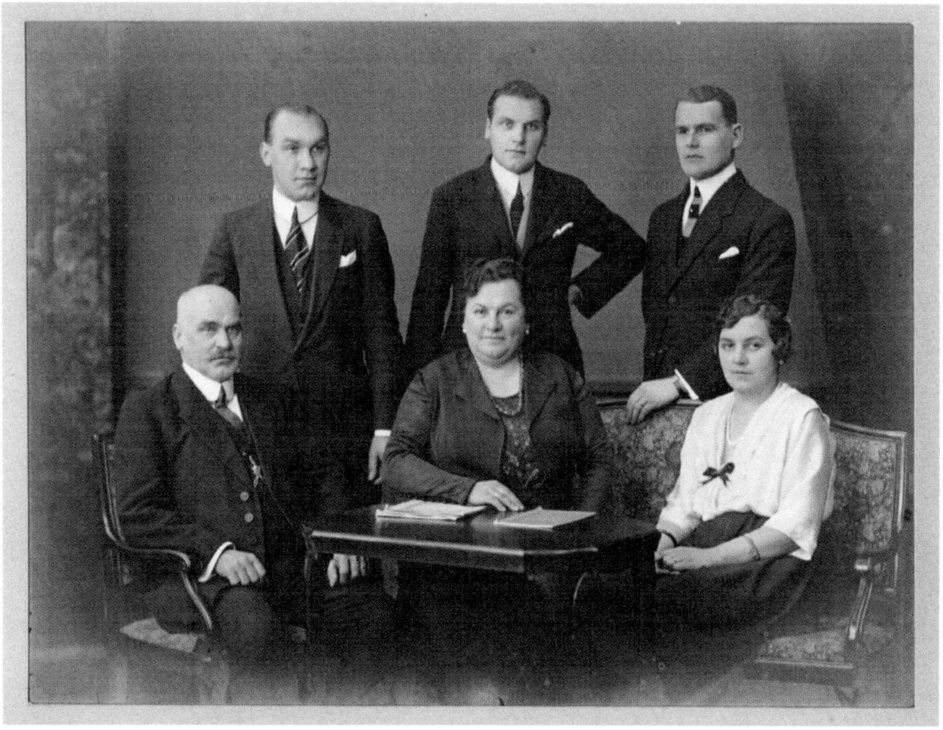

The Bock family with Maria „Mizzi“ Doswald-Bock (front, right) and Adolf Doswald (back, right) in Winterthur, Christmas 1921

current attitude towards life and is at the same time a powerful energy that lends itself to artistic and curatorial processes and discourses. *Landscapes of Desire* operates at this point of friction and interface; the artists' interventions are designed to engage with the past of the present. Following Paul Gaugin's epochal work, the basic questions of the condition humaine are: "Where do we come from? Who are we? Where are we going?" The 4th Industrial Art Biennial is thus an exhibition project which, starting from contextual realities, reflects on history and tells stories – autobiographical, collective, unknown, hypothetical, dreamed and hoped for. Whoever wants to deal with the future must first develop an idea of the past, must create a constructive, even creative way of dealing with it. The framework of this exhibition is particularly suitable for this purpose.

Right next to the large industrial port in Pula, where from 1856 the Austrian naval ship yard was located, there is a small green area, directly by the main road. Almost unnoticed there are some stone sarcophagi from Roman times lying in the meadow, which were probably unearthed during an excavation and deposited there for lack of other options. Next to the spectacular amphitheatre or the imposing Temple of Augustus, these stone coffins, marked by the ravages of time, look completely insignificant. Sometimes a passerby strolls through the meadow with his dog and the animal uses the stones as a tree substitute.

But the sarcophagi are extremely interesting in terms of their historical significance for art and industry, or rather for the art industry. Because the stone coffins do not all come from Pula, but partly from Asia Minor, probably from Aphrodisias. Since the 2nd century BC, there existed an important school of sculpture and a flourishing stonemasonry industry, which distributed their products, namely sarcophagi, throughout the Mediterranean. On this basis, Turkish conceptual artist and sculptor Seçkin Pirim has developed a project for the Industrial Art Biennial that draws on this "industrial" manufacturing of antiquity with 21st century methods. Seçkin's sculptures, centrally installed in front of the Augustus Temple, are based on digital designs. The stele-shaped columns are made of synthetic material; and the marble stones, also from Aphrodisias, were milled from the stone using high-tech machines.

A significant connection between art, culture and industry can also be seen in the monumental intervention by Spanish artist Lara Almarcegui. Almarcegui addresses the cultural economy of building, the issues of sustainability, energy, money and representation that underlie the urban world. At the point in Pula where the ferries from Venice dock at the harbour pier and drop off the streams of day tripping tourists, the artist has had a work of art constructed of Istrian limestone blocks stacked on top of each other. Although deliberately piled up and placed in an odd, non-functional way, it is unclear whether it is a work of art or, in fact, or a temporary storage facility for stones. The Istrian stone industry, which provided the stone blocks, has a long tradition that goes back centuries. Just like the sculptors from Aphrodisias in ancient times, today the Istrian quarry operators export their valuable products all over the world. Istrian stone products have been used, for example, in the construction of the Hilton Hotel in Budapest or for the facade of the Science & Technology Museum in Shanghai. Much better known than these buildings is another use of the "pietra d'Istria", as the stone is called in technical jargon: La Serenissima, the lagoon city of Venice, is largely built of the white stone, which is both beautiful and resistant. Almarcegui addresses this transfer of knowledge, aesthetics, money, and power between cultures with a minimalist gesture at the port of Pula, thus pointing to the still burning topicality of these issues. The synchronization of economic and cultural globalisation of aesthetics is a central theme in the work of Brazilian artist Fernanda Figueiredo. Starting from her own biography and thus from the influence of Bauhaus Modernism on contemporary, Brazilian culture after 1945, Figueiredo deals with analogous themes in other cultures. The almost blind faith in progress, prosperity, and modernisation is evident not only in the numerous futuristic buildings from the Italo-Fascist period, but also in the pioneering Yugoslav architecture found in Pula and Rijeka. These buildings, erected during the Tito era and in many cases now in poor condition, are a reminder that architecture once had a broader social responsibility in shaping society. When Figeuireido deals with this loss in a group of paintings created especially for the Biennial, she gives new relevance to the theme. Her message: it is important to return to the qualities of these urbanistic settings.

Unlike Pula, which has a long history, the past of the mining town of Raša covers only a short time frame. Initiated by Benito Mussolini and planned by Jewish architect Gustavo Pulitzer Finali, the town was created on the drawing board and built in just 547 days between 1936 and 1937. For the Duce, Raša was to become the "ideal fascist city": For this (propagandistic) reason, the city planning included a public swimming pool, a hospital, a

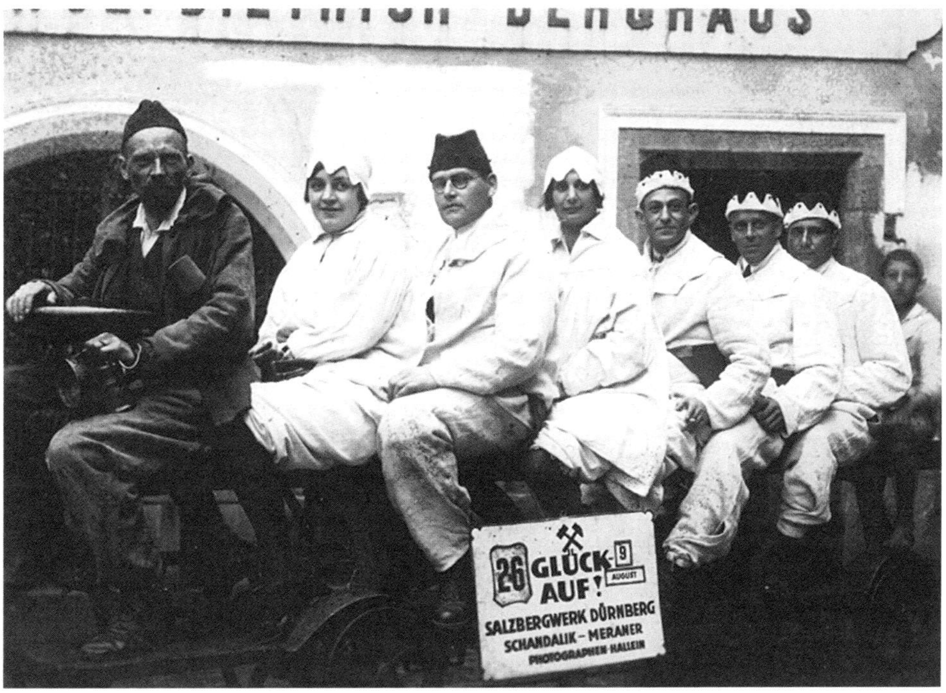

Visit of salt mine in Dürrnberg/Hallein near Salzburg, 9.8.1926

cinema, a hotel and all houses were equipped with central heating and telephone connection. Pulitzer Finali understood the construction of the town as a universalistic task and designed for the houses a furniture range, which today is offered for sale at design auctions. Anyone visiting Raša today encounters a time capsule. Although the paint is peeling here and there and the walls of the houses show signs of damage, in terms of urban planning everything is completely unchanged: With the decline of coal mining, the economic and thus also the structural dynamics for change were missing. Olaf Nicolai has addressed this specific context with a sound intervention. During the Industrial Art Biennial mysterious, delicate children's voices with Italian timbre sound from the abandoned main portal to the former coal mine, accompanied by a piano and the cool breeze from the depths of the old mine tunnels. The music is provided by the children's choir of the Comunita degli Italiani di Albona, Labin's Italian-speaking community that wants to preserve the cultural heritage of the past for the present. In Olaf Nicolai's sound intervention, titled *KO LI AJA*, the Foucauldian theory of the heterotope, the presence of the absent manifests itself as a wonderful poetic manifesto.

The fact that the Jewish architect Pulitzer Finali finally emigrated to the USA in 1938 to decorate Italian restaurants in New York and the villas of film stars in Hollywood, before returning to Trieste after the war and being responsible for the interior design of famous transatlantic steamships (namely the Andrea Doria), is another chapter in this eventful history of the *Landscapes of Desire*. Starting from these futuristic furnishings and public architecture still present in Raša, Labin and Pula, Cristian Andersen has developed an artistic reappraisal of the aesthetics of everyday life in Labin's vacant Pescheria (fish shop) from today's deconstructivist point of view. His sublime designs, analogous to the Futurists, oscillate between everyday practicality and beauty and exhibit that optimistic spirit that seems to have been lost in the wars of the 20th century in Istria.

A few steps away from the Pescheria is the central piazza of Labin, a neo-classical ensemble built by Italian architects. There, Gregor Hildebrandt has placed a bronze sculpture almost five meters high, modelled on the figure of the pawn in the game of chess. Like the urban setting in which it stands during the Biennial, the figure's design dates from the 19th century. Named after the English chess master Howard Staunton, the pieces were patented and put on the market in 1849: "The pieces generally are fashioned with convenience to the hand; and it is to be remarked, that while there is so great an accession to elegance of form, it is not attained at the expense of practical utility. Mr. STAUNTON'S pattern adopts but elevates the conventional form; and the base of the Pieces being of a large diameter, they are more steady than ordinary sets," reads the newspaper advertisement of September 8, 1849. Hildebrandt is fascinated by the globalised variety of forms that have emerged since then, despite design standardization. He collects the pawns, puts the collection on display in specially made showrooms, ambiguously calling it the "Pawn Shop". This play with ambiguities and context-shifted readings is consistently continued in Labin: While the milieu of the former Piazza Vittorio Emanuele III pays homage to the urban bourgeoisie, Hildebrandt's artistic gesture points to a context that is often misunderstood and neglected – the economic importance of agriculture (in German the name of the chess piece is farmer [Bauer]). Against the backdrop of the Ukrainian grain crisis and the discussion about sustainable food production, this work of art is highly topical.

With a similar focus but different approach, Sandra Knecht worked on the context of the Istrian peninsula. The artist undertook a large-scale research in the summer of 2022 at the farmers' markets of Pula and Labin to learn about traditional products and produce. Conversations with old peasant women and shopkeepers, forays into the overgrown surroundings for herb-gathering events, and an examination of the question of what is "typical" are all reflected in Knecht's oeuvre. With her research, the artist secures old techniques of food preparation that would be too unprofitable or inefficient for the food industry. This results in art and pleasure projects, such as a three-course menu with "barley, nuts, potatoes, chard and sucuk (for the non-vegetarians)" as the main course. In local restaurants – in Labin at Peteani and in Pula at Amfiteatar – this menu will be part of the food list during the Biennial and will be inscribed in the landscapes through everyday but essential activities such as enjoying, eating and digesting.

English artist Charlie Billingham explores the psychosomatic effects of the first wave of industrialisation in the late 18th century. In 1765, James Hargreaves invented the spinning machine ("Spinning Jenny") and built factories. From then on, the abstraction of the realities of people's lives began. While the lives of peasants had previously been shaped by natural cycles, the new factory workers had to organise their daily routines according to the

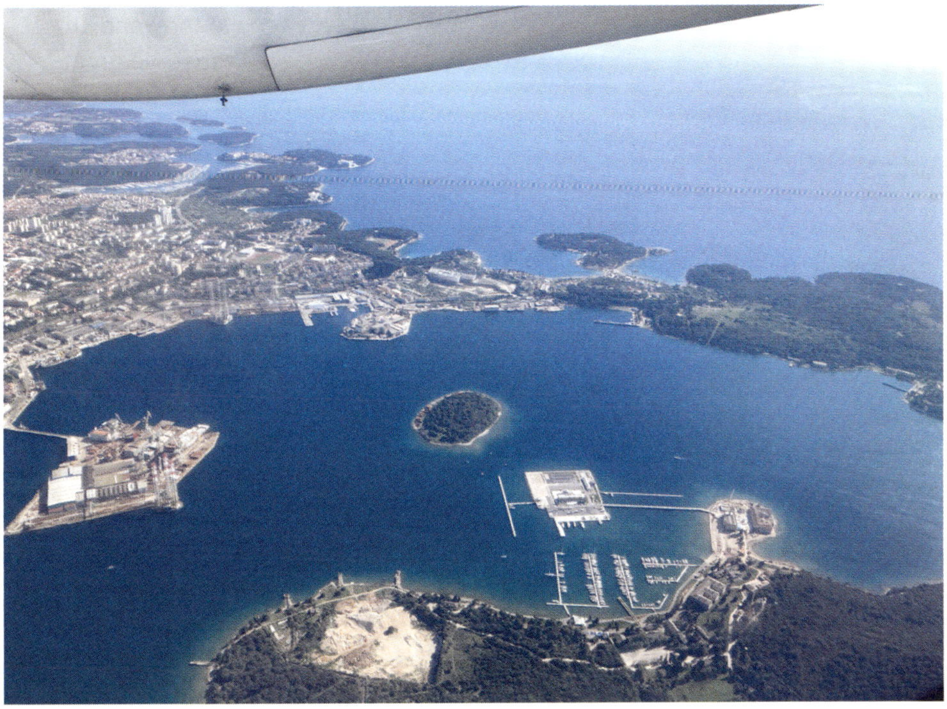

View from the plane (Pula harbour), 19.4.2023

clock. This disruption of the concept of time, the pressure to perform and the destruction of social structures led to massive disturbances of the psyche. Sigmund Freud pointed out the sublimation strategies through alcohol and entertainment as early as 1908 in his essay *The 'Cultural' Sexual Morality and Modern Nervousness.* Literature "brings pathological figures, psychopathic-sexual, revolutionary, and other problems before the mind of the reader; our ear is excited and overstimulated by intrusive and noisy music administered in large doses; the theatres capture all the senses with their exciting representations; the visual arts, too, turn with predilection to the repulsive, the ugly, and the exciting, and are not afraid to place before our eyes in repulsive reality even the most hideous things that reality offers." The starting point for Charlie Billingham's artistic exploration of social disruption is the satirical caricatures of Isaac Cruikshank (1764–1811) and James Gillray (1756–1815), which provide a critical view of living conditions in England and capture the consequences of industrialisation in drastic images. Billingham extracts particularly catchy gestures from these pictorial worlds, enlarges them into the monumental, and with this abstraction points to an overarching question: What social effects emanate from particularly disruptive inventions, currently digitalisation?

The feminist and social pedagogue Giuseppina Martinuzzi (1844–1925), to whom Anna Piva dedicates a comprehensive artistic research, also belongs to this temporal context. Martinuzzi was born in Labin, worked from nearby Trieste with her writings and journalistic works, and advocated pacifism and ethnic integration. Anna Piva's exploration of Martinuzzi's early feminist writings, combined with Istrian poets Isabella Flego's writing, has expanded to include other female positions, that had also pioneered women's rights in other cultures and countries. The result is a text-image collage that traces a fundamental question beyond the boundaries of narrowly defined national territories.

Christian Jankowski gives the sculpture park in Dubrova an artistic facelift. Created as an act of remembrance for the 50th anniversary of the "Labinska Republika", the legendary 1921 anti-fascist miners' strike, and opened in the presence of Josip Broz Tito, the park comprises almost 100 sculptures made of Istrian stone on an area of more than 33 hectares. On this site, which is used by the local population as a recreational facility, Jankowski creates a temporary 9-hole golf course during the Biennial and organises a golf tourna-

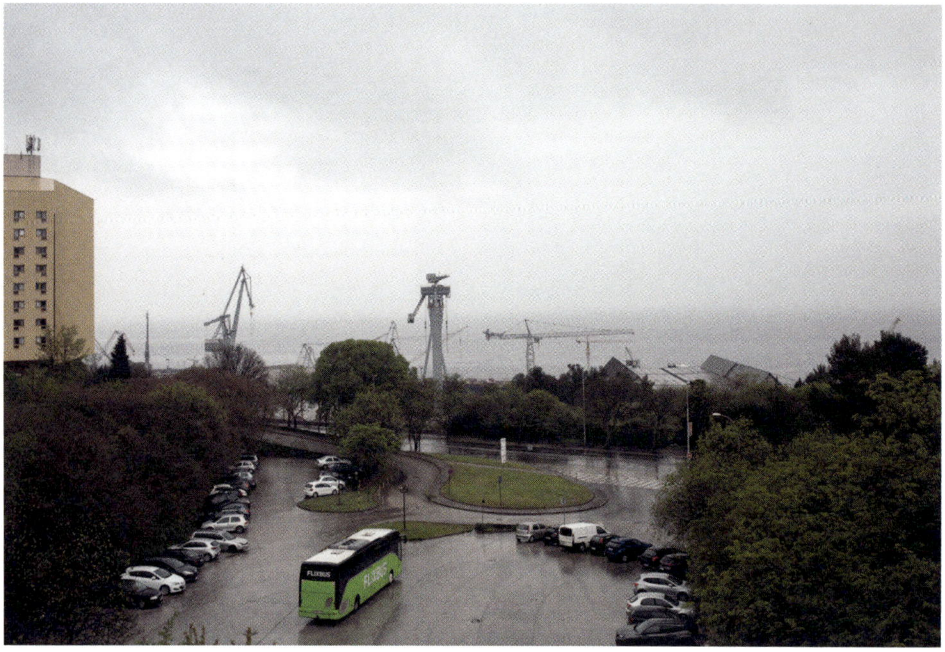

Rijeka

ment, the "1st Industrial Golf Open", in the run-up to the exhibition. With the help of a professional TV journalist, a television report is produced during the tournament, documenting the unique events for posterity. By superimposing art and sport, Jankowski creates a new, updated perception for the wonderful sculpture park. In addition to this performative experience of the participants, a golf sculpture remains in the park to commemorate the memorable occasion in the future.

Karin Sander's intervention focuses on the interface of digital and analogue landscape perception. On the tower of the Santa Barbara Church in Raša, the artist had the widely visible Christian cross specially marked with a band of light and framed this clerical symbol with the Google "Point of Interest" emblem, also in LED, the epitome of digital orientation. The transfer from digitality to reality is extremely disconcerting and evokes a series of questions that have a current background with the perception of realities in virtual reality. Karin Sander succeeds in pointing out and questioning ways of looking at things along a wide variety of timelines. For example, the following note from a Google optimizer site: "Your church is technically a business, so you should have the same level of tools that businesses use to grow."

"Vorrei sapere se, tenendomi vivo, truffo la vita o la morte" is written in front of a running clock on the large, brightly lit screen located on the back wall of the Archaeological Museum in Pula. "I want to know if, by keeping myself alive, I am cheating life or death". The quote that U.S. conceptual artist Joseph Kosuth uses (alongside 47 other quotations) for his monumental intervention comes from Italo Svevo, a writer from Trieste who embodies the multiple dimensions of cultural, political, social and economic dislocation found in Istria. Born Aron Hector Schmitz in 1861, with an Austrian father and Italian mother, of Jewish faith, he was educated in a boarding school near Würzburg and trained as a merchant. When his father's business went bankrupt, Schmitz's ambition as a writer staid unfullfilled. He had by then adopted the pseudonym Svevo, but needed to take a job at a bank. Later in his life, he married the daughter of a wealthy family and was then able to focus on writing again, although this remained unsuccessful. Svevo became friends with James Joyce, translated Sigmund Freud's *The Interpretation of Dreams* into Italian, and studied psychoanalysis. Thanks to his friendship with Joyce, he finally achieved his literary breakthrough before dying in a car accident in 1928.

This one life – an existence between bread and art, between utopia and reality, between Austria and Italy – exemplifies the many narratives, stories and biographies that gather in the *Landscapes of Desire* to trigger a fruitful discourse on the present and the future.

Croatia 2023 and the Historical Traces

Marie-Janine Calic

Croatia is the youngest member of the European Union. Ten years after accession, it adopted the euro as its national currency in early 2023. At the same time, the country on the Adriatic has joined the border-free Schengen area. Both should primarily help tourism, Croatia's most important economic sector. The former Yugoslav republic became independent in 1991, and its people are happy to be closely integrated into European structures today.

While most Croatians generally welcome the introduction of the euro, many fear that price increases will now follow. The global financial crisis had already triggered a severe recession. After a short recovery phase, the corona pandemic created new socio-economic upheavals. In 2020, economic output fell by more than eight percent; only in Greece, Spain and Italy was the slump even deeper. While the economic situation has now largely normalized, the country is facing new challenges in view of the war in Ukraine.

The aftermath of the Ukraine war

Croatia has strongly condemned the Russian attack and also supports the sanctions imposed by the US and the EU. The country is showing solidarity and has already taken in more than 20,000 refugees from Ukraine. On the anniversary of the Russian attack, the Ukrainian flag was hoisted at parliament and government buildings. However, as everywhere in Europe, consumer prices have risen sharply; moreover, most of the Russian tourists expected in 2022 stayed away. The impairments in the energy supply, on the other hand, are weaker than in other European countries. A liquefied natural gas (LNG) terminal went into operation on the island of Krk in 2021, so just over a quarter of the natural gas consumed in Croatia is sourced from Russia.

Above all, the Russian attack on Ukraine brings back bad memories of the Yugoslav war of disintegration. After Croatia unilaterally declared independence on June 25, 1991, the Serb minority rebelled. Irregular Serb armed forces, in conjunction with the Yugoslav People's Army, took control of a third of Croatia's territory in a matter of weeks. They expelled about half a million people and proclaimed the Republic of Serbian Krajina. On January 15, 1992, after six months of fighting, Croatia was recognized as a sovereign state by the member states of the European Union. A ceasefire agreement was signed, but part of the country remained occupied. UN blue helmet troops were supposed to secure the peace and mediate a political solution, but this did not happen. In 1995, the Croatian army recaptured the disputed regions in Operation Thunderstorm, smashing the Serbian parastate and expelling more than 150,000 Serbs from Croatia. With the withdrawal of the last blue helmets in 1998, territorial sovereignty was fully restored. The war has cost the lives of more than 10,000 people; around 3,000 people were missing and tens of thousands were left uprooted. The political, legal, and psychological consequences of war are felt still today.

Official Croatia regards the so-called "Homeland War" of the 1990s as a war of national unification and a state-founding event. Although the former Yugoslav republic has only around 4 million inhabitants, it is more diverse than almost any other European country. Centuries of foreign rule by various powers and mixed cultural influences have left their marks. The area around Zagreb and northern and eastern Croatia belonged to the Habsburg monarchy, while on the coast, in Dalmatia and Istria, you can see the close connection with the culture and history of Venice. In addition, there are historically grown regional identities that also shape the political culture. On the coat of arms of the national flag you can see five symbols above the white and red checkerboard pattern, which stand for central Croatian Zagorje, the former Merchant Republic of Dubrovnik, as well as Dalmatia, Istria and Slavonia. Croatians who think nationally would like to undo the roughly 70 years of belonging to the multi-ethnic state of Yugoslavia. They prefer to refer to the Middle Ages, when the Croatian kingdom was once a respected regional power.

Political divisions

The national-conservative forces, which won the majority in the first parliamentary elections after the collapse of communism, cling to the dream of national greatness. The sole ruling party in 1990 was the Croatian Democratic Community (HDZ), founded by the former general of the Yugoslav People's Army and historian Franjo Tudjman. He was the first president to rule independent Croatia for a decade with an authoritarian style of leadership. After his death in 1999, a centre-left coalition won the parliamentary elections the following year. The Croatian constitution was amended and the excessive powers of the president were restricted. Croatia then embarked on a resolute Europeanization and reform course, which was rewarded with EU accession in 2013.

To this day, Croatia is divided into two roughly equally strong ideological camps that alternate in government. On the one hand there are conservative, Catholic and nationally oriented forces, on the other left-wing liberal and social-democratic ones. In addition, a number of smaller parties and interest groups have established themselves, which will tip the scales in the parliamentary elections. Domestically, Croatia has recently been facing similar challenges to those of many other EU countries: populist Eurosceptics as well as ultra-conservative, nationalist and right-wing extremists are on the rise. You can find them not only in political parties, like the "Homeland Movement", but also among intellectuals, in social media and in pop culture.

The political and ideological division is also reflected in the attitude towards the Ukraine war. For example, the social-democratic president Zoran Milanović has repeatedly spoken out against Western arms deliveries to Ukraine, specifically against prime minister Andrej Plenković and his HDZ-party, which has governed the country since 2016. This year, the Croatian parliament also voted against training Ukrainian military personnel in Croatia.

Historical revisionism

Last but not least, the ideological rifts run through the public debates on history raging around the time of the Second World War and socialist Yugoslavia. Right-wing politicians, emigrants and intellectuals relativize its interpretation by rehabilitating the fascist Ustasha, which ruled the so-called "Independent State of Croatia" at the time of the Second World War. Serbs and Jews, as well as members of the political opposition, were murdered or expelled en masse in the Croatian state by Hitler's grace. More than 80,000 people died in the Jasenovac concentration camp alone.

Yugoslavia is the only European country whose multinational partisans shook off the foreign occupation on their own, which became the founding myth of the post-1945 socialist state. The Croatian communist Josip Broz Tito coined the motto "Brotherhood and unity", but at the same time fought a terrible civil war against the Croatian Ustasha, Serbian Chetniks and other collaborators. In the spring of 1945, the "Quislings" fleeing with the Wehrmacht were liquidated en masse in Carinthian Bleiburg. Nationalist forces refer to the event as a "Croatian Holocaust", and a former HDZ Minister of Education even described the defeat of the Ustasha in 1945 as a "national tragedy". Nonetheless, veterans' associations and the Catholic Church even want the fascist Ustasha salute "Za dom – spremni!" (For the homeland – ready) to be reintroduced into the army. The historical revisionism propagated by the official side has prompted the Jewish community to repeatedly boycott the commemorative events for the liberation of the Jasenovac concentration camp. To this day, a folkish nationalism is haunting the country, making life difficult for minorities and hindering the process of coming to terms with the past.

Titostalgia

Under President Tudjman, thousands of streets and squares commemorating the "War of the People's Liberation" were given new names, and most of the partisan monuments were torn down. Thousands demonstrated unsuccessfully when the City Council of Zagreb, after years of tug-of-war, decided in 2017 to rename the representative Tito Square to "Square of the Republic of Croatia". Josip Broz Tito, long-serving Yugoslav president and frontman of the Non-Aligned Movement, is a figure who continues to divide political camps to this day. "Tell me how you think of Tito, and I'll tell you what you are!" is often heard today in what was once Yugoslavia.

Many people have positive memories of Tito, who died in 1980. He ruled the country autocratically, but there was significantly less repression than in the Eastern Bloc. His Yugoslavia seemed to promise certain prosperity, social security, ethnic tolerance, and international prestige. Therefore, Tito is now the subject of an alternative culture of remembrance. Quite a few celebrate his official birthday on May 25 or make a pilgrimage to his grave in Belgrade. For many younger people, too, Tito is the hero of their lives and the personified positive. This reflects the insecurities and disappointments that the new era brought with it. After all, many promises remained unfulfilled after the system change. Croatia's level of prosperity is still far below the EU average, and since 2013 the brain drain has driven more than 350,000 people, around 20 percent of the Croatian workforce, including many doctors, abroad. Against this background, the past remains a projection screen for an uncertain present.

This essay was commissioned by the magazine of Burgtheater (Vienna) for Tena Štivičić's *Drei Winter*"

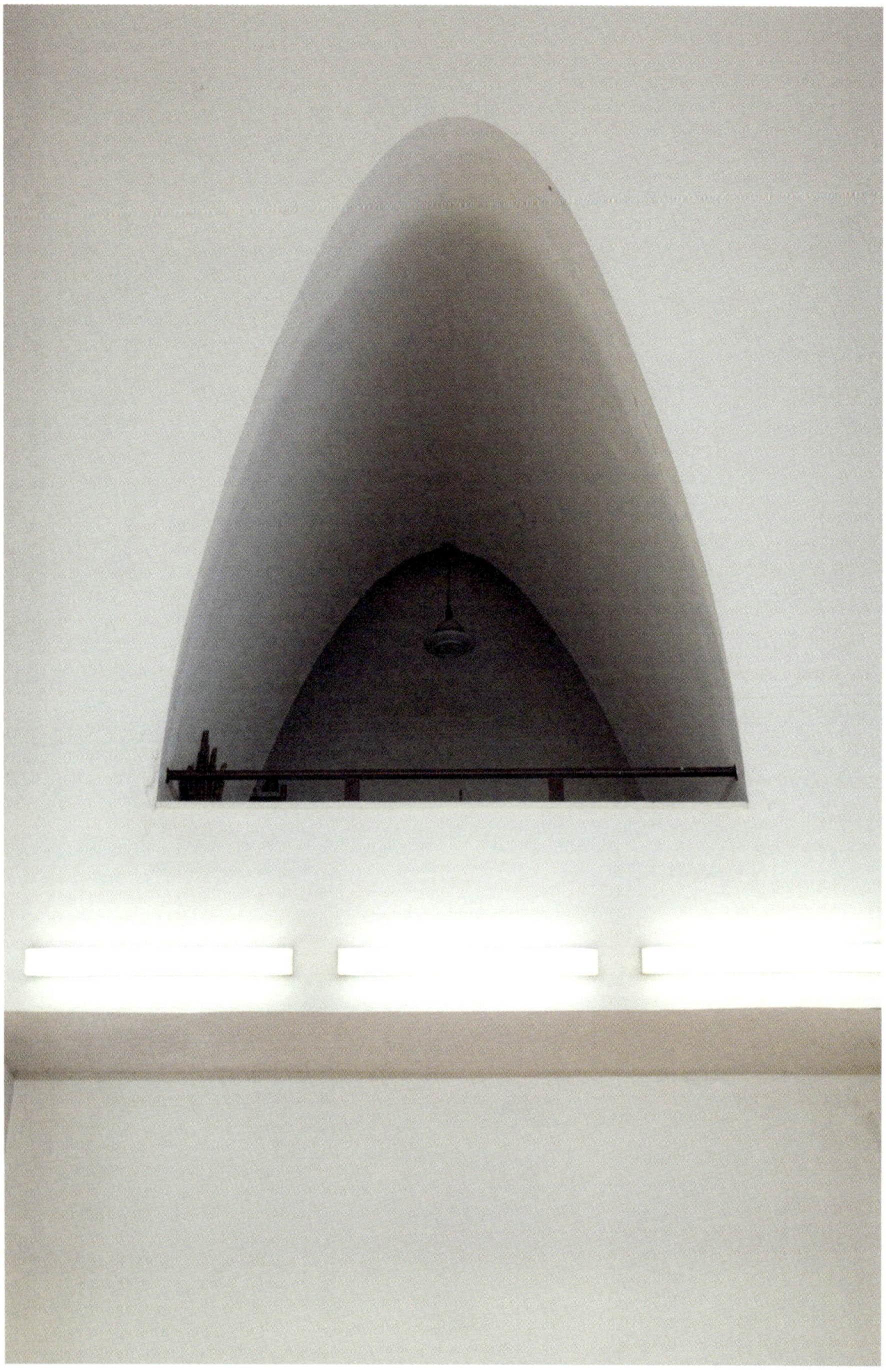

St. Barbara Church, Raša

Gesamtkunstwerk. City of Raša and the Mining Town of Labin

An Empathic Essay as a Testimony of Time from 2005*

Tatjana Gromača

The first time I saw Raša I was riding a bus from Pula to Rijeka. It was almost six years ago, just after I suddenly and on my own initiative moved from Zagreb to Istria, more precisely to Pula. I remember that trip well, especially the reason I went there – following a newspaper ad, I traveled from Pula to Rijeka, to meet a man who had been making a living for years by providing sexual services to dissatisfied (unhappy, lonely) women. I wanted to write a newspaper story about him and we agreed to meet in the center of Rijeka, at the city cafe, where I was supposed to wait for him in one of the glass-lined booths, dressed in a bright red coat. I will not use this opportunity to recount how risky my undertaking was, nor the dangerous consequences that could have followed. I will say only that I believe I was saved from the possibility of being attacked and killed by a grasshopper knife, or raped in a dark entrance opposite the railway station, by some kind of a lucky star of mine.
But my path to this story led me through Raša, a place with a beauty that fascinated me so much that I remember the first time I encountered it even more intensely than the unpleasant episode in Rijeka with the male prostitute.

The bus was descending the hill along sharp turns, gliding slowly towards the bay of Raša, its landscape possessing an unusually rare atmosphere that we might call "satisfied serenity". The narrow road followed the gently winding course of a small river, overgrown with wild sedges and reeds, traces of the former marshland. On one side of the river, not far from the concrete bridge, two wooden boats rested. One beautiful old three-storey house, probably once a manor, filled its side of the coast with mystery. Its walls were wrapped in a barely visible, greenish veil of moisture. On the washing line stretched in front of the house clothes fluttered in the wind – old-fashioned and stiff women's brassiereas and dirty-white cobweb curtains, resembling, from a distance, the torn dress of a bride who fled from the wedding party and the groom and made her way through a damp forest and bushes.

A cramped "topolino"

The image of the river, the reeds, the boat and the house with damp walls, with transparent linen by its side, swaying in the wind, will forever stay imprinted in my memory – it has, for reasons unclear to me, acquired a particularly important place in my storehouse of memories, almost archetypal, like the experiences I remember from early childhood or particularly striking dreams whose meaning I can never fully decipher.

The road that follows that image in my memory is a kind of extension of it – a narrow, not too busy road that runs parallel to the course of the river, tall narrow cypresses and apple trees, a modest river embankment, plants that signal a well-drenched soil, a heron here and there that slowly pushes away from the ground, elevating its slender body upwards, reaching the heights of the treetops. It is actually a valley, a basin bordered on all sides by hills, whose emptiness and peace exude a meditative quality.

To drive down this road, edged by old stone curbs, decorated with small concrete bridges, is something like driving through the southern Mediterranean in an open cabriolet, or a cramped "topolino", like a scene from black and white Italian neorealist films. It reminds me of an old road in the French Riviera – though I have no concrete arguments to back this up, since I've never been to France. I don't know if it comes from a passage in a book, a photograph, or a TV movie that I may have watched, or if it's simply a personal chimera that I can't seem to resist.

Harmony and aesthetics

After passing the embanked river and a row of tall apple trees that look like an empty chessboard, a small town called Raša appears. The sight is unique – the road we are travelling is on the same level as the upper floor windows and rooftops. The town is in a unique location, and as we approach it we see its ground plan, the unusual regularity of houses and their rooftops. This creates an almost hypnotic effect – because only a few seconds later do we realise that the houses are all the same, like a painter's scrawl, an enchanted circle, or a strange labyrinth of homes that are also unusually beautiful.

The first time I saw those houses, I fell enduringly in love with their unique harmony and aesthetics. Something within them absolutely won me over, as a kind of a "breath" of past times, a taste and style that contain proper elegance, quite discreet hints of nobility, immersed in simplicity and functionality. I fell in love with these houses as I have fallen in love with houses countless times before, mostly with similar characteristics and nuances. Houses (though never new ones) are one of my permanent fascinations – houses with their own histories that I can immerse myself in, without knowing anything about them, with the desire to at least intuitively appropriate a piece of their essence.

But the story of Raša and its houses is something special, it is a town of about two thousand inhabitants in which absolutely every building radiates "something" that could only be understood in relation to a larger whole.

Repetition and loneliness

I visited Raša many times after that first fatal meeting, without a specific reason. I didn't know anybody there. Its emptiness and absence filled me with anxiety and pensive dullness: this artistry filled environment did not lead me to do something, to act, but only to wander the streets absent-mindedly, to absorb the colours of facades, the lines of buildings, the silent collision between my gaze and the gazes of curious residents. Tired of walking, frightened by a wave of despondency that would inevitably hit me after only a few moments spent in that town, I indulged myself in a short respite, an escape into the interior of one of the three shops, where my vital energy and shaken morale slowly returned only after buying something, like a small tin kettle.

In hindsight, however, nothing could correct that anaemic image of that beautiful but dying town which I fell in love with; its entire atmosphere underlined a lack of life; the ominously empty square, a car or a resident occasionally crawling down its deserted streets; a hairdressing salon with a dusty window and a jar with three small dried violet flowers placed in its centre.

Loneliness is a kind of spiritual constant here. The very configuration of this place suggests solitude, rows of identical house fronts, the inevitable monotony of life rituals, repetition. But isn't he who can transcend solitude and repetition by perceiving and accepting them, and thus resist being subjected to them, at an advantage? It is certainly possible to train yourself in this spiritual discipline by living here, this place where the panoramic view and the timeless, unmoved atmosphere are reminiscent of scenes from the paintings of Giorgio de Chirico (1888–1978). The de Chirico-like poetics were once suppressed by the noise from mining shafts, the hustle and bustle of miners and their families on Raša's streets, the noise of trucks, buses. Today, Raša is like a frozen painting out of some European museum, its poetics composed by an interplay of sunlight and shadows, of empty surfaces where, occasionally, a bony dog will slowly pass by, or a child, or an old miner, who originally came from Central Bosnia.

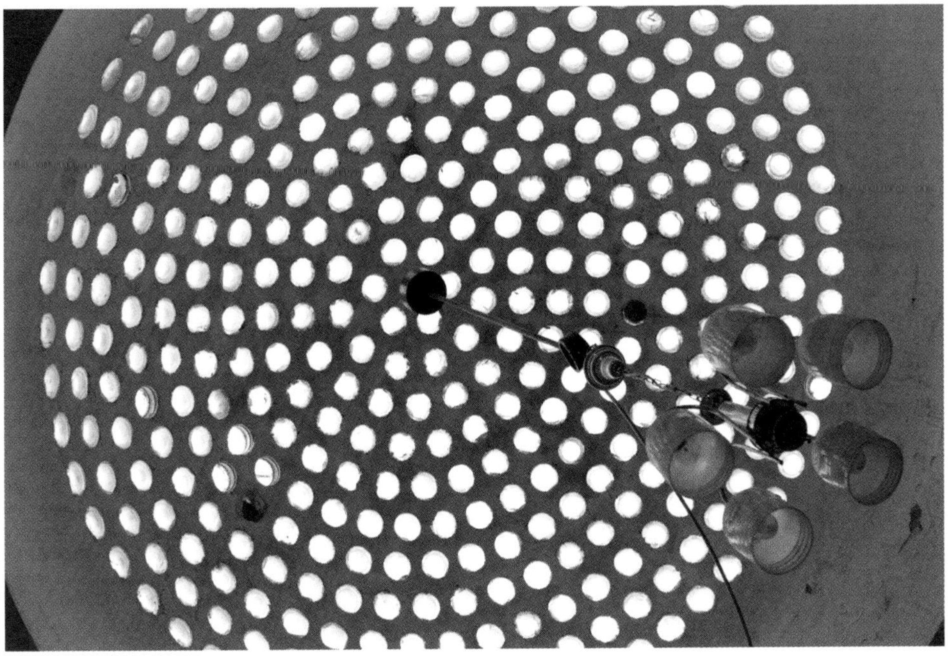

St. Barbara Church, Raša

Gustavo Pulitzer Finali

Did Raša's Italian architect, Gustavo Pulitzer Finali, also have such a pure artistic vision of Raša? Did he believe in the eternal life of a perfect mining town? The story that follows is the story of a unique town – an artistic creation of single man. Gustavo Pulitzer Finali was born in Trieste, 13 years before the end of the 19th century, from a marriage between Caroline Finali, a woman of Jewish descent, and Geza Pulitzer, the owner of a trading company of Hungarian origin. Pulitzer's parents met in Vienna, where Mrs. Finali was a singer in the Vienna Opera. It is unknown how Mr. Pulitzer came to Vienna, but the Finali family, whose descendant is of unusual importance for this story, lived in Trieste, which was the largest Austrian port at the time. Traces of the Austro-Hungarian Monarchy can be seen in every street in Trieste – judging by its architecture, one would presume that Trieste is not an Italian city, but an Austro-Hungarian one. Along with Rijeka, which back then was better known as "Fiume", Trieste was a city that was called a home by people of various cultures. It was a lively, open city, with cargo ships with unusual flags sailing in and out of its harbour. Those who disembarked and remained were waiting for a better future, and the atmosphere of intermingling and the constant influx of the "new" truly made this seem possible.

The education of an architect

As early as 1908, at the age of twenty-one, Gustavo Pulitzer Finali enrolled in the Polytechnic of Munich. This was a very respectable study programme whose very name was a guarantee, not only of the acquisition of knowledge, but also of the possibility of using the knowledge it offered to traverse new horizons. It can be said that this study had a reputation as a place of advanced minds, where free thinking and research were not hindered, but nourished and supported. The "Deutscher Werkbund", an association whose efforts were intended "to unite art, applied art, craftsmanship and industry", was founded in Munich just one year before the young Pulitzer arrived there. One of its founders, Theodor Fischer, played an important role as a professor in the Pulitzer's apprenticeship.

All is one

During the following years Gustavo Pulitzer often went on so-called "study trips", during which the

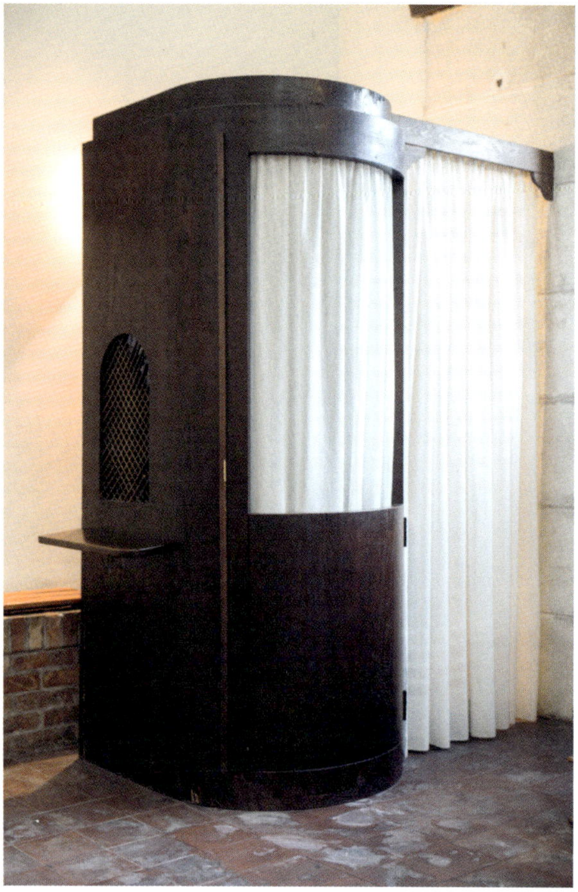

St. Barbara Church, Raša

young architect would get to know and explore the architecture of major cities around the world, until this was abruptly interrupted by the turbulent beginning of the First World War. Pulitzer would often travel to southern Italy, Greece, Spain, England, the United States, Norway, Finland. He stayed in each city for as long as his studies permitted, absorbing not just the appearance of the cities, but also their internal structure, rhythm, and the rhythm of their breath.

It is quite possible that these research trips made the still young and inexperienced Pulitzer aware of the fact that in art, all is actually one. All is one, Gustavo Pulitzer probably reasoned while observing the pediments of the Pantheon, the windows of the White House in Washington, or a street corner in some English province. He certainly realised something equally important: "everything is permitted". Everything is permitted in art, just like in love.

The spirit of the place

During his studies in Munich Finali learned another very important lesson in construction – respect for tradition, local architectural peculiarities, and what is called the "spirit of the place". The spirit of the place, one of the fundamental axioms of good architecture – a builder who was not endowed by nature with such a nuanced sensibility that he could perceive the spirit of a place, could be a good builder, but not an exceptional one. The books about Finali and his masterpiece speak of how he was influenced, along with his contemporaries like Jože Plečnik, Max Fabiani, Carl Seidl or Viktor Kovačić, by what is known as the "spiritual planting" of Late Historicism, Late Secession and the Wagner School; not strictly belonging to any of these stylistic formations, but operating in the in-between.

Fascism and cities

We will skip the chapters that discuss Finalis' return to Trieste and the progress of his career, which was on a rapid, upward trajectory. We will pause in 1935, right before the beginning of the Second World War, when Fascism was already operating in full force in Europe. Finali's country was one of the harbingers of Fascism, and its soldiers were already stationed in Syria and Africa.
One of the things Fascist "visionaries" were very fond of was the external demonstration of their strength and power. Architecture at that time

was considered to be a "gentleman's art", and architects were "the only true gentlemen among artists". An architect is the one who initiates order and balance, the perfect mediator between man and society, the one who works to create a utopian future.

Building large yet aesthetically impressive buildings, was one of the ways in which all former great empires demonstrated their power. Mussolini was particularly fond of this idea – to be a leader who raised a town from nothing, an "ideal town" intended for "the man of the new age". Now doesn't that sound fascinating, worthy of our deepest respect?

An ideal mining town

The real war was yet to come, preparing for war meant more than just possessing an army and weapons. It was necessary to reserve safe sources of stone ore and lignite, which at that time were important raw materials for the powering of ships, railways, and for the army.

Istria, the westernmost Croatian province, a peninsula annexed by Italy 1918 after the fall of the Austro-Hungarian Monarchy (to which it previously belonged) possessed mines rich in this raw material. Mussolini decided that the "ideal mining town", which would accommodate 2000 miners and their families, should be built near Krapan and the mining shafts "Franz Jozef", "Salamon" and "Carlotta". He entrusted the entire task of the urbanisation, architectural solution and execution to Gustavo Pulitzer Finali from Trieste. Pulitzer Finali thus got a unique opportunity to put in practice the meaning of a "Gesamtkunstwerk", being granted the unique opportunity to be the total artist who will project and design everything – the entire town, its architecture, its urban and interior fittings.

To begin with, it was necessary to drain the valley, the large barren swamp of Krapan bay, which lay at the dishevelled mouth of the Raša river, but was also flooded by the sea.

A short and superficial history of the mine

Regular ore production was established in Istrian coal mines in 1785, during the Venetian administration.

In 1807, it was appropriated by Napoleon.
In 1813, after Napoleon's army retreated, his Illyrian provinces, including Istria, were returned to Austria.

The mines remained under Austrian administration for a whole century, before they came under Italian control in 1918.

Mining fever

Mining fever took hold of the population in the Labin region during the 1830s. Both the impoverished locals, scattered among the nearby hills and newcomers prone to adventure, frantically searched for coal, hoping to get lucky quickly.
At the same time, there was another kind of mining fever, although not a literal one, and it took place in the mines themselves. In the wider Labin area, contracts were being granted to open new coal mines and quotas were enlarged. In between 1819 and 1829 production almost doubled in the Sveta Barbara mine in Krapno near Raša – the annual average grew to one thousand tons. Ore from the Istrian coal mines made its way to the Trieste market, and it was most likely used in the Trieste refinery. In 1830, the new owners of the coal mines arrived in Krapan – trading houses M. A. Rothschild, Gaymüller, Stametz, Neuwall and Wartheimstein. Mining in the Austrian monarchy was regulated by a special law, and trading companies received a contract for the exploitation of hard coal in Dalmatia and Istria for the next 99 years.

Republic of Labin

We will pass over the numerous mining accidents, the strikes by miners forced to work 12 hour shifts, with a one-hour break at noon and midnight; the transfer of the Labin mines to "Trifailer Kohlenwerks-Gesellschaft." company, based in Vienna, which directly connected the tunnels of Vinež, Krapan and Štrmac mines (the total length of all the mining corridors was more than 100 kilometers); World War I and the "Labin Republic" – the complex 1921 strike, organised by miners of various nationalities (Poles, Czechs, Slovenes, Croats, Austrians) who, blasting the entrances to the mine shafts, briefly took over the Labin coal mines.
We will also skip over the fact that the mine was often in an extremely difficult situation (due to floods, snow and inefficiency), and that it had to be shut down on several occasions.

We will skip all that so that we can arrive as soon as possible at the year 1935, when the construction of the "ideal mining town" began under the supervision of engineers Pulitzer and Ceppi in the place where the bed of the dead sea – the

Krapan lake and the lower course of the stem Raša river – had until recently lain (this is why that region was rich in both sea and fresh water fish).

The life work of Gustavo Pulitzer Finali

It is not known how long Gustavo Pulitzer Finali spent on his life's work – creating a plan for construction of a mining town that was originally supposed to be called Liburnia. Judging by the result, a "pearl of modern architecture" that has been declared a "cultural monument" in its entirety, it is clear that Raša came to be through meticulous and inspired work that did not leave a single loggia, garden, window pane or mansard to chance. Finali knew that he was given an opportunity that wasn't afforded to any other architect – the possibility to create an entire town. He dedicated all his knowledge, talent and his open, modern spirit to that creation, seeing things in their totality and never in isolation.

The three great European cultures

While he was working on Raša, Finali had to be aware of the fact that Istria is not an area dominated by one culture, but a place where three great European cultures – Romanic, Slavic and Germanic – constantly touched and mingled for centuries.

Finali combined these three traditions, thus creating new value, respecting the local, Mediterranean spirit. A symmetrically perfect and stylistically uniform, strictly rational, town only at first glance, the observer will feel that Raša reminds him of something, but he will never be able to say with certainty what that is. This is because they will recognise in it moments of modernism, Italian Rationalism, New Classicism, Novecentismo, Ruralism or Art-Deco, but none of these styles are so strongly present that a meticulous observer could settle on them. Ultimately it is clear – Raša is still too original a creation of one artist to be attributed to any one of these tendencies.

A town built "overnight"

The construction of Raša began at the end of April 1936. The entire town, including the houses that accommodated 2,200 workers and special villas for the administration erected on steep slopes, slightly above the town so as to function as an observatory, with a hostel for single workers, squares, bridges and transverse arches, a school, a kindergarten, a cultural centre, administration buildings, a swimming pool, a large town square, a fountain, a thermal power plant, electricity, water, lighting, a hundred telephone numbers for communication above and below the ground and an impressive church – all this was created, as in Russian fairy tales, almost overnight.

Already on November 4, 1937, a little more than a year later – 547 days to be precise – a month before the date the works were due to be completed, the town was built.

Someone endeavoured to calculate the number of working hours invested in the construction of the youngest town in Istria – and the total they reached was 380,000 hours.

Duce's restrictions and disappointment

The construction of the city of Raša is dominated by Istrian stone, lime, marble, and then wood and tiles. Iron was used very sparingly, because of the restrictions imposed by Mussolini due to his wars of conquest in Africa.

When he visited Raša, which was still under construction, on the 7th of August, 1936, Il Duce was not pleased with the architect's choice of location. Pulitzer Finali situated Raša in a valley, as close as possible to the mining shafts. According to Mussolini, the ideal mining town (three were built during his reign, the other two, Raša's twins, are Podlabin or Pozzo Littorio in Labin, and Carbonia in Sardinia) must be located in a sufficiently elevated place to assert its dominance. It should be imposing and "loud", signifying the greatness of the regime, which a valley is certainly not.

The first inhabitants

The town came to life on November 27th, 1937, and soon became a municipality by the decree of king Victor Emmanuel III. The first inhabitants of Raša were Italian miners from Sardinia, Sicily, Puglia and Friuli, who remained in Raša until the fall of the Italian regime in September 1943, when, together with the defeated army, they began to leave the mine and retreat home.

Church of Santa Barbara

The Church of Santa Barbara in Raša is also the work of Gustav Pulitzer Finali. Some think that Finali wanted to "discreetly" show his own attitude towards Fascism. Although, one should not lose sight of the fact that the investor carefully supervised and paid attention to every detail in the ar-

chitectural and interior decoration of Raša, which, above all, was supposed to testify to the power of the "Third Rome". "There were strong tendencies to put Fascist symbols on the church", said one resident of Raša, "but this was not allowed."
The Church of Santa Barbara is certainly one of the most unusual churches in the history of sacral architecture. From the outside, it resembles an overturned coal wagon, while inside it feels as if the visitor is in a mining shaft. The church has no windows, nor richly decorated stained-glass, light enters only through narrow glass openings. The robust bell tower is abruptly cut off – suggesting the shape of a miner's lamp. The porch next to it is covered with three semicircular arched openings, like the medieval loggias in front of the city walls – the place of trade and gatherings. In front of the church are a large concrete town square, buildings with colonnades, a fountain.

De Chirico and the square in Raša

The emptiness of the concrete square is frightening. The purity and simplicity of its clear geometric lines, the colonnade on the surrounding buildings, together with the almost always empty square, create a specific atmosphere of "internal tension". It is about a kind of intellectual, almost metaphysical tension that suggests the rigidity of time, and, simultaneously, eternity. It is very difficult to "locate" the square in Raša in time. To which time does it belong, to which present? If the observer observes only the square, in its concrete bareness, it is almost impossible to answer that question. There is a certain similarity of this city square with the paintings of the painter Giorgio de Chirico (1888–1978), who studied in Athens and came originally from the Greek city of Volos. De Chirico described his art as metaphysical, because it depicts the world that is hidden behind reality. The typical motifs of de Chirico's paintings are scenes of a timeless, immobile atmosphere. Mysterious, deserted squares surrounded by shadowy colonnades, empty, inhospitable buildings, emptiness filled with menace. They say that Raša has a "De Chirico atmosphere", the atmosphere of glowing Greek or Sicilian and southern Italian squares, desolate cities whose population was driven North in the era of industrialisation. In summer the square is simmeringly hot, but because of the mountains the sun sets earlier here than in the South.

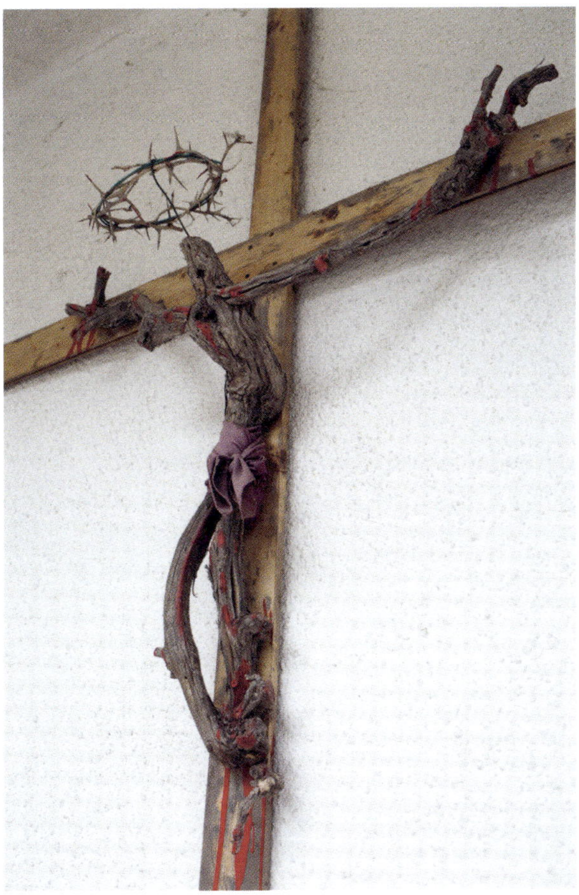

Raša

Slogans on Raša's walls

"We will be able to build our country only through intense work!"
"Long live Tito!"
"This is Yugoslavia"
"Raša, the pride of Socialism"
"Heroes of hard work"
"Raša will give its all"
"Every ton of our coal – a contribution to building a better future and a blow to our enemies"

Good luck!

When the mine was in need of new miners, trucks with wooden partitions that were converted into buses were sent to Bosnia and Kosovo to find them. The square in Raša, otherwise known for its ominous emptiness, was brimming with buses, sometimes 50 a day, during the first, highly productive years in the newly formed socialist Yugoslavia. Workers were brought in and immediately sent to wait in lines for a health check-up. The new miners underwent a brief training course, were given work equipment and descended into the mine shafts in elevators. In front of the entrance to the shafts, there was an inscription on a large white board: GOOD LUCK!

Patriotism and striker badges

Back then, miners were considered "heroes of labour", one of the most responsible for the rapid reconstruction of Yugoslavia after the Second World War. The revenue from the Istrian coal mines helped not only in the construction and renovation of the surrounding towns, but also in the construction of large cities, such as the capital of Yugoslavia at the time, Belgrade or Zagreb. The miners who worked in the mines at that time were well rewarded – high wages, four daily meals, and at the end of the year, an additional, thirteenth wage.

Being a miner meant being a great patriot at that time. Miners competed to break production norms, new mining records were set. The most skilled ones received decorations, special miners' achievement medals, which were personally awarded to them by the president of the country, Josip Broz Tito, in Belgrade (then the capital of the country).

Slow death

Since the mine shut down until this day, Raša has slowly been dying. The machine tool factory, Raša's knitwear and clothing factory, the first factory in the area to mainly employ women, and even the doll factory, the first of its kind in Yugoslavia at the time – nothing survived. Mining has failed. Agriculture has collapsed. A well built port terminal has largely shut down. The Raša area has almost a longer coastline than Slovenia, but nobody cares about that. The mine, which is very unusual, and which could be a technical museum, is falling into disrepair. The city library is leaking, the book purchase fund doesn't exist. The kindergarten, which had three groups until recently, now has only one. The school has only ten pupils per grade.

Today (2005)

It's impossible to buy a postcard of Raša anymore. If anybody even wanted it in the first place the "competitive market" would have already taken care of that detail.

The newly decorated city cafe on the square welcomes new visitors – young people who don't have time for anything. Nevertheless, they sit in front of the cafe comfortably reclining in aluminium chairs through the long morning, absentmindedly typing text messages into worn out, silvery mobile phones. In the afternoon, they lazily drag themselves to their houses, the mothers having already packed their lunches, and after that, they drag themselves in their rustling Bermuda shorts and flip-flops onto small "motorcycles" and go to the local football field, the only site of collective support and prosperity.

The generation of miners was replaced by a generation of trained waiters and cooks, football players – amateurs with a pronounced tendency towards professionalism. Their primary goal is to do as little as possible, so their brain cells don't get overworked and there's enough of them left for flipping the daily newspapers and typing text messages. And also to lie down, eat, sleep and watch TV.

Nothing in Raša impresses them, maybe only the newly renovated cafe, because of the aluminium chairs. Given the first opportunity they will escape, and wherever they escape to, they will lie and say that they are from the neighbouring, much larger, Labin town. They will never admit to themselves that they're ashamed of coming from Raša,

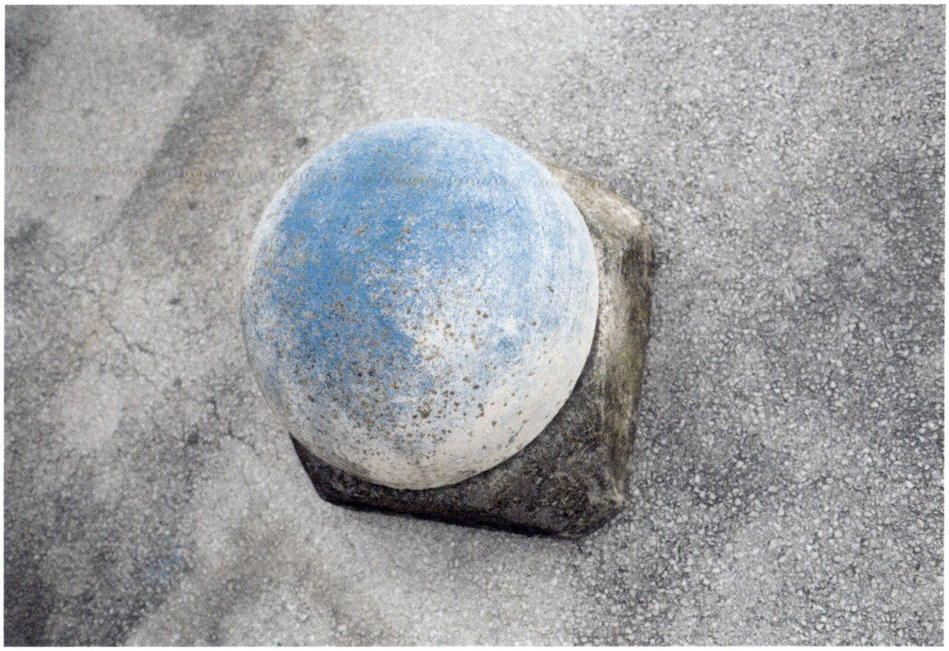

Raša

a pit that no one cares about, with holes full of desperate Bosnian people, former miners in deep depression, many of whom committed suicide a long time ago.

In 200 years' time, when the last cat from the abandoned streets of Raša finally dies, and its once-glistening architecture rots away as a toothless jaw of an old man, some sensitive individual will write sad epitaphs to this town and cultural monument, now overgrown, due to carelessness and disinterest, by "the weeds of oblivion". He will be sincerely saddened that "nothing was done to save this pearl of architecture"; although, a more attentive reader will surely perceive the author's subtly trembling satisfaction, due to the serendipity of stumbling upon such a rich theme in a part abandoned town, not to mention coming up with the phrase – "the weeds of oblivion".

* In July 2005, the writer Tatjana Gromača visited the ideal city of Raša, which was built in 547 days in 1936/37. Her essay, written not with nostalgia but with empathy, appears here in a greatly abridged English version. The original in Croatian remains unpublished. Instead, a version in German has been published: Tatjana Gromača, "Die ideale Stadt kehrt heim ins Grün – Raša" (The ideal city returns home to green – Raša), in: *Last & Lost. Ein Atlas des verschwindenden Europas* (Last & Lost. An Atlas of Vanishing Europe), edited by Katharina Raabe and Monika Sznajderman, Suhrkamp Verlag, Frankfurt am Main 2006, pp. 266–286. We consider the text worth reading as a testimony to the time in which it was written, and to the history of Raša, but it is important to note the following here. Since the text was written in 2005, the situation in Raša has changed. There are signs of recovery, including the restoration of the heating plant chimney, its strong role in all editions of the Biennial and the work to restore the cinema and the Karlota mine entrance, which is planned as a future exhibition space.

La Galleria della Memoria

Isabella Flego

Entro con arcano stupore in un angolo di mondo sotterraneo

Gli occhi si aprono su di esso, entrato in me con emozione dall'interno della rimembranza

Sulle bocche delle pareti indebitate di respiri si posa lo sguardo

Il silenzio al quale sta ancorata la voce di mio padre avanza

Tanto silenzio risale, portando in vita un linguaggio nel midollo della terra generato

Fermo sulla faccia dei muri e in ogni altra cosa presente radicato

Segni erosi e passi incisi sul suolo, dalla poca luce mangiati, riprendono a respirare con il tempo, insieme a tante parole perse nel mondo dentro di me

Altre ferme su attrezzi e utensili in sosta che hanno servito viaggi verso smorti orizzonti tra cavità nere e lucide

Anche se superati dal tempo nel secreto della loro forza muta hanno in se sul letto di polvere una lingua escoriata che interpretare la può chi l'ha vissuta

La galleria che mi lascio alle spalle nel fulgor del ricordo di vite passate al piano astrale respira l'eternità ed è come se dovesse rinascere, ingrandirsi di parole frugate nei pozzi conquistati e persi

Parole della riconoscenza che nessuno cerca più. Parole forti, capaci di sbrecciare la cava, e di codificare il messaggio di ogni voce sepolta nelle crepe della vena nera più profonda

Uscivi dal buio, dalla galleria che nuda si erge e conduce all'apparir del sole

A passo lento avanzavi, la lampada in mano

Entravi come la luna in cielo stellato nella luce del giorno

La cipria impalpabile che tutto avvolge

Istante sublime, gioia al minatore portata nel cuore

Come fosse l'unica a onorare l'esistenza e sentire i battiti della vita

Là dove regna sempre la notte vestita di luce da sepolcro, l'aria grossa tramena

Il gioco di vita e morte alimenta desideri di sole e di mare

Ogni suo soffio prezioso e dolente è respiro

E come un serpente si infila nei polmoni

Fiori di roccia ornati di neri confini

E quando anche la bocca si fa di pietra

Il minatore inventa sorsi d'aria per l'aurora di un nuovo giorno

The Tunnel of Memory

Isabella Flego

I enter, strangely bewildered, into a corner of the underworld

My eyes open, aware, filling me with an emotion flooded with memories

My gaze rests on the mouths of the walls and their strained breaths

The silence to which my father's voice is anchored, becomes present

A deep silence surfaces, bringing into life a language generated from the kernel of the earth

It hangs motionless, held in the walls, rooted in the heart of everything

Eroded signs and steps etched into the ground, absorbed by the faint light, begin to breathe in time along with the many words, lost in the world that I hold inside

Words poised on the abandoned tools and machinery that have served journeys towards the dim horizons among the black and shimmering tunnels

Even when overtaken by time, secret in their silent strength they have embedded a language on a bed of dust, that only those who lived it could understand

The tunnel I leave behind me with the flash of a memory of past lives, passed onto the astral plane, breathing eternal life as if it should be reborn, become greater through words forged in the mine shafts both conquered and lost

Words of gratitude that no-one utters anymore. Powerful words, strong enough to fracture the walls of the pit and to bring to life the message of every voice buried in the fissure of every black vein

You came out of the darkness from the tunnel that stands before you naked and leads you in to emerging sun

Slowly moving forwards, the lamp in your hand

Arriving like the moon in a starry sky at the light of day

The imperceptible dust that engulfs everything

Transcendent moments captured in the miner's heart

As if it were the only one to honour its existence and hear the beat of life

There, where night adorned in sepulchral light always reigns, the air hanging heavily

The game of life and death nourishes the desires of the sun and sea

Blowing each breath both precious and piercing

And like a snake it slips into the lungs

Flowers on the rocks decorated with blackened edges

And even when the mouth becomes stone

The miner imagines sips of pure air for the dawn of a new day

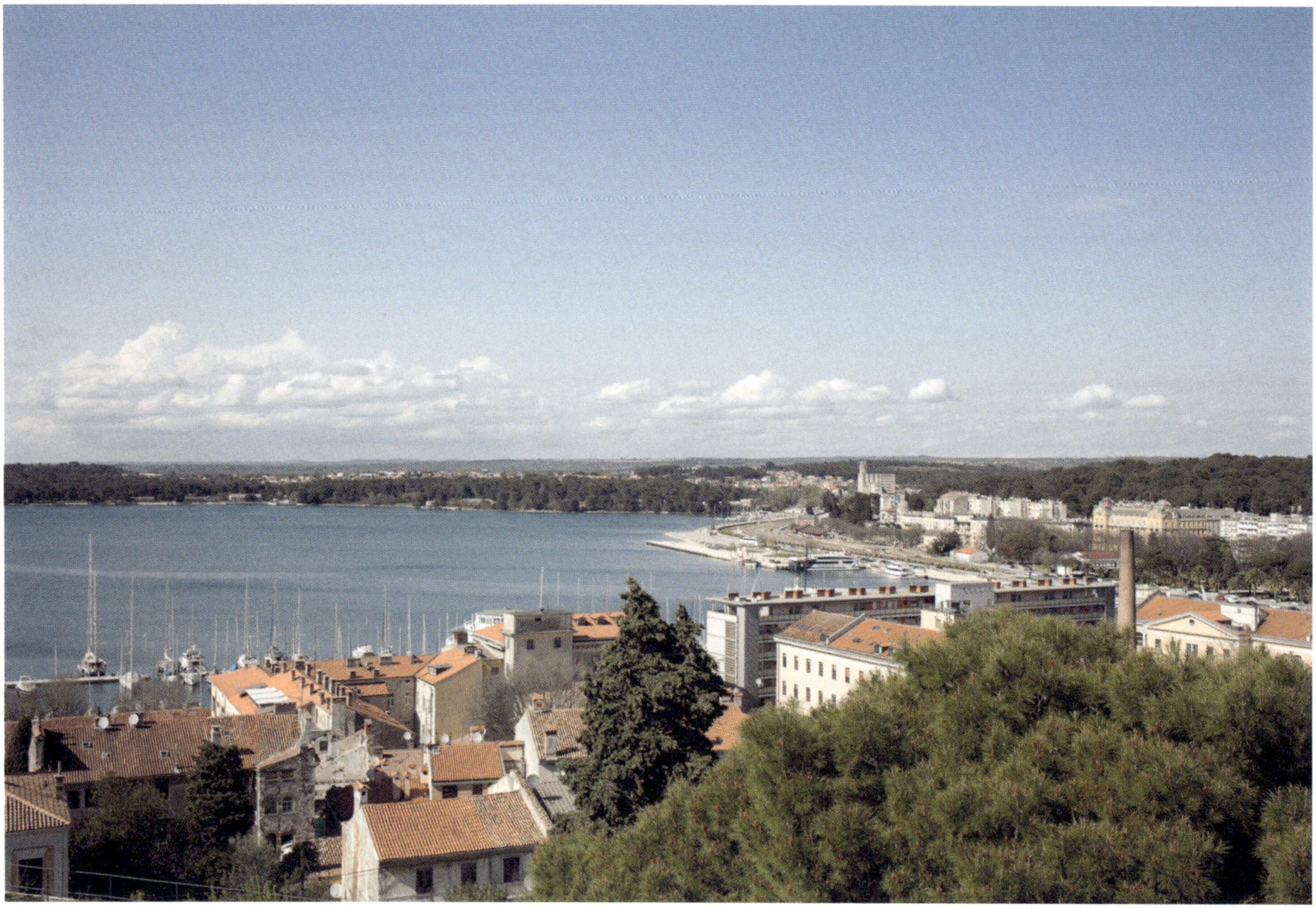

A view of the city, train station and harbour basin, Pula

Becoming Landscape

Paolo Bianchi

I

We live on Kolodvorska Street. The residential complex is called Münz houses, a magnificent Art Nouveau building from the century before last. It is named after the builder Jakob Ludwig Münz (1853–1930). The facade of the Münz-Häuser is crumbling menacingly, yet one enjoys the floral patterned house entrances and cornices. The upper-class apartments, some with balconies facing west, toward the sea, can be rented as vacation homes. We reside on the first floor, overlooking a small "pita house" and the water.

As co-curator of the Industrial Art Biennial, I have a temporary "home" here. I can come to myself. Experience my connection to the Istrian landscape. Let the extended forays through the peninsula have an effect. As a leitmotif for our doing and being, we find, first gradually and then with a leap of thought, the coherent expression *Landscapes of Desire.* As curators, we set in motion a multi-layered process. It is about finding out how artistic impulses, hopes, longings and new utopias can connect with the Istrian landscape in order to unfold in it and beyond.

II

The French sociologist Bruno Latour (1947–2022) speaks of the fact that we should question fundamental things, that we should examine what is desirable and what is not. We should work on the location of the self. We should let a "landscape of our desires" emerge, and not shy away from lines of conflict, controversy, and opposition.

It is only possible to overcome the ideology of progress and space grabbing, through a "landing", through an arrival, through a becoming at home, that is not nationalistic and exclusionary.

The Biennial project *Landscapes of Desire* shows what significance art can play in this arriving and landing. And that the question "Where and how do we want to land?" basically refers to the central questions of human life: "What forms of life do we want?" And, "How can we self-determine our own lives?" Because our dignity and happiness depend on it.

III

From our apartment on Kolodvorska Street we walk a few steps to the small bar by the train station. The 19th century building of the station has a pink facade and a green canopy. The conversa-

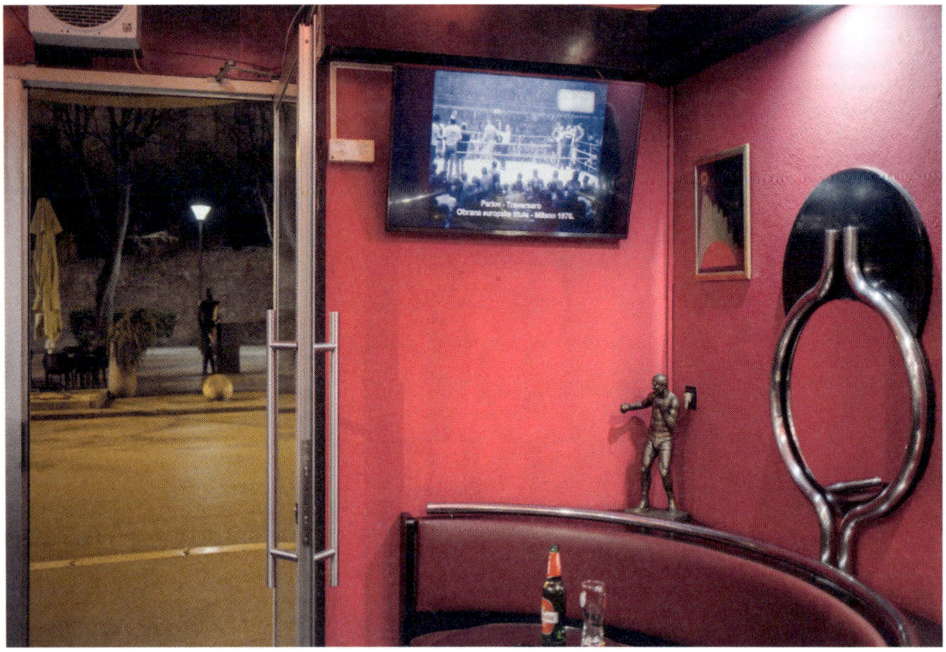

Mate Parlov Bar, Pula

tions with Noel mostly revolve around questions about the implementation of the planned artworks. How can art be shown in public space? We quickly realise: What is needed is thinking and acting in contexts, as well as constructive cooperation with all the stakeholders involved (the list is long).

While sharing an espresso right next to the railroad tracks that end in this sleepy train station, the focus is on technical variations as well as on the moment of dialogue. How can we relate to a social and media public through art? How can we create a lasting event with art? How do we succeed in communicating the self-will of works of art?

With *Landscapes of Desire* we hope that the multitude of artworks presented on public ground will transform the respective places into an agora – a place for the formation of opinion, the expression of opinion and the transfer of opinion. These works of art have a vital presence. The encounter with them opens up an in-between and arouses interest: Real interest is a true elixir of life.

IV

Opposite our apartment is a harbour dock, the ferries and ships to the Croatian islands as well as to Venice leave here. A few steps further in the direction of the city center stands the mighty Hotel Riviera, also built by Münz. Today the house is closed and awaits its revival. The former grand hotel impresses with its yellow, neo-baroque facade, the continuous balconies and terraces and the imposing corner towers.

The current city area, conquered by Romans in 177 BC, was a Roman colony under the name Colonia Pietas Iulia Pola. During the reign of Emperor Augustus, the amphitheatre was built directly on the sea, today one of the main sights of the city. In the catacombs of the amphitheatre there are display boards, on which the trade routes of the Romans are depicted. One route, on which olive oil, wine, salted fish and preserved fruit were transported in amphorae, leads from Pula to Vindonissa.

Vindonissa was the name of a Roman legionary camp on the territory of today's municipality of Windisch (Switzerland). As if by chance, I live in Windisch on a tiny peninsula. When I go for a walk in the floodplain outside my front door or visit the archaeological sites, it reminds me of Pula, of my visit to the Amphitheatre Museum. There the Istrian amphora is exhibited, it has the shape of an egg. Its appearance testifies to a far-reaching, already at that time well-organized trade. The basis of this trade was the amphora, the container of antiquity. The amphora now undergoes a transformation, our "container" is the landscape. Its content the desire.

V

The basis of our actions as curators and artists in the project *Landscapes of Desire* becomes exploring and being interested in the Istrian landscape. Landscapes are part of human existence, they shape our memories and our selves. We cannot live outside of landscapes. Our lives are woven into landscapes. The landscape invades human life and at the same time this life expands into the landscape.

The Istrian essayist, activist and educator Giuseppina Martinuzzi (1844–1925) speaks of a "piccola patria" – meaning her beloved little homeland Istria. She envisions a place of transnational and cross-cultural encounters. With *Landscapes of Desire* we tie in with these values.

In the Kunstkafe Cvajner on Forum Square in Pula, I leaf through the cultural magazine Lettre. One article fits well with the basic idea of *Landscapes of Desire*. It is about freeing landscapes from the opposition of nature reserve and overexploitation. It pleads for landscapes as a territory for living communities, so that a general benefit can take the place of profit.

VI

In the Kunstkafe Cvajner I meet the Croatian writer Tatjana Gromača, who lives in Pula, she comes with her cheeky black poodle Otto. I had written to her that *Landscapes of Desire* could be about dystopias. However, it would be more interesting to be devoted to positive utopias (i.e. eutopias). She responded with the following words: "I see in the idea of eutopia a very good way with which it can perhaps continue here in our country. Eutopia means creating good places, places that can bring us a new perception of life, a kind of hope, in contrast to the fears and resignation of the modern world. This reminds me of Ernst Bloch's 'Philosophy of Hope'. He says that our dreams are not our reality, but our reality can be corrected by our dreams."

At Gallery Kunstkafe Cvajner we also talk about Michel Foucault's concept of heterotopia. He uses it to describe spaces such as gardens, cemeteries, brothels, cinemas, theatres, museums, libraries, and more, which are different from natural spaces. As counter-spaces, they form "places beyond all places," according to Foucault. The artworks in the project *Landscapes of Desire* can also be experienced as counter-spaces. They create places where things appear different than usual. They show that people are looking for new and utopian landscapes. This longing, as Gromača notes, helps us to survive.

VII

Back in the apartment, the artists report on their discoveries and experiences. A dish is cooking in a pan with fresh ingredients from the market: barley, black trumpet mushrooms, wild herbs, vegan sour cream, potatoes, chard, pumpkin seeds, hazelnuts, smoked paprika chilli oil.

As we eat happily together at the kitchen table, I remember my youth. My mother, a Venetian, sometimes told me about Trieste as a commercial and financial metropolis on the Adriatic Sea. It was in Trieste that coffee prices were determined. The city was a transshipment point for the flow of goods and foreign exchange between the Orient and the Occident. With a trilingual daily newspaper: Hungarian, Czech and Italian. I remember her mentioning the Istrian hinterland as well, it was (and still is) populated by different ethnic groups.

The history book says that the majority of the rural population were Croats and, in the north, Slovenes; in the former Venetian coastal towns of Istria lived mainly Italians. For well over a thousand years, the Adriatic region was inhabited and cultivated jointly by Italians and Slavs as a plurinational habitat. However, due in part to the centuries-long domination of Venice, a social and economic imbalance prevailed. In the years before the war, the social antagonisms between the rich Italian townspeople and the poor Slav peasants, to put it simply, escalated dangerously in the nationality conflict.

VIII

The project *Landscapes of Desire* will take place in 2023. In summer, the peninsula is always in a vacation mood. Istria offers more than the pleasures of bathing, as Georges Dsrues notes in his guidebook *Istria and Rijeka for advanced travellers* His beautiful conclusion is almost a hymn of praise: "In truth, Istria is a gift to Central Europe: a nearby and easily accessible stretch of Mediterranean land, still partly unspoiled, with sleepy stone villages in its interior and picturesque fishing ports on its coast. A jewel surrounded by the Adriatic Sea, which shines in the light of the south not only during the summer months, full of southern *joie de vivre*, with rich culture, exciting cuisine and sunsets that expand the heart. And on top of that, a crossroads of cultures and languages, during whose visit you, as a Central European, always learn something also about your own history and therefore about yourself."

For *Landscapes of Desire,* I wish that visiting the artistic interventions will bring our guests closer to the meaning of culture. Culture is indispensable for our life, where as a life without flour, salt and sugar is hardly imaginable. It is the basis, it gives energy. It surrounds us ubiquitously in the form of architecture, music, images and words. It is a deep human need to explore the world in which we live in a creative way.

Our Biennial project *Landscapes of Desire* shows that art is counterworld. It is what emerges in creative, purposeless aesthetic power. It is a space for thought and playfulness and a workshop for the future. It is thanks to the artists that they confront us with longings, hopes and dreams. They give us the freedom to think beyond the familiar and the self-evident and to allow new worlds to emerge. In other words: we become landscape!

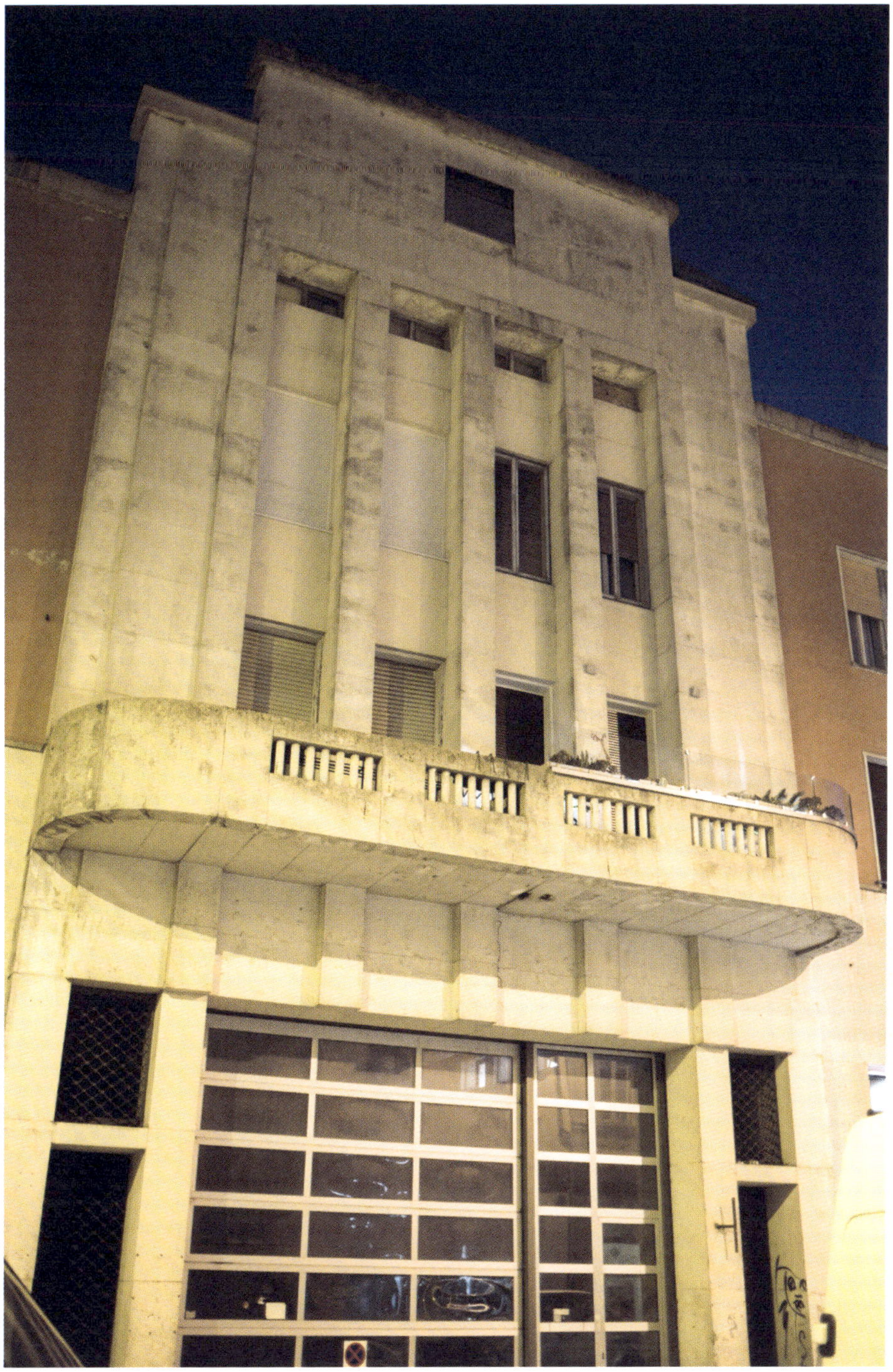

Palača Banke Italije u Puli (Palazzo della Banca d'Italia a Pola), 1937

Catalogue of the Exhibition

Lara Almarcegui

Istria limestone, 2023
Port of Pula

①

Courtesy of the artist,
supported by Mondriaan Fund

Lara Almarcegui is a conceptual artist whose work explores building materials and their potential decay. Both themes are linked to Almarcegui's interest in urban transformation processes brought about by political, social and economic changes – ideas she began to study intensively in the mid-1990s. She considers urban planning and architecture as phenomena that often interfere with spatial and social freedoms and mask the natural potential of the human habitat. Her projects reveal the geophysics and temporality of the built environment, for example by calculating and depicting the raw materials for cities or buildings, highlighting their decay and dilapidation. Or by exploring what is hidden beneath them. "Brownfields are important," says the artist, "because they are the only places in the city that remain without definition."

She became known to a larger audience in 2013 with her participation in the Venice Biennale. There, with large piles of rubble inside the Spanish Pavilion, she accumulated the materials with which the building had once been constructed. In some projects, she bundles the information she has collected into "guides" about the past, present and future of certain sites. In others, she presents installations of building materials in orderly stacks or mountainous piles.

At the point in Pula where the ferries from Venice dock at the harbour pier and drop off the streams of day tripping tourists, the artist has had a work of art constructed of Istrian limestone blocks stacked on top of each other. Although deliberately piled up and placed in an odd, non-functional way, it is unclear whether it is a work of art or, in fact, a temporary storage facility for stones. The Istrian stone industry, which provided the stone blocks, has a long tradition that goes back centuries. Today the Istrian quarry operators export their valuable products all over the world. Istrian stones have been used, for example, in the construction of the Hilton Hotel in Budapest or for the facade of the Science & Technology Museum in Shanghai. Much better known than these buildings is another use of the "pietra d'Istria", as the stone is called in technical jargon: La Serenissima, the lagoon city of Venice, is largely built of the white stone, which is both beautiful and resistant. Almarcegui addresses this transfer of knowledge, aesthetics, money, and power between cultures with a minimalist gesture at the port of Pula, thus pointing to the still burning topicality of these issues.

Lara Almarcegui (*1972 in Zaragoza, Spain) lives and works in Rotterdam. Her works have been exhibited among others at Secession, Vienna (2010), Art and the City, Zurich (2012), CAAC, Sevilla (2012), Manifesta 9, Genk (2012), the Spanish Pavilion at the Venice Biennale (2013), Casino Luxembourg (2016), Graphische Sammlung ETH Zurich (2019), IVAM, Valencia (2019).

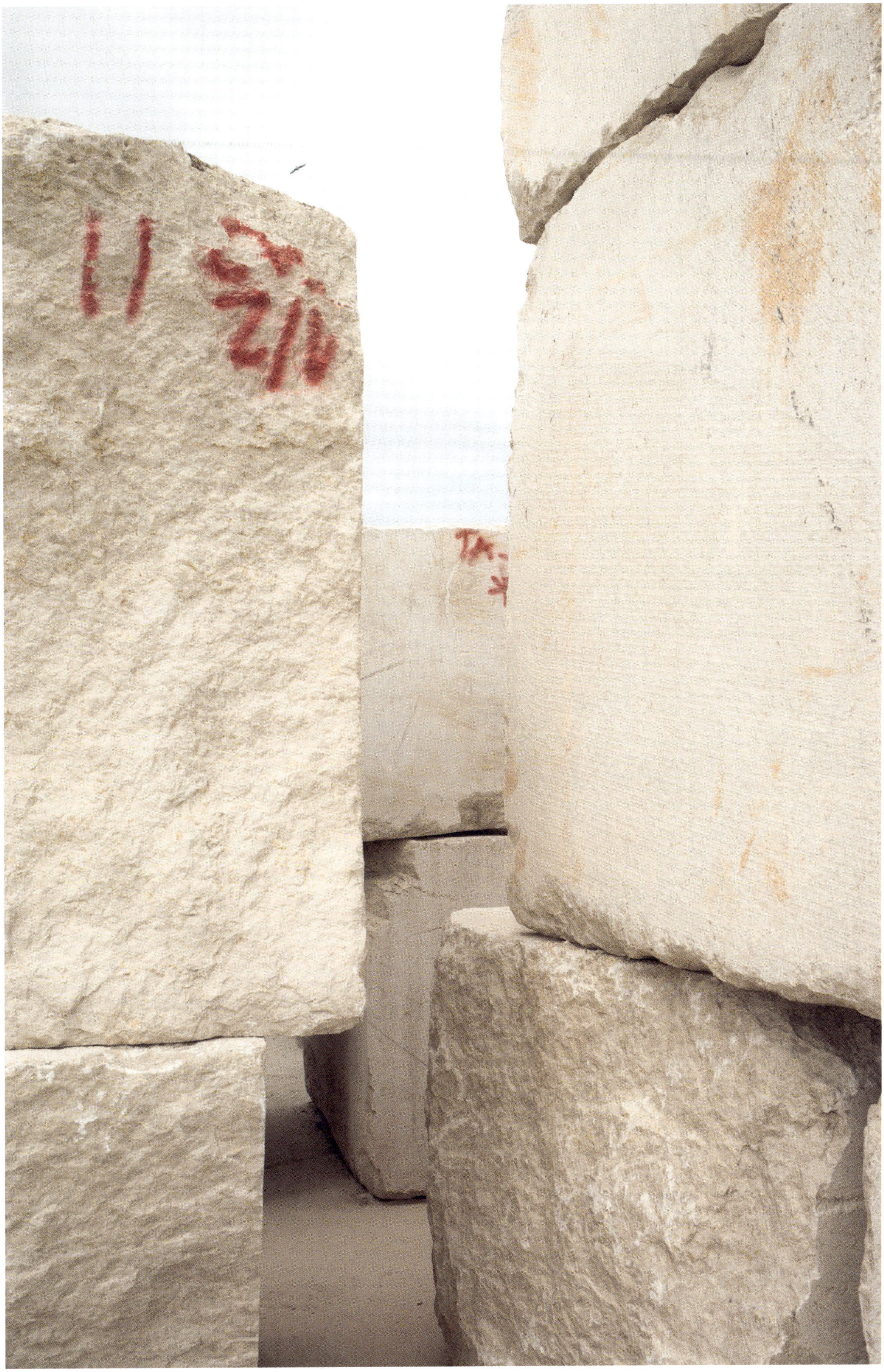

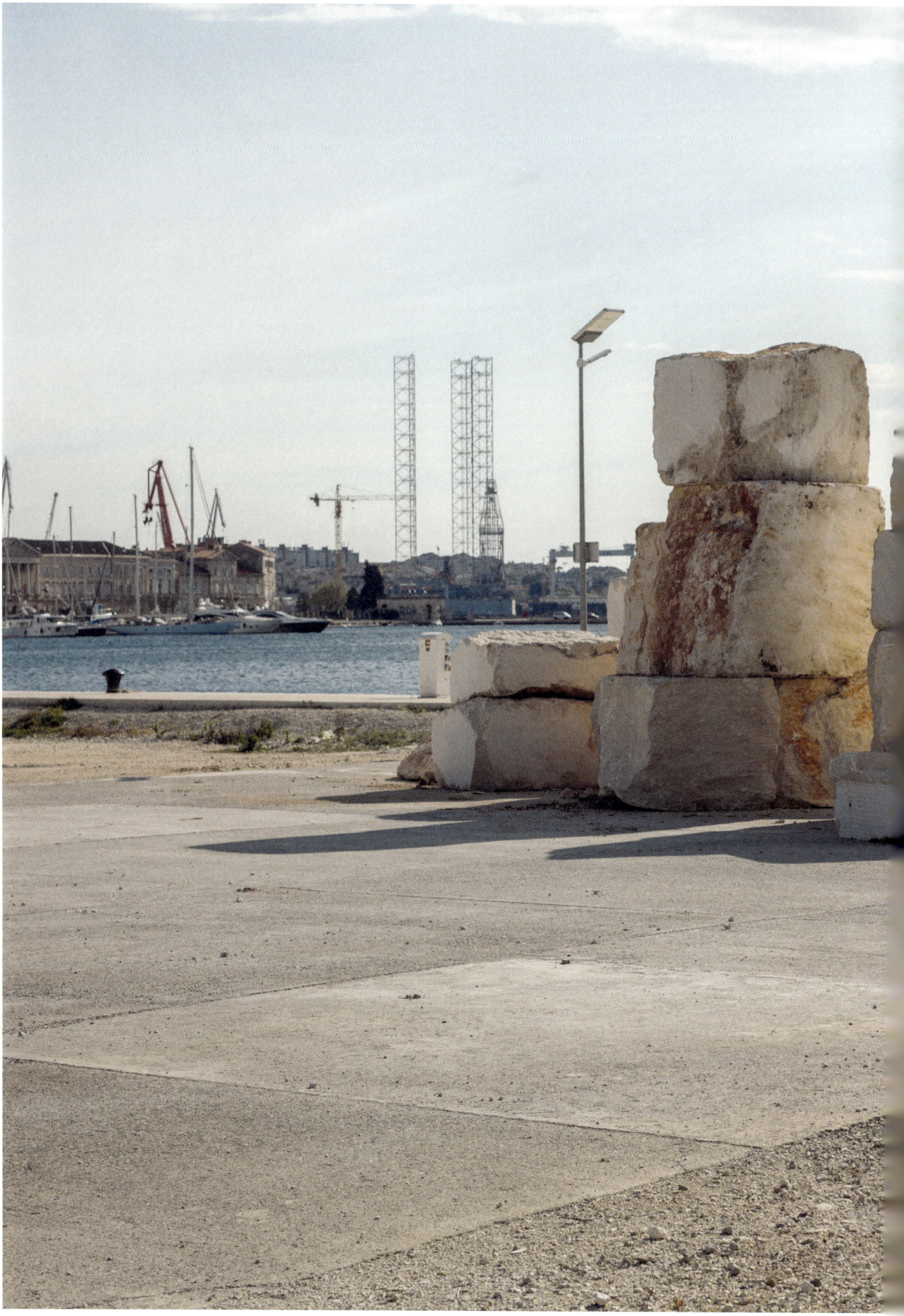

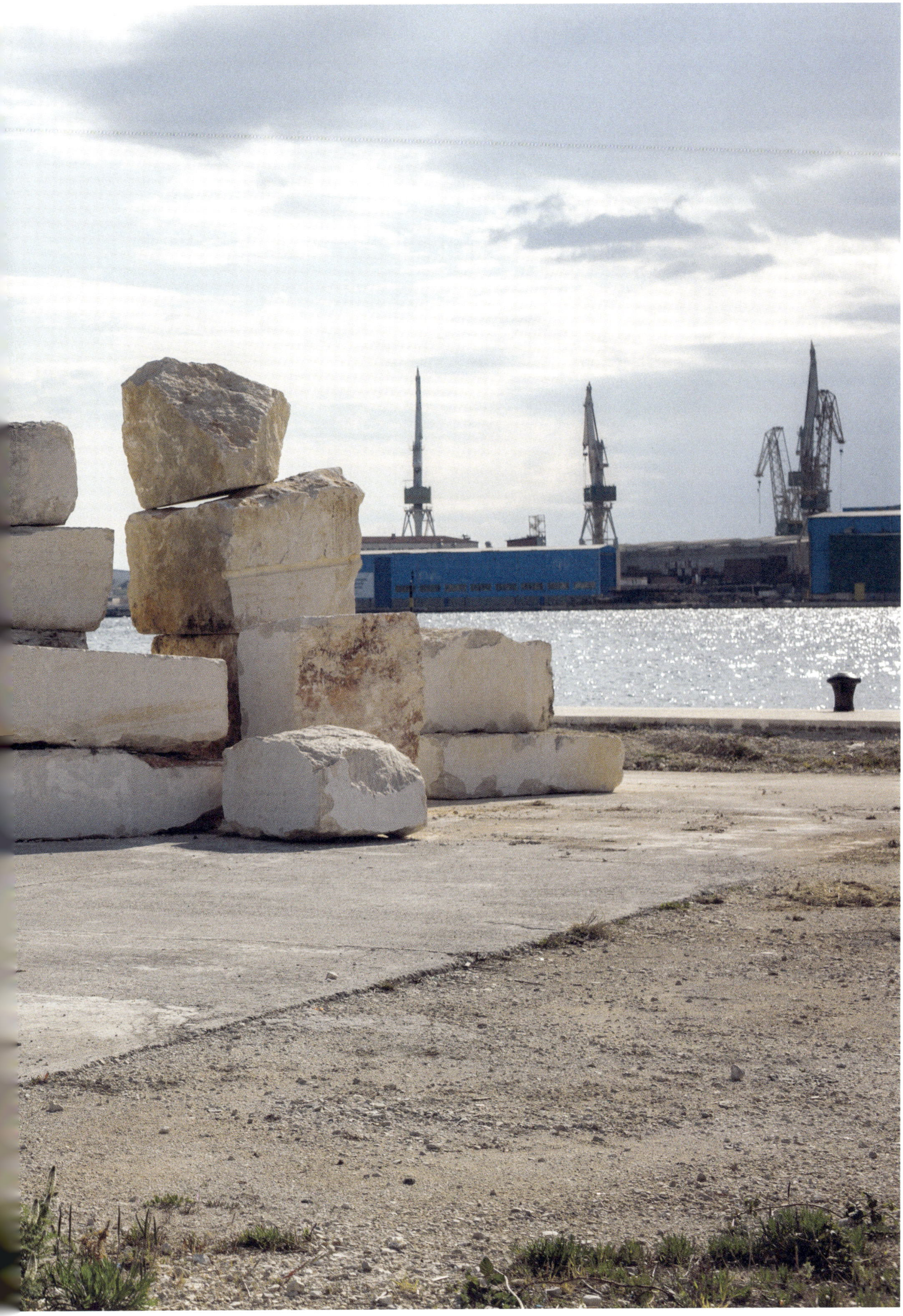

Cristian Andersen

Milk for flowers, 2023 ②
Former Pescheria, Labin

LED tubes, steel, aluminium, wicker, industrial ceramic

The Jewish architect Gustavo Pulitzer Finali, who designed the masterplan of Raša for Benito Mussolini, emigrated in 1938 to the USA to decorate Italian restaurants in New York and the villas of film stars in Hollywood. After the war he returned to Trieste and was responsible for the interior design of famous transatlantic steamships, namely the Andrea Doria, writing another chapter in Istria's eventful history, focussed by *Landscapes of Desire*. Starting from these futuristic furnishings and public architecture – also by nameless producers and designers – still present in Raša, Labin and Pula, Swiss-Danish artist Cristian Andersen has developed an artistic reappraisal of the aesthetics of everyday life in Labin's vacant Pescheria (fish shop) from today's deconstructivist point of view. His sublime designs, analogous to the Futurists, oscillate between everyday practicality and beauty and exhibit that optimistic spirit that seems to have been lost in the wars of the 20th century in Istria.

Andersen is known primarily as a ceramist, although his repertoire integrates painting, sculpture, installation into total installations. Ceramics and painting, largely abstract, give him the opportunity to work on "flowing transitions", on intermixtures of colour, on zones of ambivalence and exchange. These works live from the materiality of the materials, the life of forms and colours. With virtuosity, the artist makes use of objets trouvés, casts them and combines them, transforms them, takes them over as models for completely independent works. This results in illusory materialities: it looks like foam, but it is industrial ceramics. Curator Georgina Casparis provides a precise description of this artistic process: "Andersen assembles his sculptures in several stages from objets trouvés. Figurative-narrative elements meet constructive-abstract, post-minimal forms and industrial materials. The artist reassembles these set pieces by plastically exploring their spatial quality: front, back, top, bottom. In a second step, Andersen makes silicone negatives of these sculptures, which are scaffolded, encased and cast using a partially coloured, enormously dense and self-hardening industrial ceramic in a complex working process. The copies that are created in this way are now the original – and at the same time have a mimicry effect when the porcelain-like ceramic looks exactly like the foam that was originally used, for example. With irony and playful humour, the pastiche of the original sculpture changes into a new material entity."

Cristian Andersen (*1974, Denmark) lives and works in Zurich and Milano. His works have been exhibited among others at *Paradise, lost* (2019), Klöntal Triennale, Glarus (2017), Aargauer Kunsthaus, Aarau (2015), Art Altstetten Albisrieden, Zurich (2015), Kunstraum, Baden (2009), Kunstverein, Bregenz (2008), Musée d'Art Contemporain, Lyon (2004).

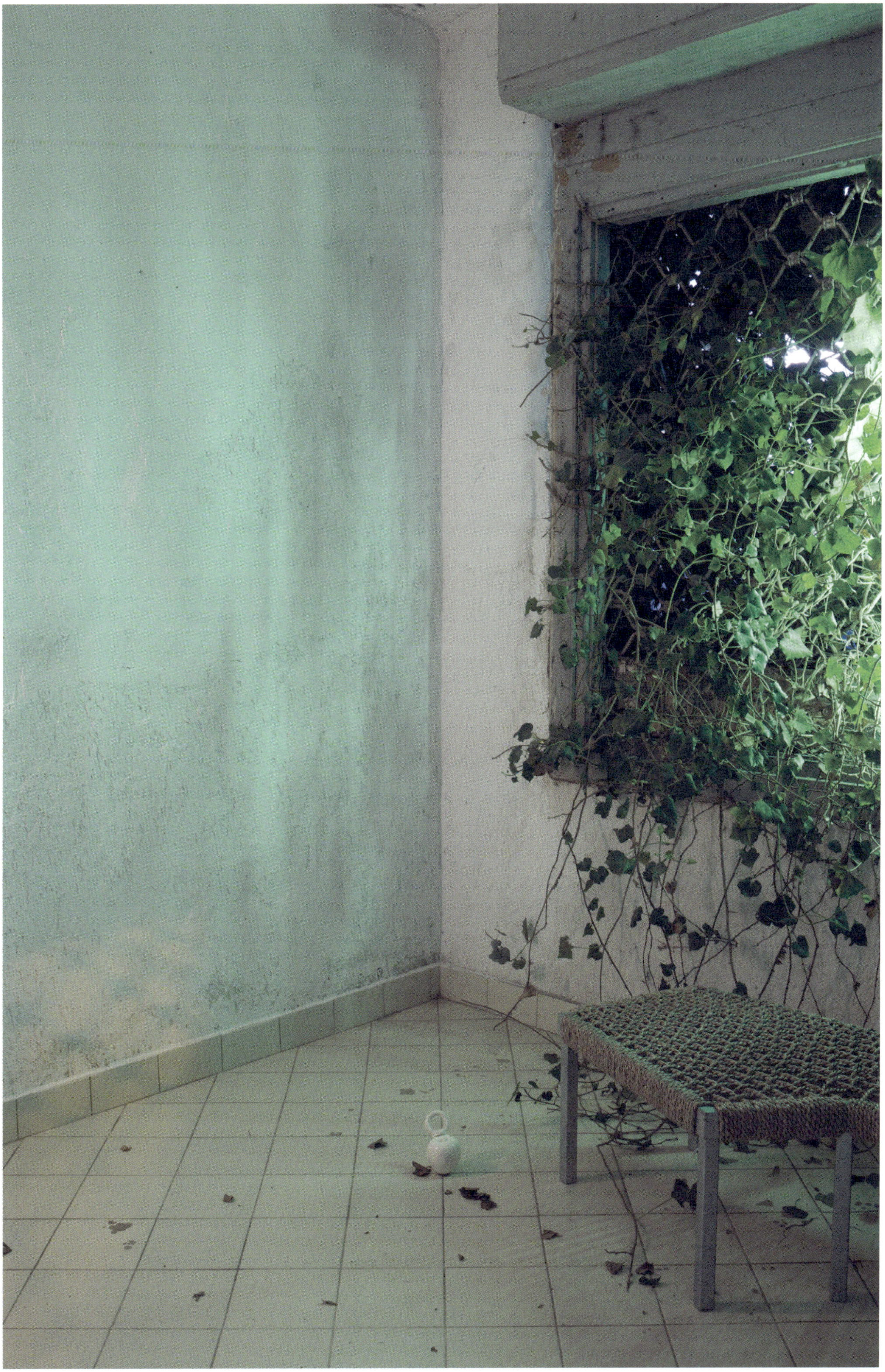

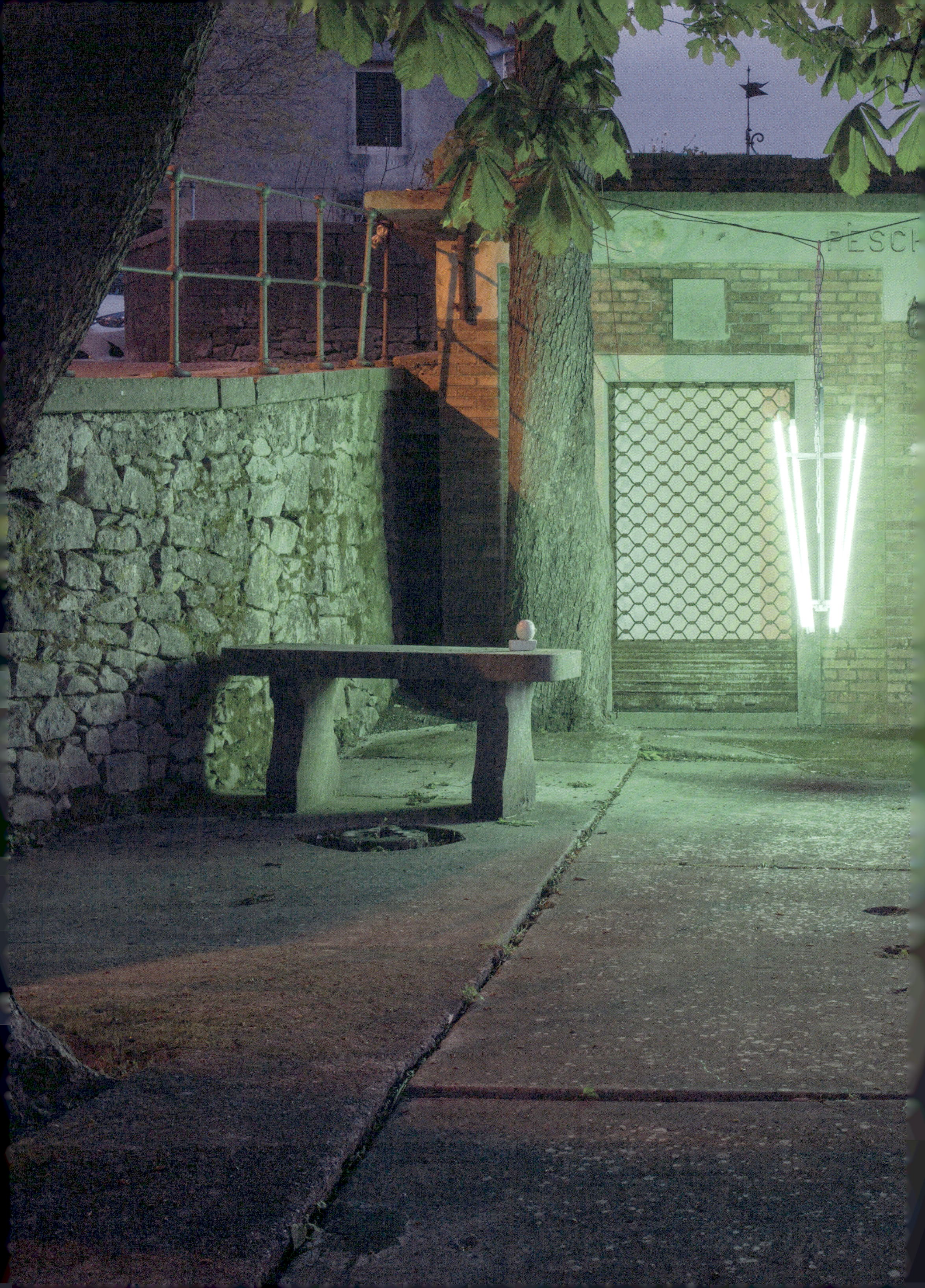
PESCH

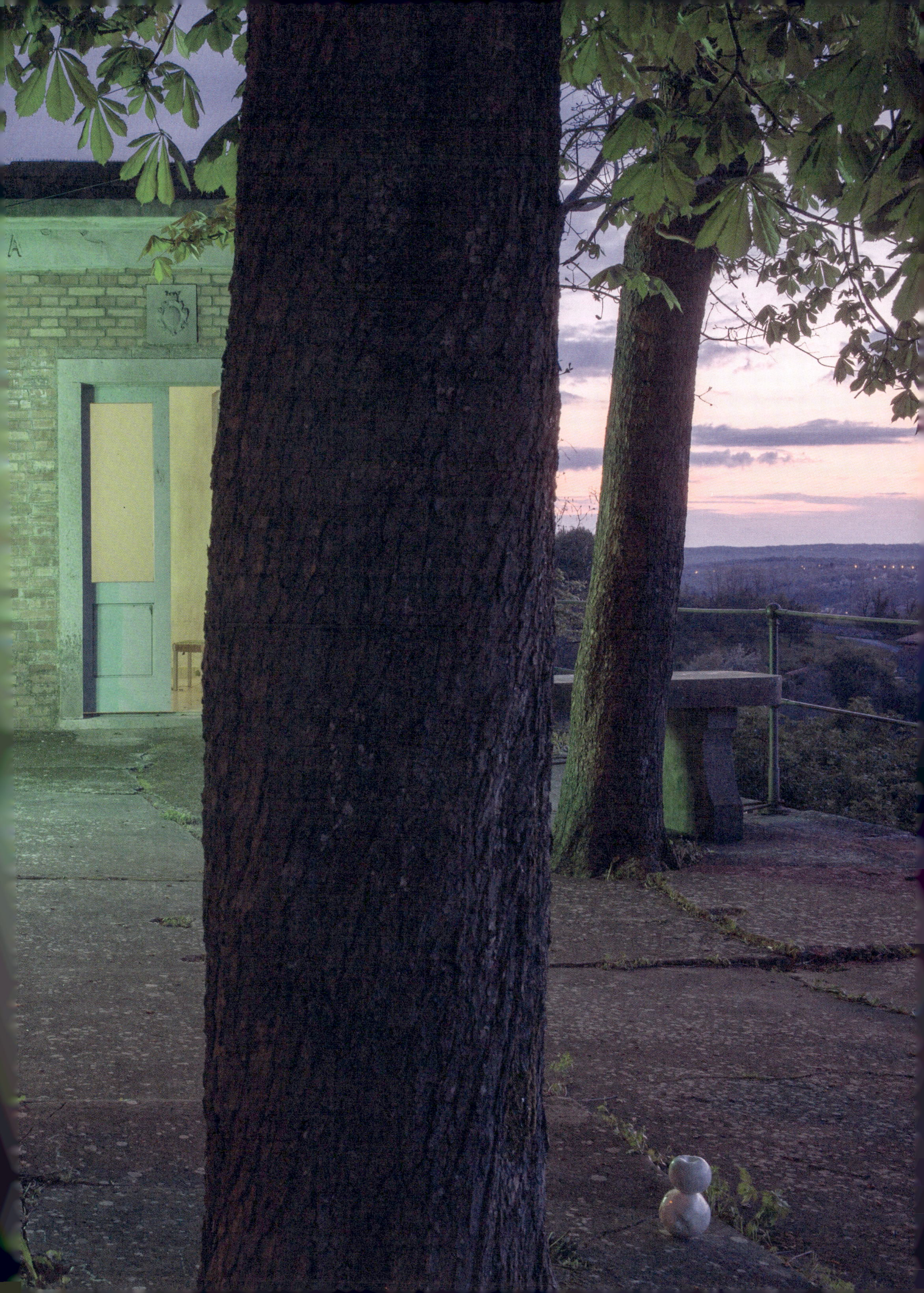

Charlie Billingham

Narodni Muzej, Battiala-Lazzarini Palace, Labin, Labin ③

English artist Charlie Billingham explores the psychosomatic effects of the first wave of industrialisation in the late 18th century and thus creates valid metaphors for current discourses on disruption and affiliation. In 1765, James Hargreaves invented the spinning machine ("Spinning Jenny") and built factories. From then on, the abstraction of the realities of people's lives began. While the lives of peasants had previously been shaped by natural cycles, the new factory workers had to organise their daily routines according to the clock.

This disruption of the concept of time, the pressure to perform and the destruction of social structures led to massive disturbances of the psyche. Sigmund Freud pointed out the sublimation strategies through alcohol and entertainment as early as 1908 in his essay *The 'Cultural' Sexual Morality and Modern Nervousness.* Literature "brings pathological figures, psychopathic-sexual, revolutionary, and other problems before the mind of the reader; our ear is excited and overstimulated by intrusive and noisy music administered in large doses; the theatres capture all the senses with their exciting representations; the visual arts, too, turn with predilection to the repulsive, the ugly, and the exciting, and are not afraid to place before our eyes in repulsive reality even the most hideous things that reality offers."

The starting point for Charlie Billingham's artistic exploration of social disruption is the satirical caricatures of Isaac Cruikshank (1764–1811) and James Gillray (1756–1815), which provide a critical view of living conditions in England and capture the consequences of industrialisation in drastic images. Billingham extracts particularly catchy gestures from these pictorial worlds – titled e.g. *Crying Woman, Brobdingnag, Slur the corrupted conman*, or *Brawlers* – enlarges them into the monumental, and with this abstraction points to an overarching question: What social effects emanate from particularly disruptive energies, currently digitalisation and globalisation?

Charlie Billingham (*1984 in London, U.K.) lives and works in London. His works have been exhibited among others at *New Order,* Saatchi Gallery, London (2013), *Forever Now,* Capodimonte Museum, Naples (2014), Travesia Quatro, Madrid (2017), Museo de Arte de Zapopan, Mexico (2019), SCAD Museum, Savannah (2020), Fabian Lang Gallery, Zurich (2021).

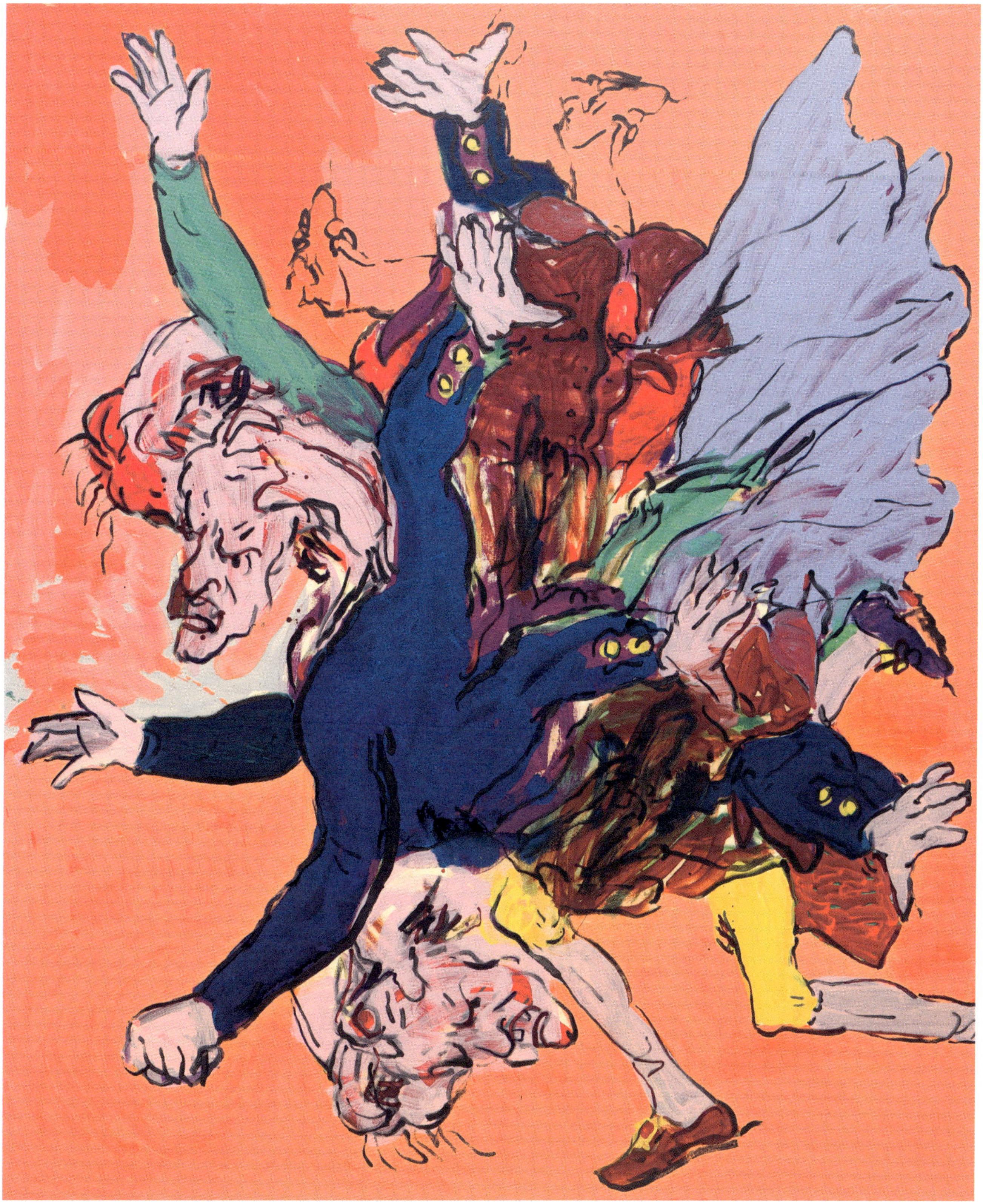

Slur the corrupted conman (7), 2020
Oil on linen, 190 × 160 cm
Courtesy of the artist and Galerie Fabian Lang, Zurich

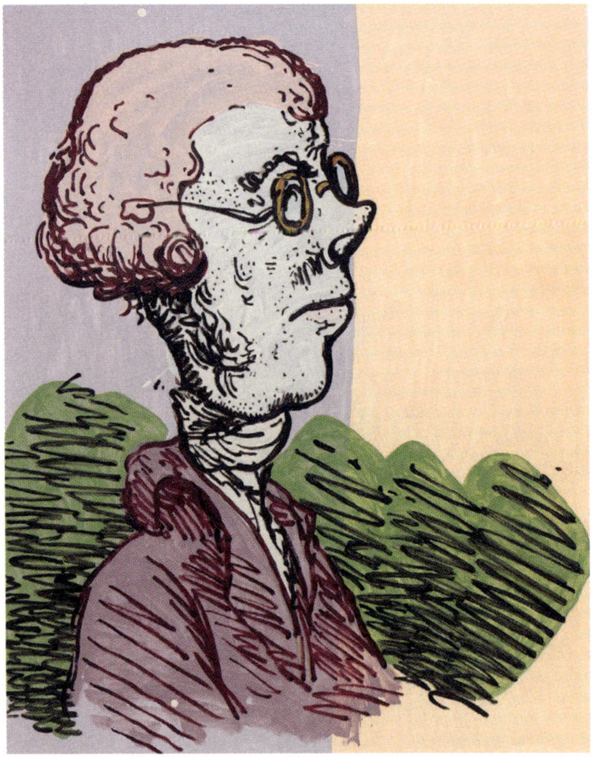

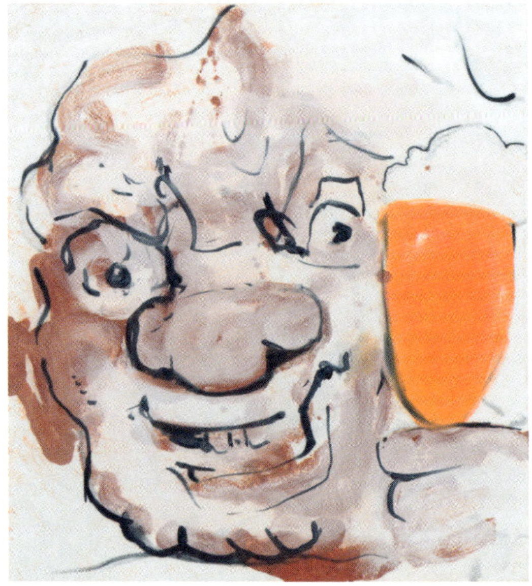

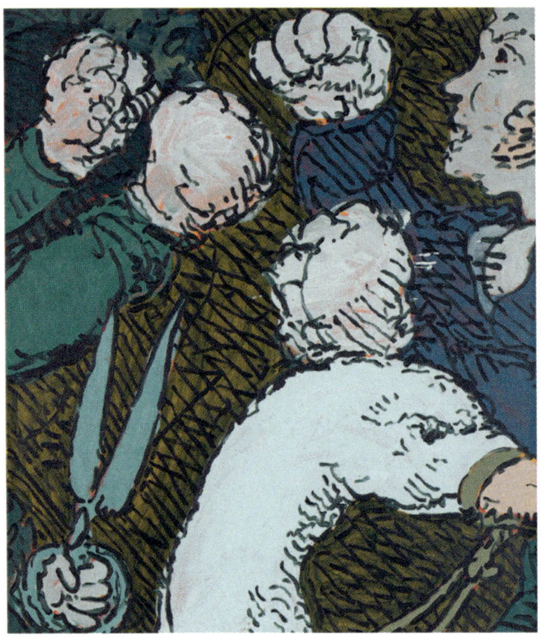

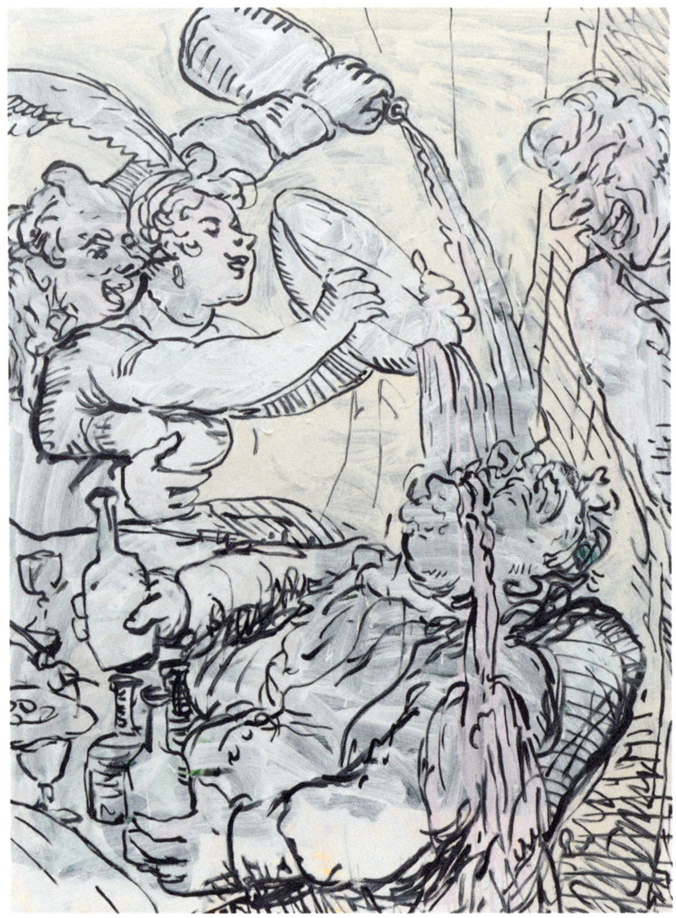

What Will You Do With This Room, 2016
Oil on linen, 100 × 80 cm
Courtesy of the artist and Galerie Fabian Lang, Zurich

Ballers, 2016
Oil on linen, 80 × 70 cm
Courtesy of the artist and Galerie Fabian Lang, Zurich

I Am Too Profound, 2015
Oil on linen, 60 × 55 cm
Courtesy of the artist and Galerie Fabian Lang, Zurich

Guns are raised at this game (4), 2021
Oil on linen, 120 × 90 cm
Courtesy of the artist and Galerie Fabian Lang, Zurich

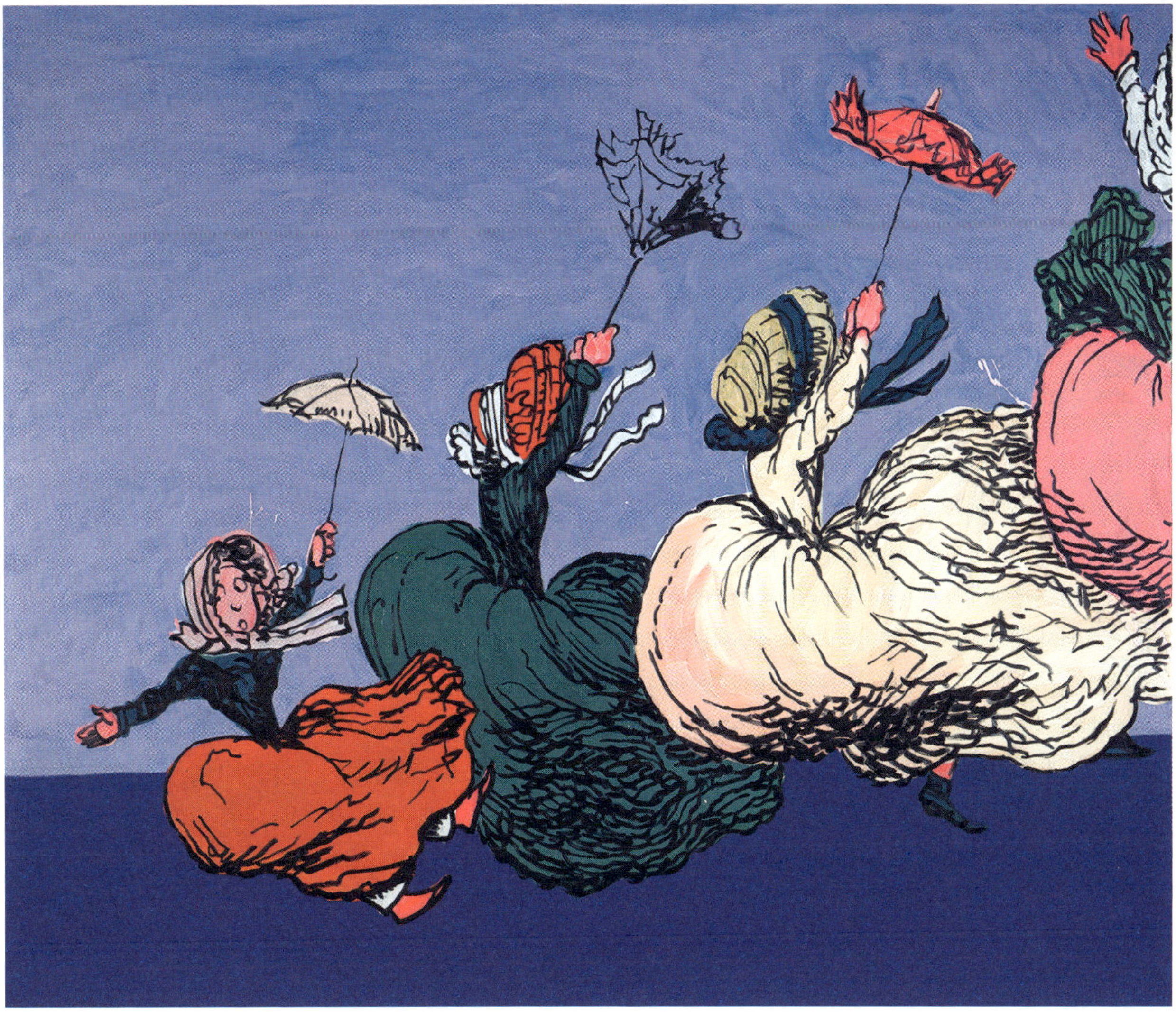

The Prevailing Wind, 2019
Oil on linen, 150 × 180 cm
Courtesy of the artist and Galerie Fabian Lang, Zurich

Vanessa Billy

A Hole in the Sky, 2023 ④
Pijacal, Labin

Rubber conveyor belt

Since April 2023, a long belt has been hanging from the 40-metre-high chimney in Labin that can be seen from far and wide: a discarded rubber conveyor belt. Like a broadband noodle ("papardelle"), the long black-grey belt encompasses the uppermost part of the structure, winds its way eastwards, westwards, southwards or northwards, depending on the wind conditions, and offers viewers a constantly changing spectacle. The industrial chimney becomes a sculpture in the sense of Constantin Brâncuși, the conveyor belt is a "readymade" in the spirit of Marcel Duchamp. *A Hole in the Sky* is a fascinating art intervention that cannot be perceived in its entirety from any perspective – neither from above, nor from below, nor from the sides. Viewers are forced to imagine the invisible for themselves, to fathom the mysterious reverse side of the artwork with their own imaginations, thus virtually completing it.

Artist Vanessa Billy, the creator of this striking intervention, works with the relationship or balance and tensions between opposing materials: with their textures and possible forms, the linguistic means for describing them as well as their effect on the viewer. In an interview with Mousse Magazine in 2019, Billy said: "I work with matter and materials as a way to relate to the world, as a way of being in the world, as an attempt at finding sense. How to compose an object, how to decompose it."

The artist investigates the effect, function and aesthetics of industrial materials with verve, leaving a lot of room for chance. Billy develops artistic experimental arrangements whose form of appearance only emerges at the moment when a situation crystallises, solidifies or even temporarily sets in. These aggregate states often manifest themselves as ephemeral moments, but can also finally end in a fixed form. This is the case, for example, in the series *Meet me* from 2011. Billy discovered the unusual shape of a piece of concrete, reminiscent of a pancake, while cleaning the concrete mixer – when she folded up the semi-liquid cement residues to be able to store them in a space-saving way. Based on such precise observations, the artist has developed a multi-layered and consistent oeuvre over the past few years that asks us, with a wink, to walk through our living environment with open eyes. The partly minimally invasive artistic interventions operate precisely at the interfaces of flawlessness, perfection, coincidence, and error. Billy comments: "I learn from accidents. And often I have to realise that I can't realise what I want – but what the material wants."

Vanessa Billy (*1978, Geneva, Switzerland)) lives and works in Zurich. Selected exhibitions: Kunsthaus Baselland, Muttenz (2011), Kunsthalle Marcel Duchamp, Cully (2014), Kunsthalle St. Gallen (2016), Centre Culturel Suisse, Paris (2017), Weiertal Biennale (2019, 2023), Centre Pasquart, Biel (2021), Museo Villa dei Cedri, Bellinzona (2023).

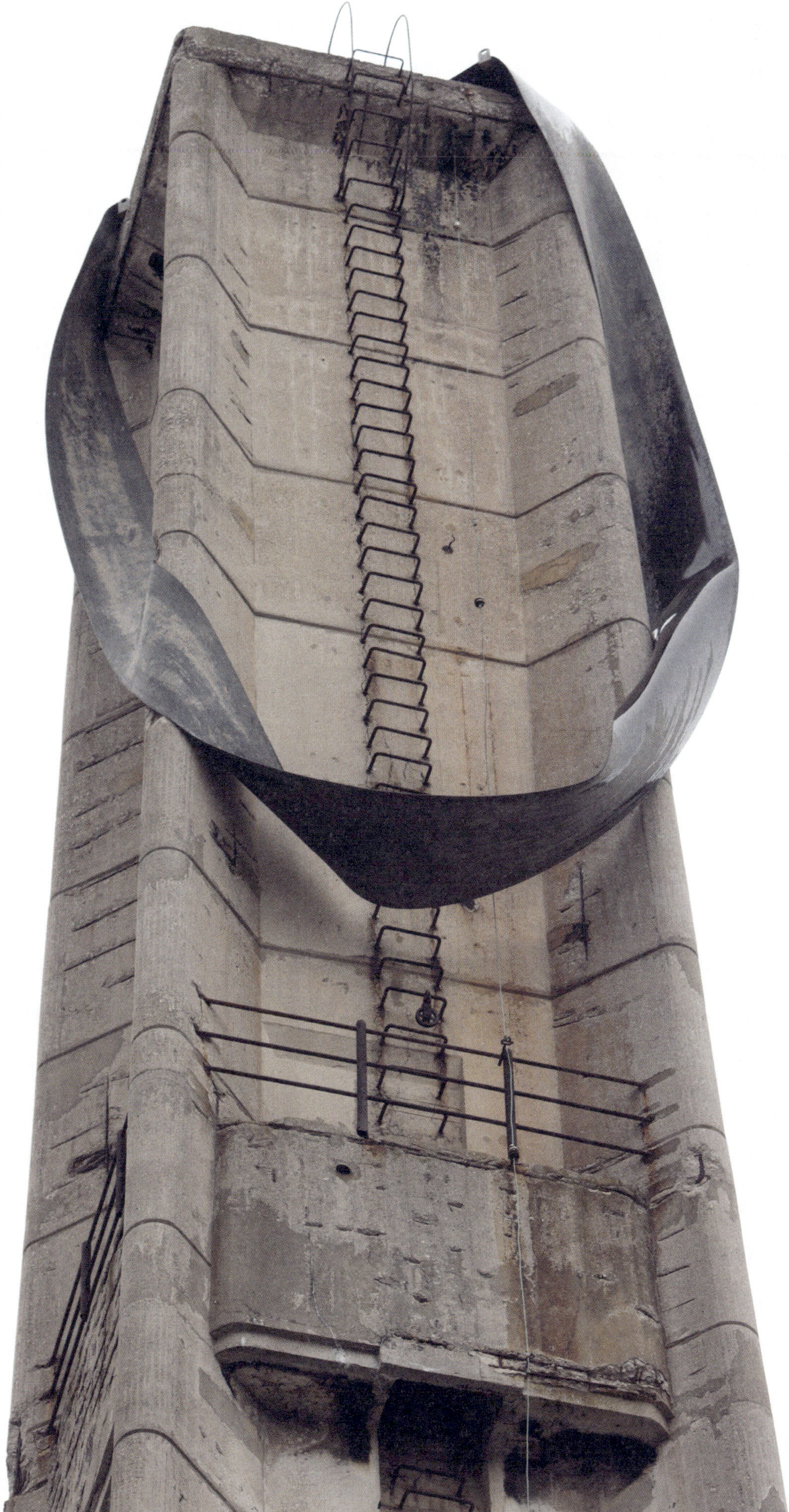

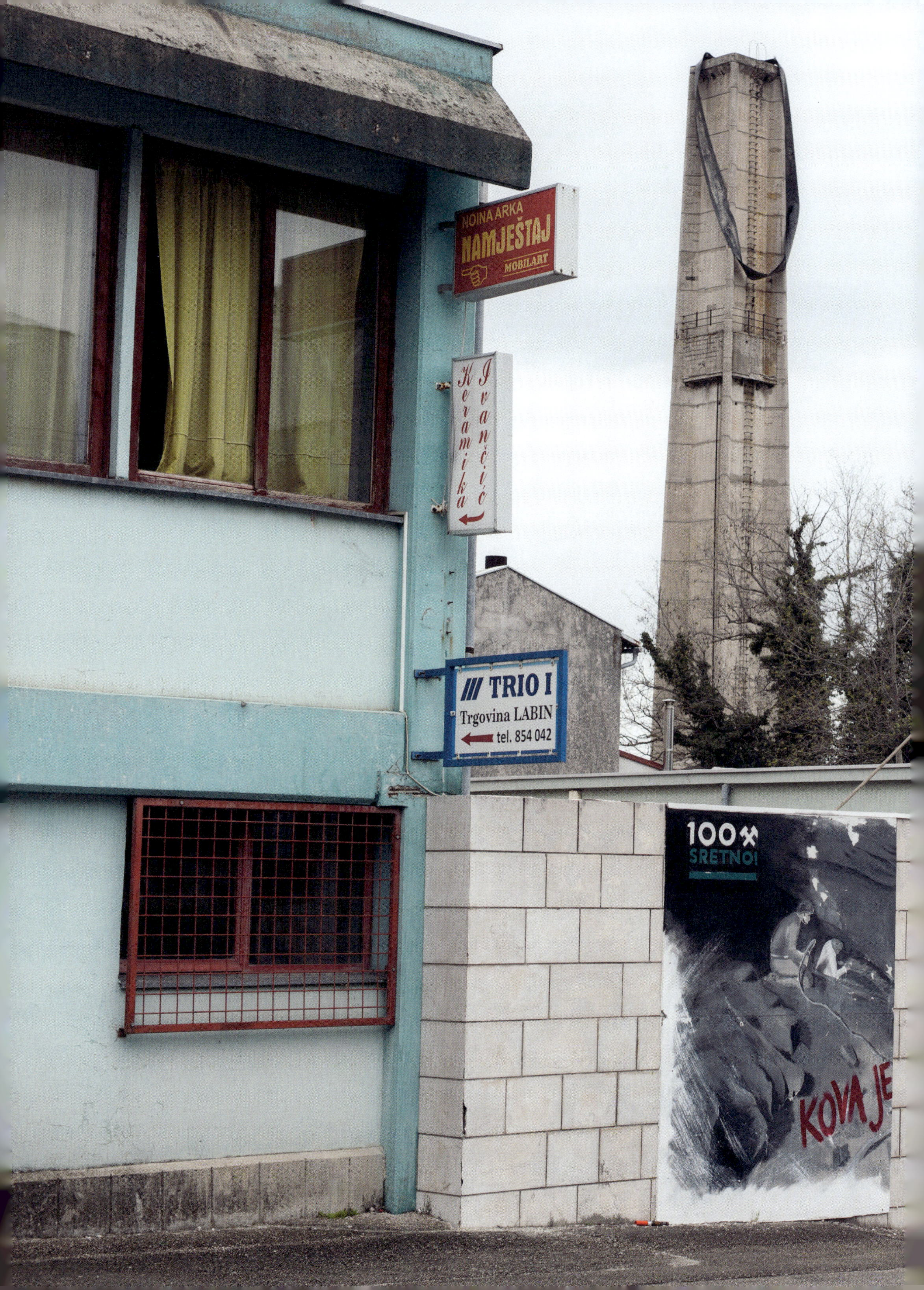
NOINA ARKA
NAMJEŠTAJ
MOBILART
Keramika Ivančić
TRIO I
Trgovina LABIN
tel. 854 042
100
SRETNO!
KOVA JE

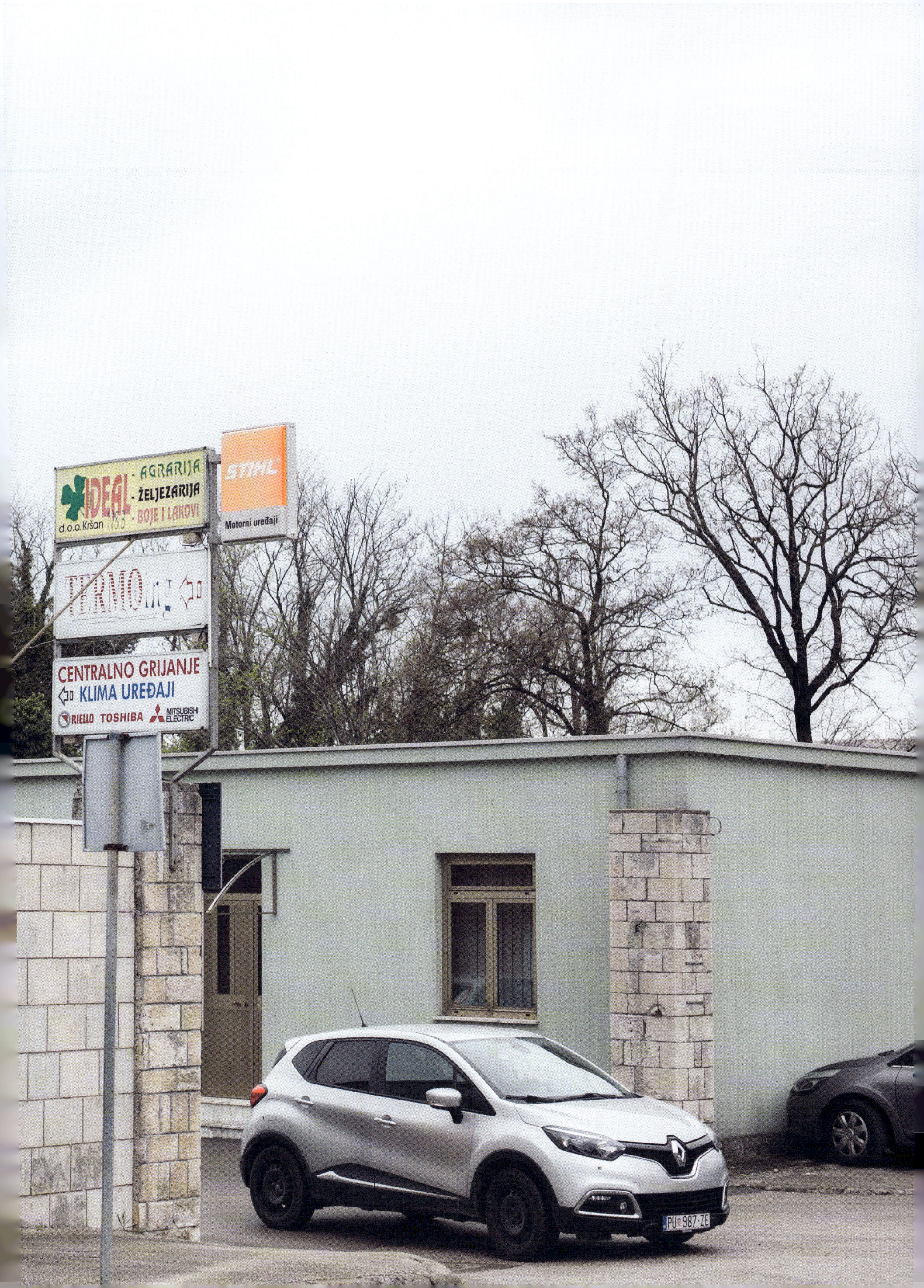
IDEAL
- AGRARIJA
- ŽELJEZARIJA
- BOJE I LAKOVI
d.o.o. Kršan
STIHL
Motorni uređaji
TERMOing
CENTRALNO GRIJANJE
KLIMA UREĐAJI
RIELLO
TOSHIBA
MITSUBISHI ELECTRIC
PU 987-ZE

Werner Feiersinger

Untitled, 2022 ⑤
"4. obrok" canteen, Raša
Lamparna, Labin
Gallery Amphitheater, Pula

Archival inkjet print, 200 × 150 cm (each)
Courtesy of the artist and Galerie Martin Janda, Vienna

Werner Feiersinger studied sculpture and also works regularly in three dimensions. But he does not do this solely in the installative or sculptural sense, but is generally concerned with spatial perception, conducts spatial research. "My work is about the symbolic and about contours," says the artist, "about the metaphorical and the ambiguous aspects of objects." As a logical consequence of this open concept of spatiality, Feiersinger works as a photographer parallel to his sculptural work. Together with his brother, the Viennese architect Martin Feiersinger, he spent a long time studying post-war architecture in Northern Italy. This resulted in the elaborately designed books *Italomodern 1* and *Italomodern 2*, as well as a series of exhibitions.

The precise observation of the world of things is at the beginning of the artistic discussions that Feiersinger tends to conduct openly in all directions. He crosslinks what he sees, reproduces it, reworks it, and uses it to develop and design new objects and spaces. His perspective has been trained over decades on the modernist vocabulary, but also on art historical aesthetics that go back further. Feiersinger is interested in discovering and establishing connections that are valid across epochs. That's why the Salzburg Museum commissioned the artist to deal with the important Baroque master builder and architectural theorist Johann Bernhard Fischer von Erlach (1656–1723) who designed impressive buildings in Salzburg's city centre. In response to this invitation, Feiersinger has developed a curatorial-artistic overall view that shows the Baroque master from the perspective of a sculptor and photographer rooted in actuality.

This integral approach to the spatial also forms the starting point for the complex of works comprising several hundred photographs that Werner Feiersinger developed for *Landscapes of Desire.* Starting in spring 2022, he travelled the Istrian peninsula in several stages and on these excursions examined both the industrial interventions, structures, architectures and ruins, as well as observing their relationship to the topographical framework. In Feiersingers' cycle we see and recognise the ruins of futuristic utopias, the decay of Yugoslav Brutalism, the fragments of infrastructures destroyed by war or neglection, the consequences of globalised capitalism and the results of the exploitation of nature over the millennia. The result is an archive of images whose melancholic power and artistic intensity returning the Istrian landscape the energy and gravitas it has lost through economic exploitation. Thanks to precise exhibition displays, which Feiersinger develops with great meticulousness, the connection between cultural, formalistic and economic phenomena becomes clear across all temporal-historical dimensions.

Werner Feiersinger (*1966, Brixlegg, Austria) lives and works in Vienna. Selected exhibitions and projects: Raum Aktueller Kunst Martin Janda, Vienna (1999), Secession, Vienna (2008), 4th Beijing International Art Biennial, Beijing (2010), Fundació Antoni Tàpies, Barcelona (2011), CAC, Vilnius (2011), O&O Depot, Berlin (2013), Fundação Gulbenkian, Lisbon (2014), Kunst Meran, Merano (2016), Belvedere, Vienna (2018), mumok, Vienna (2022).

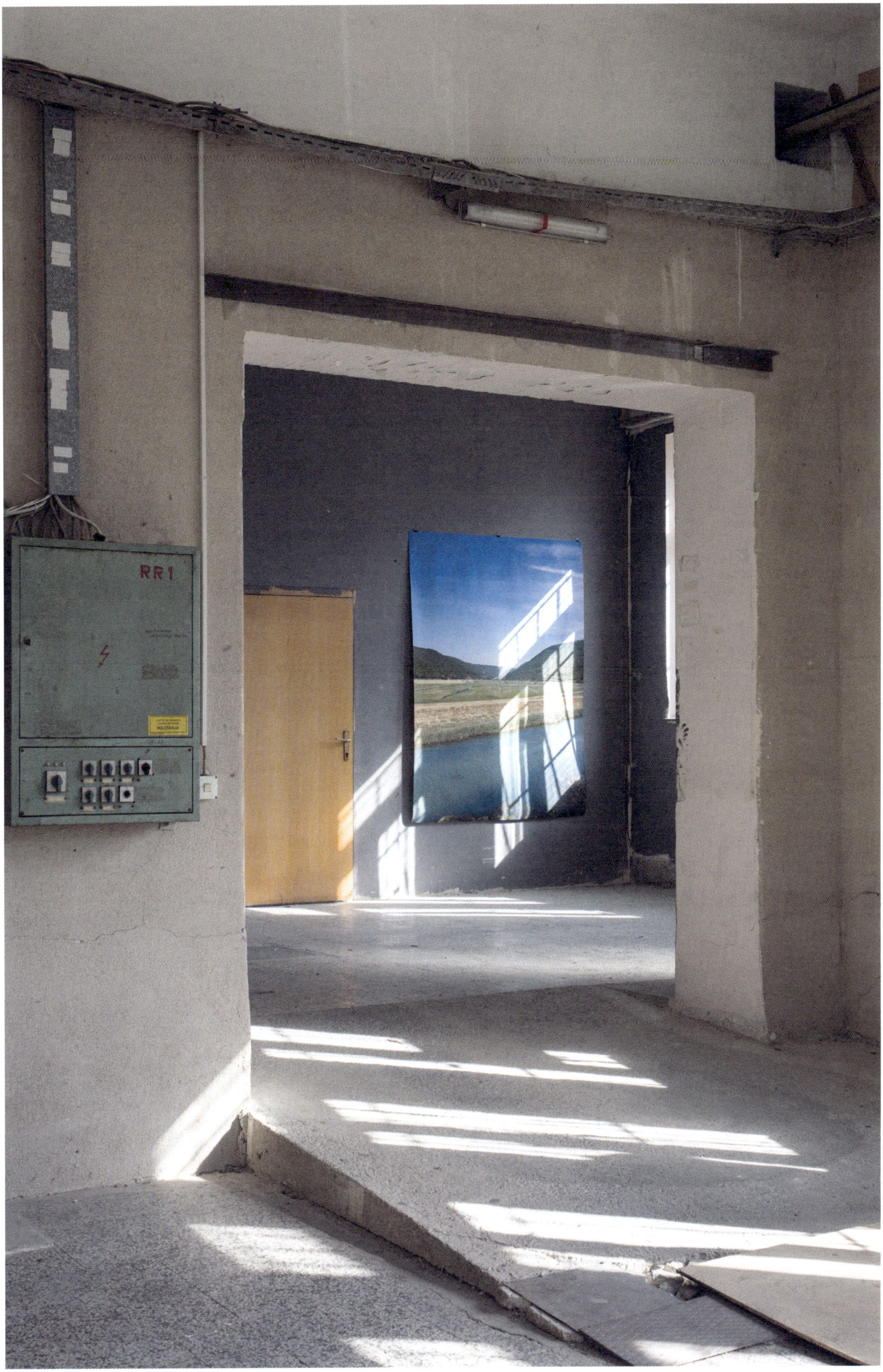
RR1

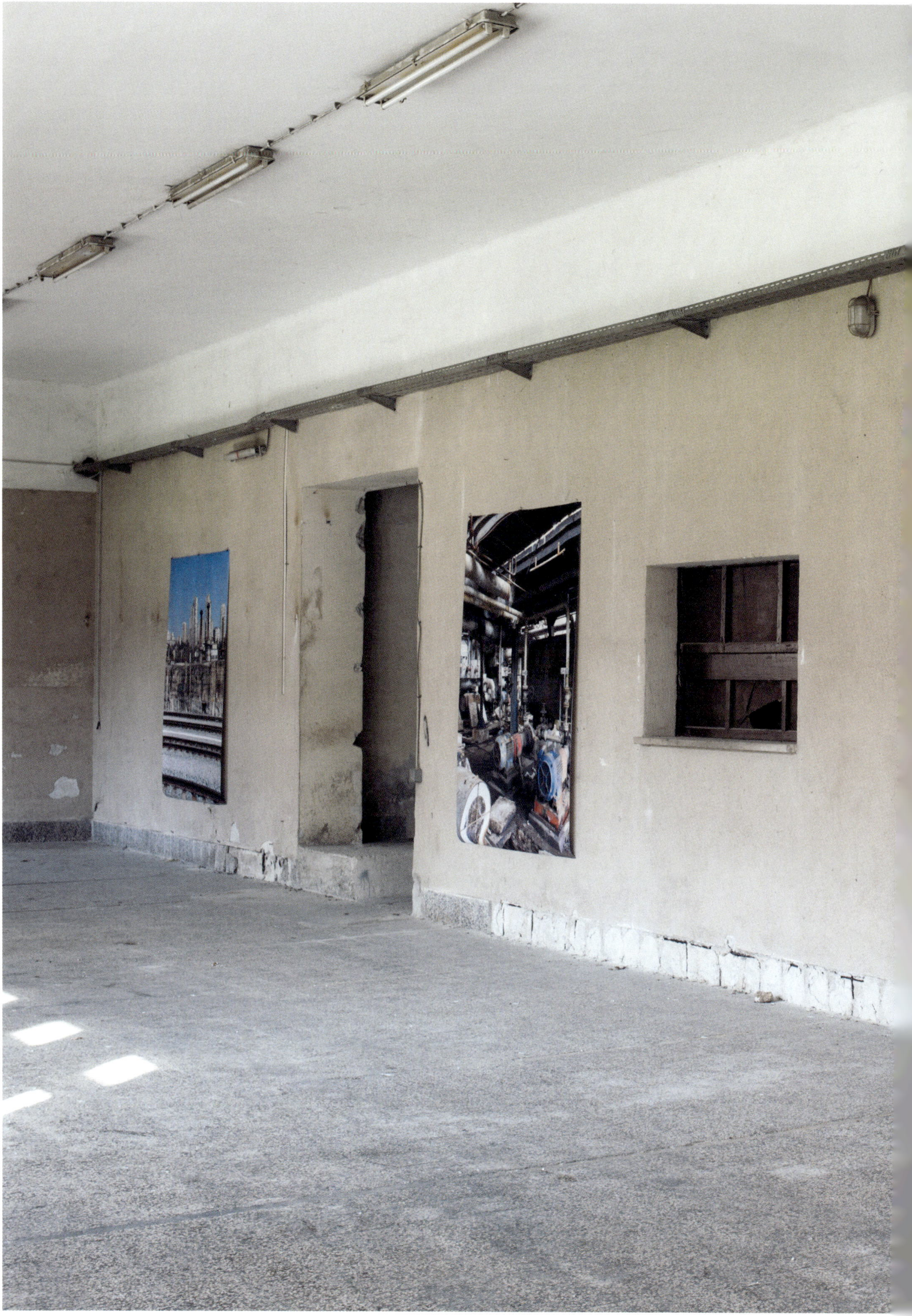

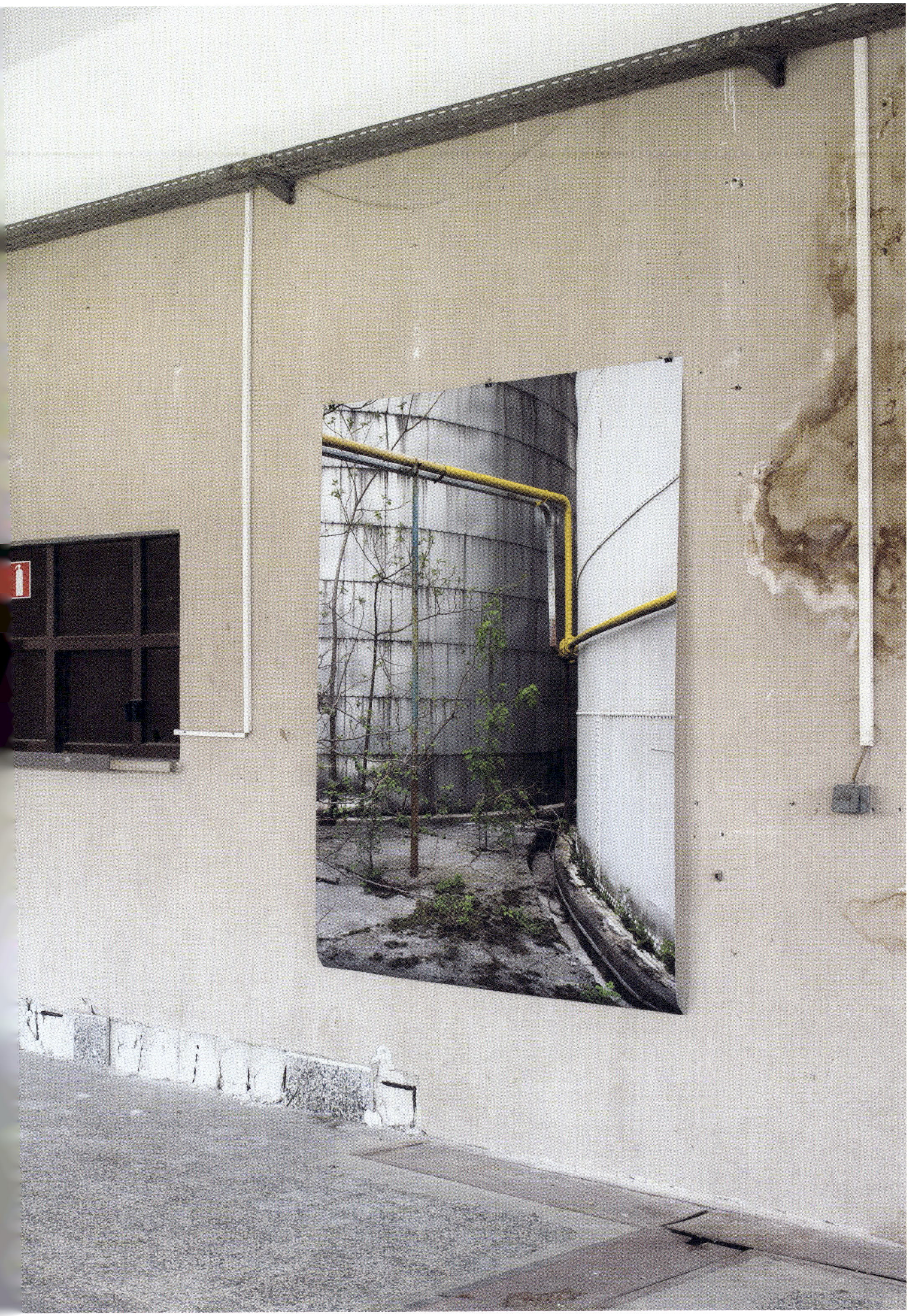

Fernanda Figueiredo

If it's been done before, perhaps we can do it again, 2022
Gallery Cvajner, Pula ⑥

The synchronization of economic and cultural globalisation of aesthetics is a central theme in the work of Brazilian artist Fernanda Figueiredo. Starting from her own biography and thus from the influence of Bauhaus Modernism on contemporary Brazilian culture after 1945, Figueiredo deals with analogous themes in other cultures. The almost blind faith in progress, prosperity, and modernisation is evident not only in the numerous futuristic buildings from the Italo-Fascist period, but also in the pioneering Yugoslav architecture found in Pula and Rijeka. These buildings, erected during the Tito era and in many cases now in poor condition, are a reminder that architecture once had a broader social responsibility in shaping society. When Figueiredo deals with this loss in a group of seven paintings created especially for the 4th Industrial Art Biennial, she gives new relevance to the theme. Her message: it is important to return in the future to the qualities of these urbanistic settings.

Figueiredo herself states: "This work is about the sense that Modern Architecture had in its imagination social and political change, but over time came the nostalgia for past achievements and a feeling of frustration. Just like Modern Architecture in Brazil, the project of socialist Yugoslavia was a utopian project, playing architecture a decisive role in the goal of projecting a better future for the society. That future, however, never materialized. The architecture reflects this former idea of the future, while the surfaces and layers of human interventions reveal the reality of its current conditions. These places still irradiate utopia, but with contradictions in their context and our own.

The title then proposes an ambivalent perspective. On the one hand, optimistic, since we always have the chance to be utopian and try it again. I believe that Modern Architecture continues to fascinate because it serves as a reminder that imagining different politics and society are possible. At the same time, it's sad decay speaks to the ultimate failure of this project, while cyclic authoritarianism and nationalism resurge in many places that experienced utopian Modernism."

The work comprises seven paintings on canvases. I designed four small ones using as references Yugoslavian pavilions built at world fairs of technology, art, and modern lifestyle: Milan, 1931 / Paris, 1937 / Brussels, 1958 / Montreal, 1967. The influence of these Modern Yugoslavian pavilions on eastern and western architecture was substantial, and they are internationally considered as a reference in innovation and uniqueness. The larger paintings are composed using references I gathered in Labin, Raša, Rijeka, and Pula during my research period: Modern architecture, vintage advertisement posters, graffiti, native vegetation, and landscaping to create friction between dystopian and utopian elements."

Fernanda Figueiredo (*1978 in São Paulo, Brasilia) lives and works in Berlin. Her works were shown at Museu de Arte de Blumenau (2014), A Gentil Carioca, Rio de Janeiro (2019), Galeria Kogan Amaro, São Paulo (2020), Oficina Cultural Oswald de Andrade, São Paulo (2021), Chromatica, Miami (2022).

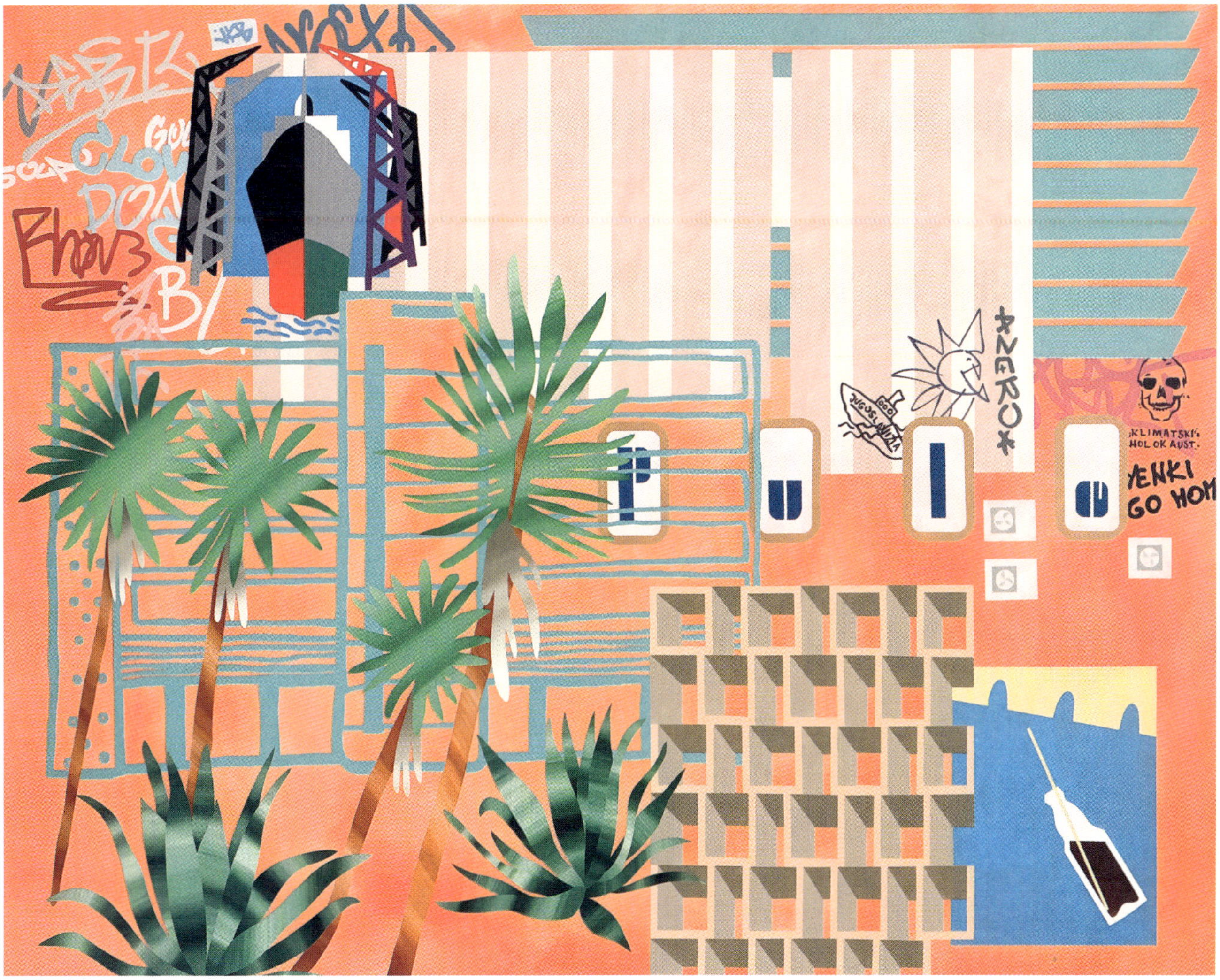

If it's been done before, perhaps we can do it again (Klimatski Holokaust), 2022
Acrylic on canvas, 123 × 160 cm

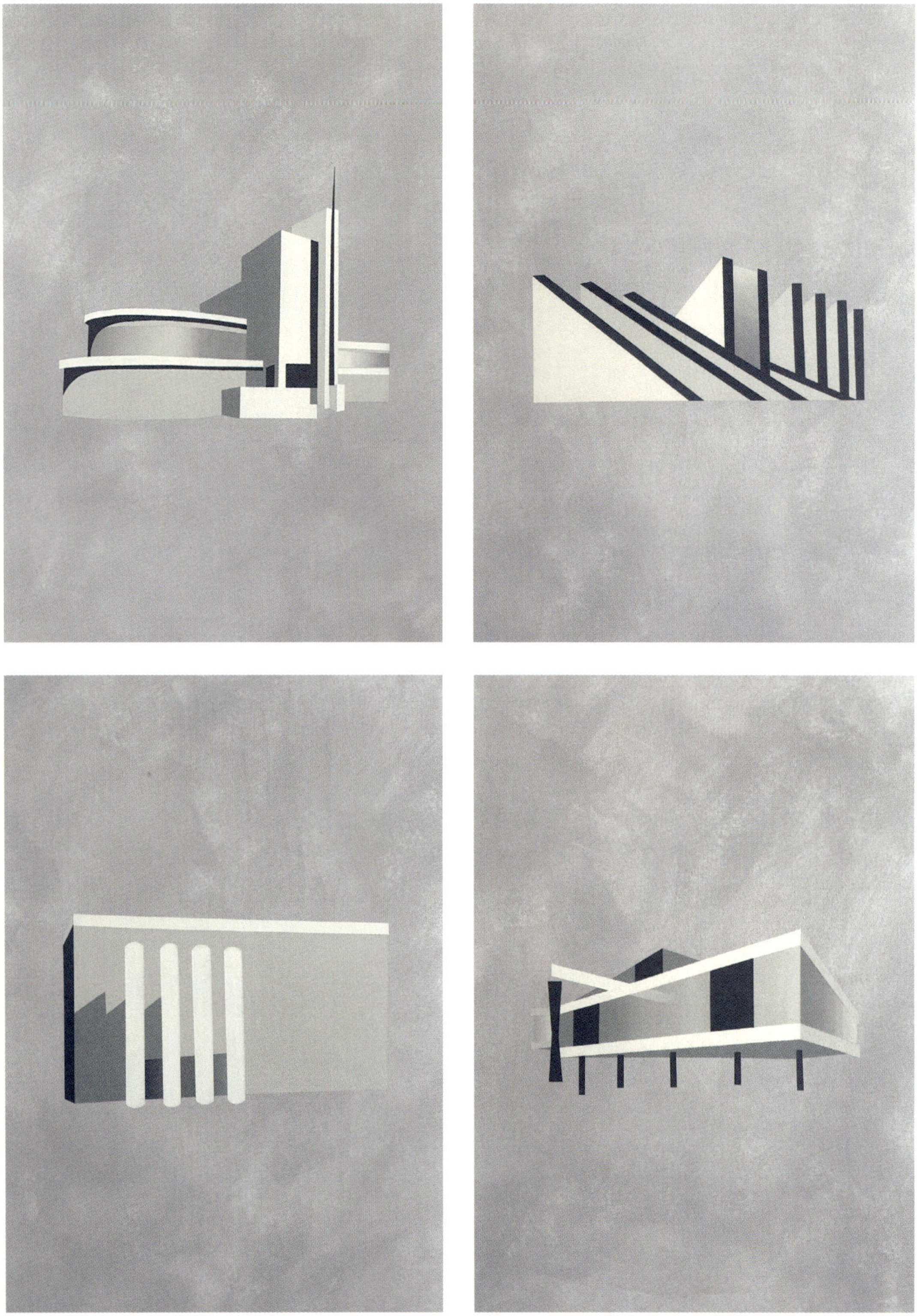

If it's been done before, perhaps we can do it again (Pavilions), 2022
Acrylic on canvas, 70 × 50 cm each

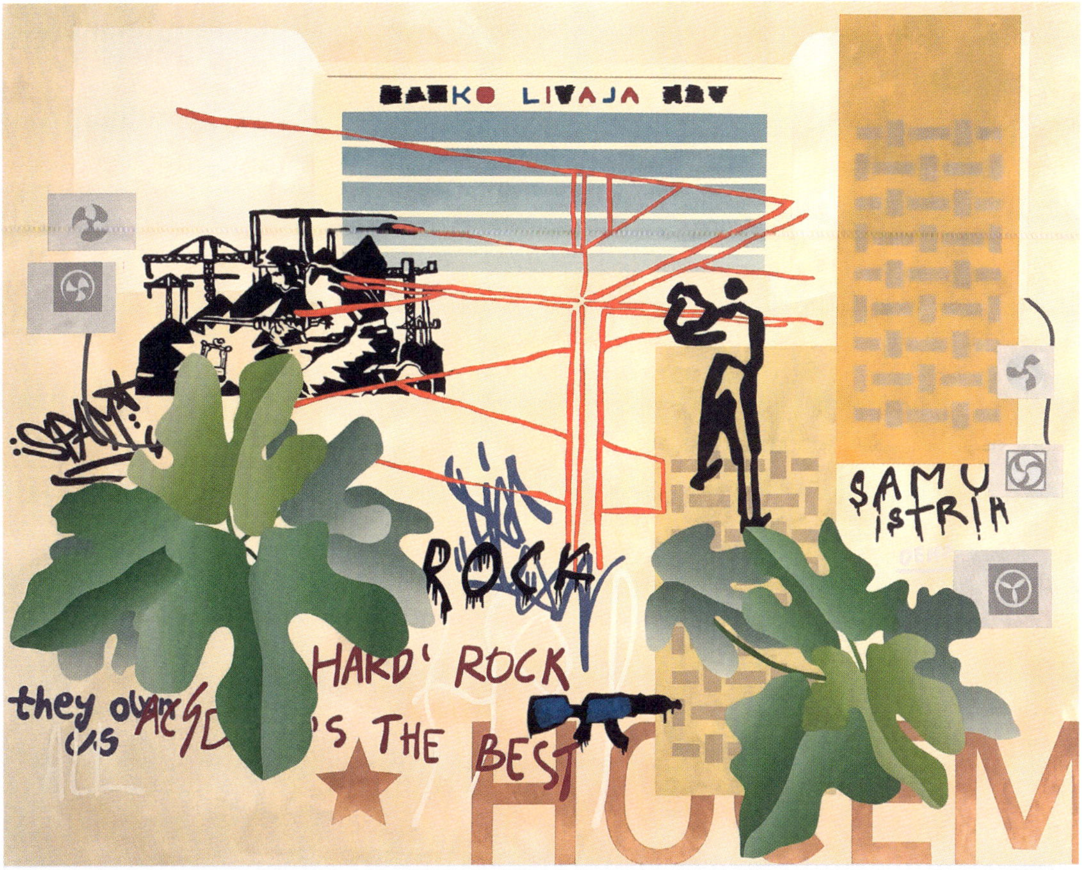

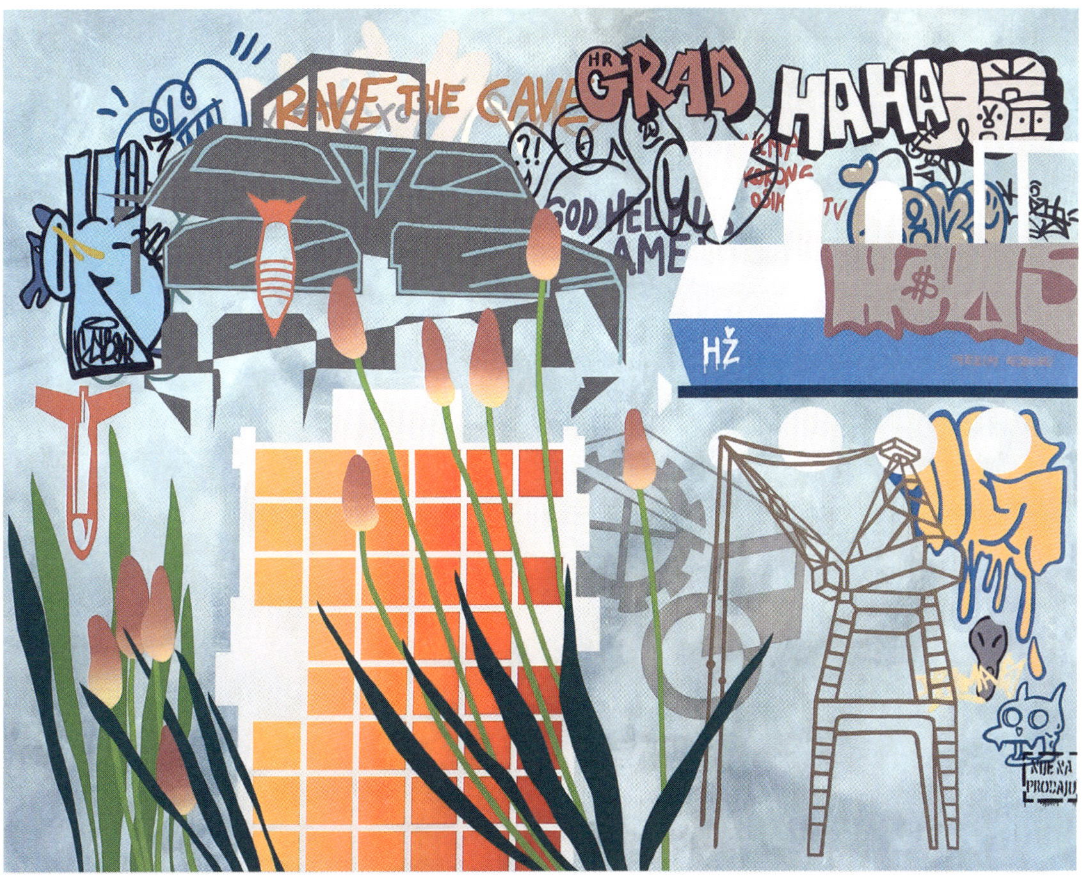

If it's been done before, perhaps we can do it again (Marko Livaja HŽV), 2022
Acrylic on canvas, 123 × 160 cm

If it's been done before, perhaps we can do it again (HŽ Building), 2022
Acrylic on canvas, 123 × 160 cm

Clare Goodwin

Ceramic Whispers, Include, Conclude, 2022 ⑦
Untitled, Object Furniture, 10 stools, 2023
Annex of St. Barbara Church, Raša

Approx. 260 individual hand-cut and glazed ceramic "whispers", ca. 220 × 510 cm
Courtesy of the artist and Lullin + Ferrari, Zurich

Handpainted stool, unique, acrylic on birch plywood, 47 × 45 × 36 cm (each)
Courtesy of the artist and Lullin + Ferrari, Zurich

The title of the solo exhibition of Clare Goodwin's work at the Centre Pasquart in Biel (as well as the monograph of the same name) was *Constructive Nostalgia* and is both an affirmative reference and a (self-)ironic iconoclasm. The Zurich-based conceptual artist, who originally trained in painting, moves in this energy field, but in recent years has increasingly developed installative, spatial interventions and also worked as a curator. The starting point of her artistic practice is hard-edge painting and the geometric pictorial structures of the Constructivists, which she recontextualises in the most diverse aggregate states, as large-format murals, room furnishings, sculptures and floor and wall reliefs. Rebecca Geldard aptly calls this the "investigation of the past as the aesthetic currency of the present".

In the spacious loggia of the church of St. Barbara in Raša, the artist deals with an icon of art history: *Guernica*, the monumental painting that Pablo Picasso painted in 1937 as a reaction and commentary on the fascist bombing of the Basque town and exhibited for the first time at the World's Fair in Paris in the same year. Picasso said at the time: "I am convinced that an artist who lives and deals with spiritual values cannot be indifferent in the face of a conflict in which the highest values of humanity and civilisation are at stake."

The blending of the source of the image (Picasso) and the spatial context (Raša), both created in 1937, is striking and is further reinforced by the architectural framing in the style of Italian Rationalism. War, destruction, politics, beauty, art and painting discourse overlap in the pavilion annex of the church to form an impressive memento mori. Goodwins wall relief adapts Picasso's original grey colour palette and abstracts the war atrocities he depicted into some 260 ceramic elements. "Clean of form, these individual ceramic pieces in monochromatic and subdued tones, collectively create a pictorial vista, allowing narrative and poetic possibilities to arrive through the process of abstraction. Essentially it operates much like a painted image, if one that materialises over a fractured ceramic surface." (Goodwin)

Complementing the relief already created in 2022, the artist has developed ten specially designed stools for the pavilion that invite visitors to stay and contemplate. Here, too, the design triggers a formal echo, as the seating is reminiscent of the legendary *Ulmer Hocker* by the Swiss artist, architect, designer and politician Max Bill. The multifunctional piece of furniture was developed for the students of the Ulm College of Design. Opened in 1953, the educational institution was intended to train a new generation of urban planners, designers and graphic artists in such a way that the reconstruction of modern Europe after the Second World War could be realised with aesthetic aspirations – similar objectives to those expressed by the Futurists a generation earlier.

Clare Goodwin (*1973, Solihull, Birmingham, U.K.) lives and works in Zurich. Goodwin studied at Winchester School of Art from 1993–1996 (BA Painting) and at the Royal College of Art, London, from 1996–1998 (MA Painting). Selected exhibitions and projects: Prague Triennale (2008), Kunsthalle Winterthur (2012), Centre Pasquart, Biel (2016), *Concrete Present*, Haus Konstruktiv, Zurich (2019), Haus der Kunst, Solothurn (2020), Atelier Hermann Haller, Zurich (2022).

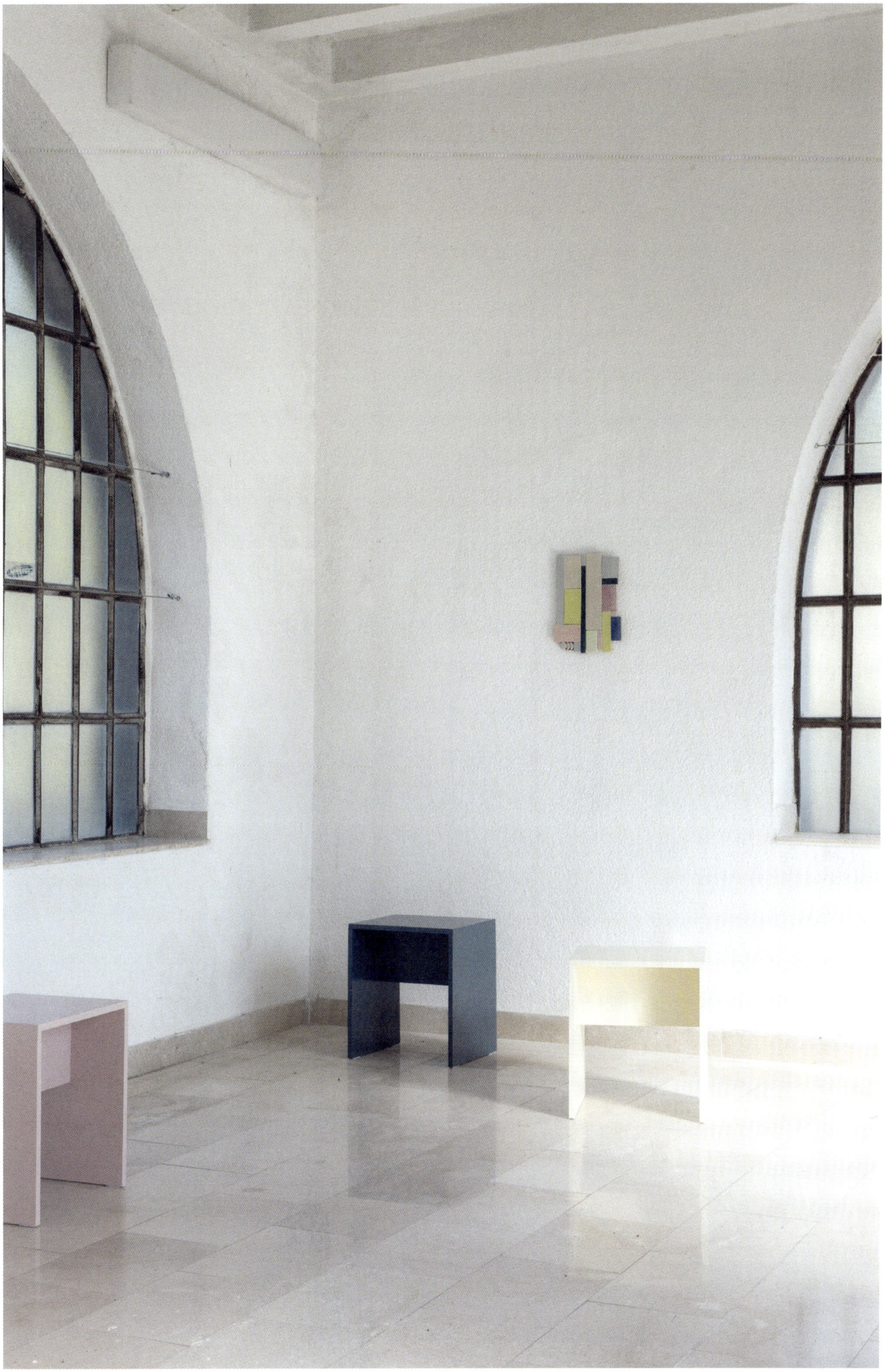

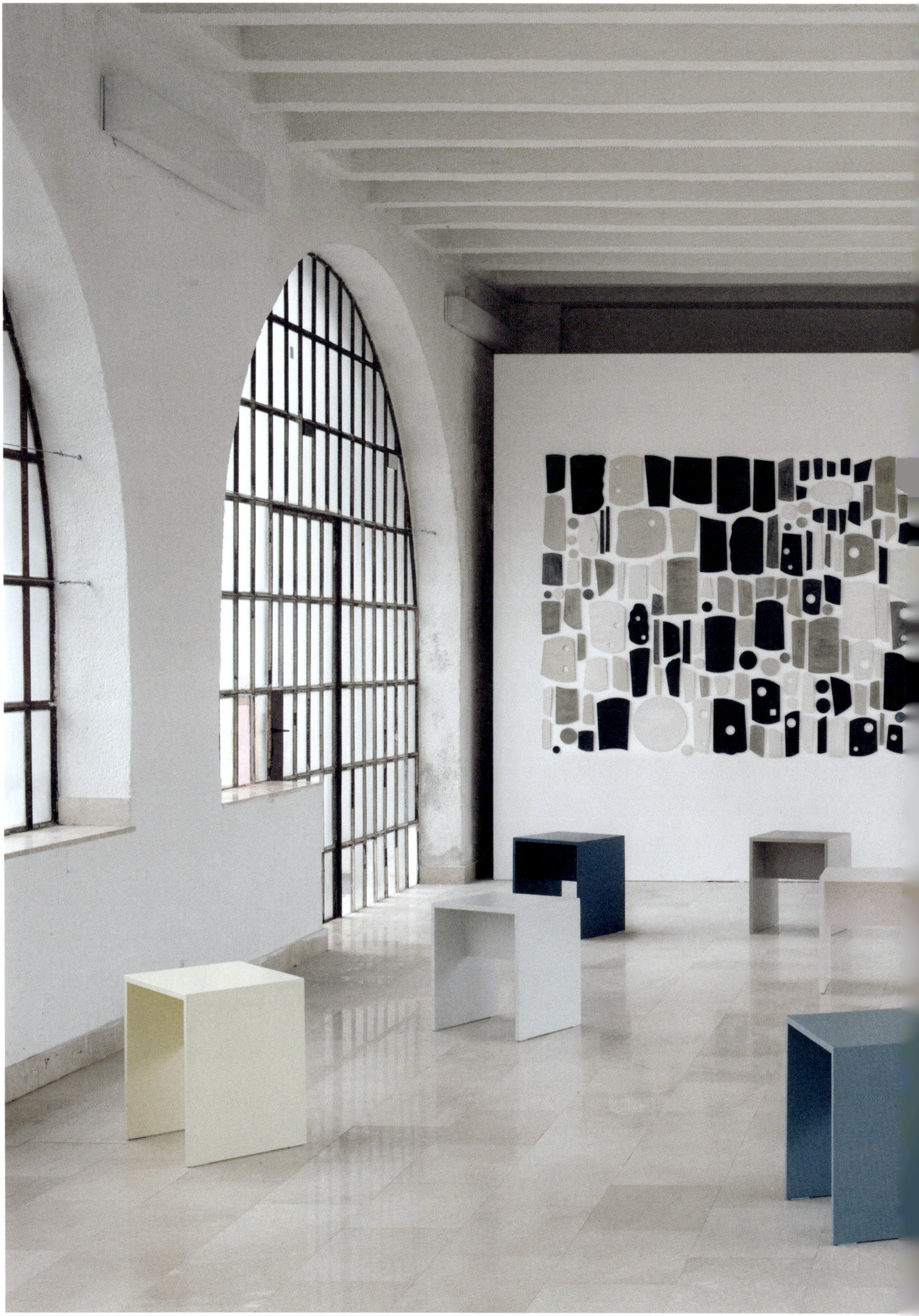

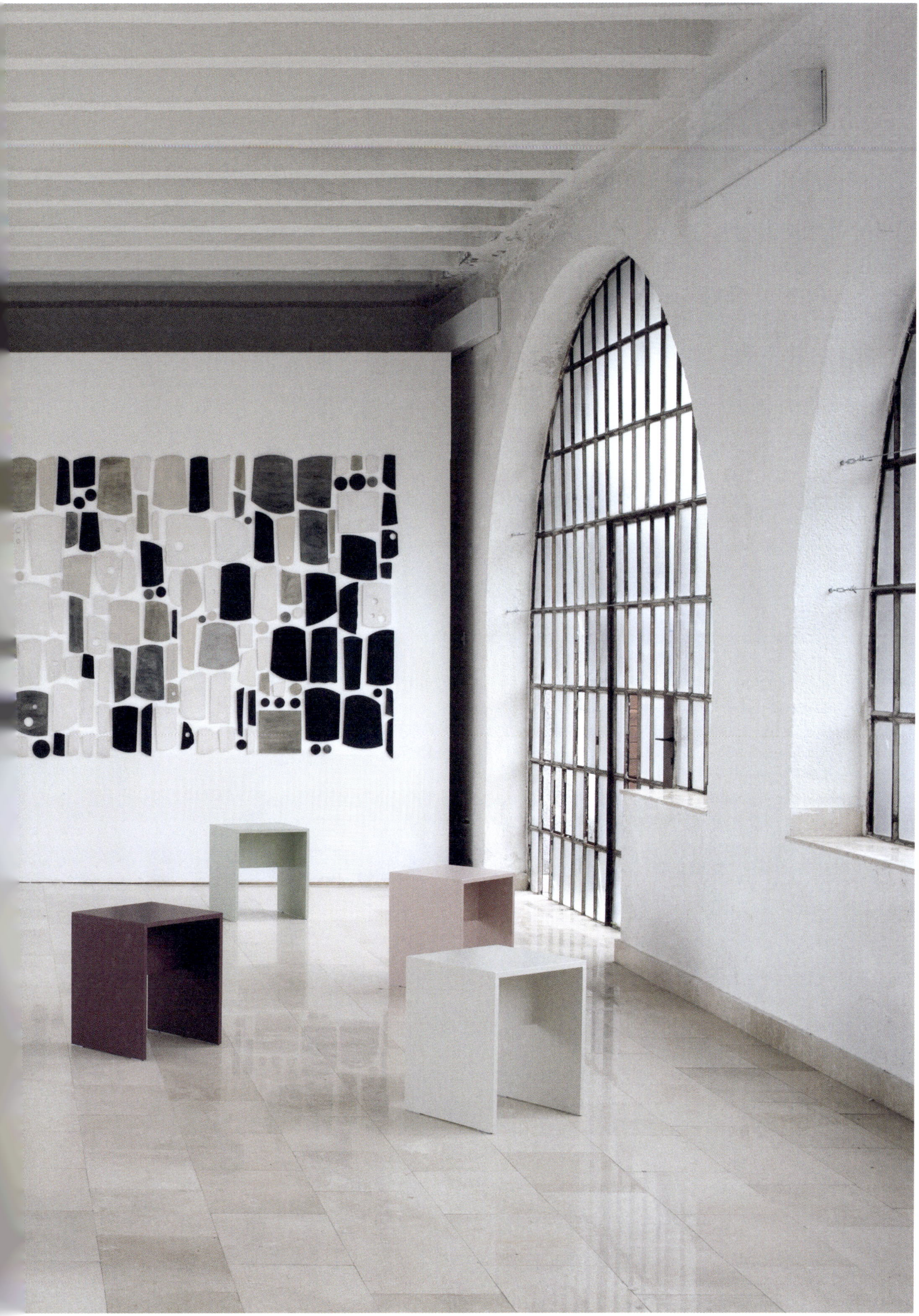

Tatjana Gromača

Nepoznati fragmenti / Unknown fragments, 2022–2023
Flaciusova ul., Pula

Billboard poster, 300 × 1800 cm
Courtesy of the artist

(8)

The writer Tatjana Gromača, who lives in Pula, is one of the quietest and at the same time most haunting voices in recent Croatian literature. Her three *Unknown Fragments* (2022), which can be read on a large billboard in public space, appear like ironic comments on reality. The whining tendency to wallow in self-pity seems to be a common behavior in Croatia.

When Gromača, in a fragment towards the end, suddenly speaks of a mimosa that is in bloom, that is a meaningful symbol. The leaves of the mimosa have the property of folding up when touched or shaken. The folding of the leaves happens in a matter of seconds after contact. The plant then rests in this position for about thirty minutes before unfolding again. For this reason, the mimosa is often referred to in English as the "touch-me-not" plant. Due to this property, the adjective "mimosa-like" has become established in general usage. Gromača writes that one should imagine the blooming mimosa in winter, i.e. in the snow. This is highly absurd, because the mimosa flowers between May and September. The mimosa as a plant and symbol thus acquires a resilient power in its text.

In the Mediterranean climate, the mimosa flowers very early, before spring, usually in February. This is the first flowering after winter – and at the same time in Croatia many people go north to the mountains that are still snowy. This leads to an opposing movement between nature and man.

The three fragments of Gromača are always about contrasting experiences. Suffering is followed by a cry for freedom and the lies of rulers are followed by breaking out of the silence of injustice, which masquerades as justice. From this perspective, the three fragments provide current mental images of a world that has gone haywire.

PS: The three text fragments by Tatjana Gromača were designed by typographer Karin Engler into a large "wall newspaper", almost an anti-poster compared to the convention of advertising. The typeface for the coloured Croatian text is called Mote and is by Croatian type designer Hrvoje Živčić. The black font for the English translation is called Punta and was developed by the two Croatian designers Marko Hrastovec and Nikola Djurek.

Tatjana Gromača (*1971, Sisak, Croatia) studied comparative literature and philosophy at the University of Zagreb. In 2001 she received a grant from the Berlin Academy of Arts. From 2000 to 2008 she worked as a journalist for the political-satirical weekly Feral Tribune (Split) and for the daily newspaper Novi list (Rijeka). Since 2017 she has been writing literary reviews, essays, travelogues and humanities articles for Croatian radio. She has published five novels, three books of short prosa, one book with selected reportage stories and a book of poetry. A second poems book will be published in May 2023. Tatjana Gromača lives in Pula, in a small creative community with her husband Radenko Vadanjel, also writer, and their daughter Marta.

Blago vama, vi putujete!

Da, opća povijest gadosti, opća povijest nepravednosti, opća povijest ubijanja, muljanja, zločina, opća povijest podmićivanja, opća povijest pokradenih novaca, posjeda, kuća, stanova, opća povijest protjerivanja i doseljavanja, opća povijest osvajačkih apetita, opća povijest prekrajanja prostora, opća povijest patriotskih nebuloza i nacionalizama, opća povijest potkupljivanja – čovjek ne vidi gdje bi svemu tome mogao biti kraj, zar ne? Jer sve se, udruženim snagama, nastavlja, u istome ritmu, tonalitetu, snazi, i sve bespovratno završava u teškim, debelim govnima, u brdima leševa po kojima plaze strvinari. Okrenuti se sunčanom nebu, procvaloj grani? Mimoza koja samo što nije procvala, zamislite to gospođo, usred zime! A vi se vraćate sa skijališta, vi i vaši, cijela obitelj? Blago vama, vi putujete!

You travel, oh lucky you!

Yes, the general history of ugliness, the general history of injustice, the general history of killing, conniving, crimes, the general history of theft, the general history of stolen money, property, houses, apartments, the general history of banishment and immigration, the general history of conquering appetites, the general history of cutting up territory, time and time again, the general history of patriotic delusions and nationalisms, the general history of bribery – one cannot see how all this could come to an end, right? Because everything, in all its force, continues in the same rhythm, tonality, strength, and everything irrevocably turns to heavy, thick shit, into the hills of corpses crawling with scavengers. To turn towards a sunlit sky, a branch in full bloom? A mimosa on the verge of blossoming, imagine that, Sir, in the middle of winter! And you are coming back from the ski resort, you and your kin, the whole family? You travel, oh lucky you!

Ništa manje niti više od toga!
O ljudska žalosti, ljudska bijedo, o biće zatočeno u tuđoj koži, o lakovjerno i blagorodno napuštanje onoga što zbiljski jesmo, uvijek iz nekakve svemirski diktirane poslušnosti, iz bogobojaznosti samih pred sobom, samih pred vlastitim visokim porijeklom koje se iznutra buni, udarajući nas, zatočeno, neukaljano, grozničavo vapeći za disanjem kao slobodom – ništa manje niti više od toga.

Nothing less, nothing more!
Oh human grief, human misery, oh being imprisoned in someone else's skin, oh gullible and benevolent abandonment of what we really are, a kind of cosmically decreed obedience, God-fearing in front of ourselves, alone before our own noble ancestry, which rebels from within, striking us, imprisoned, untainted, feverishly yearning to breathe like it yearns to be free – nothing less, nothing more.

Mir nebeski vama!

I tko više ima, više vrijedi, i tko je goropadniji i ružniji u svom ophođenju s drugima, taj zaslužuje našu poniznost i pažnju – on je, zapravo, jedna vrst vođe kojemu se tiho podčinjavamo. I učiniti ćemo sve za njegovo zadovoljstvo, i najveći besmisao, na vlastitu štetu, jer tako se dokazuje pripadnost pravoj strani. Da, moćne, prezira vrijedne vladare volimo i želimo, neotesane i grube, sirove, koji siju nepravdu, mržnju, ako treba i smrt. Mi smo alat u njihovim rukama, predajemo im se dobrovoljno, za radi dokaza naše bezuvjetne ljubavi. Nikada ništa ne opovrgavamo, ne ustajemo protiv neistine i nepravde, šutimo, tako reći, jer tako je najbolje, i povlađujemo kada je potrebno. Oh, oh, poniznost je slatka i slatko je kutriti za leđima kakvog ubojitog zmaja, koji riga vatru na nejake, i na šaku jadnika koji su mu se usprotivili, a koji mu ne mogu ništa, baš ništa, jer on je ustoličen snagom svoje odvratnosti, snagom svoje ružnoće i nepravde, koju će predstaviti kao vrhunsku, nebesku pravdu. A vi, jadno stado, koji ste mu se pokorili, glupost je snaga vašeg uznesenja, mir nebeski vama!

Heavenly peace to you!

And whoever has more is more valuable, and whoever is more ferocious and vile to others deserves our meekness and full attention – in fact, this is the kind of leader to whom we tacitly submit. We will do everything for his pleasure, even the greatest absurdity, and to our own detriment, because that's how you show allegiance to the right side. Yes, we love and want powerful, detestable rulers, uncouth and rough, raw, who sow injustice, hatred, and if necessary death. We are a tool at their disposal, we surrender to them voluntarily, in order to prove our unconditional love. Never do we confront anything, we don't stand up against untruth and injustice, we keep quiet, so to speak, because it is for the best, and we grovel whenever necessary. Oh, oh, how sweet is humility, and how sweet it is to cower behind the back of a blood-thirsty dragon, who belches fire on the weak, and on the handful of poor souls that stood against him, but couldn't do anything to him, anything at all, for the power of his abomination exalts him, the power of his ugliness and injustice, which he will unveil as supreme, heavenly justice. And you, miserable herd, who bend before him, in stupidity you shall ascend, heavenly peace to you!

Igor Grubić

How Steel Was Tempered, 2018 ⑨
Kino Raša / Cinema, Raša

Igor Grubić is one of Croatia's most accomplished and internationally acclaimed artists and is known for using art as a tool for activism. His photographs, films, and symbolic actions in public space have addressed social, political, and economic concerns, often referring to significant historical events and drawing attention towards marginalized groups and unlikely heroes. For the 4th Industrial Art Bieninal Grubić was invited to exhibit a re-adaption of a project he already displayed in the Croatian Pavilion of the Venice Biennale, in 2019. *Traces of Disappearing* is key for the latest developments in Croatia and a symbol for an artful dialogue with the past. Katerina Gregos, curator of the Croatian Pavilion, stated:

"*Traces of Disappearing in Three Acts* (2006–2019), was thirteen years in the making. It consists of three inter-related photo essays and an animated film, set in a specially designed mise-en-scène. The project began in 2006 when the artist began documenting post-war, transitional reality in Croatia, particularly the fundamental shift from socialism to capitalism, from a central, stated-planned to a free market economy. It explores how this has affected changes in habitation, the urban fabric, public space and social relations.

Wild House, the first chapter or 'Act', examines changes in homes, living and public space with the privatisation of property and the consolidation of neo-liberalism in the country; *Filigree Sidewalk (Act II)*, looks into traditional vocations such as local handcrafts and specialist workshops, highlighting which professions survive and which not in the new economic circumstances. Finally, *Deconstruction of the Factory (Act III)* presents a series of defunct factories, monumental reminders of the transition from industry to post-industry, and changing conditions of work. The latter also becomes the setting for Grubić's short film, *How Steel Was Tempered*, which weaves together issues of worker history, family bonds and generational shifts, suggesting also the importance of fruitful future relationships based on solidarity, shared social space and creative, collaborative working."

Igor Grubić (*1969 in Zagreb, Croatia) lives and works in Zagreb. Grubić represented Croatia at the 57th Venice Biennale and has participated in Manifesta 4 and 9, the 11th Istanbul Biennial, and the 20th Gwangju Biennale, as well as in numerous film festivals. His work has been acquired by Tate Modern, the Museums of Contemporary Art in Belgrade and Zagreb, MWW – Wroclaw Contemporary Museum, Kunsthaus Zurich, FRAC Champagne Ardenne, Kontakt Collection Vienna, and Kadist in San Francisco, among others.

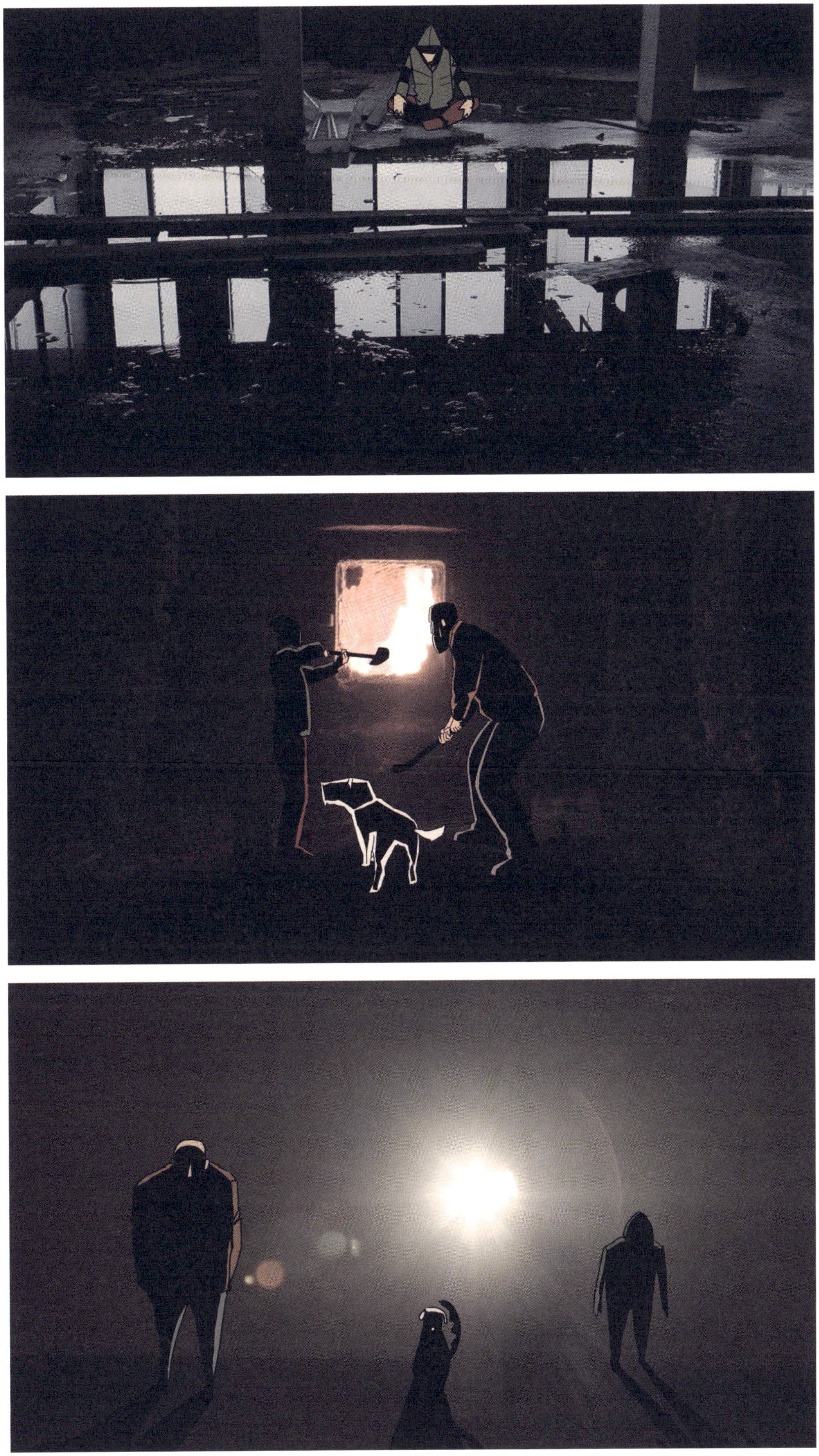

Stills from the animation
How Steel Was Tempered, 2018
mixed technique, 12 min. 40 sec.
Courtesy of the artist

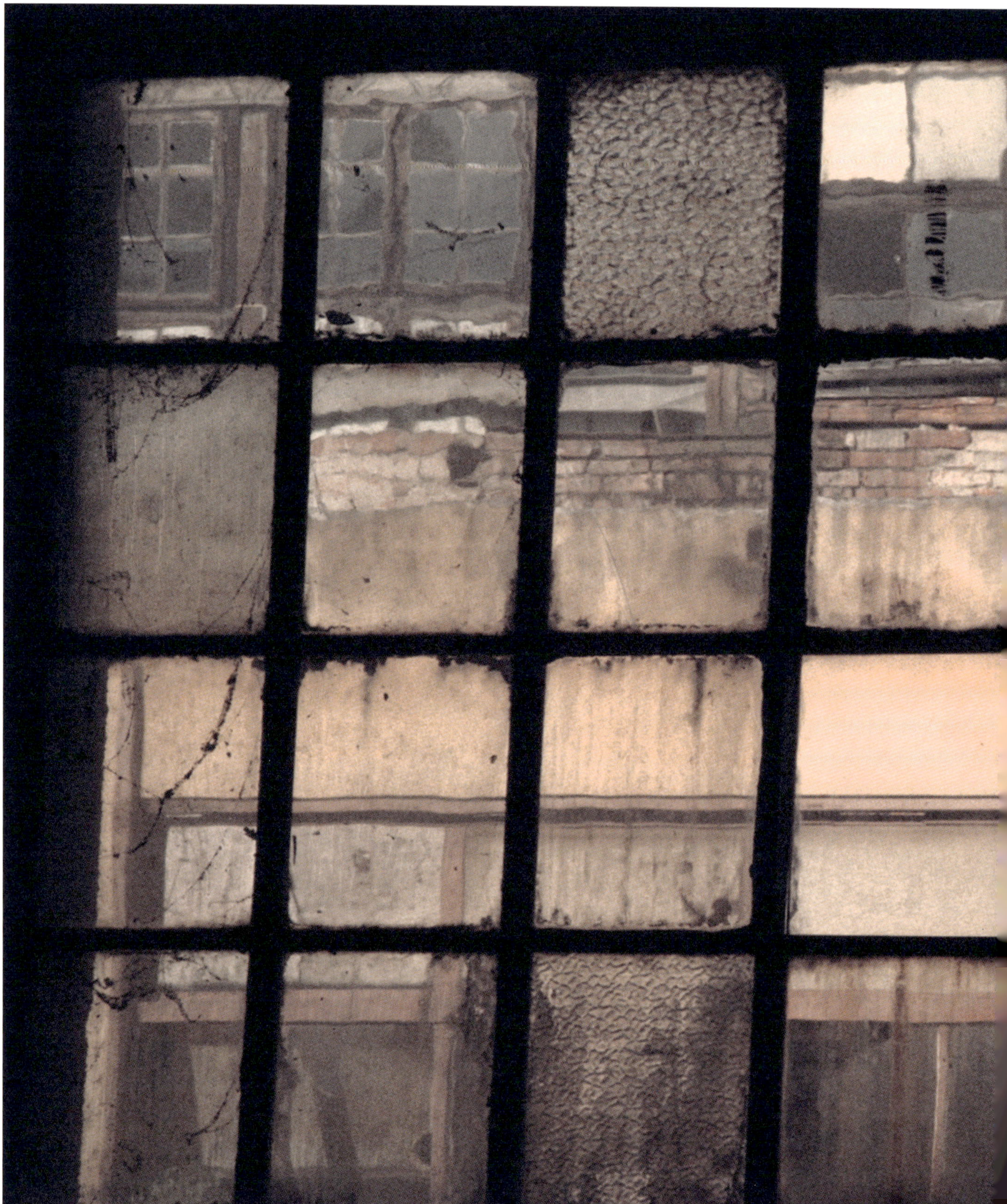

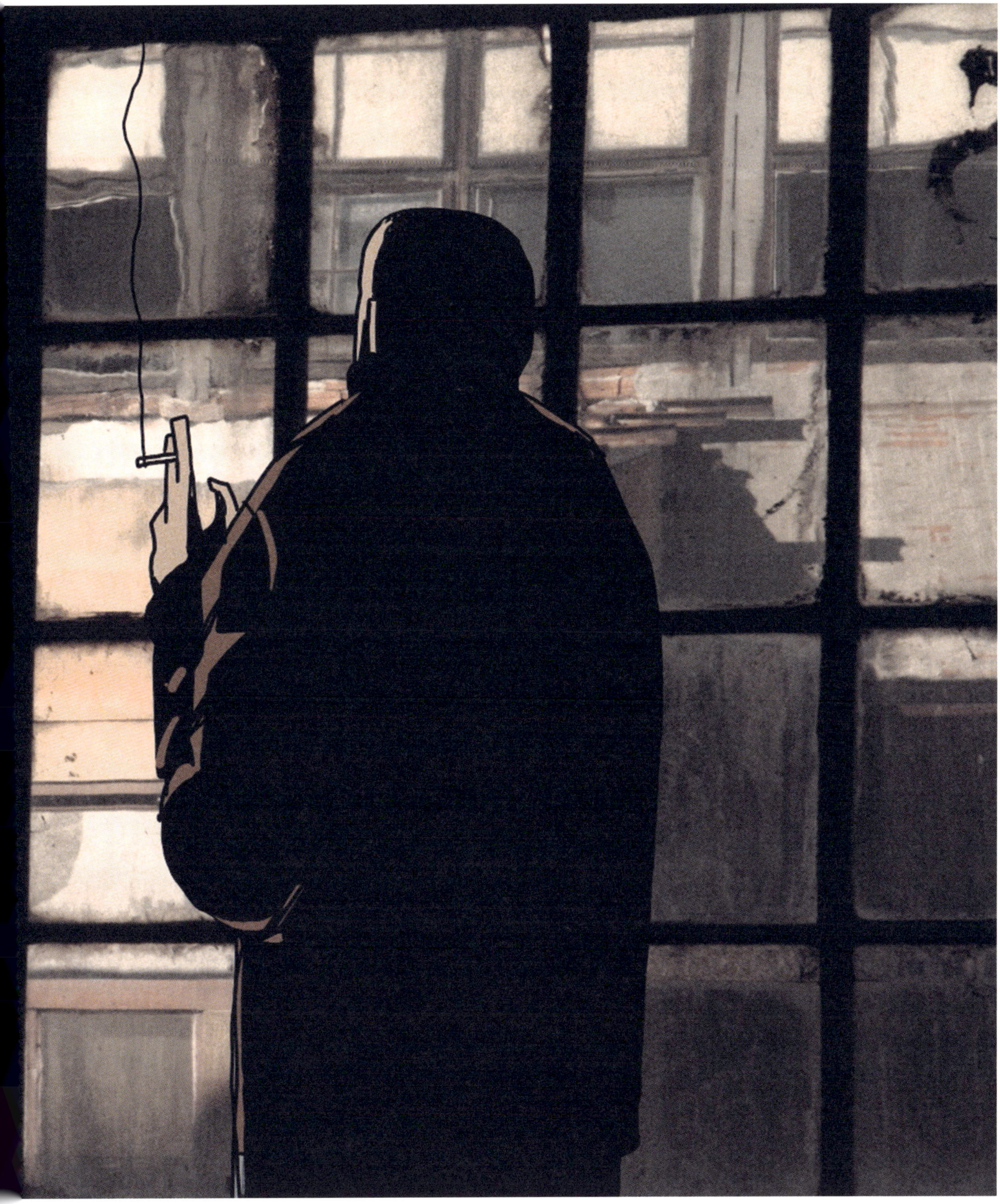

Manaf Halbouni

Dreamland, 2023
Kino Labin / Cinema, Labin

(10)

Painted wood, 200 × 1200 cm
Courtesy of the artist

With his highly acclaimed installation *Monument*, consisting of three upright buses, presented in 2017 in front of the Frauenkirche in Dresden and then in front of the Brandenburg Gate in Berlin, Manaf Halbouni took a socially critical stance on the war in Syria, global conflicts, and migration. Other central themes in his works are colonialism and military violence, borders and uprooting. Halbouni's works are often biographically motivated, as is the word installation *Dreamland*, which the German-Syrian artist created in meter-high letters on the roof of the cinema in Labin. When contemplating this work, the land of dreams seems closer than it seems. With the lettering as a crown on it, the building is exaggerated in its importance. Because the cinema is place, space, architecture, a place of longing, of dreams, a place of culture, a place that has an important position in village and city.

Halbouni's *Dreamland* installation is specifically related to the town of Motovun in Istria. Motovun is a popular holiday destination, known nowadays as a center of hedonists from all over the world. One legend says that the mythical figures Jason and the Argonauts sailed below Motovun to the traces of the first humans around 3500 BC. The artist has a history of his own with this place.

Once, staying overnight in Motovun, he wakes up in the morning and enjoys the view of the Mirna River valley from his window. It is located in what is probably the best-known and most attractive Istrian medieval town. The Romanesque-Gothic architectural style dominates in the city, which has preserved its original form to this day. The Mediterranean breeze also blows around this part of Istria, which is why mild winters and warm summers are part of everyday life. It is not the vineyards and not the Motovun forest with its enticing truffles, nor is it the traditional Motovun game of throwing ox horns that particularly fascinates the artist. It is simply the supernatural view of a landscape full of absolute beauty that gives the artist a "point of ecstasy" (according to Nietzsche), combined with the exclamation: "I have found my dreamland." This is the landscape of his wish-fulfillment, which he now pays homage.

Manaf Halbouni (*1984, Damascus, Syria), lives and works everywhere. 2014–2016 MFA, Dresden Academy of Fine Arts (HfBK), 2009–2014 BA, Dresden Academy of Fine Arts (HfBK), 2005–2008 BA, Damascus University, Faculty of Fine Arts. Numerous solo and group exhibitions, e.g. *Friday Late Night Event* (2015) at the Victoria & Albert Museum in London and *Nowhere Is Home* (2016) at the Museum of Fine Arts in Leipzig, *The Restless Earth* (2017) at the Milan Triennale, Havana Biennale de Cuba (2019), *Ost-Wind*, Kunsthalle St. Annen, Lübeck (2020), *Zone*, Center for Persecuted Arts, Solingen (2021).

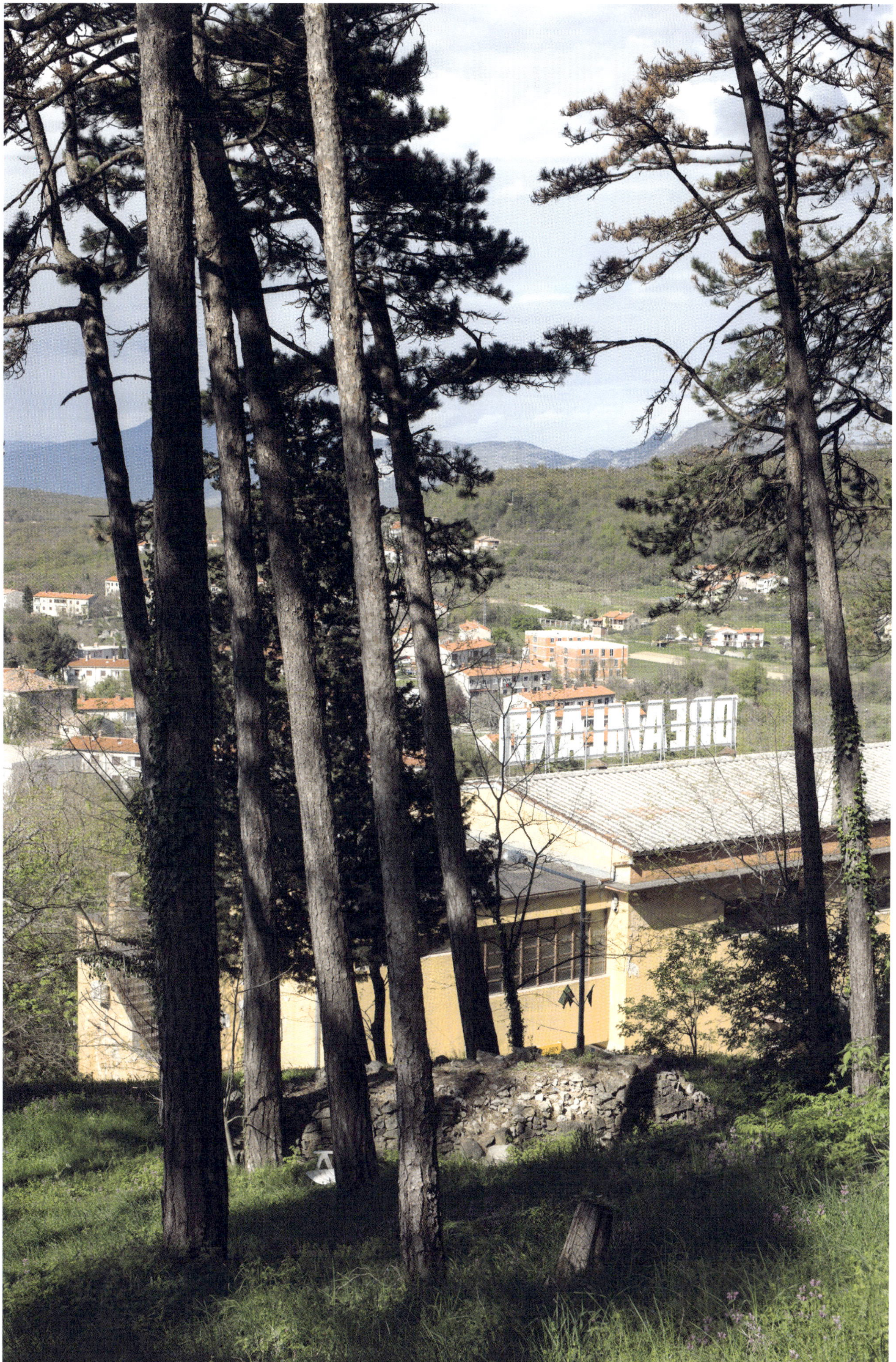

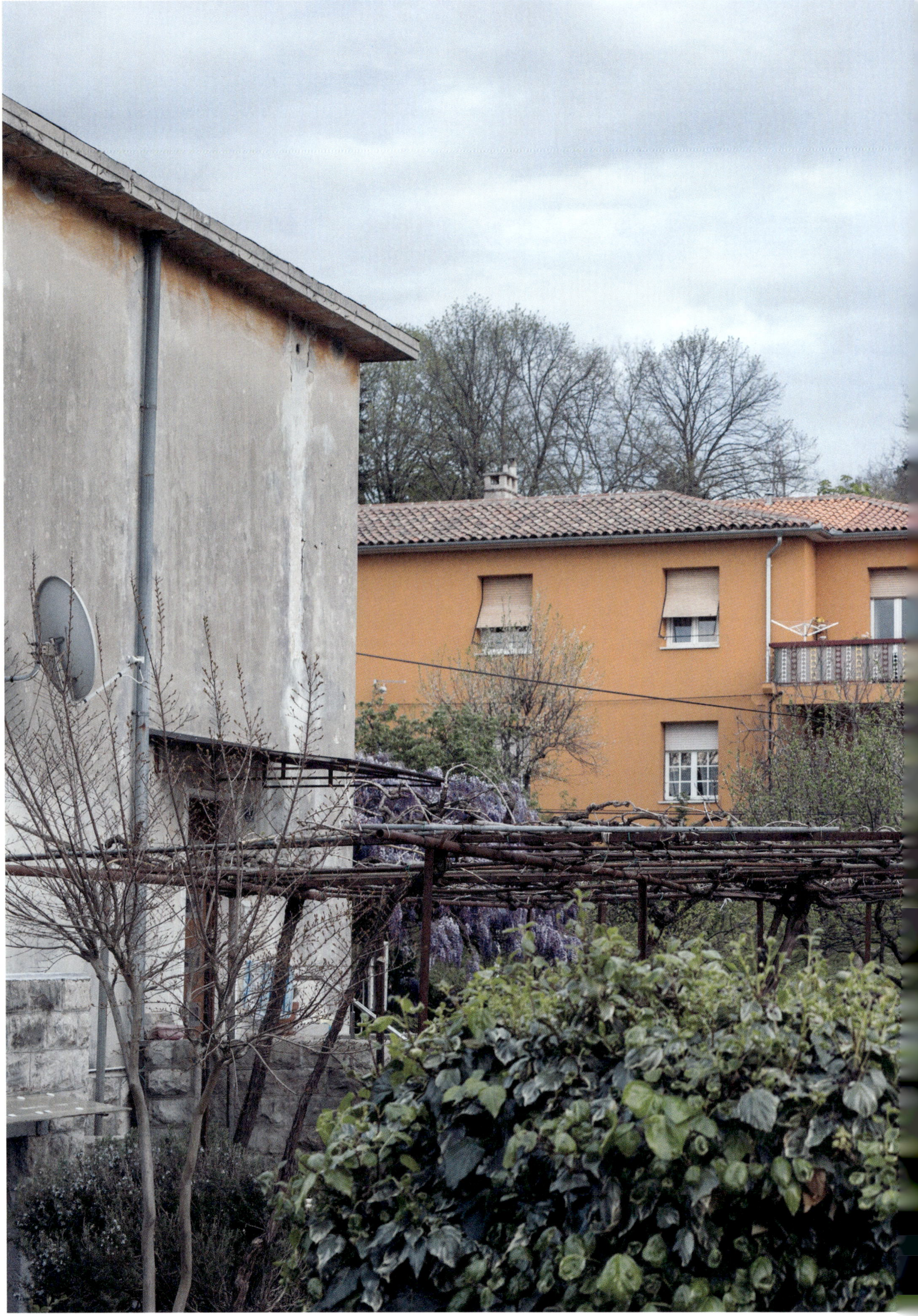

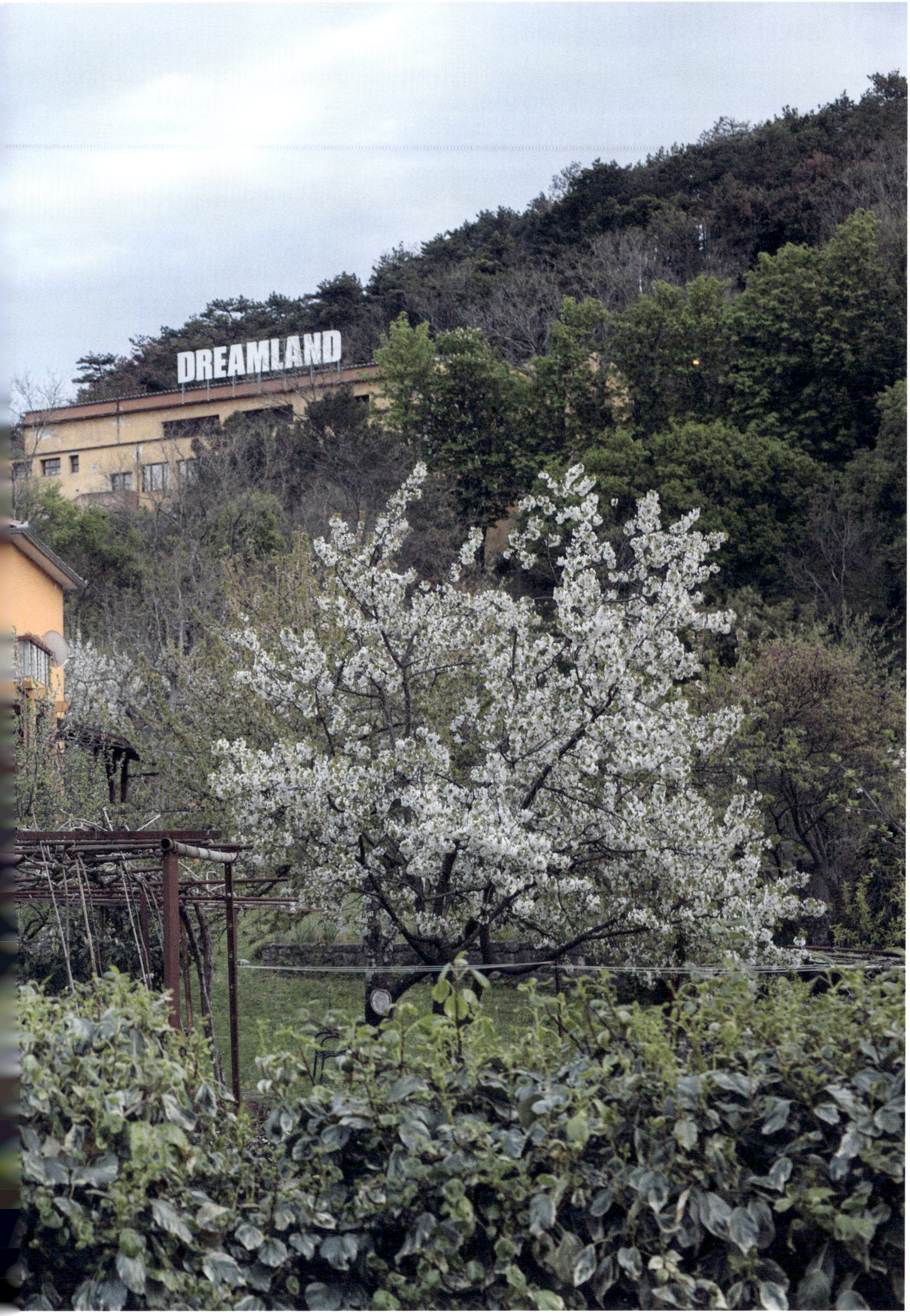
DREAMLAND

Raphael Hefti

After completing an apprenticeship as an electrical technician, Raphael Hefti studied photography at ECAL in Lausanne and art at the Slade School of Fine Art in London. This is probably one reason why a special combination of technical curiosity and a conceptual analytical approach has pervaded his work to date. Hefti often devotes himself to experimentation and research involving everyday materials, such as glass, iron or photographic paper, subjecting them to unusual processes and excessive treatment. In so doing, he produces sculptural objects of thrilling beauty, such as the impressive colourful glass-pane objects that he has developed by means of complex industrial layering processes. He has also produced large-format photograms using highly flammable clubmoss spores. Raphael Hefti's works are always intense, spectacular and poetic, all at the same time.

An excellent example of this extraordinary practice is the intervention the artist has erected in the Donišnica Valley near Raša. Between two ridges bordering a picturesque pasture for donkeys, Hefti has stretched a 320-metre-long and 20-centimetre-wide high-tech ribbon made of specially woven and coated polyethylene: While one side of the ribbon has a dark colouring, the other has a shiny silver surface. The ribbon has to be stretched across the valley with enormous tensile force to create a horizontal line that virtually inscribes itself in the landscape as a second horizon. As always with Hefti, this intervention is an experiment that explores the limits of what is possible: the tensile forces, the approval authorities, nature, technology. If things develop as planned, a new perception of nature will emerge from the many individual experiments with the help of a team of specialists. The ribbon, kept ever-so-slightly in motion by wind and weather, stretches a poetic, silvery line across this valley, which is already in itself a man-made intervention due to the various meliorations and drainage projects at the time of the Italian fascists.

as yet untitled or is it about wind, impatience, hallucination, neo-horizon, I love silver, skin veneer over a landscape whose air it splits, 2023 (11)
Dolina rijeke Raše (Donišnica)

Courtesy of the artist

Raphael Hefti (*1978, Boudevilliers, Switzerland) lives and works in Zurich. He has been widely exhibited, notably at Kunsthaus Glarus (2008), Camden Arts Centre, London (2012), CAPC, Bordeaux (2013), Nottingham Contemporary, Nottingham (2014), Fondation Vincent van Gogh, Arles (2015), Centre d'Art Contemporaine, Geneva (2015), Museum Boijmans Van Beuningen, Rotterdam (2017), New North Zurich (2018), Kunsthalle Basel (2020).

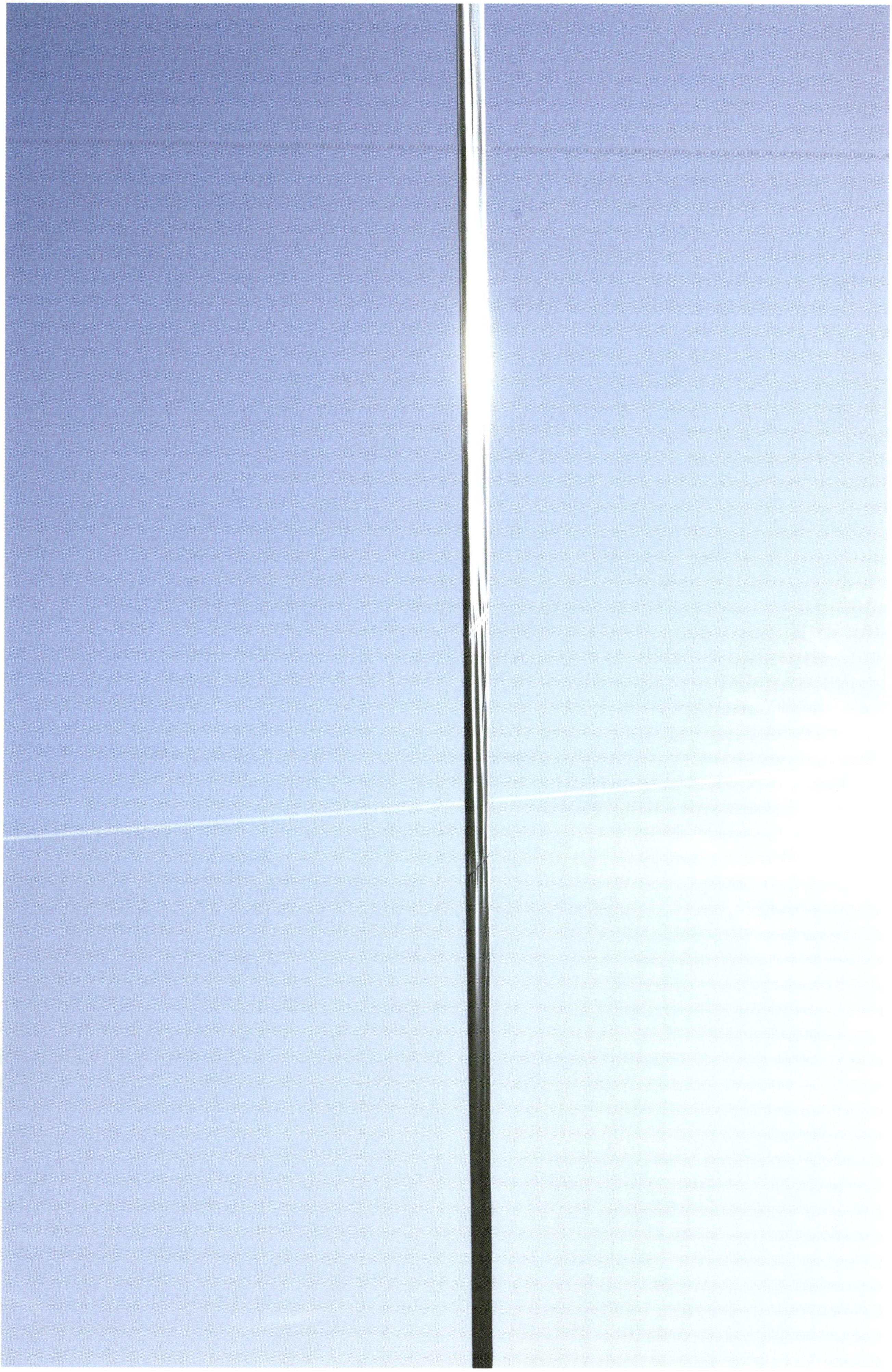

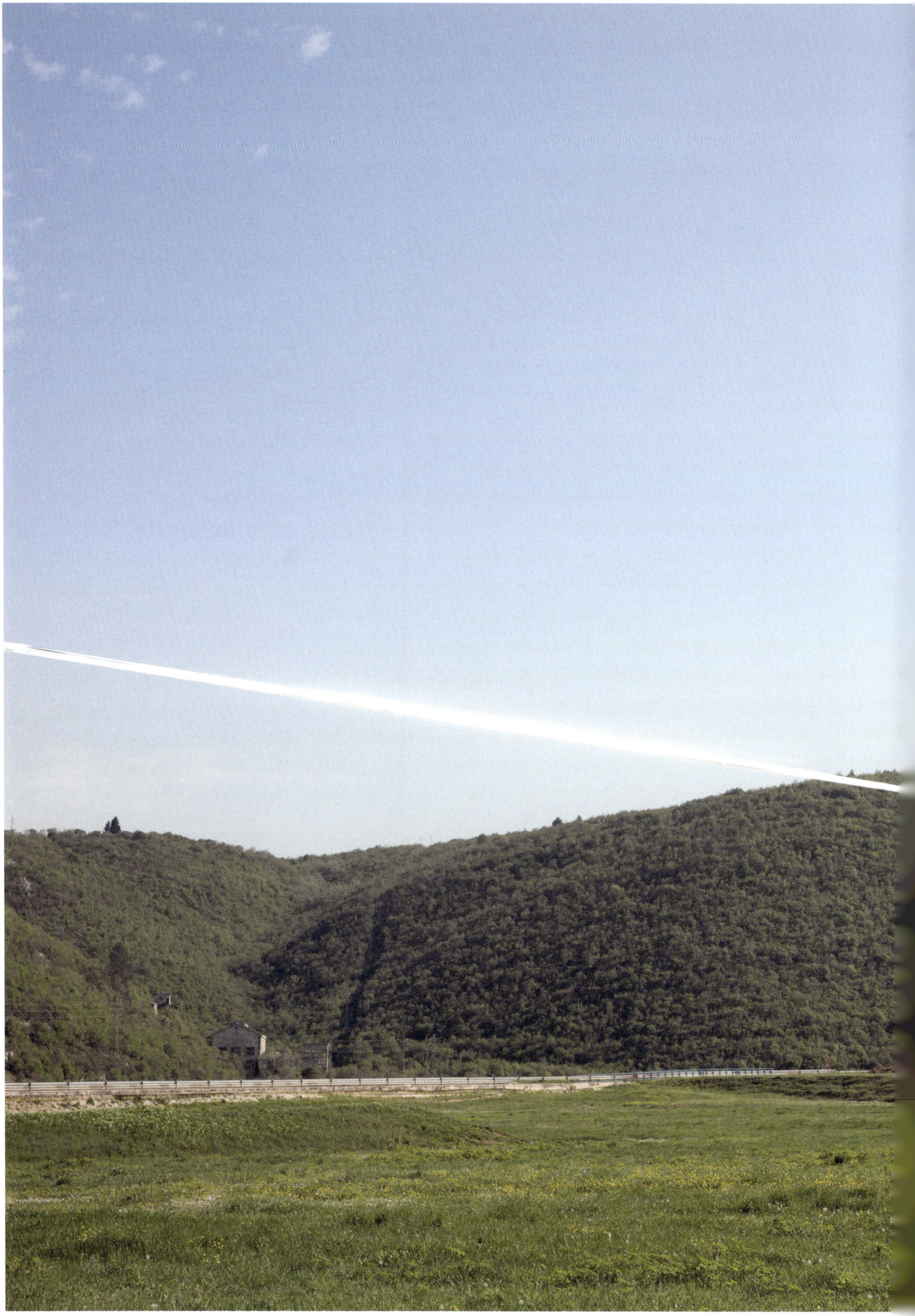

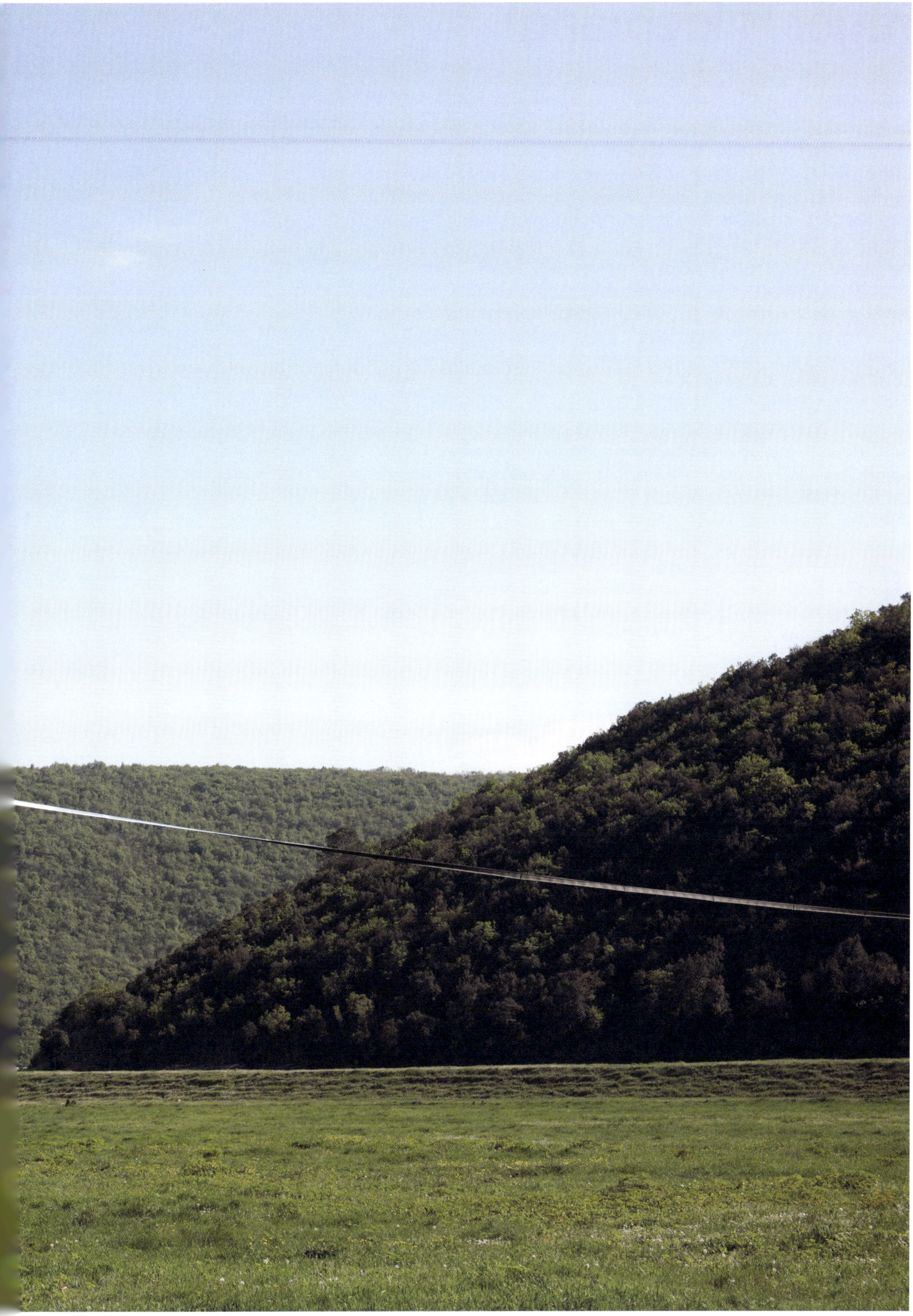

Gregor Hildebrandt

Lümmel, 2023
Titov trg, Labin

(12)

Bronze, 426 × 142 (lower Ø) × 120 (upper Ø) cm
Courtesy of the artist and Almine Rech

On the central square of Labin's old town, a neo-classical ensemble built by Italian architects, Gregor Hildebrandt has placed a bronze sculpture more than four meters high, modelled on the figure of the pawn in the game of chess. Like the urban setting in which it stands during the Biennial, the figure's design dates from the 19th century. Named after the English chess master Howard Staunton, the pieces were patented and put on the market in 1849: "The pieces generally are fashioned with convenience to the hand; and it is to be remarked, that while there is so great an accession to elegance of form, it is not attained at the expense of practical utility. Mr. STAUNTON'S pattern adopts but elevates the conventional form; and the base of the Pieces being of a large diameter, they are more steady than ordinary sets," reads the newspaper advertisement of September 8, 1849.

Hildebrandt is fascinated by the globalised variety of forms that have emerged since then, despite design standardization. He collects the pawns, puts the collection on display in specially made showrooms, ambiguously calling it the "Pawn Shop". This play with ambiguities and context-shifted readings is consistently continued in Labin: While the milieu of the former Piazza Vittorio Emanuele III pays homage to the urban bourgeoisie, Hildebrandt's artistic gesture points to a context that is often misunderstood and neglected – the economic importance of agriculture (in German the name of the chess piece is farmer [Bauer]. Against the backdrop of the Ukrainian grain crisis and the discussion about sustainable food production, this work of art is highly topical.

Hildebrandt is a master in the repurposing, renaming and reinterpretation of everyday objects. He incorporates heterogeneous elements and references from music, film, literature, and art history in his multifacetted work. The pictures of magnetic tapes, the sculptures of vinyl records, the assemblages of chess pieces evoke new and sensual experiences – tactile evocation of music, painterly representation of sound. And so the pawn on the central square in Labin, named after the former Yugoslav President Tito, also writes another chapter in the endless transformations of cultural themes, forms, media and ideas that Gregor Hildebrandt integrates into his oeuvre, which is conceived as a post-industrial echo to the idea of the Gesamtkunstwerk.

Gregor Hildebrandt (*1974, Bad Homburg, Germany) lives and works in Berlin. He is a professor at the Academy of Fine Arts in Munich, and has been widely exhibited. Selected solo shows: Contemporary Art Museum St. Louis (2008), Berlinische Galerie, Berlin (2009), Biennale de Lyon (2013), Saarlandmuseum, Moderne Galerie, Saarbrücken (2015), Künstlerhaus Bethanien, Berlin (2016), G2. Kunsthalle, Leipzig (2020), Kunsthalle Praha (2022), ASE Foundation, Shanghai (2022).

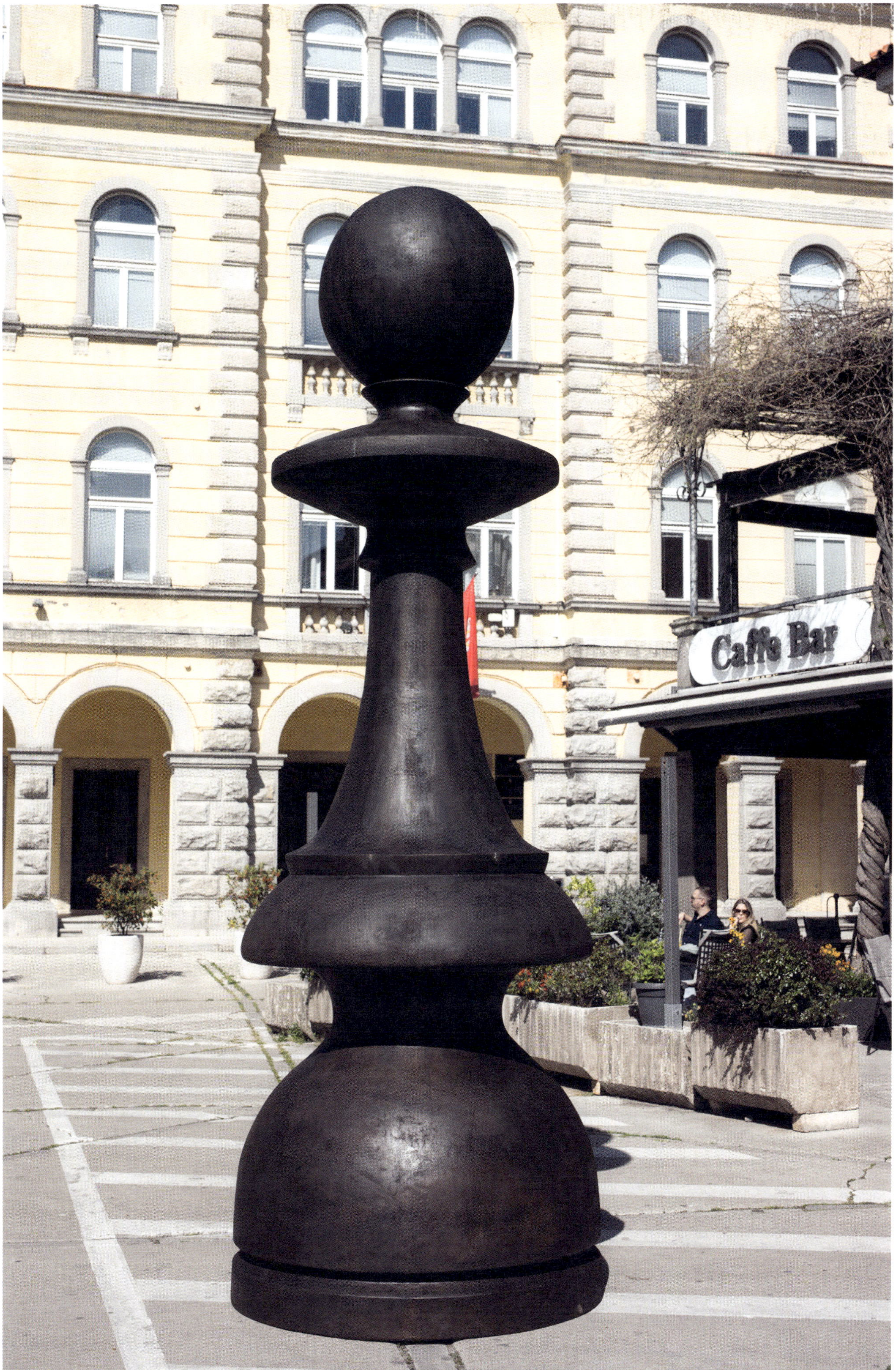
Caffe Bar

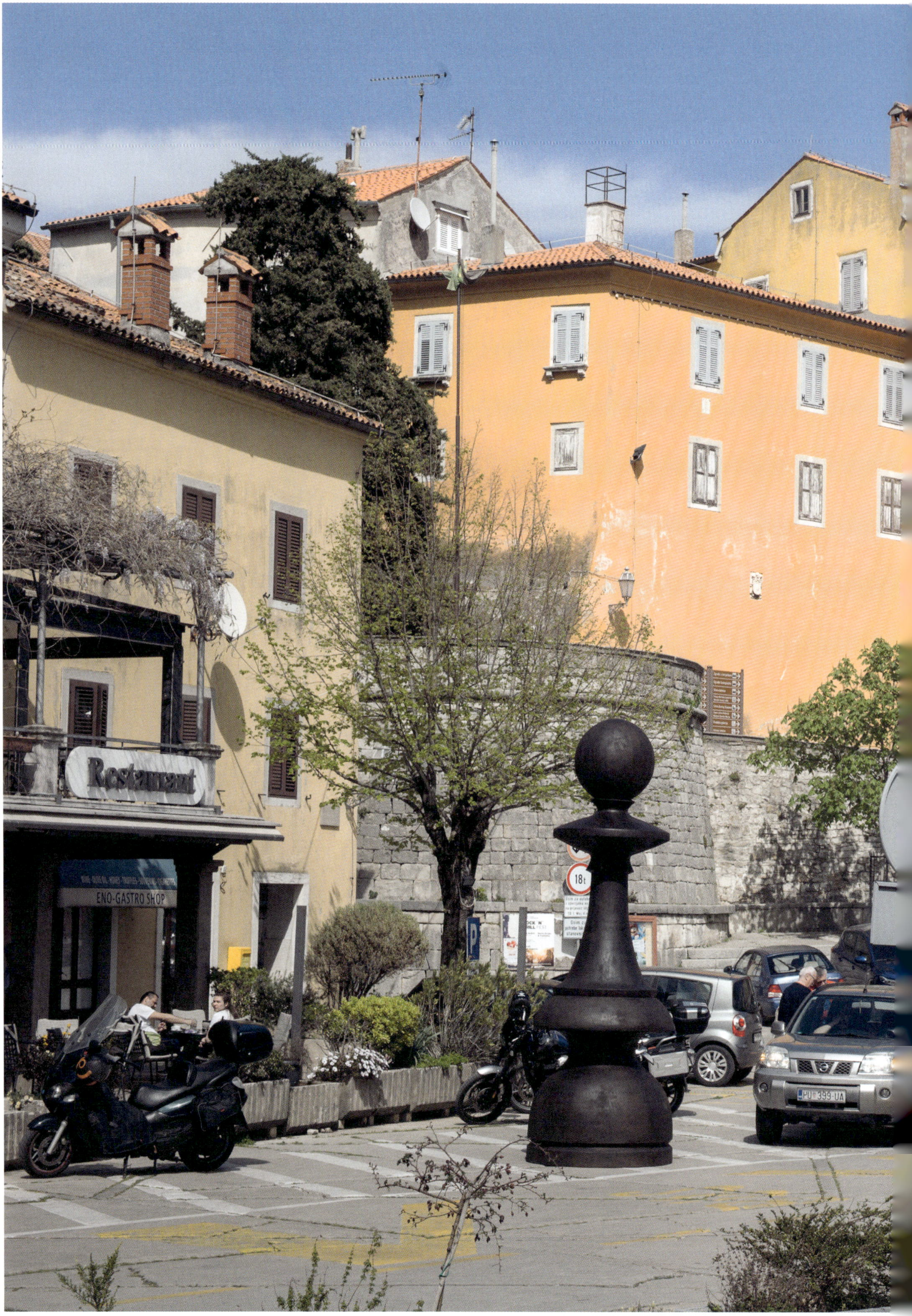
Restaurant
ENO-GASTRO SHOP
18t
PU 399-UA

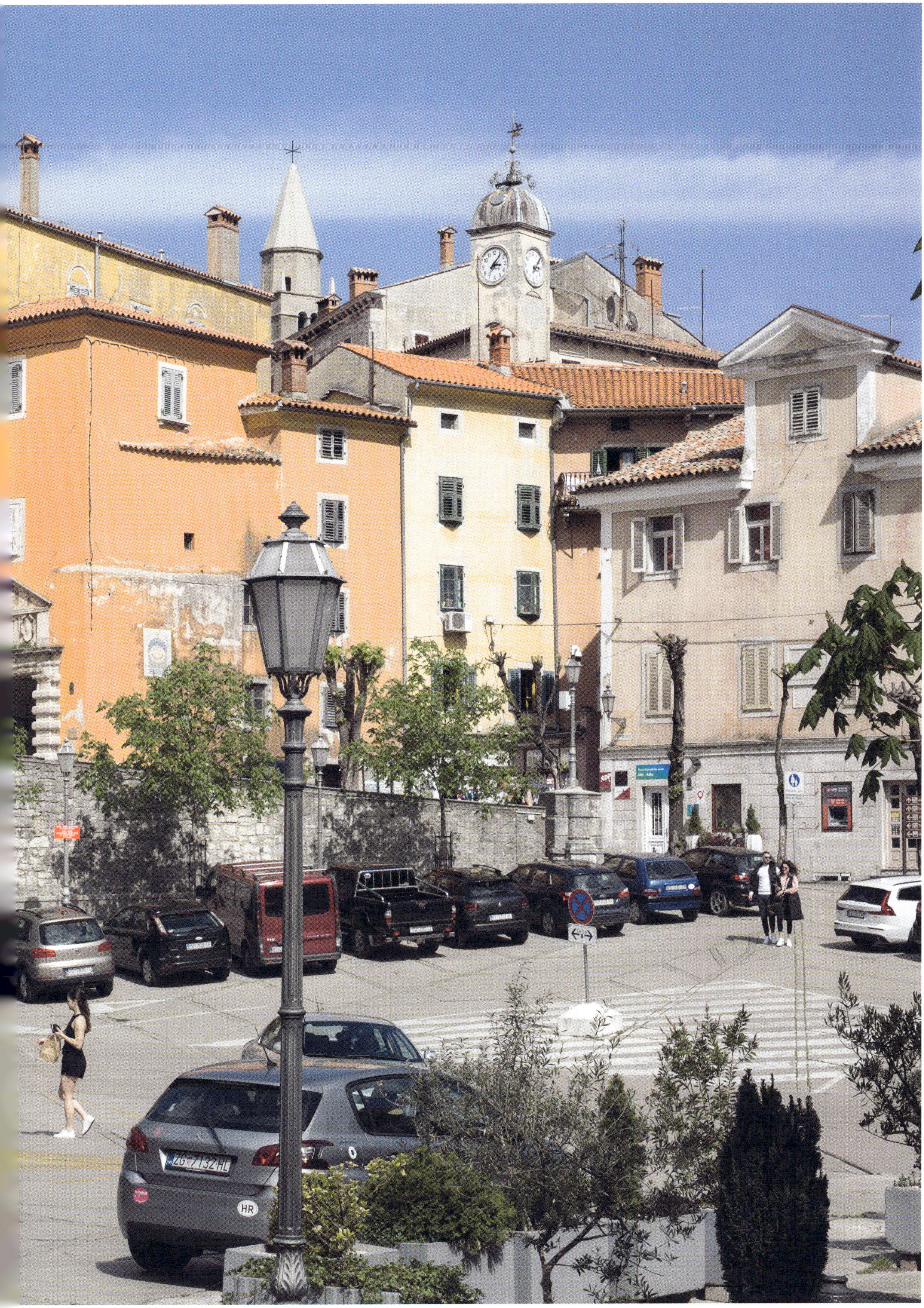
ZG 7132-HL
HR

Christian Jankowski

Industrial Golf, 2023 ⑬
Sculpture Park DUBROVA,
Štrmac, Labin

Istrian limestone, 100 golf clubs,
ca. 380 × 300 × 180 cm
Courtesy of the artist and Grieder Contemporary, Küsnacht/Zurich

In his artistic practice, Christian Jankowski deals with eco-systems, with "bubbles" as they are called today. The starting point for his research, however, remains the art system, a highly specialised and, for outsiders, slightly esoteric world. Jankowski examines this cosmos by confronting its peculiarities, rituals, cultures and economic interconnections with other, concise systems of the present day – mostly in connection with their broad media impact. For example, he made the US TV preaching scene his field of investigation (*The Holy Artwork*, 2001), the luxury boat industry (*The Finest Art on Water*, 2013), TV cooking shows (*Cooking Studio*, 2004), the rampant casting show culture (*Casting Jesus*, 2011), or the Olympic weightlifters (*Heavy Weight History*, 2013), to name just a few examples. Jankowski: "I have great interest in professions, and these specific perspectives on life and the world play a crucial role in all my projects."

For *Landscapes of Desire*, Jankowski undertook a wide-ranging research on site and finally decided – inspired by the exhibition title – to place a sculpture park somewhat off the beaten track at the centre of his project. The Sculpture Garden Dubrova is a picturesque site outside Labin, where sculpture workshops focusing on the local "Istrian stone" have been held regularly for more than fifty years. As a result of these workshops, the number of artworks continues to grow and the extensive park is populated with more and more new white sculptures, now numbering 79. For this 30-hectare site, the artist has developed a 9-hole golf course where the works of art now become inspiration- and orientation points, sometimes playmates or obstacles for the athletes. The fairways were created with the help of municipal employees and their lawn mowers; the Croatian Golf Association took over the promotion. "We are happy and proud to invite you to a spectacular golf-experience: The 1st Industrial Golf Open (IGO), which will be hosted by the Dubrova Sculpture Golf Club, a newly created golf course near Labin", stated the invitation letter.

For the site the artist himself also created a new sculpture from the white stone and 100 golf clubs to commemorate this performance and the 100th birthday of golf in Croatia; a miniature version of it became the prize for the winner of the "1st Industrial Golf Open". The corporate design of the new golf course – only the fourth golf course in Croatia – also comes from the artist, likewise the fairway design and the fairways with sculpture obstacles painted on large-format canvases. The start of the tournament on April 16 at 11 a.m., which was announced in the newspapers, was attended by the local public. But the media and a professional TV crew also accompanied the event, which invoked all the rituals of the game of golf. From this diverse pool of materials, Jankowski finally developed an overall installation that will be shown at the 4th Industrial Art Biennial. Art becomes sport and sport ends up in art. Or as Jankowski says: "Professions bring a certain vocabulary and viewpoint on the world, and they come with their own aesthetic. They also bring something unexpected and new into my art through a method of shared authorship."

Christian Jankowski (*1968, Göttingen, Germany) lives and works in Berlin. He studied at the University of Fine Arts, Hamburg, in Germany. In his conceptual and media artworks he makes use of film, video, photography and performance, but also of painting, sculpture, and installation. His works has widely exhibited, e.g. in the Portikus, Frankfurt (1998), Biennale di Venezia (2001/2013), Museum für Gegenwartskunst, Basel (2003), Centre d' Art Santa Mònica, Barcelona (2007), Kunstmuseum Stuttgart (2008), BAWAG Foundation, Vienna (2009), Museum of Contemporary Art, Rome (2012), Van Gogh Museum, Amsterdam (2015), Bundeskunsthalle, Bonn (2018), Rockbund Art Museum, Shanghai (2019).

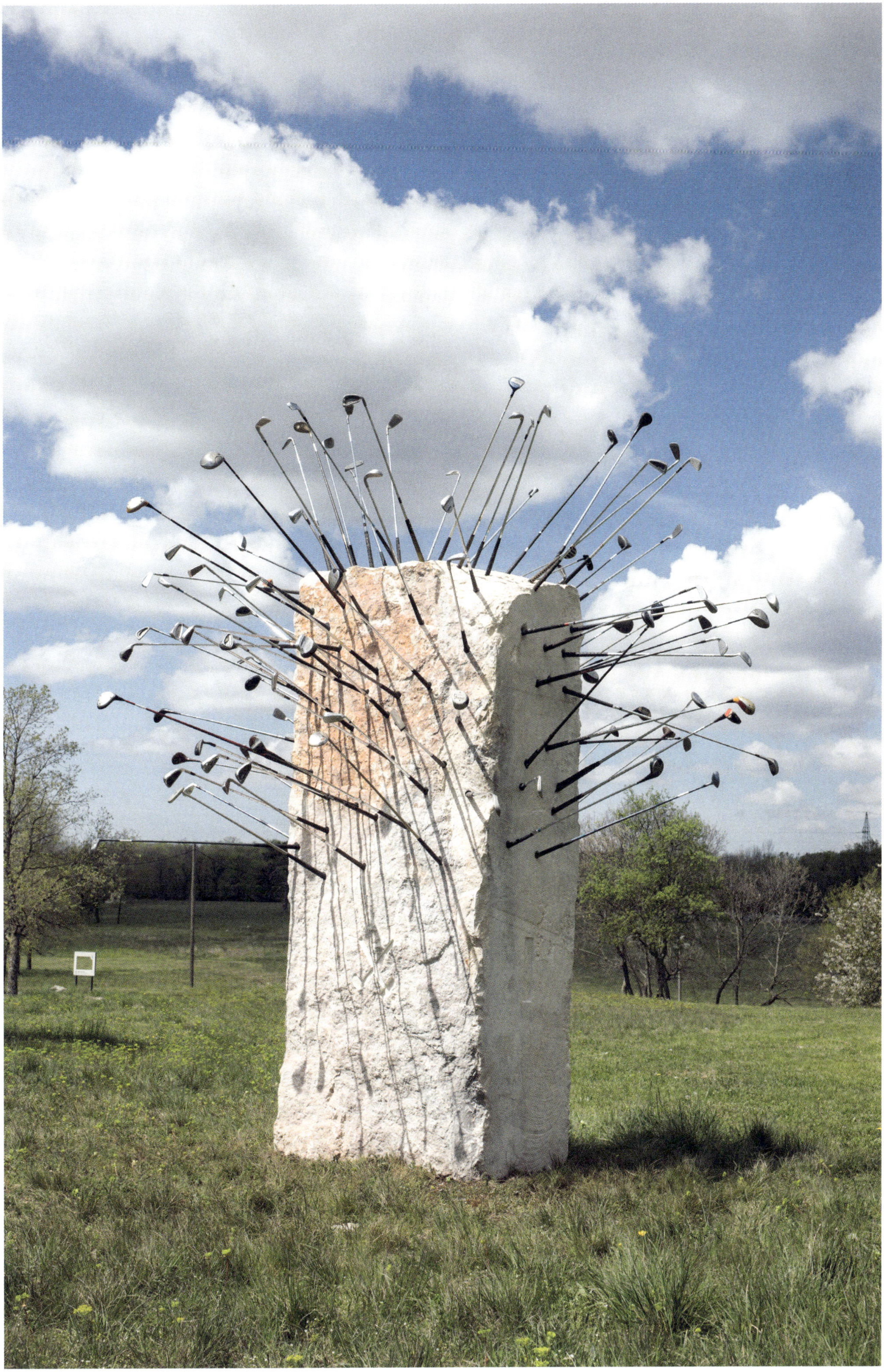

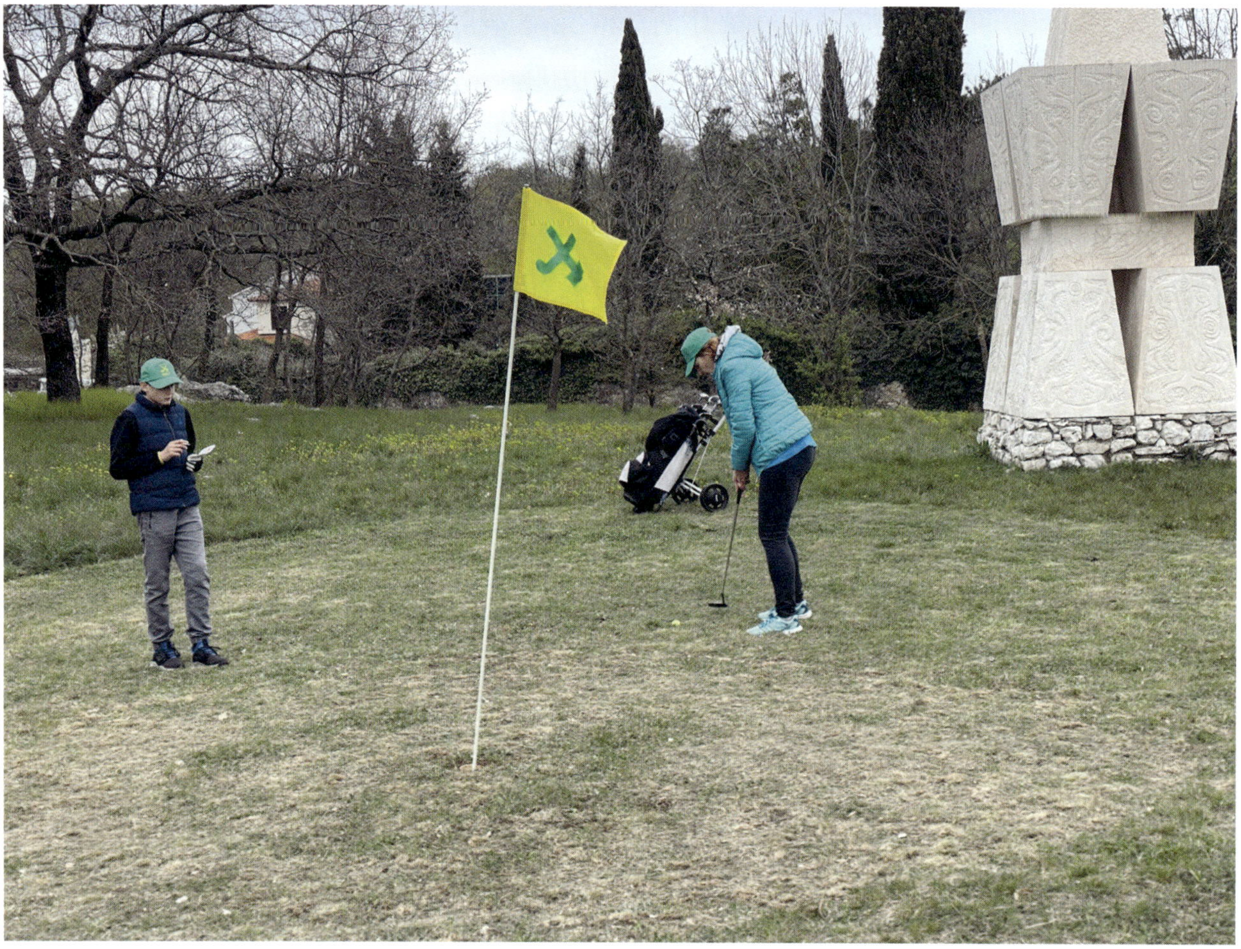

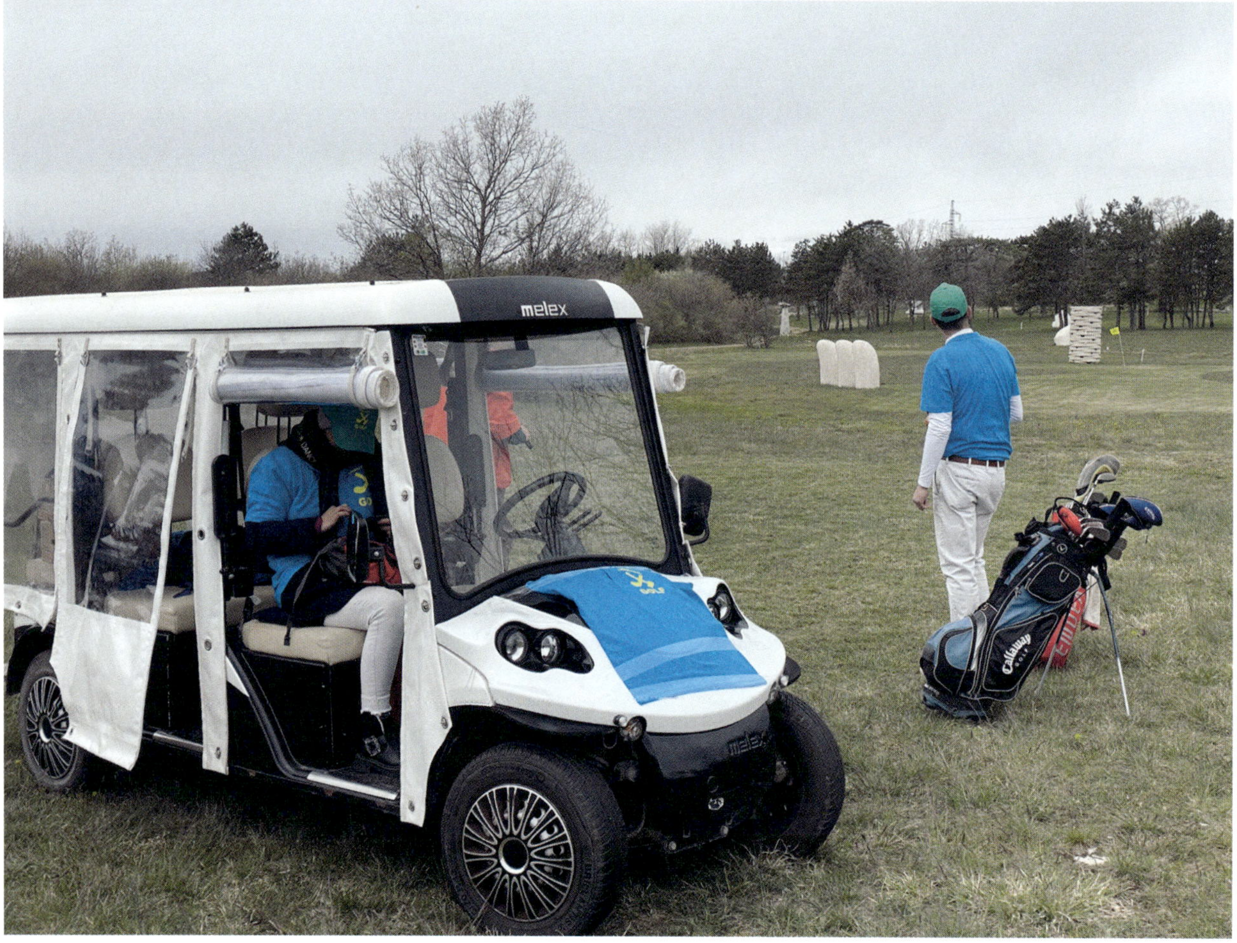
melex
Callaway

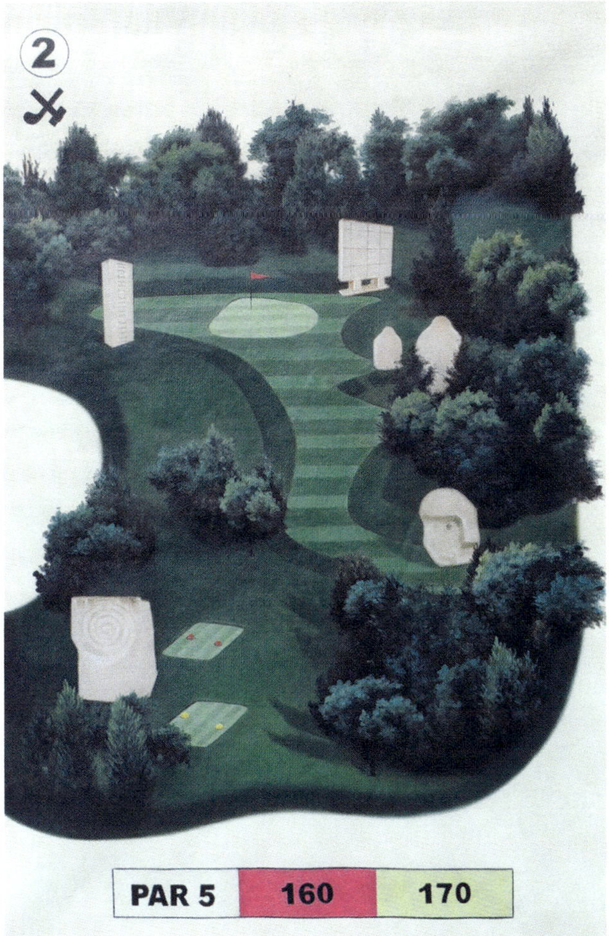

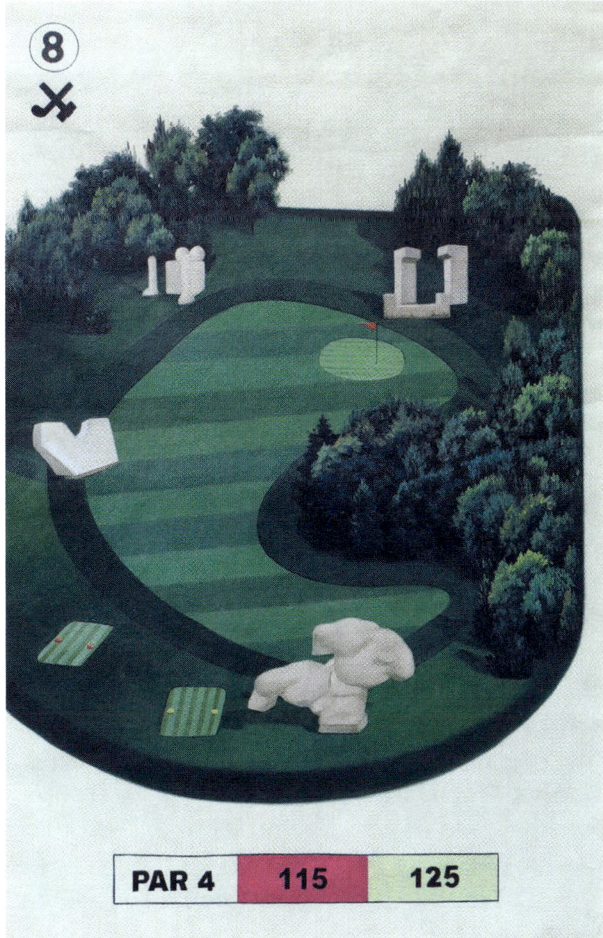

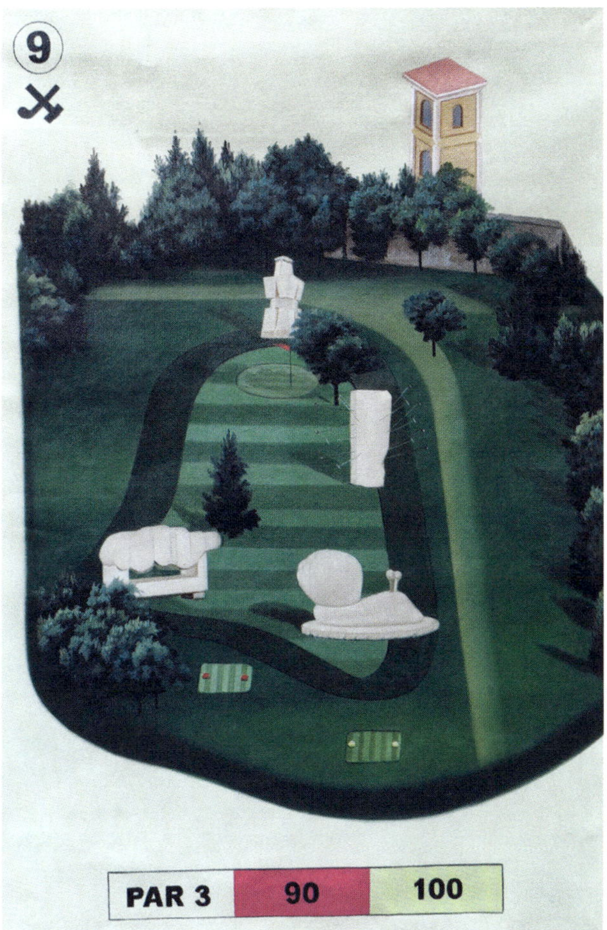

Tee Sign Landscape 2, 2023
Oil on canvas, 105 × 70 cm
Courtesy of the artist and Grieder Contemporary, Küsnacht/Zurich

Tee Sign Landscape 8, 2023
Oil on canvas, 105 × 70 cm
Courtesy of the artist and Grieder Contemporary, Küsnacht/Zurich

Tee Sign Landscape 9, 2023
Oil on canvas, 105 × 70 cm
Courtesy of the artist and Grieder Contemporary, Küsnacht/Zurich

Page 124: Industrial Golf, 2023
Video (work in progress)
Courtesy of the artist and Grieder Contemporary, Küsnacht/Zurich

Nikita Kadan

Kharkiv-Rijeka Checkpoint, 2022–2023
Korzo, Rijeka
(14)

The artist Nikita Kadan, who was born in Kyiv, regularly deals with current socio-political developments in Ukraine and their foundations in Soviet communism. In his installations, objects and pictures he refers to the suppression of the emancipatory aspects of the communist avant-garde in the present. He clarifies this by dealing with monuments from the Soviet era, which are abandoned to destruction, and advocates a differentiated view of the past and its utopias.

His latest installation *Kharkiv-Rijeka Checkpoint* refers to the war in Ukraine and uses concrete blocks of the kind used to set up checkpoints in the streets. In addition, there is a spherical shape, which has always been considered the "perfect shape". The material for the installation is raw, reused concrete. The spherical shape, on the other hand, looks newer, more polished and shiny. The general structure quotes the project of *Monument to the President of Planet Earth* by Vasyl Yermilov, the key figure of constructivist art in Kharkiv and one of the main artists of Ukrainian avant-garde of 1910th–20th. This project, actually a sketch which was never realised in material, is dedicated to the "President of Planet Earth", Russian futurist poet Velimir Khlebnikov, who spent much time in Kharkiv and influenced several young Ukrainian artists and writers. War questions the relevance of those intercultural relations, which stand aside of colonial matrix. Do we still have optics, which makes such relations and influences visible? If no, do not we loose some elements and aspects of our own cultural heritage, some logics of historical continuity? If yes, what does it mean to read Russian poetry under the Russian missiles and bombs?

In March 2022 Nikita Kadan made an appeal in the London magazine Frieze: „We urgently need your solidarity. [...] But, ultimately, this is not about saving Ukrainians only; it's about protecting yourselves, too. We are all in danger, because this is a war against the very idea of democracy and human rights." It is now 2023 and there is still a war of attrition going on. As long as the parties maintain their positions, there seems to be no basis for a negotiated peace. The fighting on the war front could drag on for a long time.

Nikita Kadan (*1984, Kyiv, Ukraine). The artist, author and activist Nikita Kadan studied at the National Academy of Fine Arts in Kyiv in the class of monumental painting until 2007. Since 2004 he has been a member of the artist group R.E.P. In 2022, Nikita Kadan won Taras Shevchenko National Prize of Ukraine, in 2014 he got the Special Award of the Jury of The Future Generation Art Prize, in 2011 the Pinchuk Art Centre Prize. In 2015 his work was exhibited in the Ukrainian Pavilion at the Venice Biennale. Also he took part in Busan Biennale. (2019), Istanbul Biennial (2015), The Kyiv International (2017) and School of Kyiv Biennial (2015).

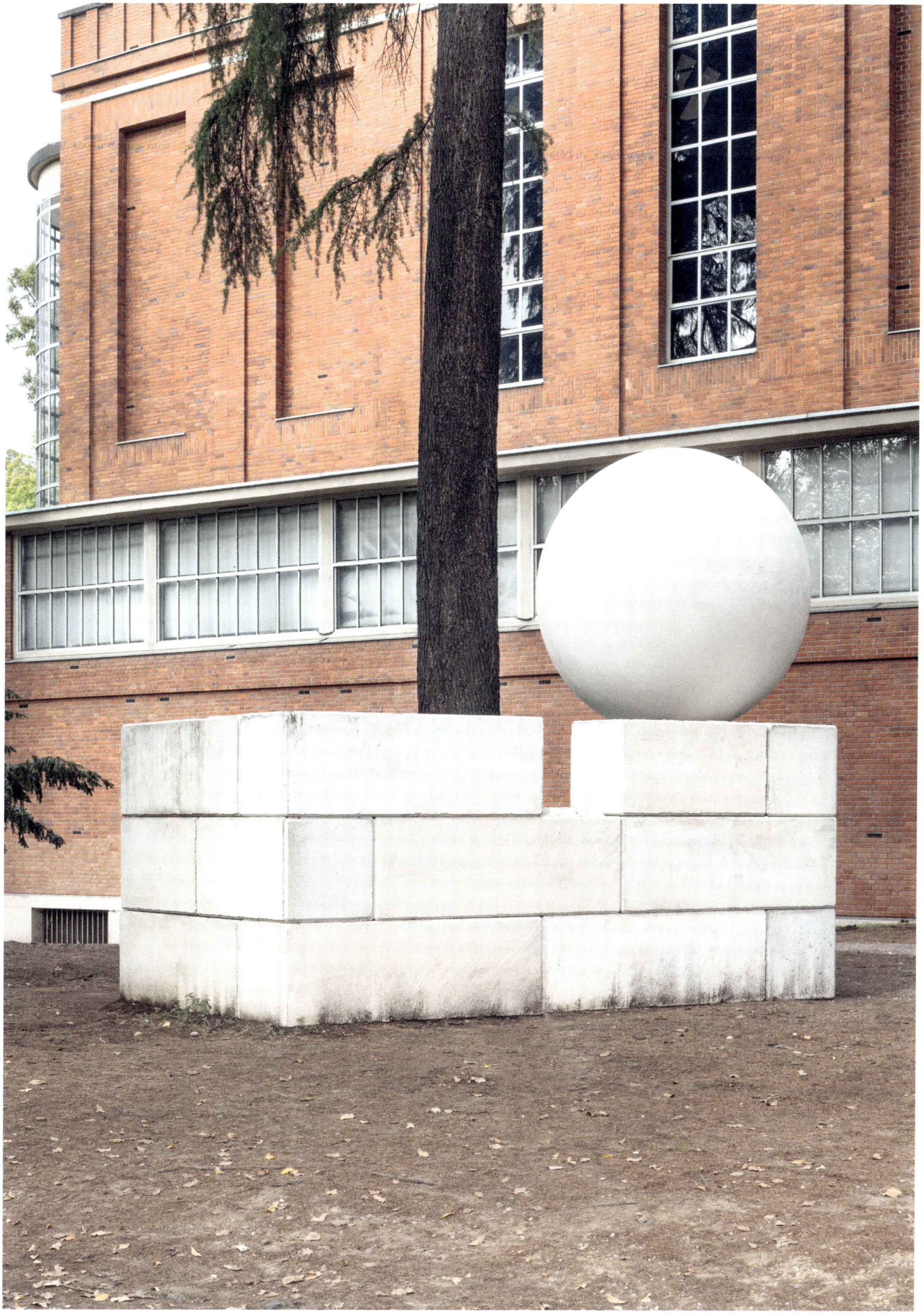

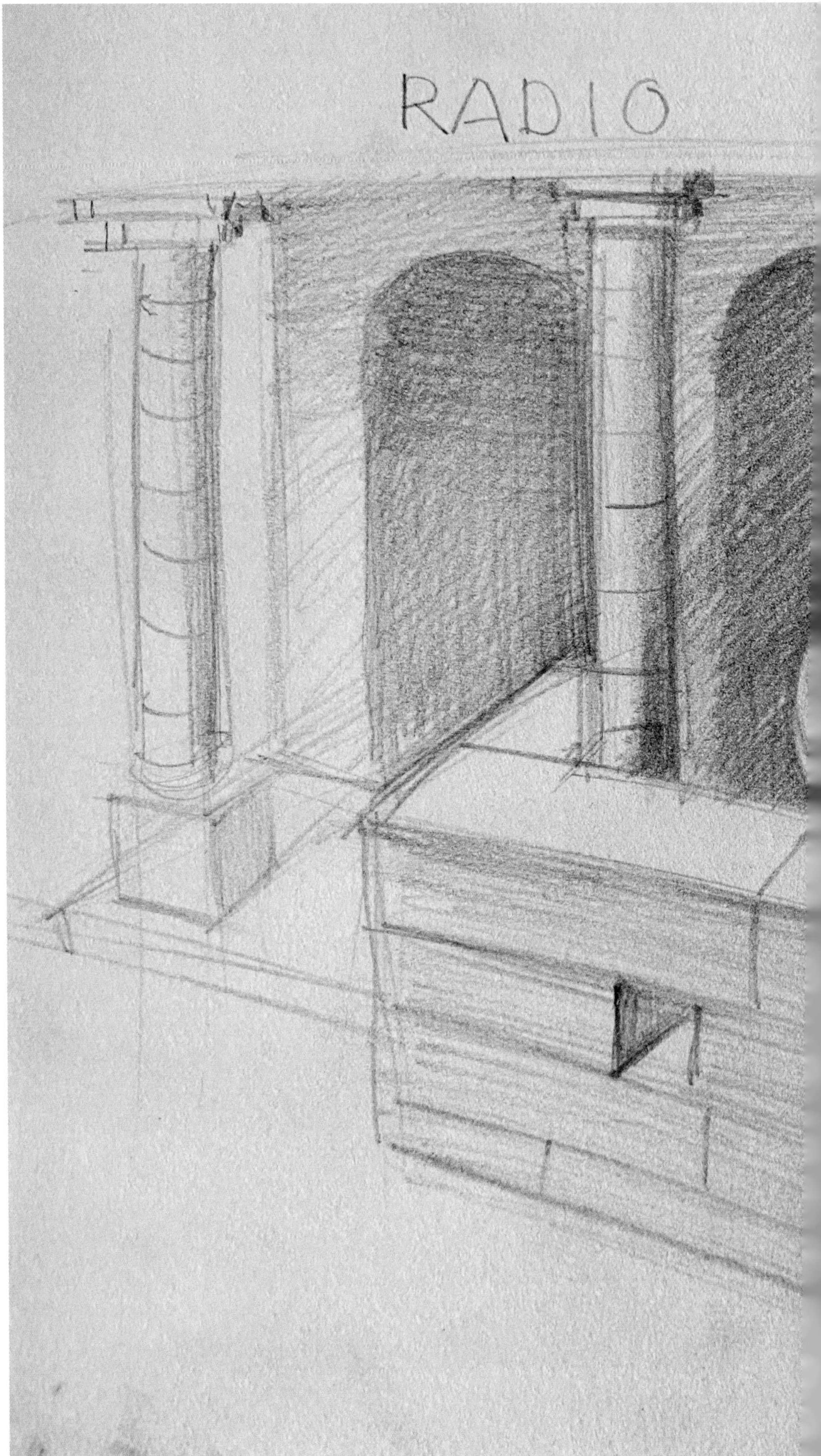
RADIO

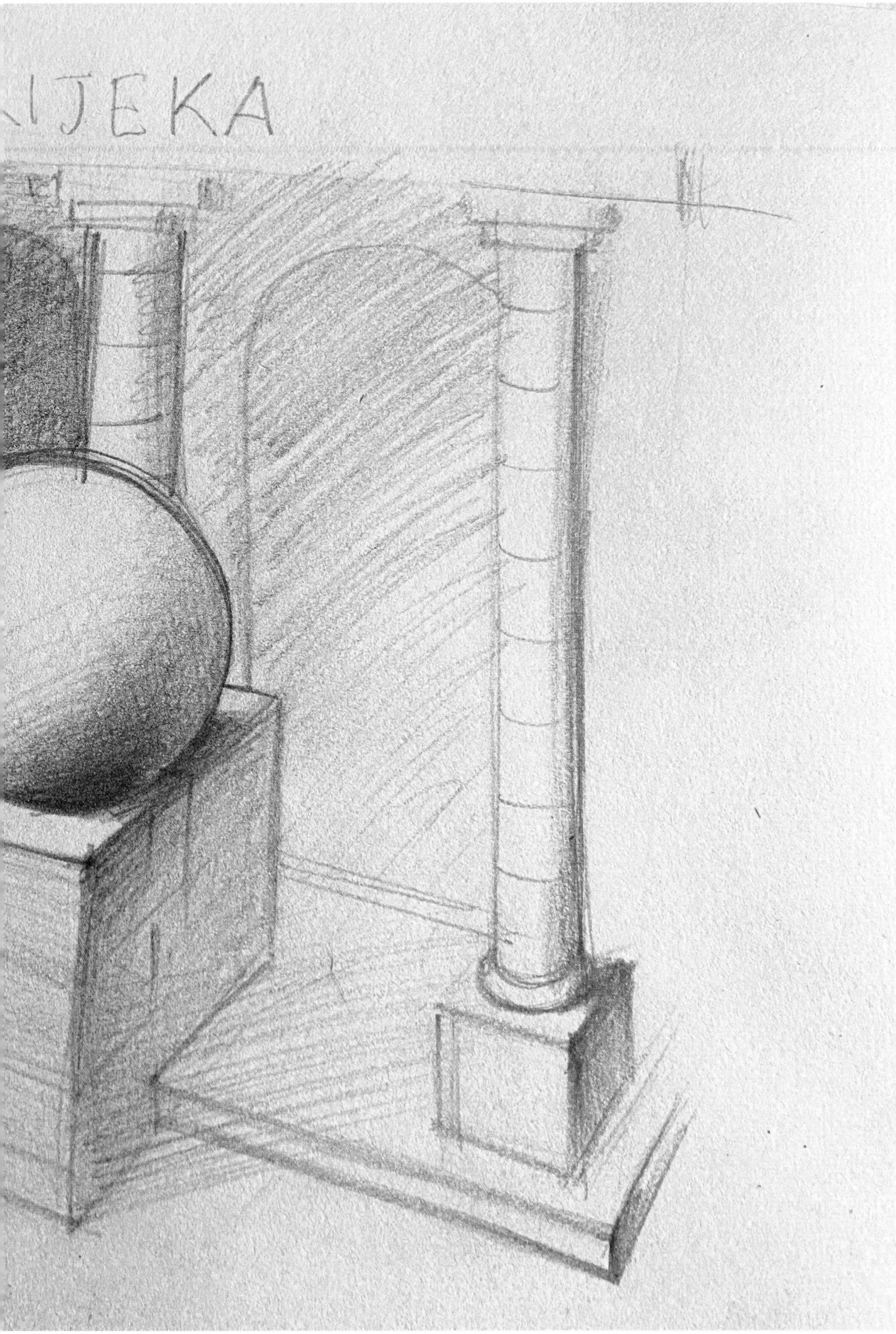
IJEKA

Sandra Knecht

Istria Homemade, 2023
Restaurant Amfiteatar, Pula
Restaurant Peteani, Labin

(15)

The socio-cultural act of eating together, its preparation and conscious experience becomes an artistic task for Sandra Knecht, for which she has created from 2016 to 2019 in Basel a special platform with her restaurant called Chnächt and the event series *Immer wieder sonntags* (Always on Sundays). She writes on her homepage: "Each dinner is dedicated to an animal, a plant or a preparation. Each dish has never been prepared before and will never be prepared exactly the same way again afterwards. The meat comes from the immediate surroundings. All the other ingredients except the spices come from no further than 10 km around Baselbiet or from friendly farmers and fishermen."

Her artistic practice focussing on food and nutrition is an elaborate strategy to discuss the normative rules of traditions and cultures, and the social values connected to it. For an outdoor exhibition in a park in Winterthur (Weiertal), the artist has developed a menu proposal for the local insects: *Gib dem Affen Zucker* (Give the Monkey Sugar) was a sculpture made of the eponymous food raw material, which, transfigured and demonised, is also a symbol of our civilisational nutritional neurosis and dissolves in the course of the exhibition. Knecht created an ephemeral food sculpture: The exhibition lasted three months and during this time the shape of the sculpture changed daily, and almost disappeared with the help of mosquitoes, beetles and bees.

With a similar focus but different approach, Sandra Knecht worked on the context of the Istrian peninsula. The artist undertook a large-scale research in the summer of 2022 at the farmers' markets of Pula and Labin to learn about traditional products and produce. Conversations with old peasant women and shopkeepers, forays into the overgrown surroundings for herb-gathering events, and an examination of the question of what is "typical" are all reflected in Knecht's oeuvre. With her research, the artist secures old techniques of food preparation that would be too unprofitable or inefficient for the food industry. This results in art and pleasure projects, such as a three-course menu with "barley, nuts, potatoes, chard and sucuk (for the non-vegetarians)" as the main course. In local restaurants – in Labin at Peteani and in Pula at Amfiteatar – this menu will be part of the restaurants' food list during the 4th Industrial Art Biennial and will be inscribed in the landscapes through everyday but essential activities such as enjoying, eating and digesting.

Sandra Knecht (*1968 in Bern, Switzerland) lives and works in Buus and Berlin. Her works have been exhibited among others at Kunsthaus Baselland, Muttenz (2018), Kunsthaus Zurich (2018), *Paradise, lost*, Weiertal / Winterthur (2019), Galerie Stephan Witschi, Zurich (2021), Swiss Art Award, Basel (2022), Dark Night, Fundacio Joan Miro, Barcelona (2022)

Artichokes with white beans and figs

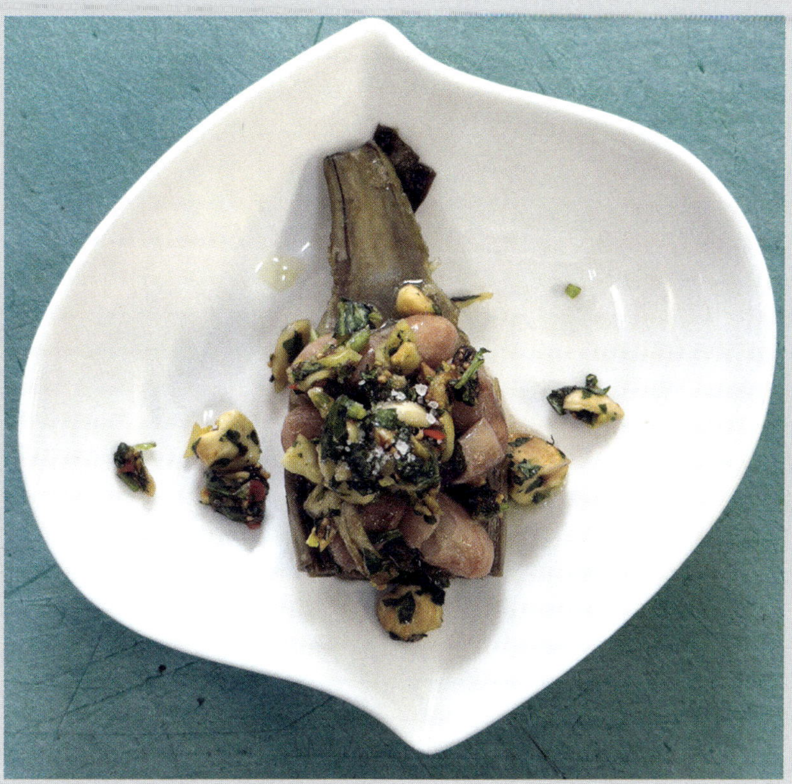

1 small fresh artichoke per person
1 handful (approx. 40 grams) wild garlic
300 ml rapeseed oil
Olive oil
Salt
Dried figs
Parsley
Roasted walnuts
1 lemon
White beans
Fleur de Sel
White mild wine vinegar

Artichokes
Peel the artichokes to light leaves. Cut off the top of the spitz to about half. After that, cut in half. Heat the frying pan with a little olive oil. Add the artichokes. Sauté on both sides until crispy light brown. Then deglaze with water a finger's width. Cover on pan and continue cooking for about 15 minutes. When the artichokes are soft, remove from the pan.

Beans
Soak beans with a tablespoon of baking soda overnight. Then rinse the beans under cold water and bring to the boil in a pan covered with water. Add a teaspoon of salt. Cook until they are completely soft. Then marinate lukewarm with vinegar and lemon juice.

Figs
Cut three dried fleshy figs into thin strips, mix well with half a cup of roasted walnuts, chopped parsley, zest of half a lemon and a good pinch of fleur de sel.

Wild garlic oil
Wash the wild garlic and dry it well. Heat rapeseed oil to 60 degrees. Add a pinch of salt and wild garlic and mix well. Let stand for 15 minutes and then filter through a very fine sieve or straining cloth.

Place artichokes on plates. On top a tablespoon of beans. Add the figs/nut/parsley mixture on top. Finally, drizzle generously with wild garlic oil.

Barley with wild herbs and sheep's cheese

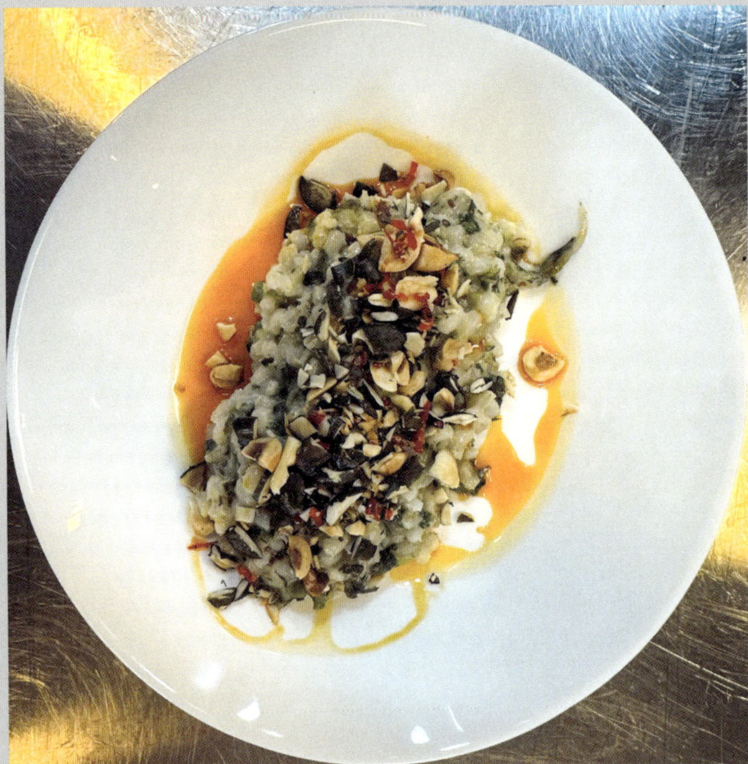

3 cups small-grained barley
Approx. 12 cups of water
3 handfuls of wild garden herbs cut into small pieces (young leaves of curly thistle, fennel green, sorrel, dandelion, cauliflower leaves, chard)
2 cups hard sheep's cheese chopped into small pieces
1 small onion
1 hot chili
1 tablespoon smoked paprika
1 cup hazelnuts and pumpkin seeds roasted and finely chopped
1/2 cup olive oil
Salt to taste
Juice of a small lemon

Barleyotto
Boil water with a little salt. Add the barley and cook until it gets a thick soupy consistency after about 30 minutes. The stye at this time should be a little more than al dente. Then add the wild herbs and lemon juice and do not let it boil for long. Stir in the cheese and put the lid on pan. Let everything steep for 10 minutes.

Chili/paprika oil
Do not overheat olive oil in a pan. Lightly fry finely chopped onion and chili. As soon as the onions are translucent, add the smoked paprika powder, let it steep at a very low temperature for about 5 minutes. Then strain the oil through a very fine sieve or cloth.

Arrange barley in a deep plate, then drizzle generously with red chili/paprika oil. Sprinkle chopped nuts and pumpkin seeds on top.

Deep-fried krafi on plum sauce with anise ice cream and caramelized walnuts

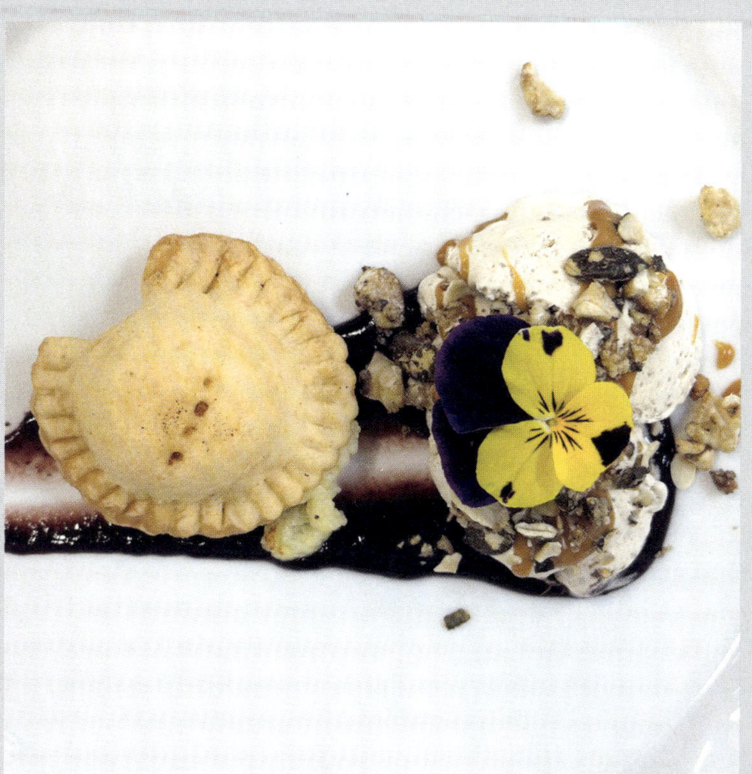

Krafi
Oil for deep-frying

Filling
300 g young sheep cheese, grated
200 g aged cow cheese, grated
150 g granulated sugar
1/2 cup raisins soaked in rum
1 whole lemon zest
1 whole egg
2 egg whites
1 packet vanilla sugar
Pinch of salt
Breadcrumbs as needed

For the filling, put all the ingredients in a large bowl and mix well. If the mixture seems a little liquid, add a little breadcrumbs.

Pasta dough
300 g wheat flour
Pinch of salt
1 whole egg
2 egg yolks
Water as needed

Mix all the ingredients together, knead the dough until it becomes elastic. After that, cover with cling film, leave in the refrigerator for at least 30 minutes.

Roll out the pasta dough thinly. Divide into two lanes. To prepare the krafi, spread an equal amount of filling every 5 cm. Cover with the second sheet of dough and press lightly around each portion of the filling so that the air in it goes out. Finally, cut out the krafi with a glass.

They can either be boiled in salted water or, as in this case, fried in deep oil.

Plum sauce
12 dried plums chopped into small pieces
3 cups of red wine
1 cup of water
1 spoonful of red balsamic vinegar
1 fresh bay leaf
4 cloves
1/2 cup cane sugar
1/2 cinnamon stick
Juice of half a lemon

First, boil wine, water with bay leaf, cinnamon and cloves for 15 minutes. After that, remove cloves, cinnamon and bay leaf. Add the plums, sugar, vinegar and continue to simmer until the liquid drips thickly from the spoon. Then puree, add lemon juice and pass through a sieve. Chill in the fridge.

Arrange the still warm krafi on a plum sauce mirror with a dumpling of anise ice cream and caramelized nuts on plates. Serve immediately.

Joseph Kosuth

Existential Time, 2023
Small Roman Theatre, Pula

(16)

One of the pioneers of Conceptual Art, Joseph Kosuth initiated language based works and appropriation strategies in the late 1960s. His work has consistently explored the production and role of language and meaning within art and art system. *One and Three Chairs* (1965) is perhaps the first, and in any case the best-known work of Conceptual Art: the three-part installation consists of a chair, the photographic image of this chair, and the lexical description of a chair. If a chair is always considered a popular example of a real object in philosophical discussions because it is supposedly particularly simple, Kosuth overturns it, if you will, and shows that here, too, complexity lurks from all sides. A linguistically powerful philosopher among artists, he has also expressed himself in numerous interviews, which in turn have become works of art for him: "My work is based on the fundamental idea that artists work with meaning and not with form and colour."

For the large screen at the back of the Archaelogical Museum in Pula, which is directly adjacent to a Roman amphitheatre, Joseph Kosuth has developed a new, site-specific version of his *Existential Time* series of works. The artist has been working on this body of work, an artist-philosophical exploration of the concept of time, since 2020. While Kosuth previously operated with analog elements – namely wall clocks whose dials feature literary text quotations – a digital version was realised for the first time in Pula. Moreover, it is the first intervention of the cycle of works in the outdoor space, within the framework of a precisely chosen context: the back of the museum, the backyard of a memory machine. As an ongoing series of reflections, *Existential Time* invites us to contemplate on our own lived experience as it flashes by or hangs heavily, leading to questions of consciousness, to what we mean within time.

The hands of a clock make the passing of time appear visible and objectifiable. And yet the experience of time depends on specific contexts, the subjective perception is unique. This is indicated by the 48 text quotations chosen by Kosuth, which show a reference to the Istrian peninsula and the Adriatic cultural area – for example: "Vorrei sapere se, tenendomi vivo, truffo la vita o la morte" ("I want to know if, by keeping myself alive, I am cheating life or death"). The quote comes from Italo Svevo, a writer from Trieste who embodies the multiple dimensions of cultural, political, social and economic dislocation found in Istria. Born Aron Hector Schmitz in 1861, with an Austrian father and Italian mother, of Jewish faith, he was educated in a boarding school near Würzburg and trained as a merchant. When his father's business went bankrupt, Schmitz's ambition as a writer staid unfullfilled. He had by then adopted the pseudonym Svevo, but needed to take a job at a bank. Later in his life, he married the daughter of a wealthy family and was then able to focus on writing again, although this remained unsuccessful. Svevo became friends with James Joyce, translated Sigmund Freud's *The Interpretation of Dreams* into Italian, and studied psychoanalysis. Thanks to his friendship with Joyce, he finally achieved his literary breakthrough before dying in a car accident in 1928.

This one life – an existence between bread and art, between utopia and reality, between Austria, Germany and Italy – exemplifies the many narratives, stories and biographies that gather in the *Landscapes of Desire* to trigger a seminal discourse on the present and the future.

Joseph Kosuth (*1945, Toledo/Ohio, USA) lives and works in Venice and New York. Selected exhibitions: Documenta, Kassel (1972, 1977, 1982, 1992), Kunstmuseum, Luzern (1973), Biennale di Venezia (1976, 1993, 1999), Staatsgalerie, Stuttgart (1981, 2017), Castello di Rivoli, Turin (2006), Museum Moderne Kunst, Frankfurt (2010), Museum Haus Konstruktiv, Zurich (2011), Musée du Louvre, Paris (2016), Palazzo Bembo, Venice (2017), Punta della Dogana, Venice/Pinault Collection (2023).

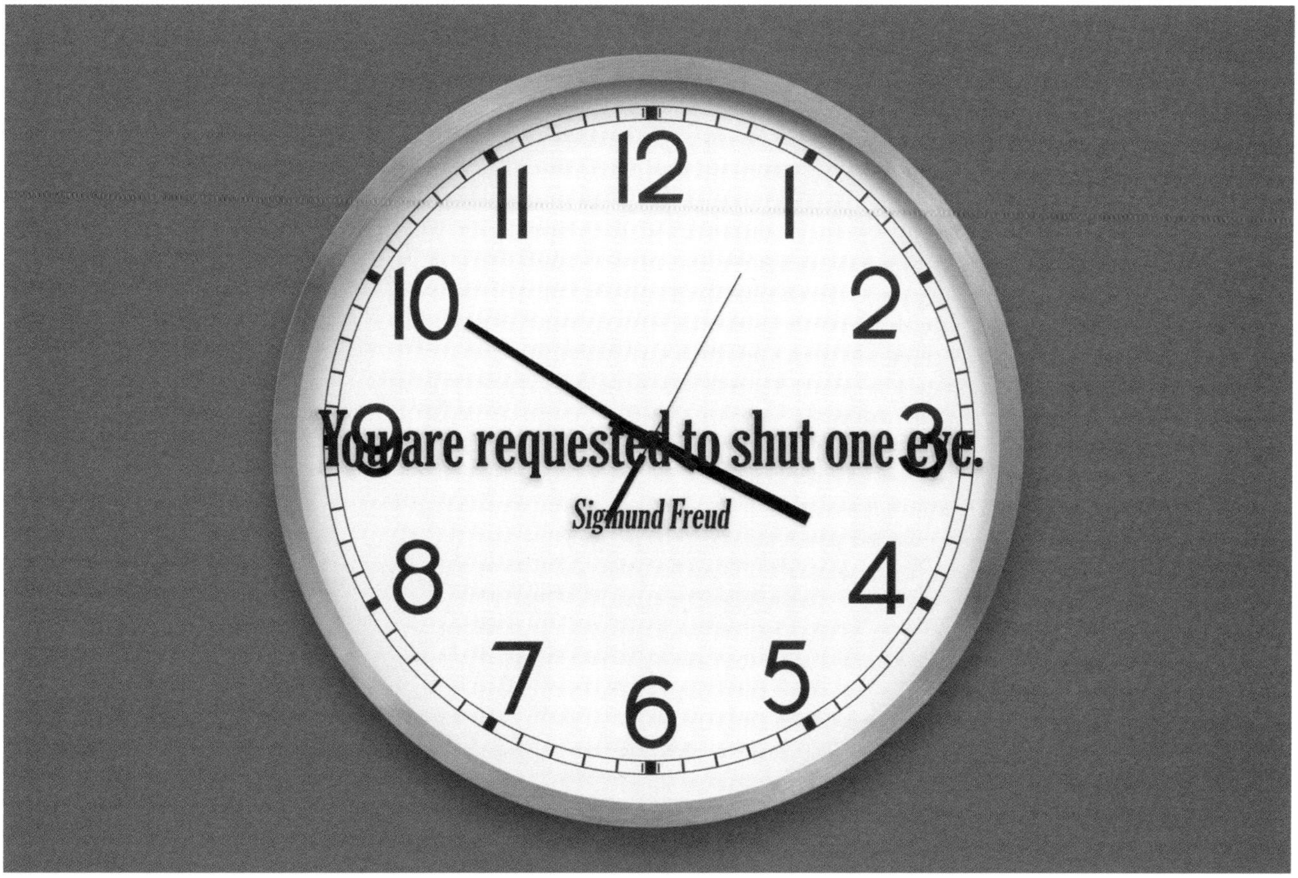

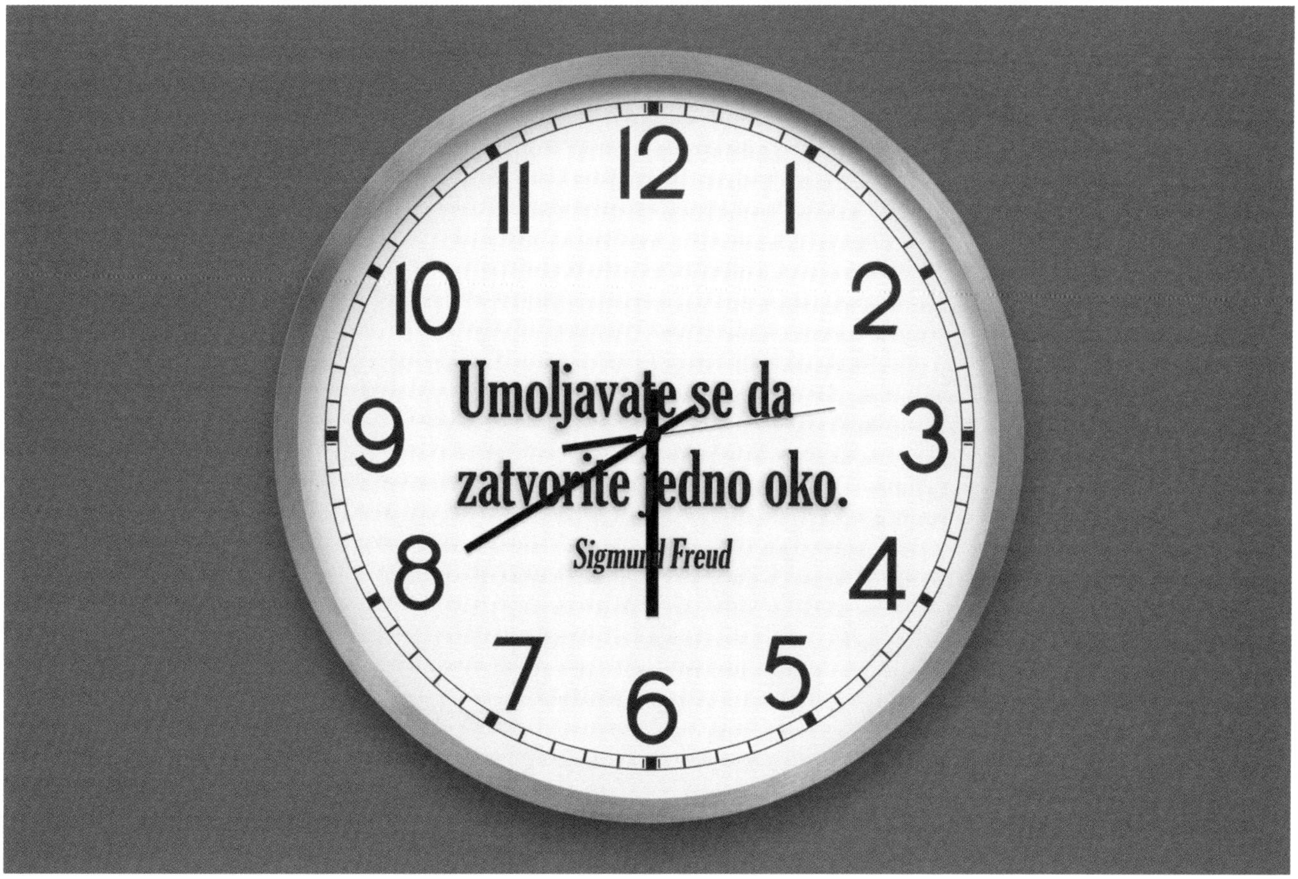

Digital animation on LED-Screen, 12 hours
Courtesy of the artist and Lia Rumma Gallery,
Milan/Naples

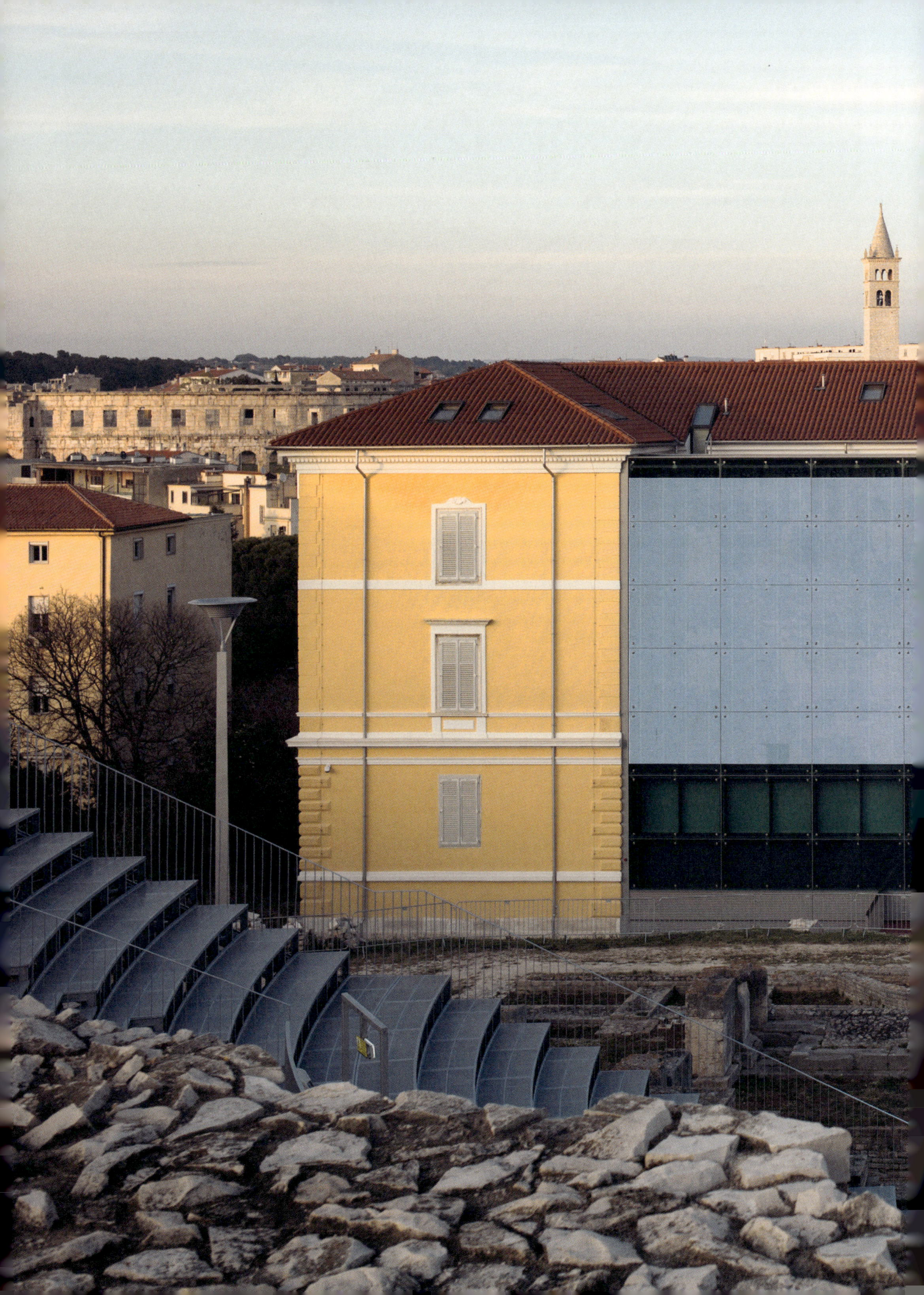

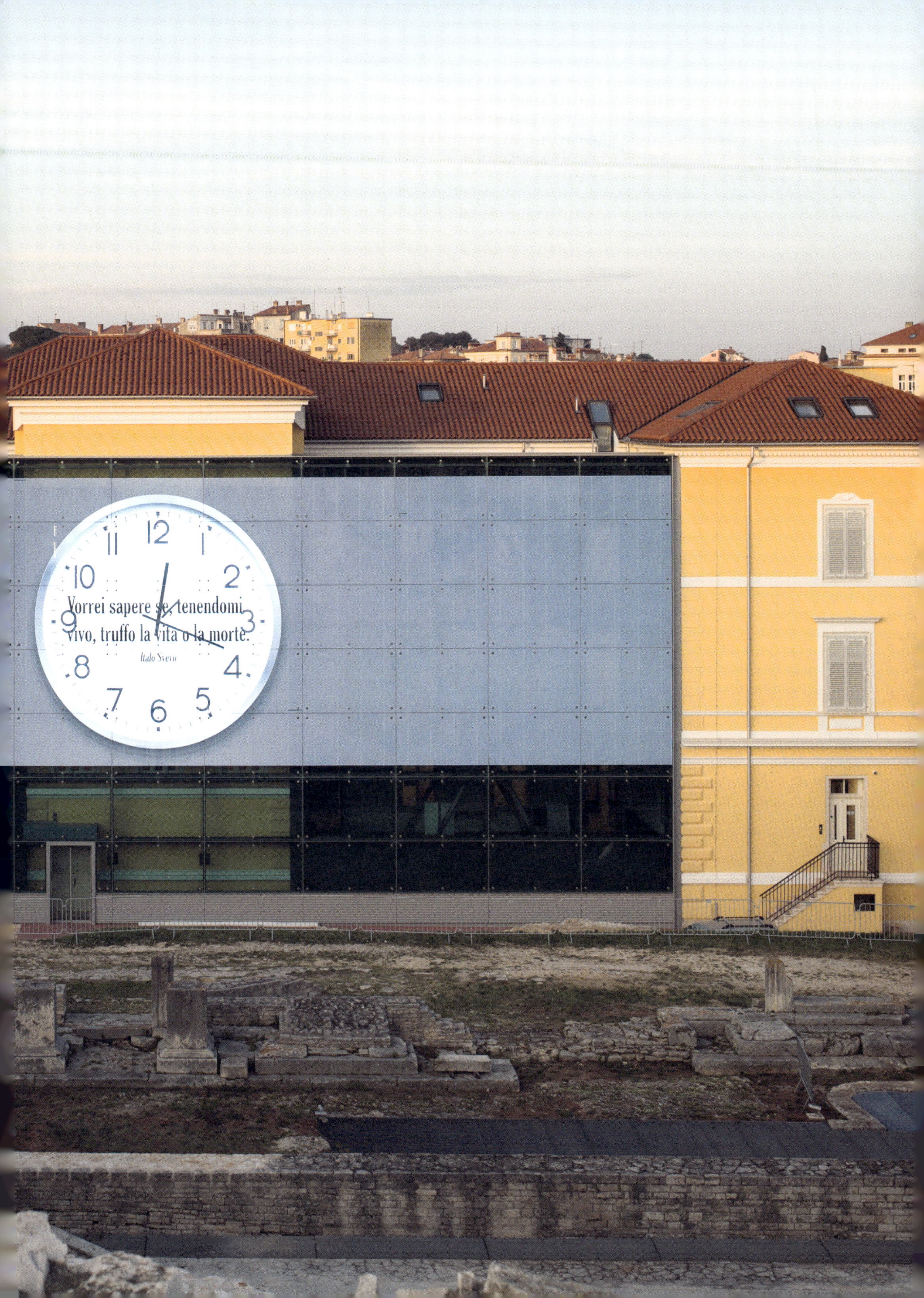
Vorrei sapere se, tenendomi
vivo, truffo la vita o la morte.
Italo Svevo

Lena Lapschina

Hadrian, 2023
Pijacal, Labin

17

The film character Hadrian does not lack earthly luxury. Nevertheless, one day he sets out in search of a better life or a better place to live. He wants to break out of routines, is driven by longing and the desire for something better. He makes an attempt to escape the previous version of his life. This demands all his strength. He wants to explore the meaning of life. He has Fyodor Dostoevsky in his ear, who says: "The secret of human life lies not in mere living, but in the meaning of life." Hadrian's journey begins in Austria and ends in Croatia. This kind of road movie is not about what happens on this journey, but what Hadrian experiences in his head.

When we watch Hadrian travel, you think that something happened to him that occurs to many young people: His heart was broken. And so he did what you can do in those situations: you try to run away from the pain. Lena Lapschina is not the first road movie filmmaker, but she is one of the few to see the purpose of travel not in discovery but in itself. Travelling for the sake of travelling. We can never understand this longing better than after this video film.

Lena Lapschina became known in 2005 for documenting the curious and impressive urban microcosm in front of her feet with a camera and telephoto lens from her bedroom window on the seventh floor of Gasometer B in Vienna. She sees the residential complex in the industrial area designed by the architects Coop Himmelb(l)au as "a kind of oil platform in the wilderness". Around 2000 photos address aspects such as work, children, animals, winter, dogs, eating, telephoning, taking photos, tinkering with the car or urinating. The artist calls her work "investigations of daily/nocturnal social behavior".

Lapschina has remained true to her artistic-ethnological view of her own and foreign cultures to this day. With her work *Hadrian*, which in the word contains the expression "Adria" as the destination of the trip, she as an Austrian "writes" her favorite country Croatia a love letter in the medium of film. A gift.

Lena Lapschina (*1965, Kurgan, Siberia), lives and works in Vienna and Lower Austria. She graduated from State Stroganow University of Fine and Applied Arts in Moscow. She has won the Austrian State Grant for Video and Media Art in 2011. She was awarded several prestigious residencies, including the Djerassi Residence Artists Program (Woodside, California), KuS (Heerlen, Netherlands), ORTung (Strobl, Austria), and Nordens Hus (Reykjavík, Iceland). She has been exhibited at leading institutions, like Kunsthaus Zurich, Museum der Moderne Salzburg, Landesgalerie Niederösterreich, Kunsthalle Wien, Steirischer Herbst, Kunsthal KAdE Amersfoort, Kulturens Hus Luleå, Museo Municipal Tecleño, Joel and Lila Harnett Museum of Art Richmond, FLACC, MAK, OK, among others.

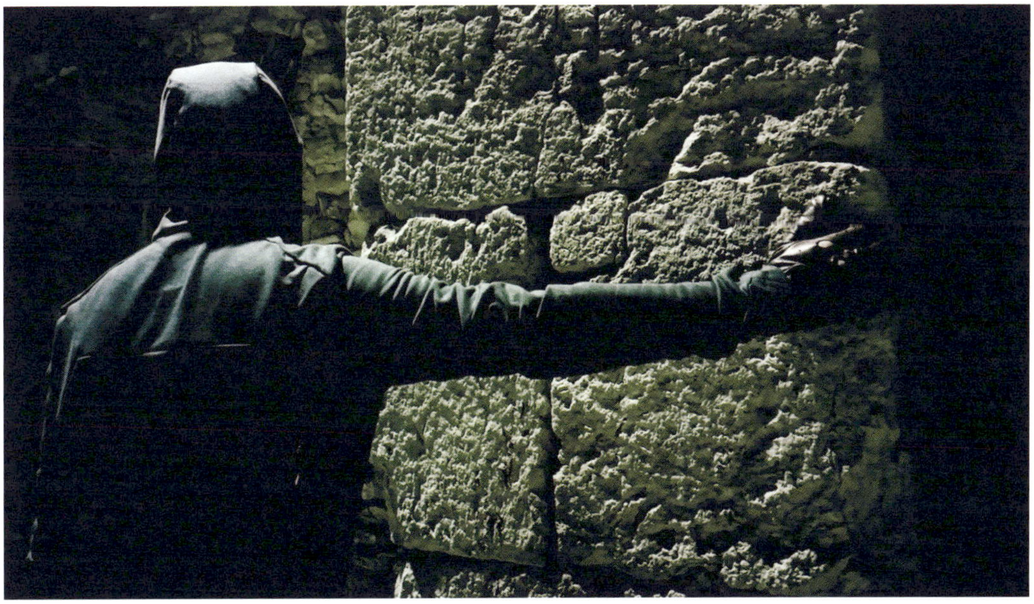

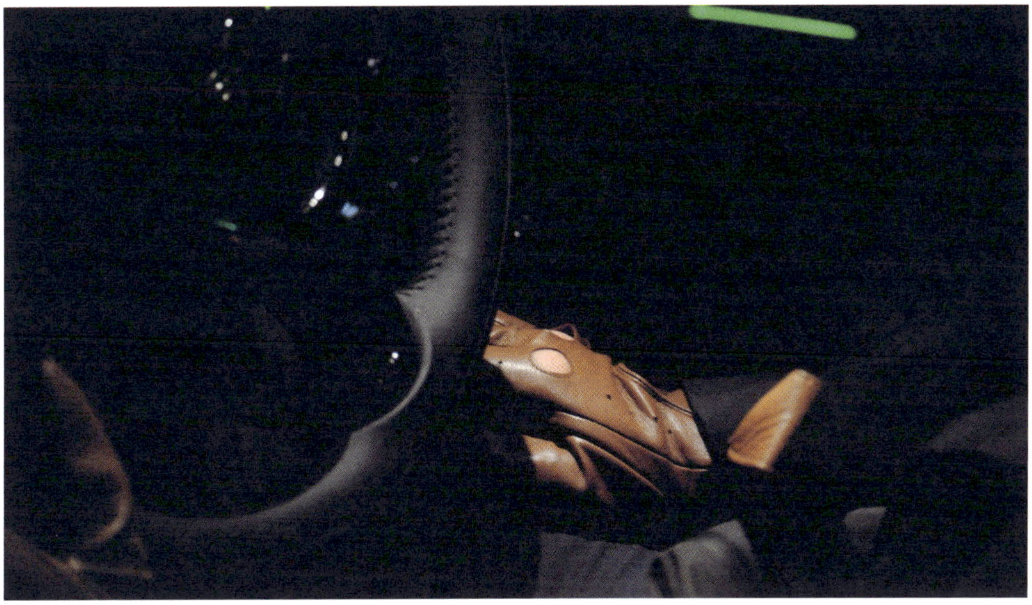

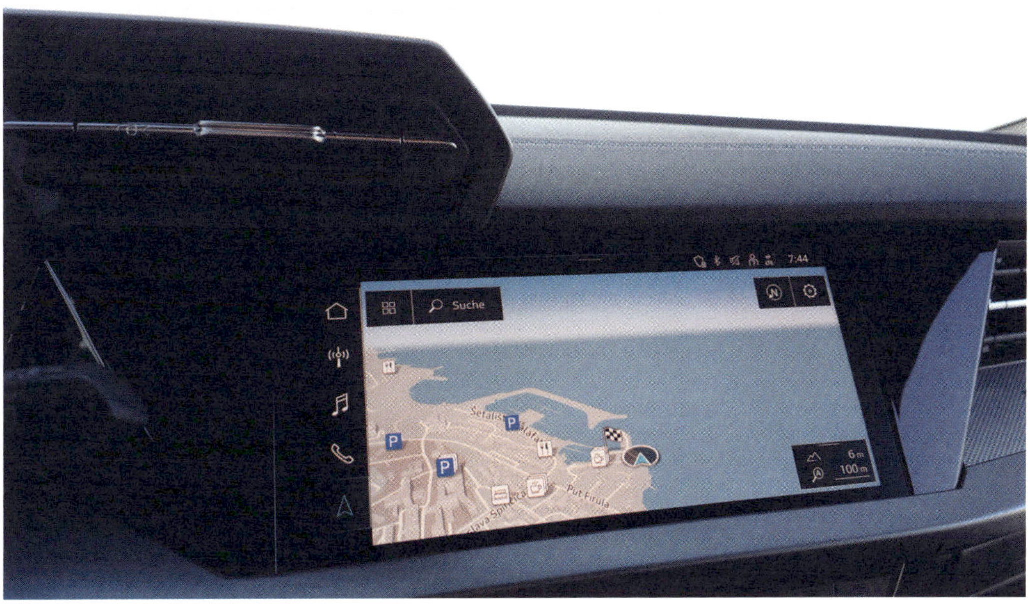

Stills from media installation, a film,
a journey in four episodes.
Total video runtime: approx. 45 min.

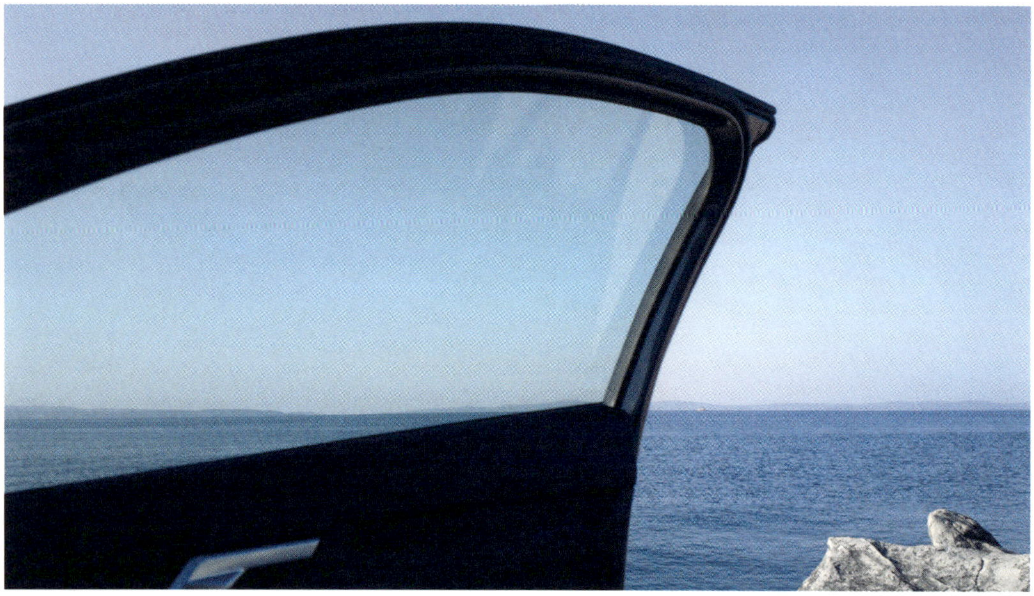

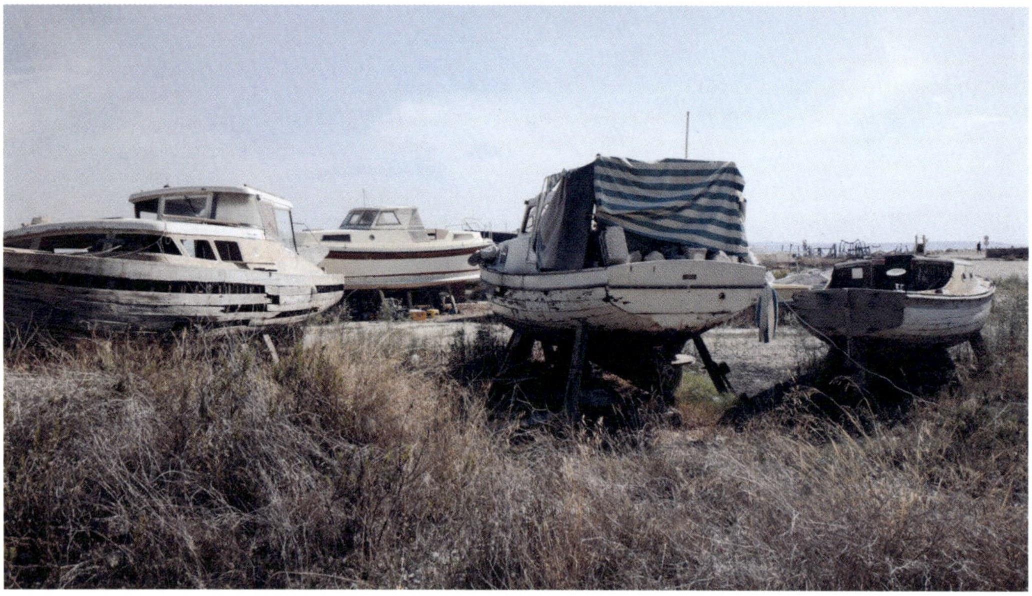

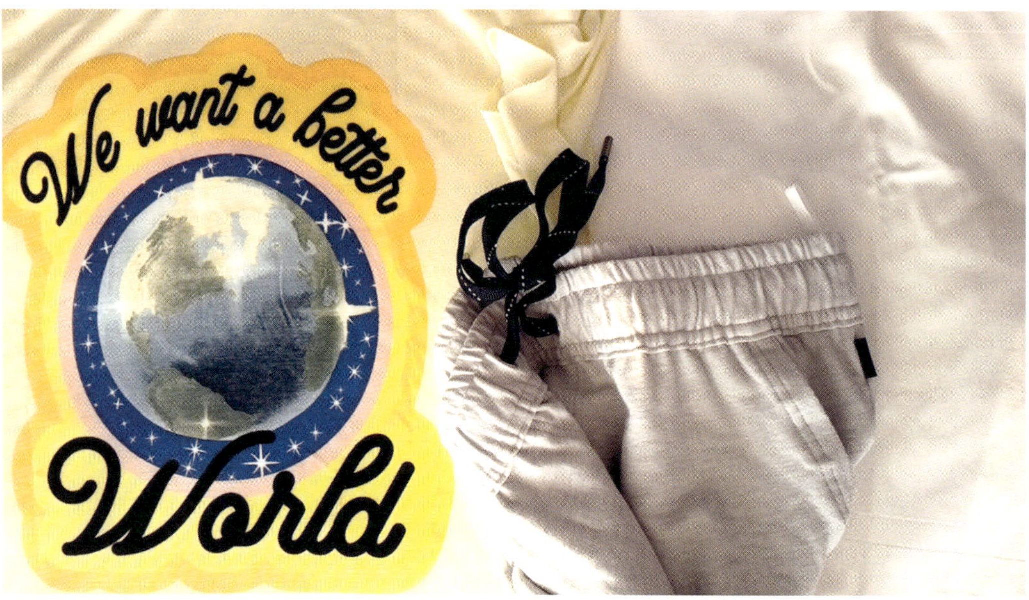
We want a better
World

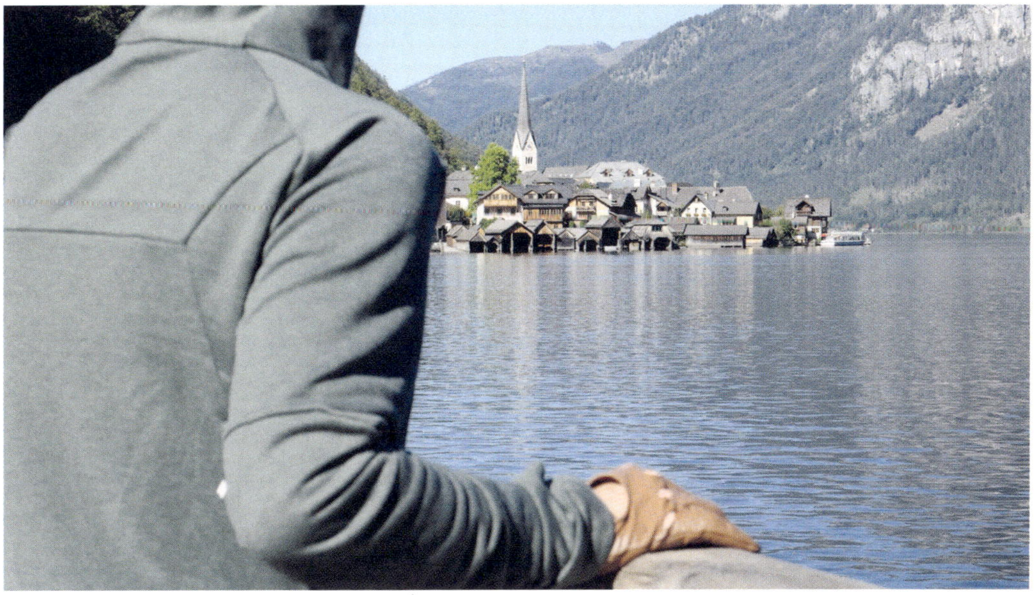

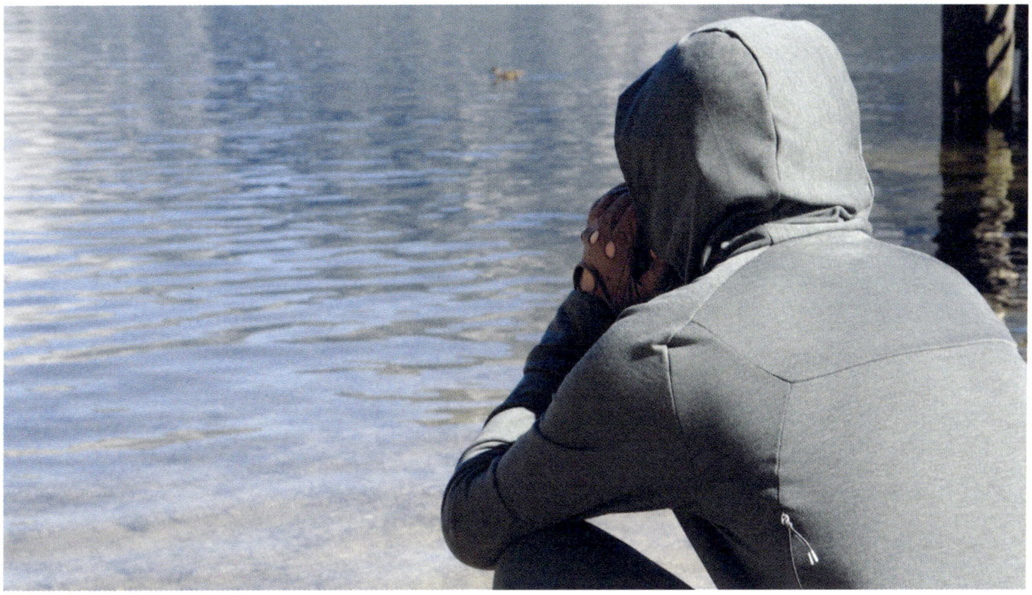

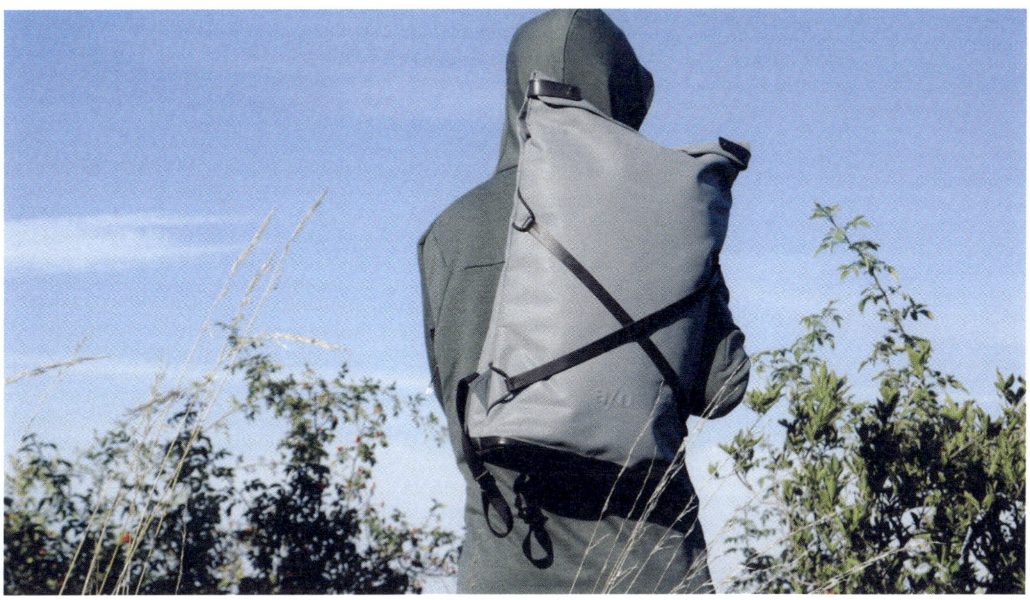

Sonia Leimer

DUST BUDDY, 2023
Temple of Augustus, Pula

(18)

> *Shouldn't we expect to find among these bodies also some that are similar to our planets? Of course, they are too far away for us to perceive them; however, probability speaks strongly for their existence. In fact, the most recent scientific research – as one of its most wonderful results – has been able to show that the entire universe, even in its most distant parts, is both controlled by the same natural laws and structured from the same material as the Earth and our solar system! At other locations within the universe, wouldn't something similar, in many cases almost the same thing, have to materialize under the same conditions (from the same matter and under the effect of the same laws) as in our case?**

Sonia Leimer's dust sculptures refer to dust particles found in the city of Pula. In cooperation with the Natural History Museum in Vienna, the collected dust was analyzed under the microscope. Inside were man-made industrial dust grains as well as cosmic stardust. While the artificial particles tell about the industrial history of the city of Pula, the stardust was created during a long journey through space and entering the Earth's atmosphere. 100 tons of such micrometeorites hit the Earth every day. Due to their original chemical composition, they are often dark in color and slightly magnetic, easily mistaken for Earth dust particles. These less than one millimeter small parts were photographed with the microscope and served the artist as a template for her bronze and aluminum casts. Leimer's sculptures make something visible that is directly related to the city, but is normally invisible. Presented in the Temple of Augustus, these enlarged dust grains now enter into a dialogue with the architecture and connect Pula, where they were found, with the city's industrial history and with the sheer endless expanse of space.

* Herman Potočnik (1892–1929) (pseudonym Hermann Noordung) was an ethnically Slovenian Austro-Hungarian Army officer, electrical engineer and astronautics theorist. He is regarded as an early theorist of modern space flight and is remembered mainly for his work concerning the long-term human habitation of space.

Sonia Leimer (*1977 in Merano, Italy) lives and works in Vienna. Her works have been exhibited, among others, at Manifesta, Rovereto (2008), Salzburger Kunstverein (2010), Moscow Biennial (2013, 2015), MoMA Los Angeles (2014), Taxipalais/Kunsthalle Tirol, Innsbruck (2017), Museion, Bolzano (2020).

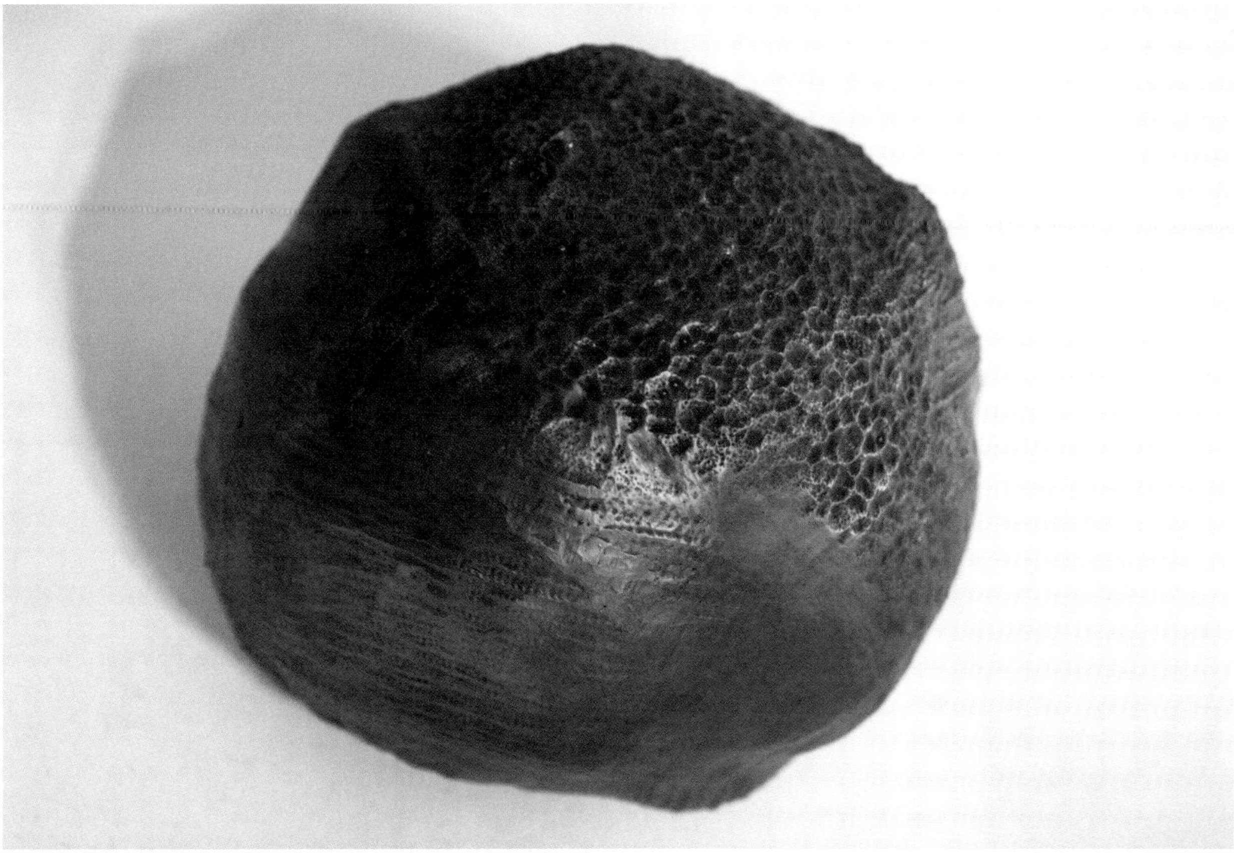

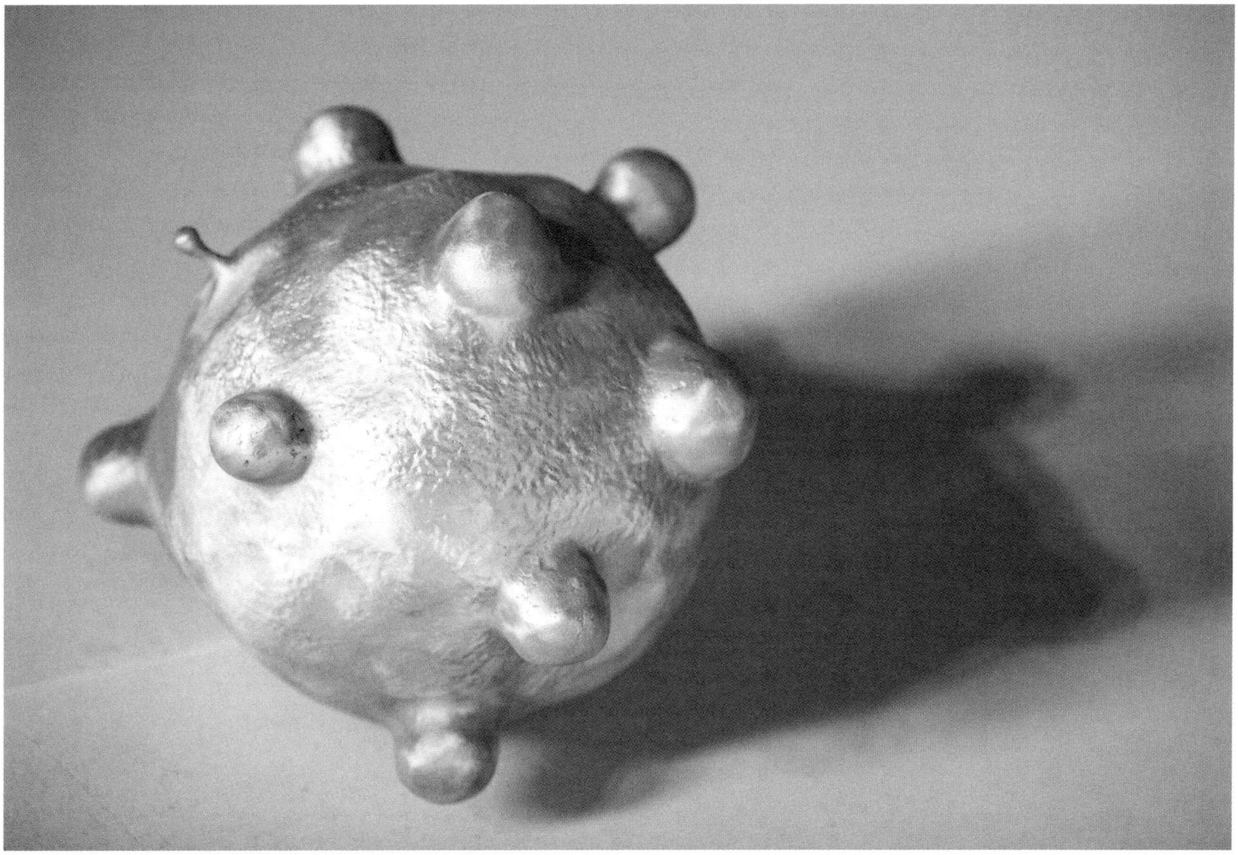

DUST BUDDY, 2023
Bronze, dark patina, Ø 27,5 cm, ed. 1 + 1 AE

DUST BUDDY, 2023
Aluminium, sand plasted, Ø 28 cm, ed. 1 + 1 AE
Courtesy of the artist and Galerie nächst St. Stephan
Rosemarie Schwarzwälder, Vienna

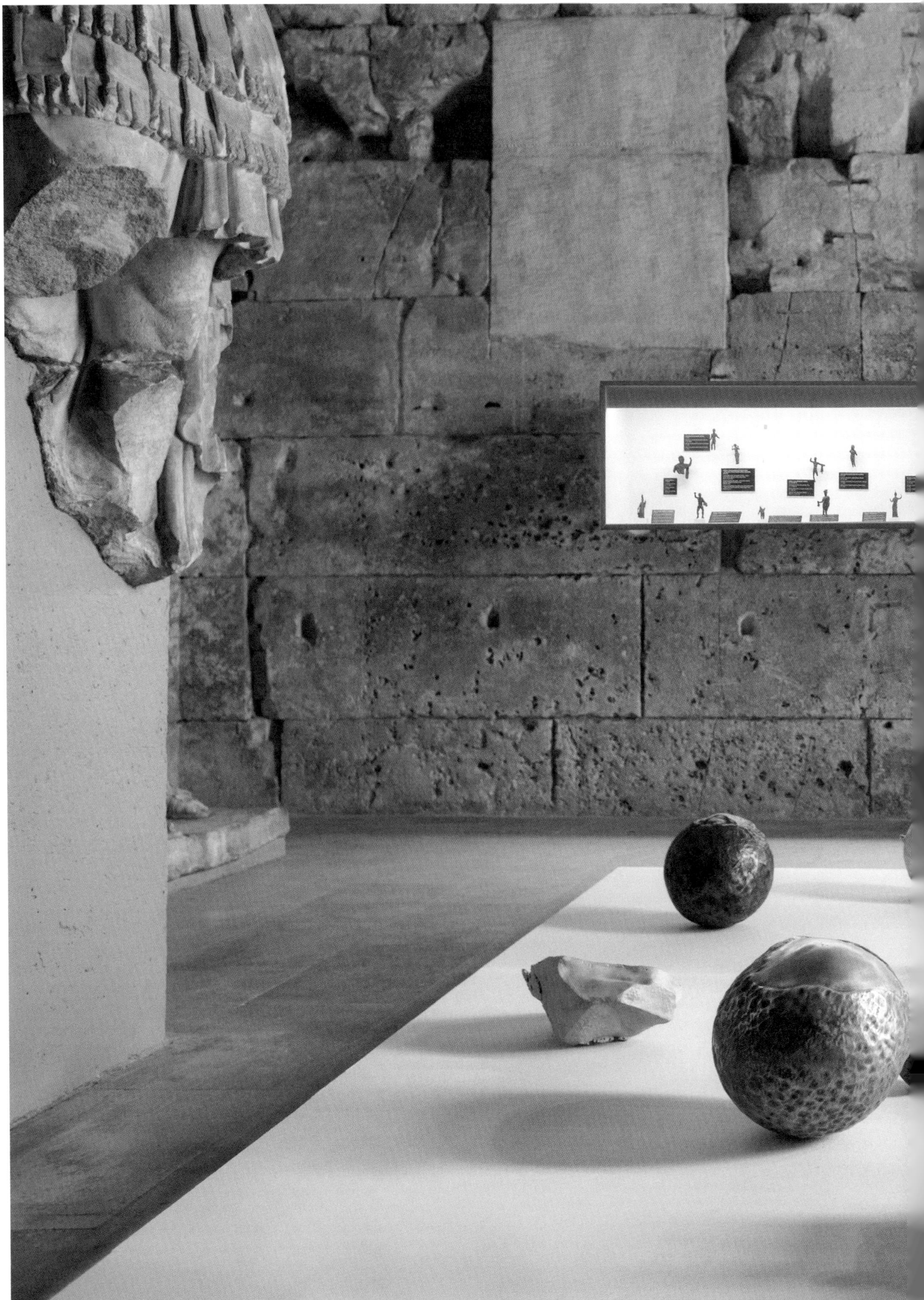

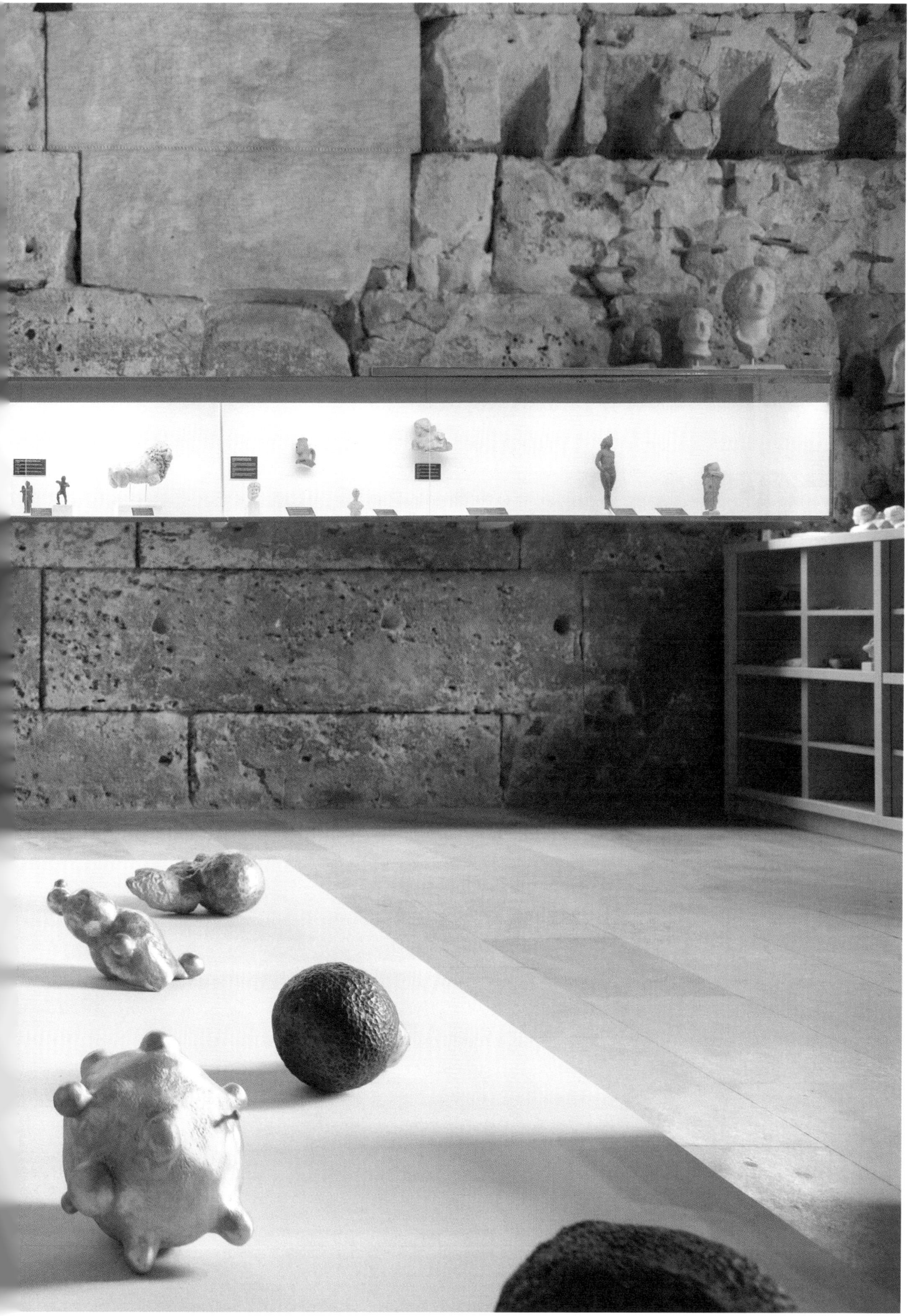

Olaf Nicolai

KO LI AJA, 2023 (19)
Prvomajska, machine factory management building, Raša

Sound installation
Courtesy of the artist and Galerie Eigen+Art, Berlin/Leipzig

Cultural interspaces and social gaps are central for Olaf Nicolai's artistic explorations. For his multi-layered interventions, he specifically evaluates those zones in which creative energies evoked by ambiguities, misunderstandings and obscurations lie dormant. "There are wonderful, beautiful thoughts," says Nicolai – and sometimes they are beautiful only "because you don't understand them. For me, not understanding is the beginning of many interesting things." Nicolai develops thus interdisciplinary projects that question the elemental experience of space, time, and physicality. Whether it be a bee house, a science-fiction novel, a piece of music, or the processes of industrial arts and crafts, the artist acts as a go-between, mediating between a given space and conceptual forms to tackle questions of social behaviour in the zone of tension between concrete experience and abstract contextualization.

During the 1930s the Raša mines were part of the company Azienda Carboni Italiani. The mines were recording a sharp rise in production due to the needs of fascist autarkic economy. The period between 1936–1942 marks an era of the largest company expansion with the mines in Raša considered as the most sophisticated in Europe, employing more than ten thousand workers and reaching the top production of 1.158,000 tons of coal in 1942. Olaf Nicolai has addressed this specific context with a sound intervention. During the Industrial Art Biennial mysterious, delicate children's voices with Italian timbre sound from the abandoned main portal to the former Prvomajska factory management building, accompanied by a piano and the cool breeze from the depths of the old mine tunnels. The music is provided by the children's choir of the Comunita degli italiani di Albona, Labin's Italian-speaking community that wants to preserve the cultural heritage of the past for the present. In Olaf Nicolai's sound intervention – titled *KO LI AJA* after the name of Croatian football player Marko Livaja, which was tagged recently by football fans over the buildings entrance – the Foucauldian theory of the heterotope, the presence of the absent manifests itself as a wonderful poetic manifesto.

Olaf Nicolai (*1962 in Halle/Saale, Germany) lives and works in Berlin. His works were shown at documenta X (1997) and at the Venice Biennale (2001, 2005, 2015), among others. Nicolai has had numerous international solo exhibitions, e.g. at Kunsthalle Wien (2018), Museion, Bolzano (2018), Boijmans Van Beuningen, Rotterdam (2016), Musée du Louvre, Paris (2013), Migros Museum, Zurich (2001).

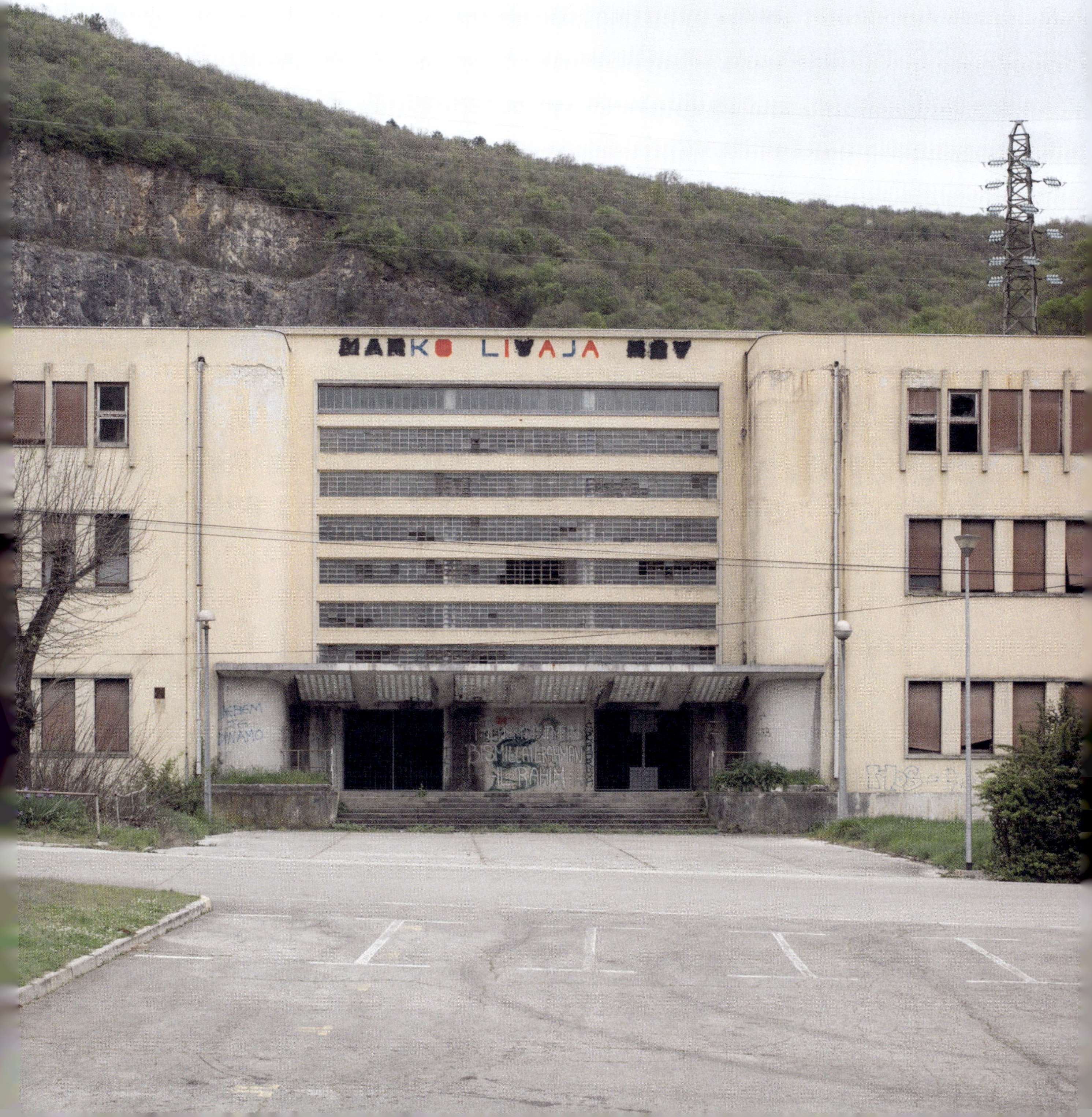
LIVAJA

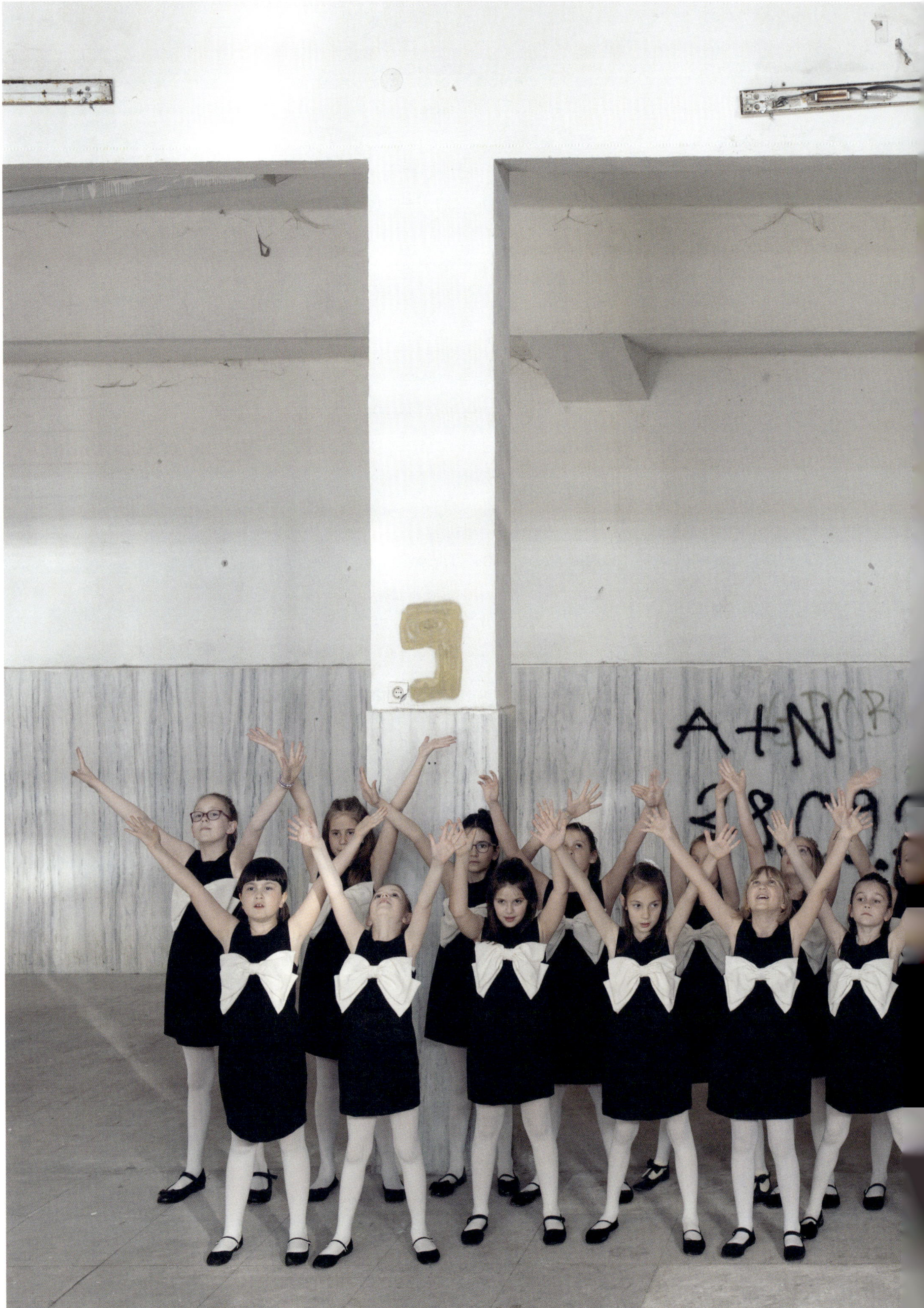
A+N

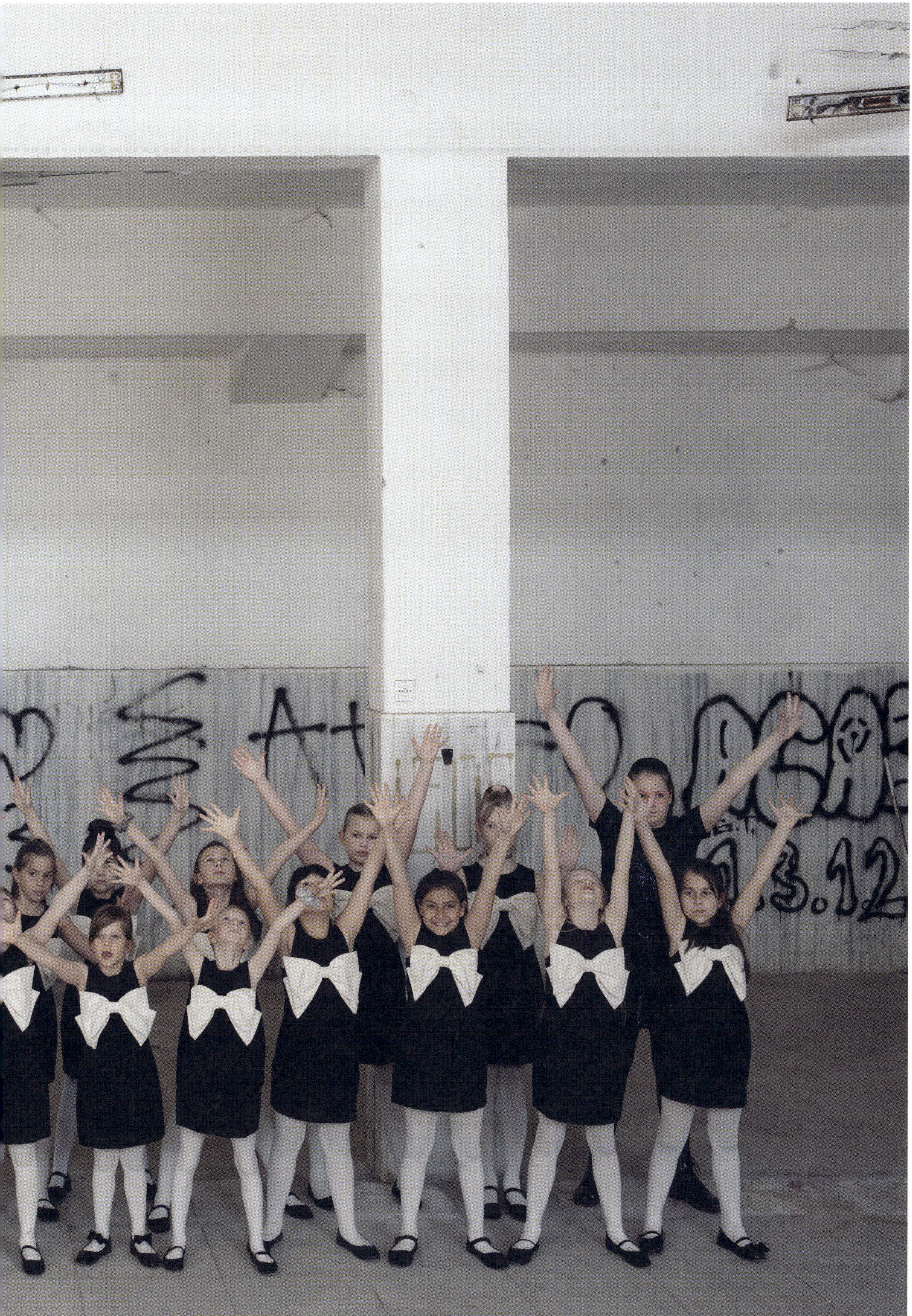

Anna Piva

Common Ground, 2023
Lamparna, Rudarska ul. 5, Labin

Spirits of the Mine, 2023
Narodni Muzej, Battiala-Lazzarini Palace, Labin

20

The conceptual work of art *Common Ground* by the artist and musician Anna Piva is a creative reading of fragments from the late works of Istrian writer, educator and socialist revolutionary Giuseppina Martinuzzi (1844–1925) through multimedia installation art.

Drawing on African-American feminist and Marxist literature, and though a montage of historical imagery, contemporary photography, environmental recordings, electronic music and spoken word, the project traces connections across time and spaces: between Martinuzzi's writings and the work of other American, Indian, African and European 19th century pioneers of intersectional feminism; and between the social histories of Labin, Trieste and Istria in the early 20th century, and histories of more recent and present global movements for social justice and emancipation.

Martinuzzi's late poetry and essays denounce the divisive and oppressive forces of patriarchial racial capitalism, nationalism and fascism present in her (and our) time; they also envisage a "piccola patria", her beloved and troubled native land of Istria as a possible "common space", a place of transnational socialism and (comm)unity in diversity, a (future) space of radical love, social justice and belonging for all people.

Anna Piva explains her approach as follows: "My interest in Giuseppina Martinuzzi and the social histories of Istria was sparked by a research in my late father's extensive postal history collection and a visit to Labin in 2021 to celebrate the centenary of the 'Labin Republic'. In that occasion I was given access to the Martinuzzi archive at the Labin Museum, and spent some time researching her work."

In remembrance of the 1921 Labin Republic and its unsung heroes, Anna Piva created the sound art installation *Spirits of the Mine,* featuring Istrian poet Isabella Flego and musicians Kikanju Baku and Moussa Dembele. The installation's soundscape comprises a reshape of historical recordings of sounds of local coal miners interwoven in an electroacoustic composition of environmental and concrete sounds, electronics and percussions, with readings by Isabella Flego. This spoken word component, recorded at Isabella's home in June 2022, consists of fragments from her text *La Galleria della Memoria* (The Tunnel of Memory), a poem by Giuseppina Martinuzzi and other writings.

Anna Piva (*1961, Italy) is a multimedia artist and musician based in London. She is a founder of the art group Flow Motion (1996–present) and the electronic music group Hallucinator, whose work was released with Berlin's electronic music label Chain Reaction between 1998–2006. Her arts research-practice focuses on the temporal dimensions of media and the transformation of archival data through digital art processes, electroacoustic composition and cross-disciplinary collaborations. In 2008–10 she was co-artist in research at the International Institute of Visual Art for the creation of promised lands, supported by a grant from Iniva. In 2015 she received a PhD in Arts and Media Practice from the University of Westminster. Her doctorate thesis, *Landscapes of the Invisible: Sounds, Cosmologies and Poetics of Space*, is available online.

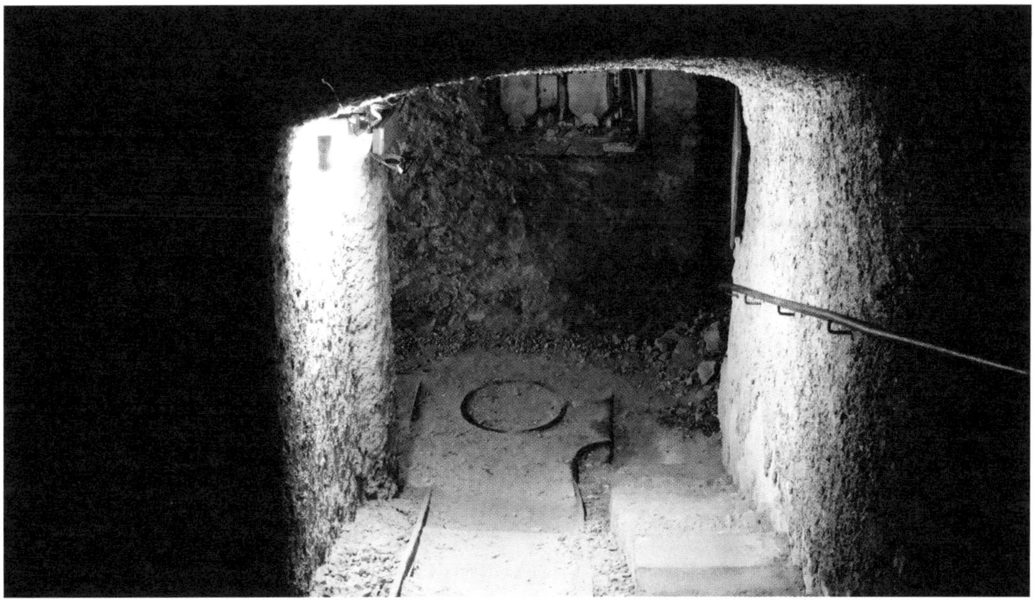

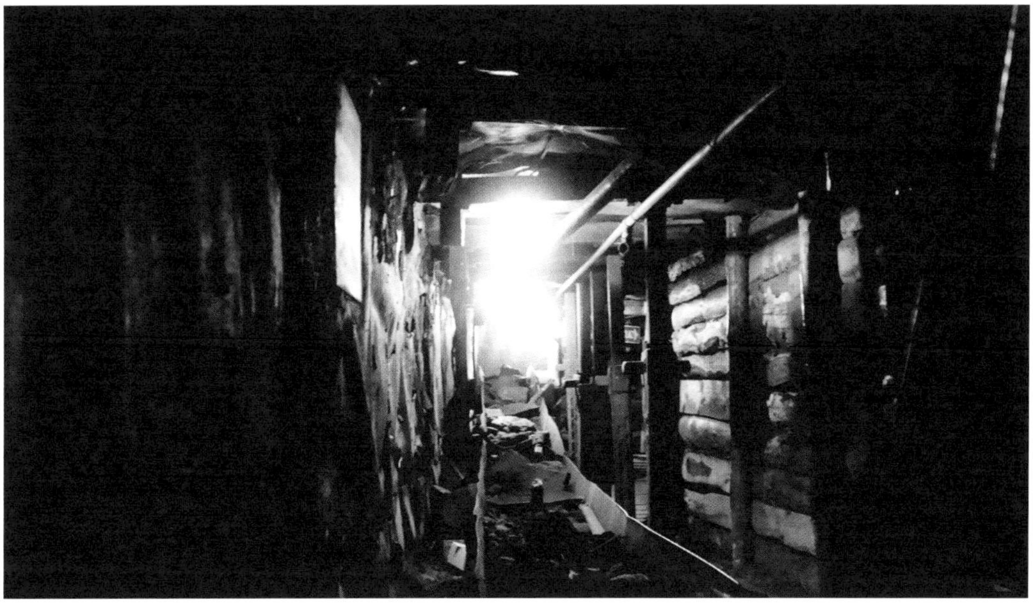

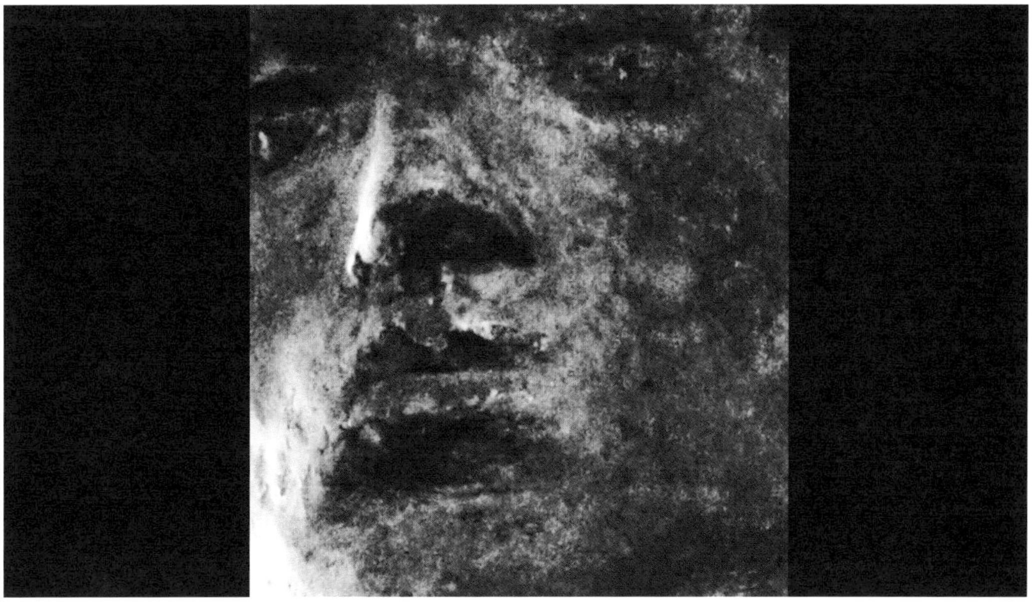

Spirits of the Mine, 2023
Sound art installation

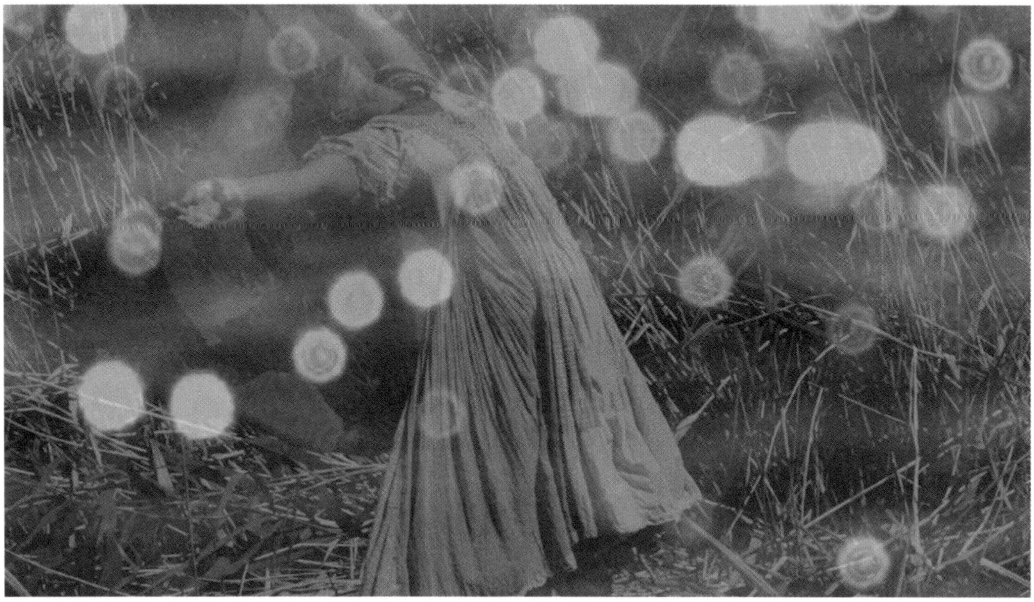

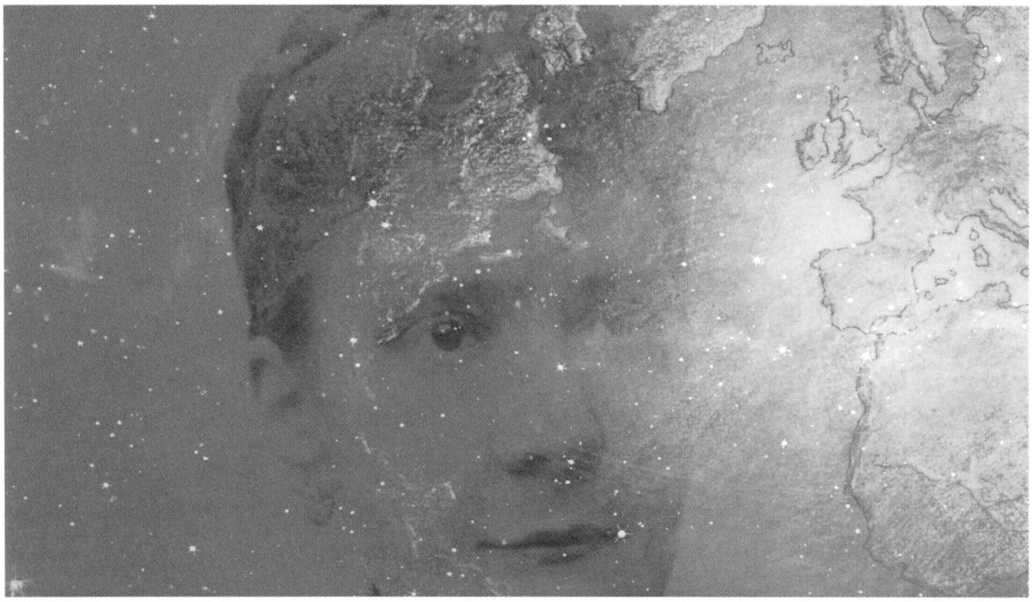

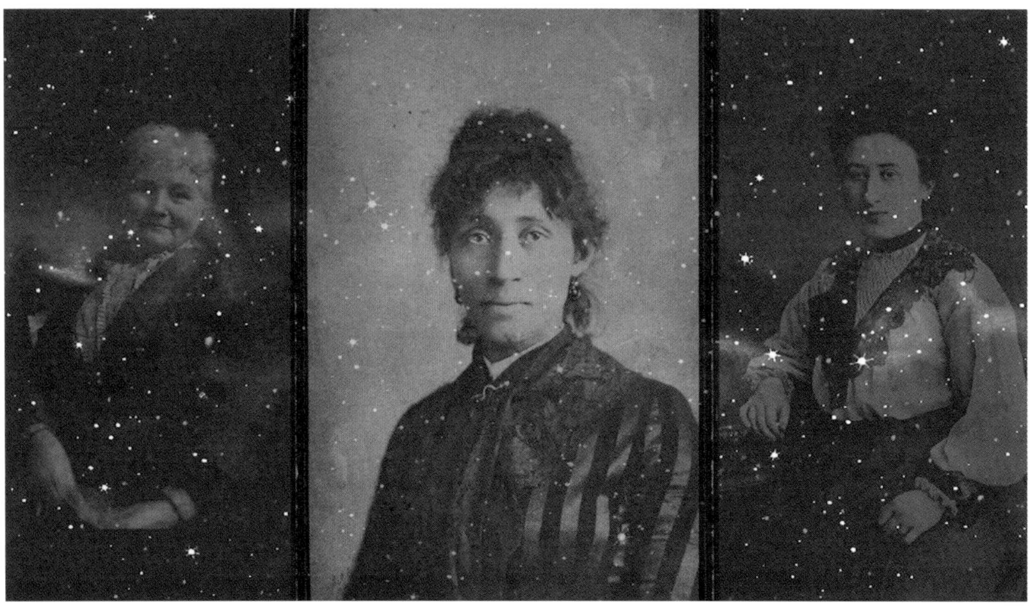

Common Ground, 2023
Stills and photographs from multimedia installation

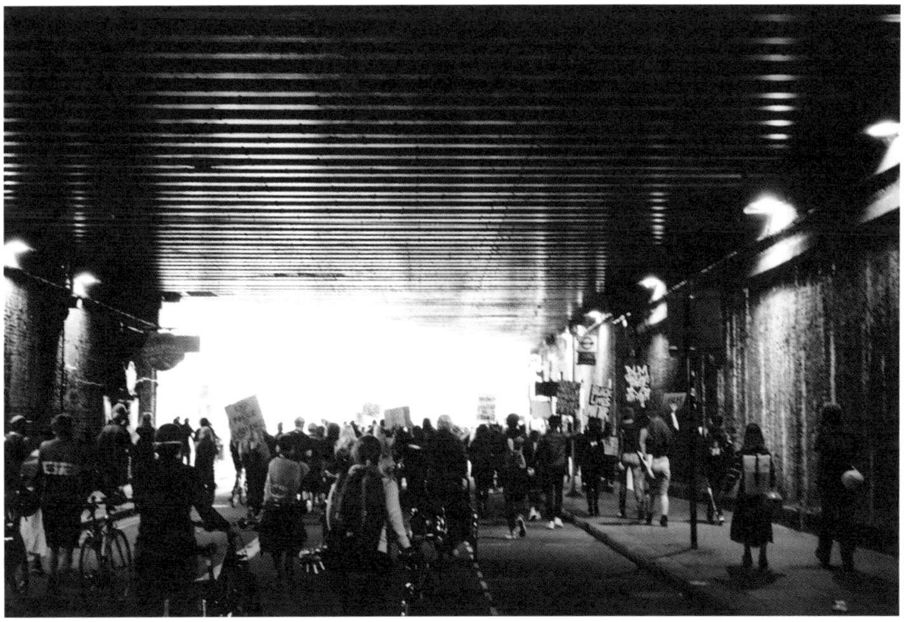

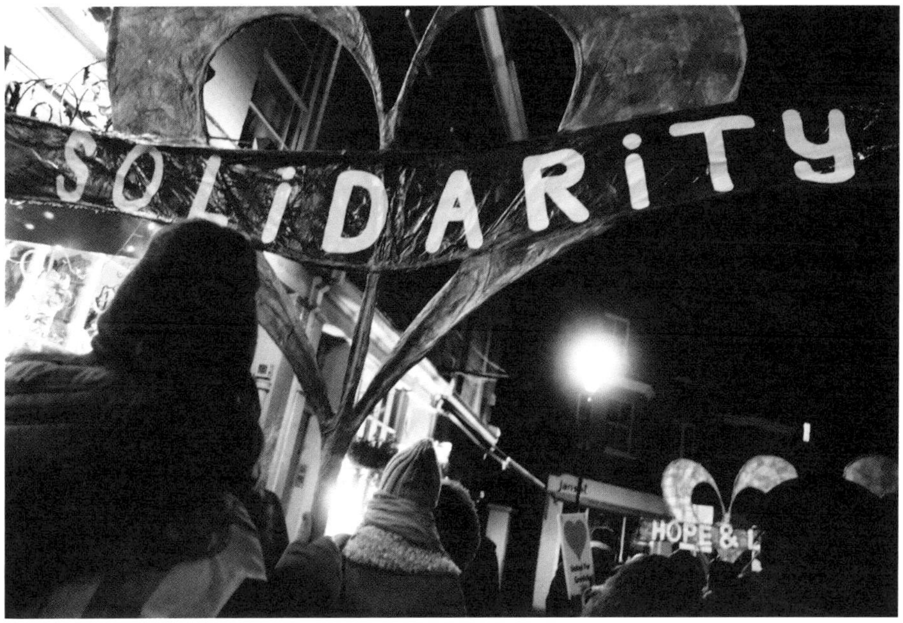
SOLIDARITY
HOPE &

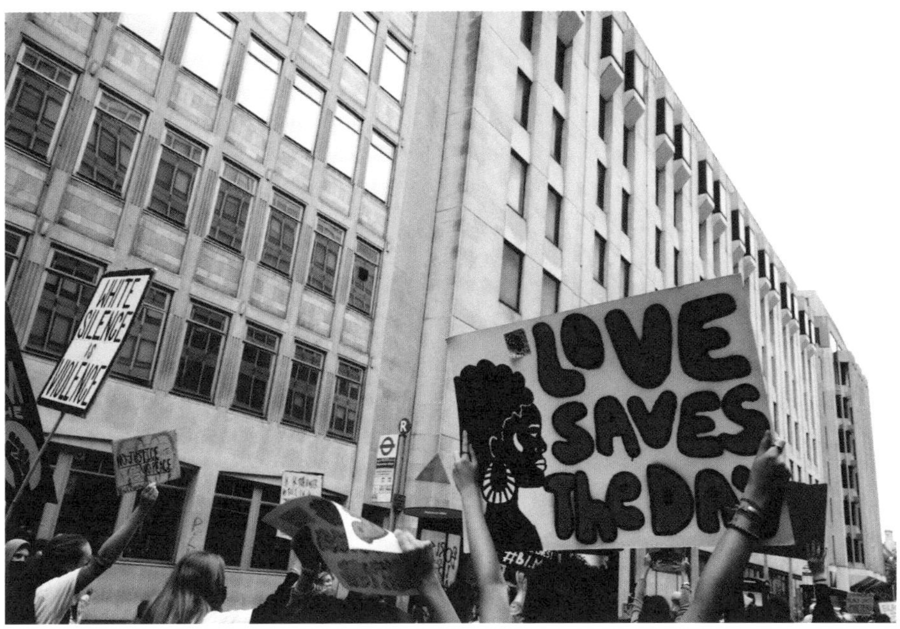
WHITE SILENCE
VIOLENCE
LOVE SAVES

Seçkin Pirim

Past, Present, 2023
Forum, Pula

(21)

2 columns, charcoal paint on polyester, 427 × 80 cm
5 marble stools, 50 × 90 cm Ø (each)
Courtesy of the artist and Dirimart, Istanbul, supported by SAHA

With his artistic practice, Seçkin Pirim moves at important systemic interfaces between architecture, design, sculpture, and museology – in other words, the way art is produced, commercialized, presented, mediated, and conserved. He works (parallel to his classical sculptural works) with sculptural means in urban dynamic contexts (e.g. for shopping centres) and he creates works for touristic architectures (hotel complexes), which decidedly ask themselves what social meaning art has today. These subtle and mostly implicit connections between today's mostly highly specialized activities that have formed within the contemporary art system (as a result of centuries-old developments) are given a historical echo space through his current project for the Industrial Art Biennial.

Right next to the large industrial port in Pula, where from 1856 the Austrian naval ship yard was located, there is a small green area, directly by the main road. Almost unnoticed there are some stone sarcophagi from Roman times lying in the meadow, which were probably unearthed during an excavation and deposited there for lack of other options. Next to the spectacular amphitheatre or the imposing Temple of Augustus, these stone coffins, marked by the ravages of time, look completely insignificant. Sometimes a passerby strolls through the meadow with his dog and the animal uses the stones as a tree substitute.

But the sarcophagi are extremely interesting in terms of their historical significance for art and industry, or rather for the art industry. Because the stone coffins do not all come from Pula, but partly from Asia Minor, probably from Aphrodisias. Since the 2nd century BC, there existed an important school of sculpture and a flourishing stonemasonry industry, which distributed their products, namely sarcophagi, throughout the Mediterranean. On this basis, Turkish conceptual artist and sculptor Seçkin Pirim has developed a project for the Industrial Art Biennial that draws on this "industrial" manufacturing of antiquity with 21st century methods. Seçkin's sculptures, centrally installed in front of the Augustus Temple, are based on digital designs. The stele-shaped columns are made of synthetic material; and the marble stones, also from Aphrodisias, were milled from the stone using high-tech machines.

Past, Present is a perpetuum mobile of multi-perspective references, which characterizes this one intervention at the Augustus Temple. It refers along the time-space-axis to a significant reference theme: the canonization of aesthetics, the standardized idealization of beauty, which is essential in the evaluation of art. In other words, when we look at art we must also always ask ourselves the following questions: Why are the works conserved? Who is showing us these works? How are they shown to us? And where are they exhibited? These confrontations with social hierarchies of value form the framework of cultural archives. Without their permanent, discursive evaluation and questioning, as Seçkin Pirim does in his Pula project, there is no progress in art and in society.

Seçkin Pirim (*1977 in Ankara, Turkey) lives and works in Istanbul and London. His works have been exhibited at Borusan Sanat, Pera Museum, Museum Haus Konstruktiv, Glory Yeh Museum & Sculpture Park, Yverdon-les-Bains and Saatchi Gallery. His works are collected by The National Art Museum of China, Istanbul Modern Museum of Art, Odunpazarı Modern Museum, Baksı Museum and Elgiz Museum.

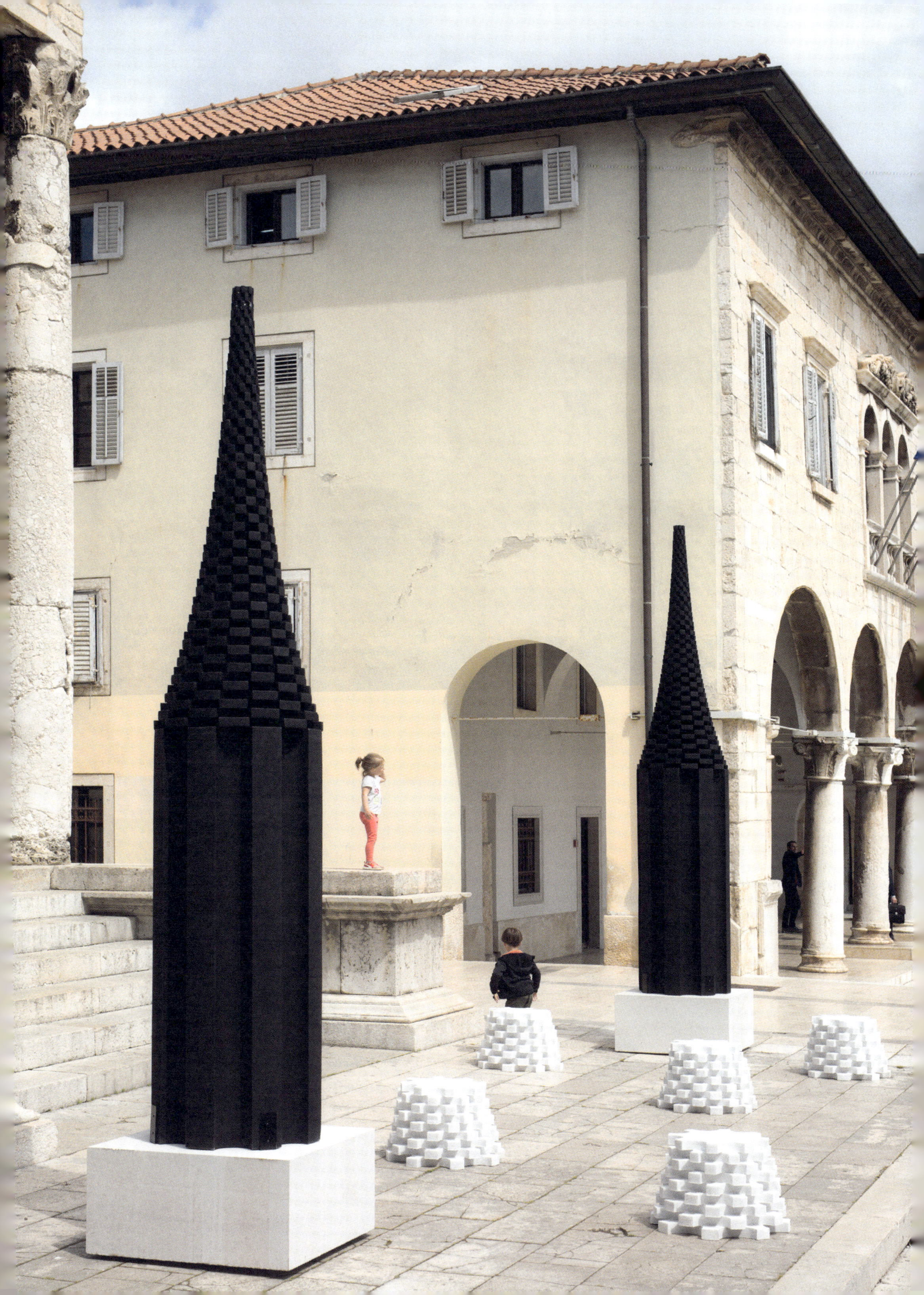

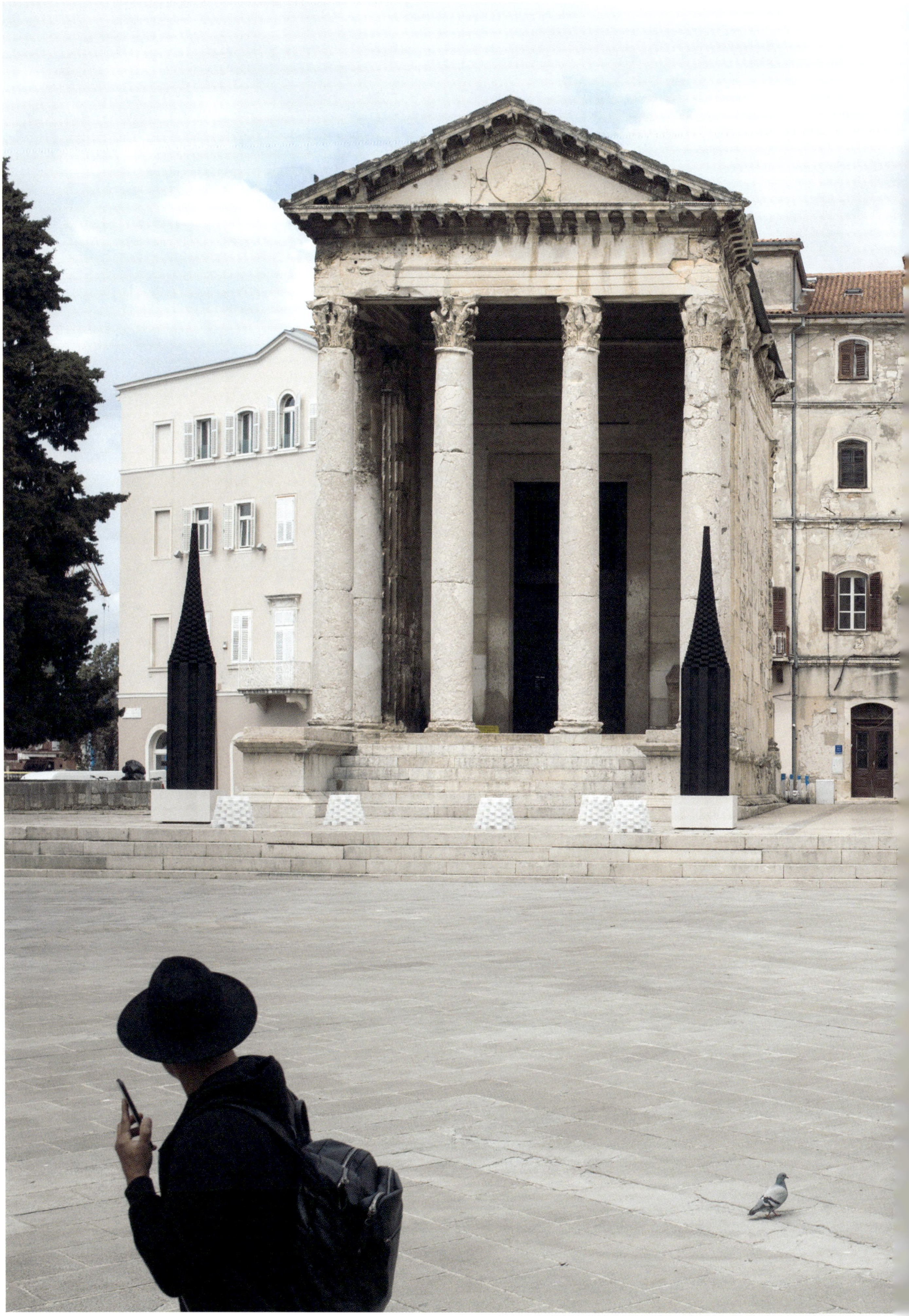

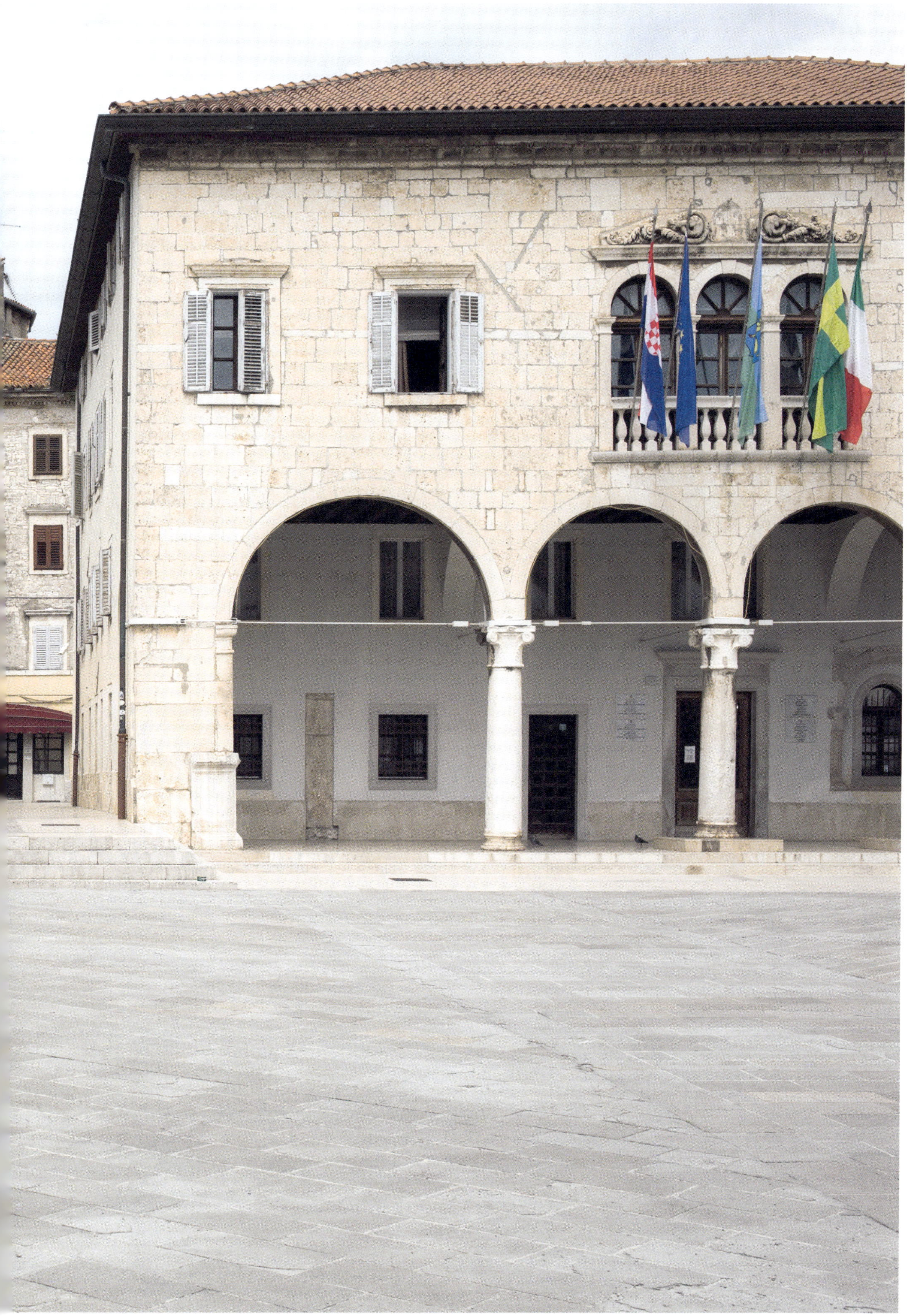

Marko Pogačnik

Introduction to the Sacred Landscape of Istria, 1986/2013
Historical and Maritime Museum of Istria, Pula

(22)

Marko Pogačnik is probably the most famous rediscoverer and mediator of modern geomancy – an ancient knowledge of the fine energetic areas of the Earth and nature, which the old master builders of the Gothic cathedrals had already applied. In all his work as a sculptor, Land Art artist and Earth healer, Pogačnik is concerned with reconnecting with our home planet Gaia – also mentally and spiritually. With his cosmograms he developed his very own language, which is intended to help this communication.

In his artistic work he harmonises the exchange of energies through targeted stone placements – lithupuncturing, i.e. something like acupuncture for the Earth. As an artist, Pogačnik has, as he says, "the freedom to venture into realms unknown to the human mind." The effect of his work can be seen, for example, when he designs the coat of arms for Slovenia with his very own language of cosmograms.

In 1986, Pogačnik, together with photographer Dušan Podgornik, published a loose-leaf book entitled *Introduction to the Sacred Landscape of Istria*. The two authors write: "Today we see around us certain mountains, certain flora and fauna, certain human communities and cultural monuments through which we perceive Istria." And further: "In this book we shall try to find an answer to the single question of how an individual landscape relates to the other aspects and dimensions of the universe." This is done with the following focus: „We are interested in the 'breathing holes' of Istria and finally in the 'breathing system' of the region as a whole. We shall try to demonstrate how humanity has, through millennia, used its creativity to mark these vitally significant points in the landscape with the aid of masonic and sacred architecture."

Humanity stands at the threshold of a new phase of Earth's planetary evolution. Breathtaking possibilities – in tune with the evolutionary path of the universe – are now available. Yet the question arises: Does humanity have the ideas, foresight and potential for action that could create a culture that corresponds to the planet's transformation? The encounter with the work of Marko Pogačnik offers the opportunity to understand more deeply that Gaia is changing and that only our reconnection with nature makes this change existentially tangible.

Marko Pogačnik (*1944, Kran, Slovenia) lives and works in Sempas, Slovenia. He worked in Conceptual Art and Land Art as a member of the OHO group during the years 1965–71. He has had exhibitions in the Aktionsraum in Munich, at the Museum of Modern Art in New York, and at the Venice Biennale. After 1979 he worked in the field of art combined with integral ecology (geomancy). His works stand in many continents of the world, including Europe, South and North America, Africa and Asia. After 1998 he developed Gaia touch body exercises to tune to the essence of the Earth and its transforming process. In 2016 he was appointed by the UNESCO Secretary General as Artist for Peace.

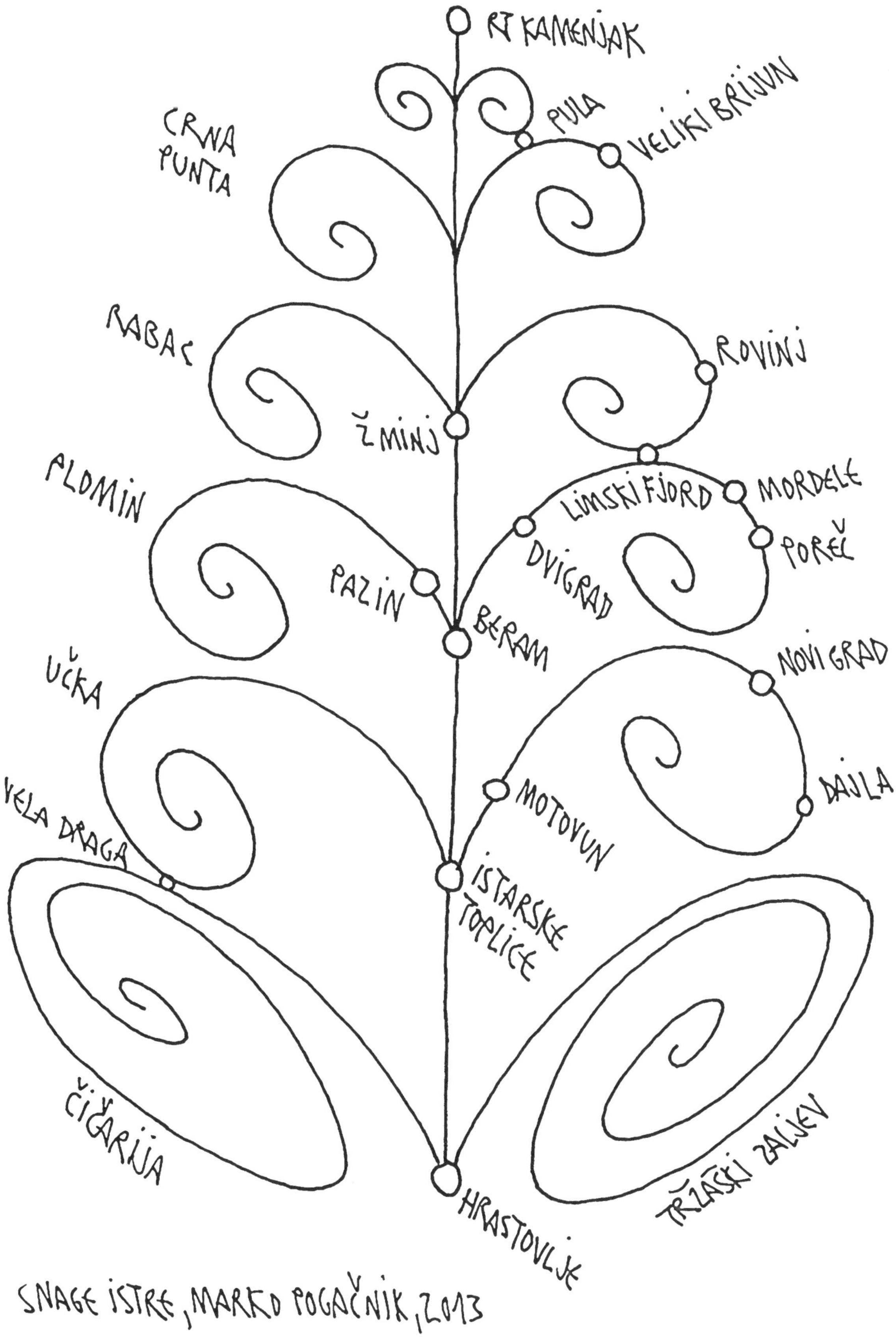

Insight into the Essence of Istria, 2013
Drawings, ink on paper, 32 × 24 cm / 24 × 32 cm

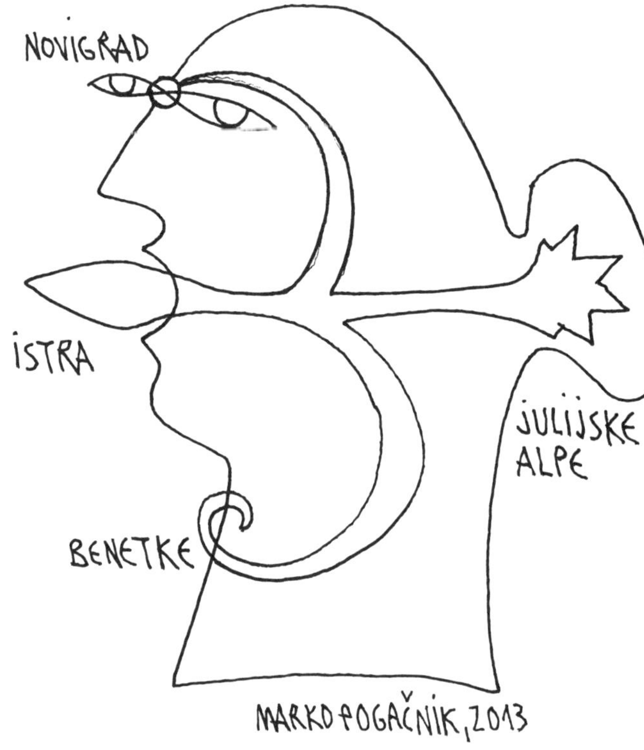

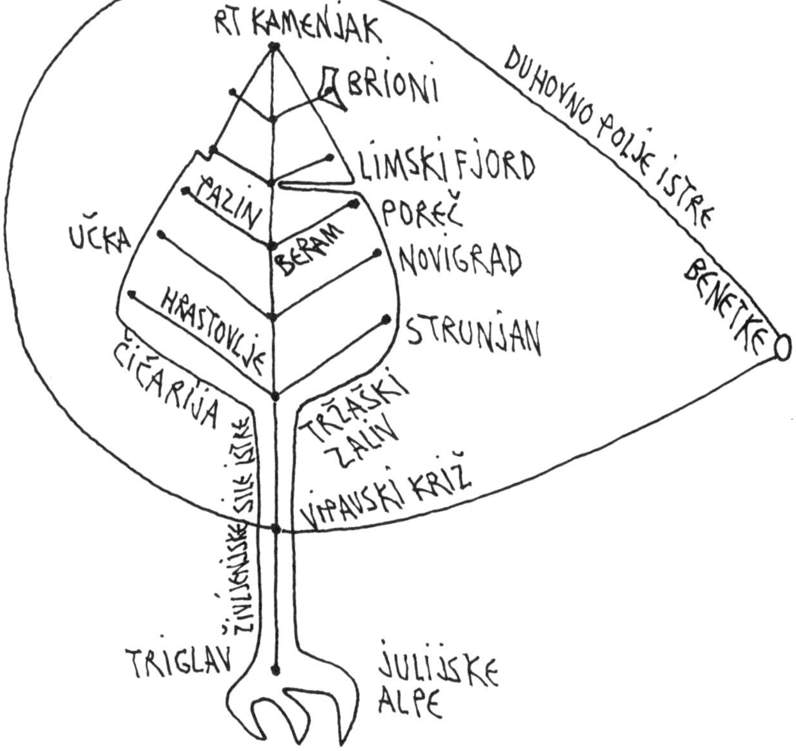

From: Marko Pogačnik (text and drawings) and
Dušan Podgornik (photographs and design):
Introduction to the Sacred Landscape of Istria,
printed material, published by the artists, Koper 1986

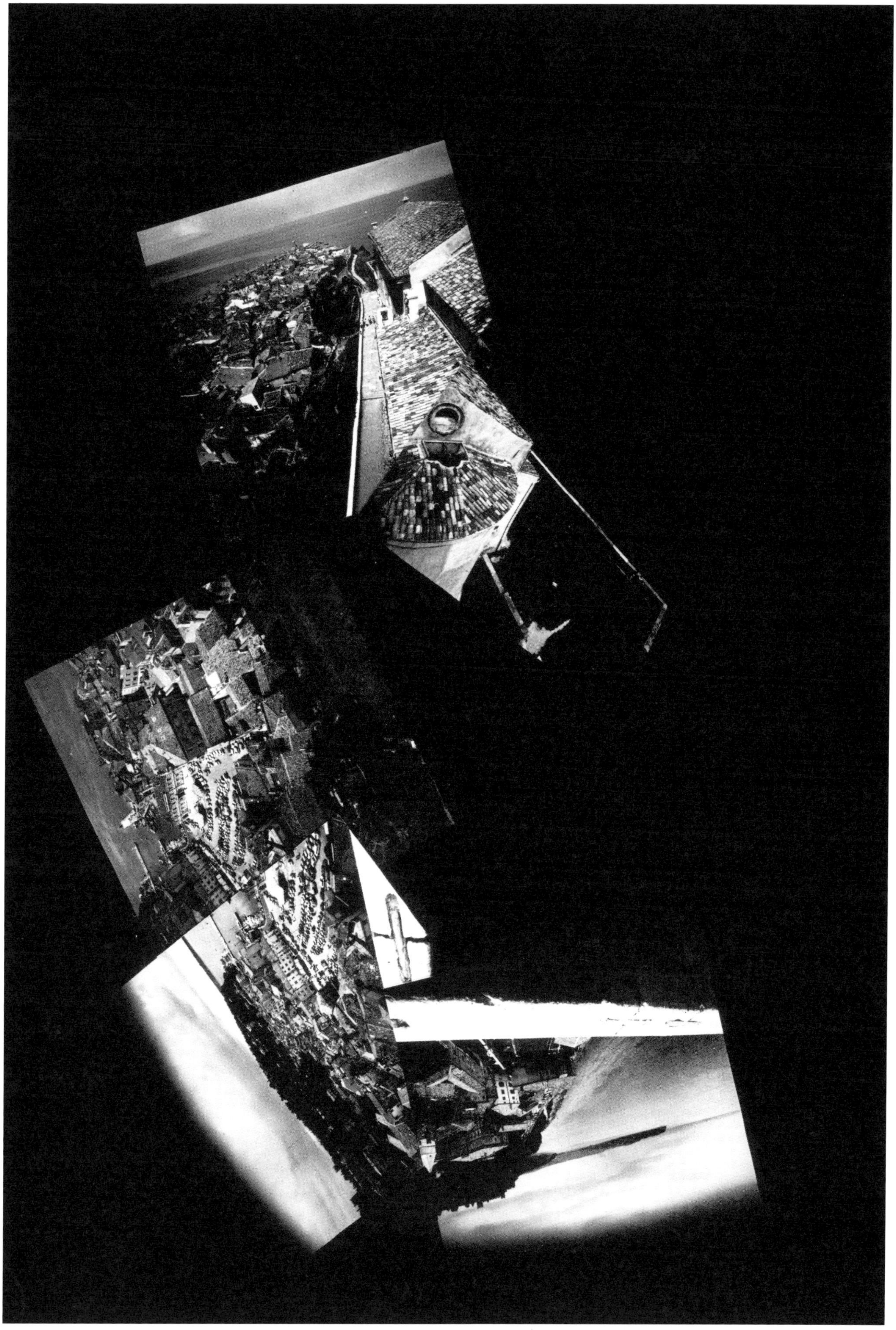

Tanja Helena Roscic

Man in the Bottle, 2023 (23)
Narodni Muzej, Battiala-Lazzarini Palace, Labin (outdoor)

Metal, willow and string, 210 × 120 cm (Ø)
Courtesy of the artist

The *Man in the Bottle* is a particularly personal work for Tanja Helena Roscic. She still vividly remembers her first "work of art". In her early childhood she developed a perfume mixed from liquids she found in the kitchen and bathroom. She wanted to recreate her father's presence in an essence after it had disappeared.

The starting point for this activity is a small perfume bottle that her father left in the mirrored cabinet in the bathroom when he left his wife and daughter. Since she applies this fragrance to her neck every night before going to bed, the contents of the bottle are soon used up. Therefore, she decides to remix this fragrance herself, as the longing for her father becomes a never-ending task for her. She wants to revive her father in a bottle as a perfume, so that she can keep him forever. The bottle embodies for her an object in which her father is present. She will not get her father back this way, but she will discover something important for herself.

Later, she realises that her childhood attempt was a transformation, an attempt to give the dishwashing liquid a higher meaning. In her work *Man in the Bottle*, Roscic fabricates a wickerwork as both an empty vessel and a shaped body. This artefact is available to accommodate something "elementary" on an imaginary level: hoping, wanting, wishing.

In 2011, the art critic Laura Arici aptly formulated the following about Roscic: "The artist transforms life moments of what has been seen, thought, felt, loved, hated into visibility. And this is where the quality of this work lies: in the transformation process as a sensitive approach to these moments in life." With her willow work, the artist is now taking a decisive step further: she reveals a vulnerable side of herself, revealing a moment of her life with which she shows us what it means to indulge in longing.

Tanja Helena Roscic (*1980, Zurich, Switzerland) lives and works as a Swiss visual artist with Croatian-Albanian background in Zurich and Zagreb. She studied Bachelor of Arts at the Zurich University of the Arts (2006–2009) and Art History, Film Studies and Eastern European History at University of Zurich (2002–2005). Selected solo exhibitions: Monica De Cardenas, Zuoz (2018); Galerie BolteLang, Zurich (2018); Gysin Studio, Zurich (2017). Selected group exhibitions: EAC Peep Show, Studio Stalder, Zurich (2020); Swiss Art Awards, Basel (2018); Refaire le Monde, Helmhaus, Zurich (2018).

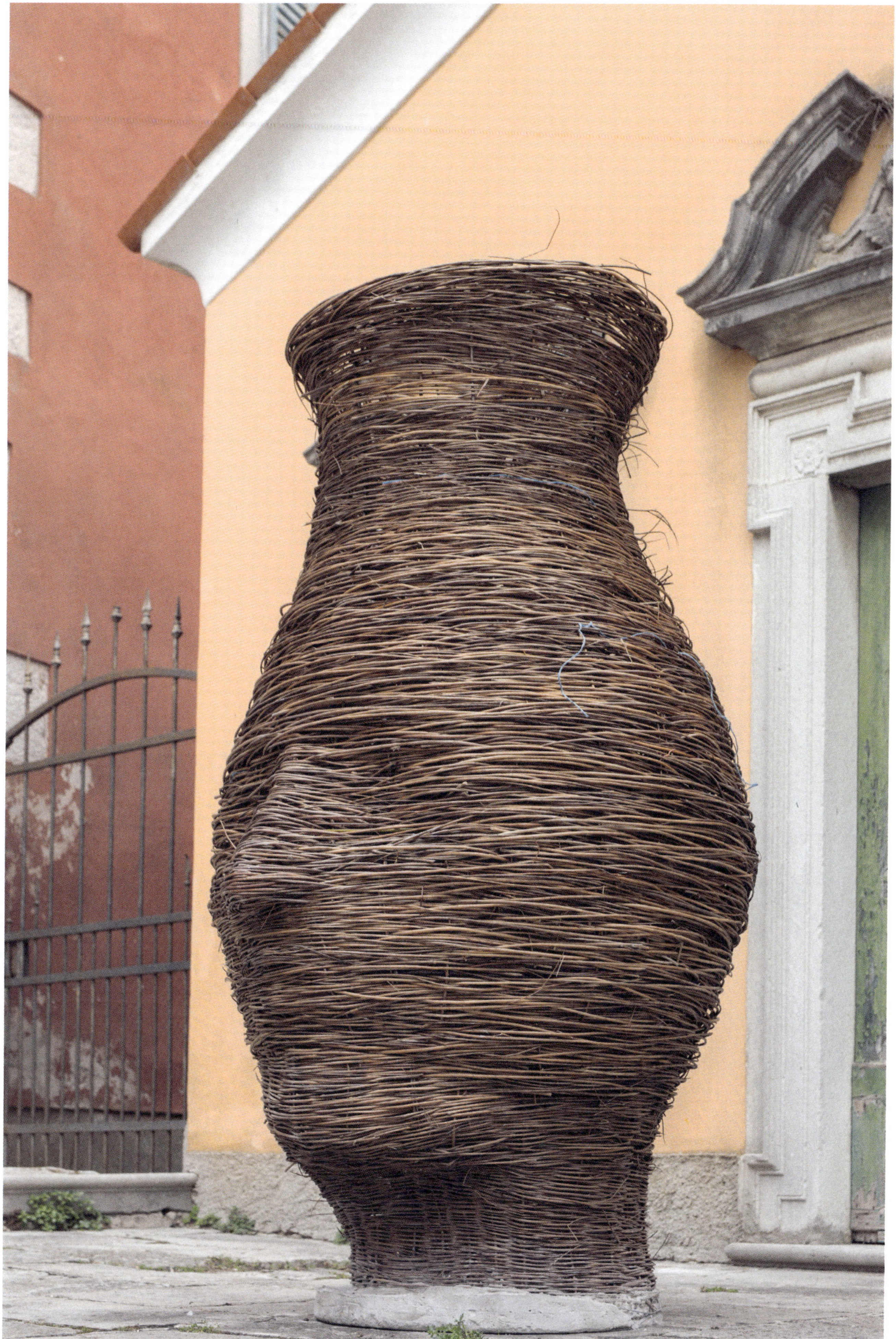

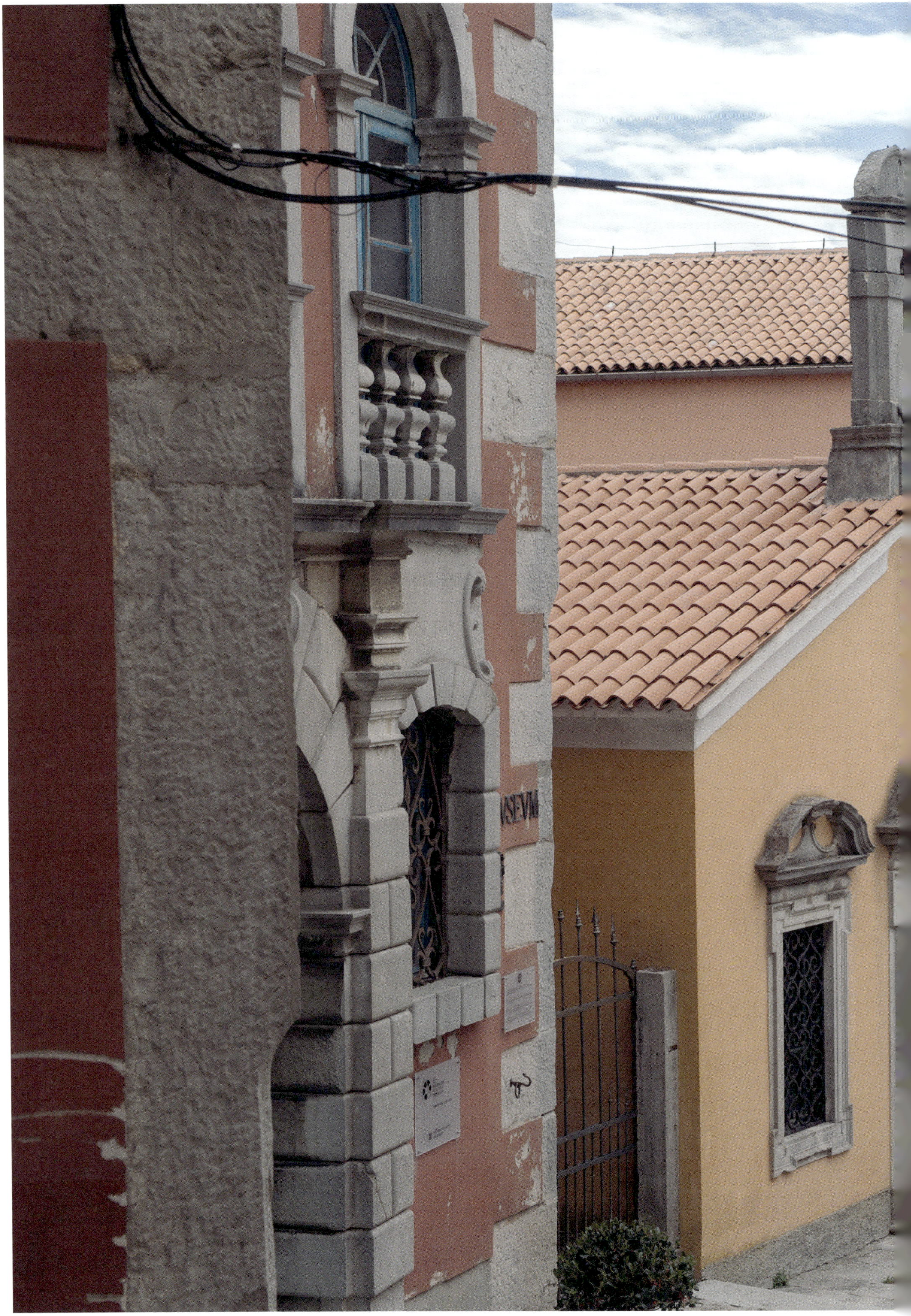

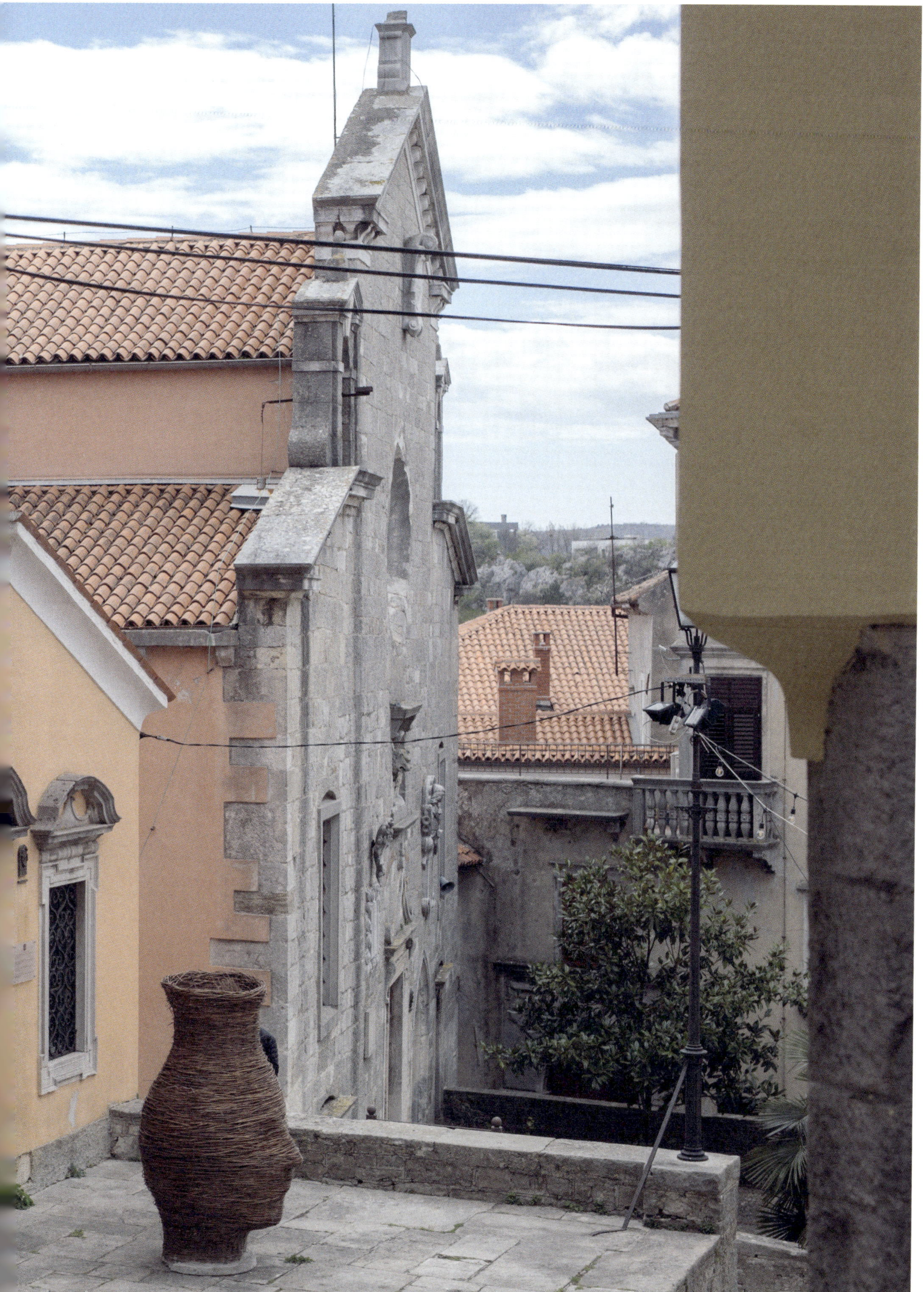

Karin Sander

Point of Interest, 2023 (24)
St. Barbara Church, Raša

LED neon, 420 × 125 cm (double sided)
Courtesy of the artist and Galerie nächst St. Stephan Rosemarie Schwarzwälder, Vienna

The categorisation of art and the art business are Karin Sander's fields of work. She adresses questions and conditions of creation, exhibition, mediation, commercialisation and curating and elevates these aspects to working fields of her own art. Sander became known in the 1990s with her *Wandstücke* (wall pieces) – polished wall surfaces in interior and exterior spaces that recalibrated the idea of the mural painting. Typical of Sander's methodology is also the series of *Mailed Paintings:* the artist sent white primed but unpackaged canvases to exhibition venues all over the world. On these journeys, which artworks usually complete in protective crates, the canvases were marked with traces of transport, "self-writing diaries that record the journey of the work", as the artist explains. "The collected patina exaggerates and mirrors the effect of the passage of time on the surface of the painting and emphasis on the environment of the exhibition and the circumstances surrounding it. Thereby the artwork is constantly in the mode of being exhibited."

The Church of St. Barbara, dedicated to the patron saint of mine workers, is centrally located in Raša. Designed in 1937 by Gustavo Pulitzer Finali, it is not only an idiosyncratic modernist sacred building, but also a monument to the eventful history of the Istrian peninsula. The formal cues for Pulitzer Finali were the everyday objects and tools of mine construction. The nave, for example, is reminiscent of an inverted tipper lorry, the 25-metre-high bell tower is modelled on a miner's lamp, as is the town's coat of arms. The cross on the tower was made from mine rails. At this prominent and highly visible location of analogue culture, Karin Sander has placed the centrepiece of digital localisation: the Google sign "Point of Interest", abbreviated POI. By superimposing, even synthesising globally recognized codes – the cross and the POI – the artist succeeds in building a surprising bridge. On the one hand, a merciless analysis of the analogy of different dogmatisms on time and faith levels and, on the other hand, a playful handling of tourist rituals.

Karin Sander (*1957, Bensberg, Germany) lives and works in Berlin and Zurich. Selected exhibitions: MoMA, New York (1994), Guggenheim Museum, New York (2004, 2011), Schirn Kunsthalle, Frankfurt (2006), Kunstmuseum Stuttgart (2012), ZKM, Karlsruhe (2013), MUDAM, Luxembourg (2014), Galerie für Zeitgenössische Kunst, Leipzig (2017), National Museum of Art, Osaka (2018), Akademie der Künste, Berlin (2019), Kunst Museum Winterthur (2019) Museion, Bolzano (2020), Kunshalle Tübingen (2021).

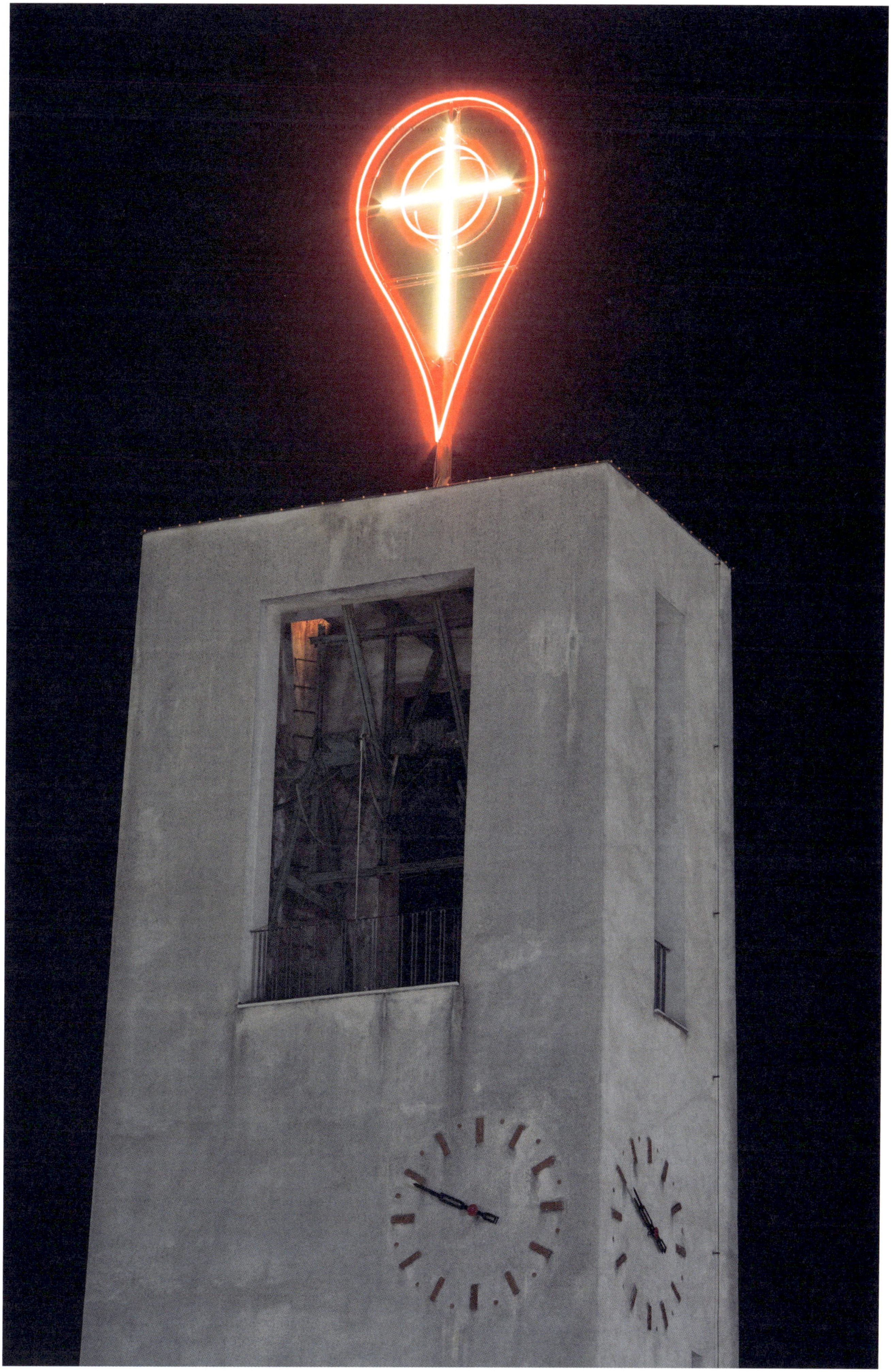

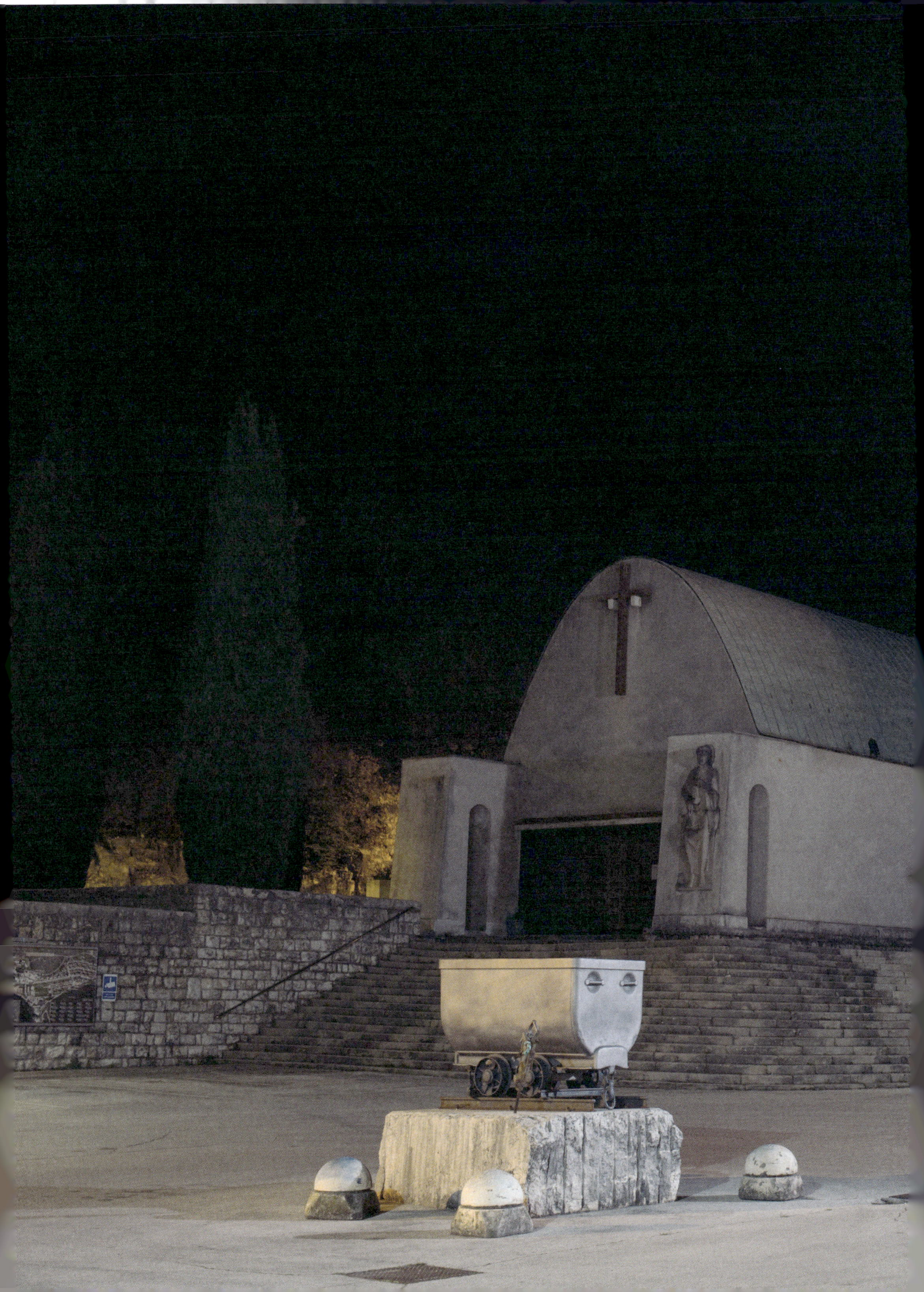

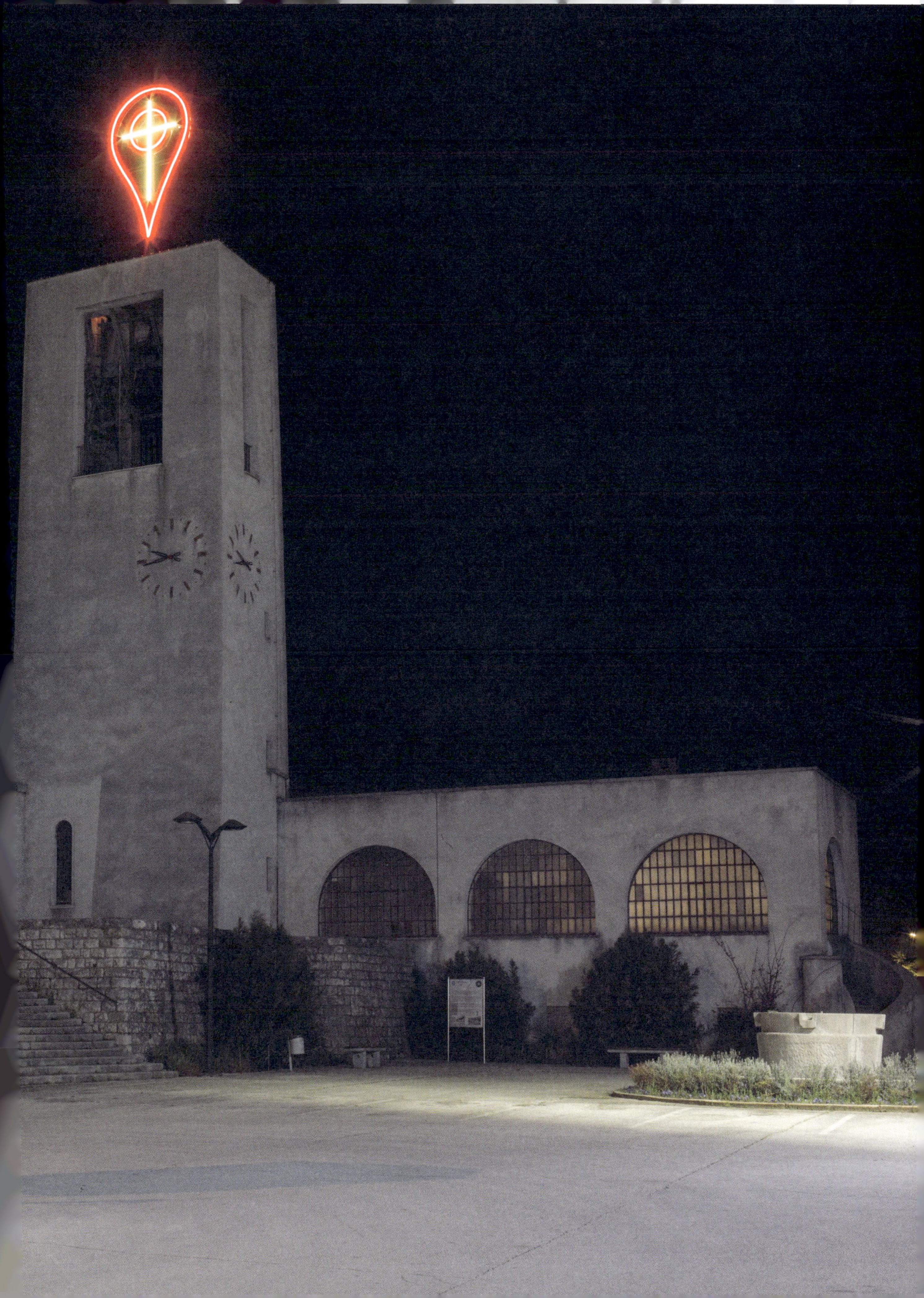

Arcangelo Sassolino

Damnatio Memoriae, 2016/2023 (25)
"4. obrok" canteen, Raša

Marble, steel, hydraulic and electric system
Courtesy of the artist and Galleria Continua, San Gimignano / Galleria dello Scudo, Verona

The expansion and questioning of the common concept of sculpture is Arcangelo Sassolino's central topic. References to Futurism and Arte povera are obvious and formative. In his oeuvre, the Italian artist focuses on industrial materials and processes, on supposedly simple, less artistic methods. His installations and objects explore mechanical processes, material behaviour and physical forces. Each work is the result of intensive research and careful preparation. The results impress, both by their purely physical presence and by forces such as pressure, gravity and friction that act on them and emanate from them in equal measure. Sassolino's works are not functional, but they work and in their functionality lies their beauty. Essential are the deliberately induced moments of reversal and feedback loop: Wood and stone are worked in an iconoclastic rather than sculptural manner. Sassolino's works make highly reduced processes, physical phenomena such as speed, pressure, gravity, friction and controlled danger visible and tangible. He exposes his materials to direct and immediate force, and force thus acquires an artistically overformed perceptibility (in ancient Greek: "aisthesis") as a physical quantity. "I examine the consequences of Modernism on contemporary life," says the artist.

In an empty room of the former cantina in Raša, Sassolino has rebuilt a work that he already developed in 2016 and has now updated for the 4th Industrial Art Biennial: *Damnatio Memoriae*. The artwork consists of two parts, a computer-controlled grinding machine and a stone sculpture – originally a marble torso, in Raša a column fragment made of local limestone. Over the course of the exhibition, the machine will systematically turn the stone sculpture into fine dust, which will settle in the exhibition space as a white surface layer. In the end, nothing remains of the form, everything has been transformed into dust. The title of the work refers to a social sanctioning measure in the Roman Empire – the erasure of a person's memory – but is a modern neologism. In antiquity itself, people still spoke of the "abolitio nominis". The names of particularly despised and hated persons in Rome were erased from all annals, all accessible portraits and inscriptions were destroyed. "It is in the wake of this custom," concludes art critic Caitlin Eyre, "that Sassolino attempts to erase the restrictive idealism of the classical tradition. In this way, the interactions serves as a revolutionary act against the oppressive and restrictive confines of an art historical narrative that prizes the Classical as the finest example of Western art."

Arcangelo Sassolino (*1967, Vicenza, Italy) lives and works in Vicenza. Selected exhibitions: Palais de Tokyo, Paris (2008), *Under Deconstruction*, Tinguely Museum, Basel (2010), MACRO Museo, Rome (2011), MART, Rovereto (2011), Art and the City, Zurich (2012), Frankfurter Kunstverein, Frankfurt (2016), *Artists & Robots*, Grand Palais, Paris (2018), Kunstverein, Hannover (2019), Villa Medici, Rome (2021), Biennale di Venezia (2022).

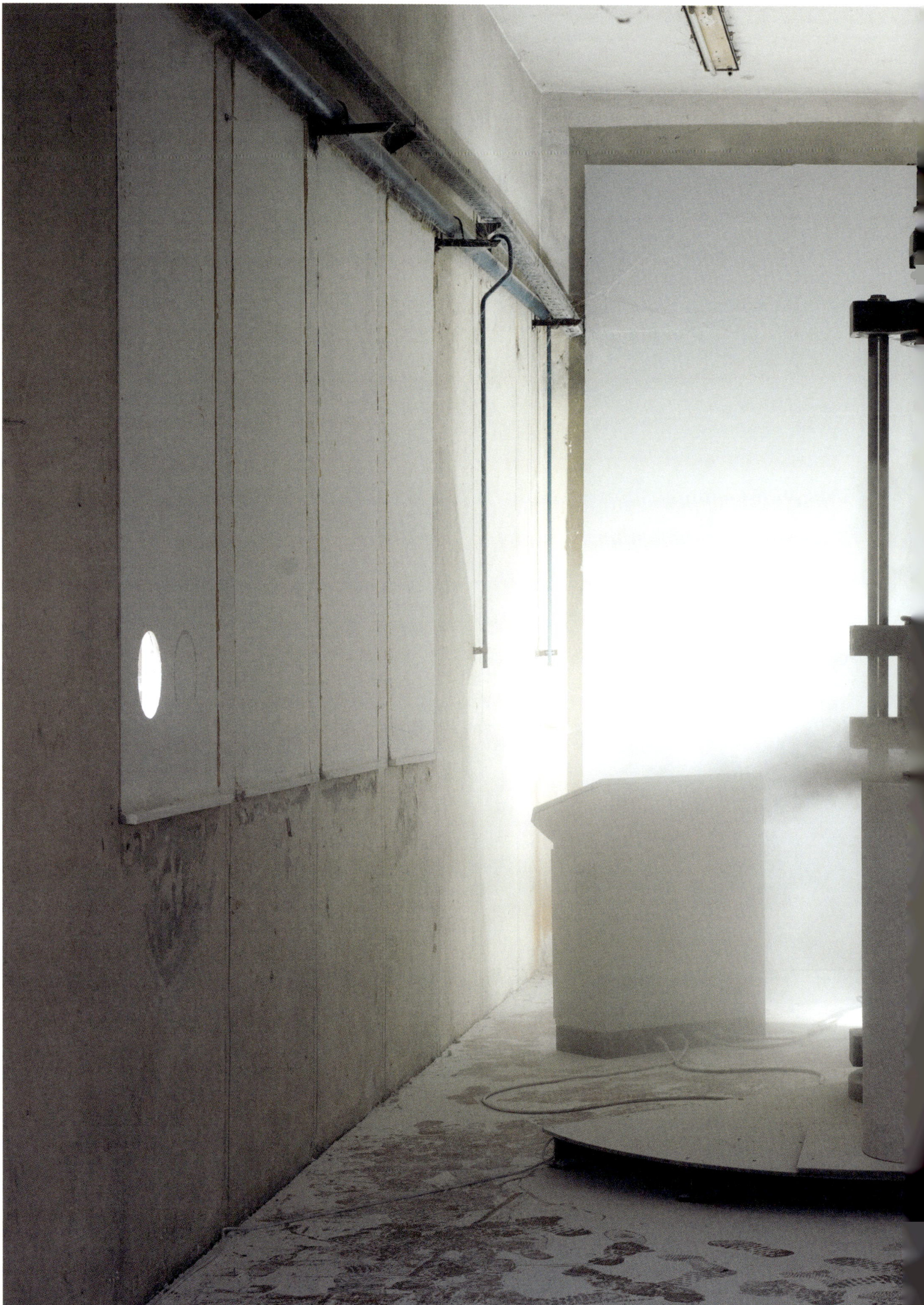

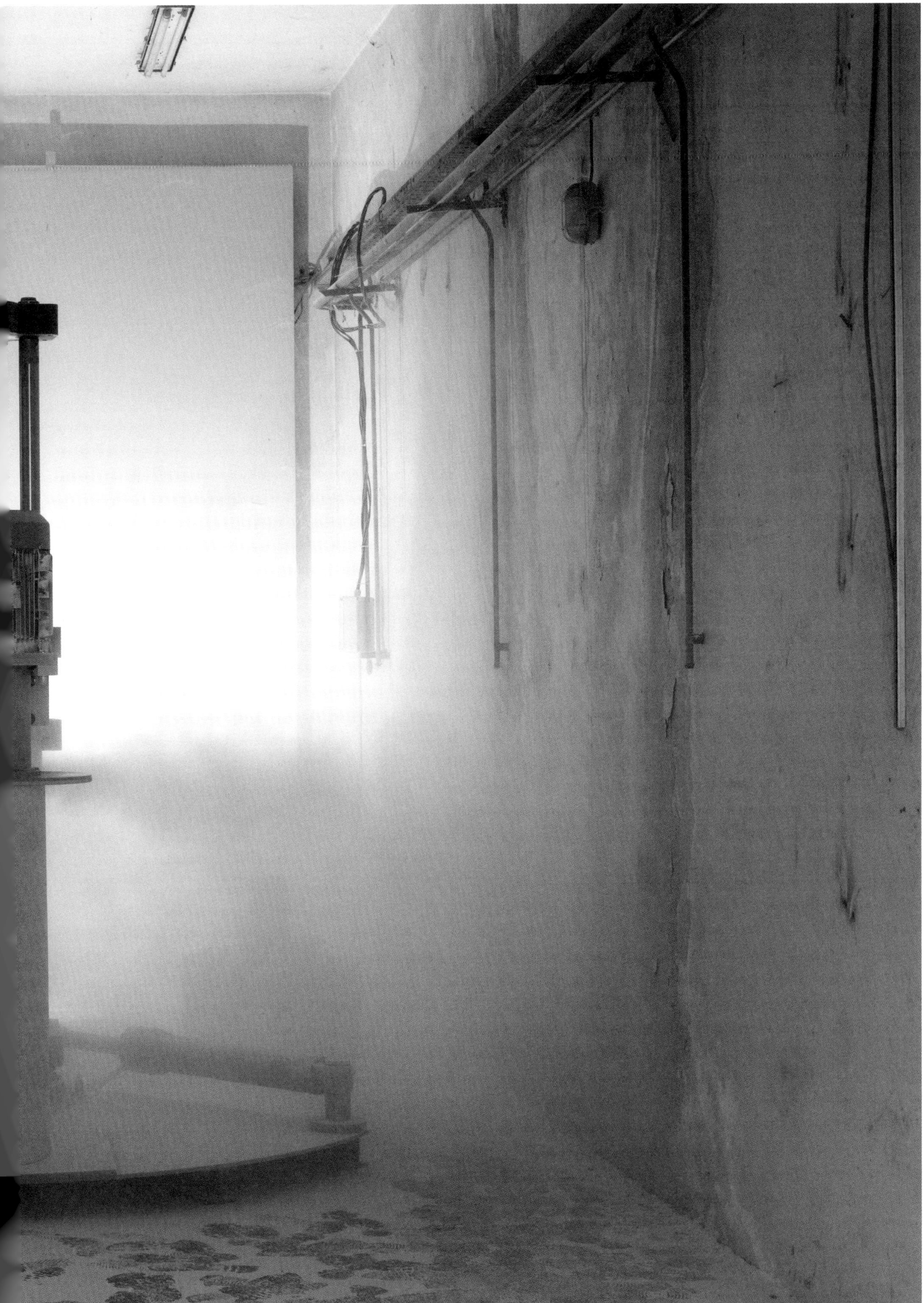

Talaya Schmid

Liquid Cuntry, 2023 (26)
Museum of Modern and Contemporary Art, Rijeka

Detail from environment with site-specific wall painting, mixed media installation
Courtesy of the artist and König Büro, Zurich

Next page: Detail from environment with site specific wall painting, mixed media installation, including *A Tent for Storytelling, Secrets and Kissing*
Courtesy of the artist and König Büro, Zurich

With her space-filling installation *Liquid Cuntry*, Talaya Schmid creates a place where visitors can flow with her works of art, penetrate its elements, be circluded by and interwoven with the *Liquid Cuntry*. It is a celebration of fluidity and change and sets a counterpoint to categorization and borders. A boardwalk leads to a tent past one of the tufted work *Infinite Pool of Love and Juices*. Underneath is a freezer with so called Rocket Ice Cream. Guests are invited to lick a popsicle while strolling through the environment. The 20-minute soundscape *Body Fluids* is part of the installation in form of a surround sound experience. This is a collaboration with the music producer and DJ Belia Winnewisser. A mixture of explicit love poems, personal stories and sounds of water that flows, drips and splashes.

Talaya Schmid's immersive environment is a homage to the cunt and all its liquids. Cunt is an ancient term that encompasses the whole gynecological sexuality and anatomy, external and internal, including labia, vulva, pudendum, vagina, and clitoris. Thus, it accounts for and allows female sexual pleasure. Etymologically, Cunt connects to kin, kinship, cunning, thought, cognate, cognitive, knowing, knowledge, king, queen and country. It has very positive, powerful roots and is about 2400 years old. The artist painted on a museum wall the mysterious figure of "Sheela na gig", she is the embodiment of big vagina energy.

Talaya Schmid sees the reappropriation of this positive and life-affirming, original meaning of the word Cunt as an empowering and healing act. Connected to this is also a social attitude towards this body part, towards women and sexuality. We learn sexual behaviour and gender performance, thus, they are both part of our cultural production and we must take them seriously and value them like we value other forms of culture. In this regard, seeking sensual, sexual and societal healing, becomes a political act by exploring the role of intimacy, individual freedom, and artistic practice.

In Talaya Schmid's *Lebenskunstwerk* we enter a landscape of desire. It is not a possessive-sexual, but it is an erotic-aesthetic desire. While possessive desire is virtually blind to the individuality of the other person, eroticism is different. It "gives us the power", writes the author Audrey Lorde, "to change things in the world." Talaya Schmid gives us the moment to experience erotic desire with all our senses.

Talaya Schmid (*1983, Zurich, Switzerland) is a playful feminist artist, activist and art lecturer. She uses tufting, originally a technique for rug-making, to create colourful soft sculptures, sculptural fashion and fluffy murals. She is a performance artist using her voice, sounds and storytelling to create immersive and welcoming spaces. Talaya Schmid is co-founder and curator of Porny Days, an annual film and art festival on sexualities and gender held in Zurich since 2012. In 2013 she finished her Master of Fine Arts at Goldsmith University of London. From 2013 to 2017, she was the publishing director of the comic magazine Strapazin, where she she was an editor and president of the association until 2022. In 2014, Talaya Schmid cooked at the canteen at the F+F School of Art and Design, where she subsequently worked as an assistant and tutor in the Fine Arts program from 2015 to 2019.

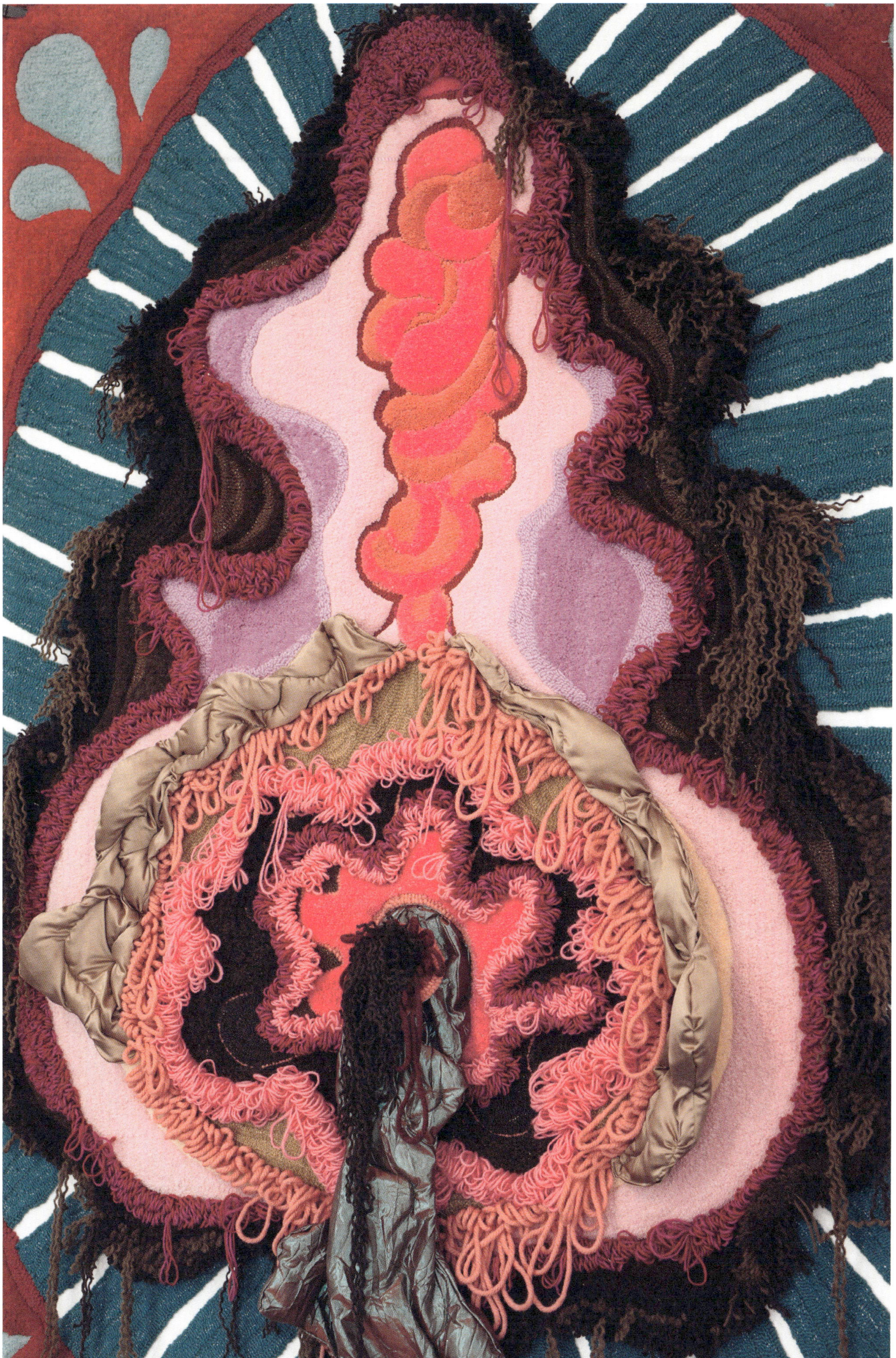

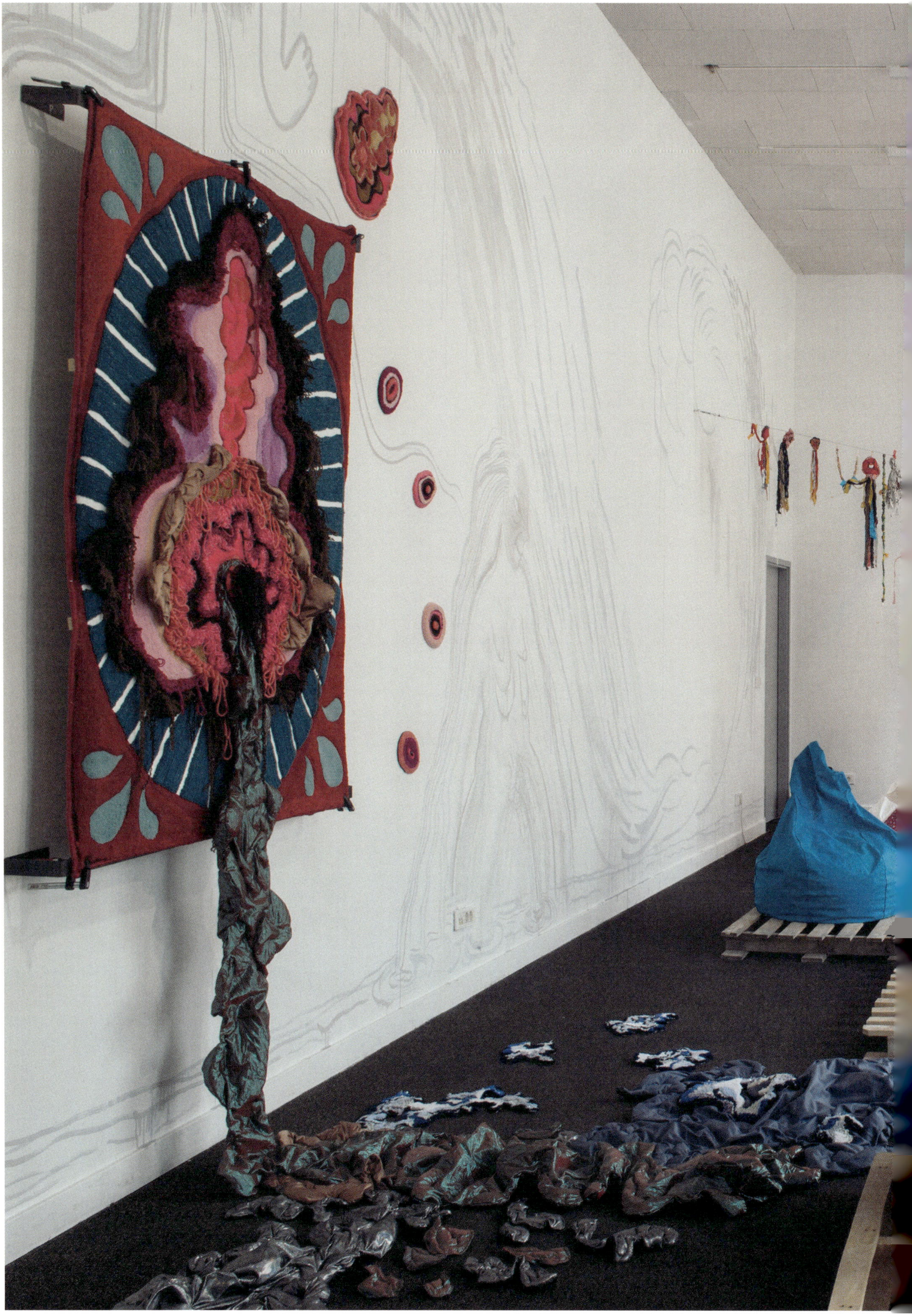

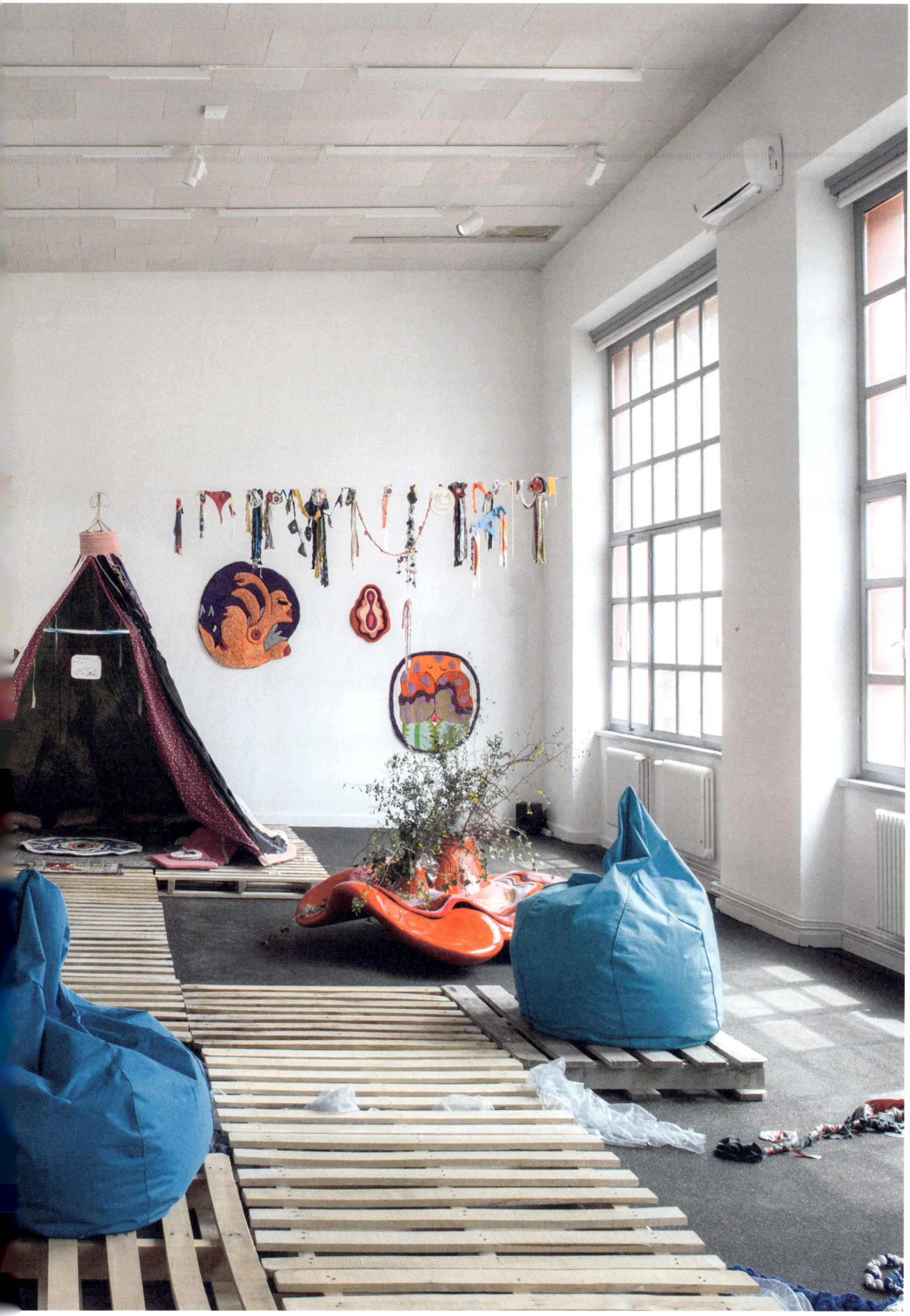

Natalia Stachon

Neither ends nor begins, 2021 (27)
Lamparna, Labin

What influence do built spaces have on the reality of our lives? What architectural traces that continue to shape us are left by past eras and generations? How do we deal with physical experiences in monumental contexts? How does power manifest itself in architecture? The conceptual artist Natalia Stachon, who comes from Poland and lives in Berlin, deals with all these relevant questions in her multi-layered oeuvre. She examines the relationship between space and the individual, the impact of consciously developed, architectural stagings. Stachon: "In my works, I repeatedly invert the everyday, pragmatic, loud and bright elements of human infrastructure into their opposite. They then appear as if shock-frozen. In the silence and concentration of these transformations, the viewer can reassemble the found elements in his or her mind and in this way draw completely different conclusions about the relationship between space, people, architecture, mobility and perception."

Absolutist, totalitarian, centralist or monotheistic cultures tend to erect particularly representative architectures in order to convey the (meta-) physical interpretive sovereignty of the system to the public in a meaningful way. Even democratic states cannot refrain from endowing their schools, courts, parliaments, hospitals or museums with special design symbolic power in order to refer to the state-bearing significance of the buildings. As a result of its chequered history, the Istrian peninsula is littered with monumental buildings – military relics and testimonies to ruling or feudalistic systems from all possible epochs from antiquity to the present day. Stachon has defined a series of eight exemplary subjects from this rich field of investigation. She had photographic templates made of these objects, which were taken at night so as not to lose focus through everyday effects. Based on these templates, the artist finally created charcoal and chalk drawings that show the place as a pure form: deserted, brutal, powerful. A haunting atmosphere emerges from the seriality of these backdrops, actual places of power of the system. Curator Dorothea Strauss aptly sums up this extraordinary interaction between image and viewer of Natalia Stachon's works: "Stachon stages an atmosphere of attention in which both the works themselves and their relation to space and audience create intense experiences."

Natalia Stachon (*1976, Katowice, Poland) lives and works in Berlin. Her works have been exhibited in many solo and group exhibitions, e.g. at Tate Modern, London (2010), Haus Konstruktiv, Zurich (2011/10), Bundeskunsthalle, Bonn (2013), n.b.k., Berlin (2015), Centre of Contemporary Art, Torun (2016), Konrad Adenauer Stiftung, Berlin (2016), ZKM, Karlsruhe (2019), Daimler Contemporary, Berlin (2020), Kunstverein Springerhof, Neuenkirchen (2020/21).

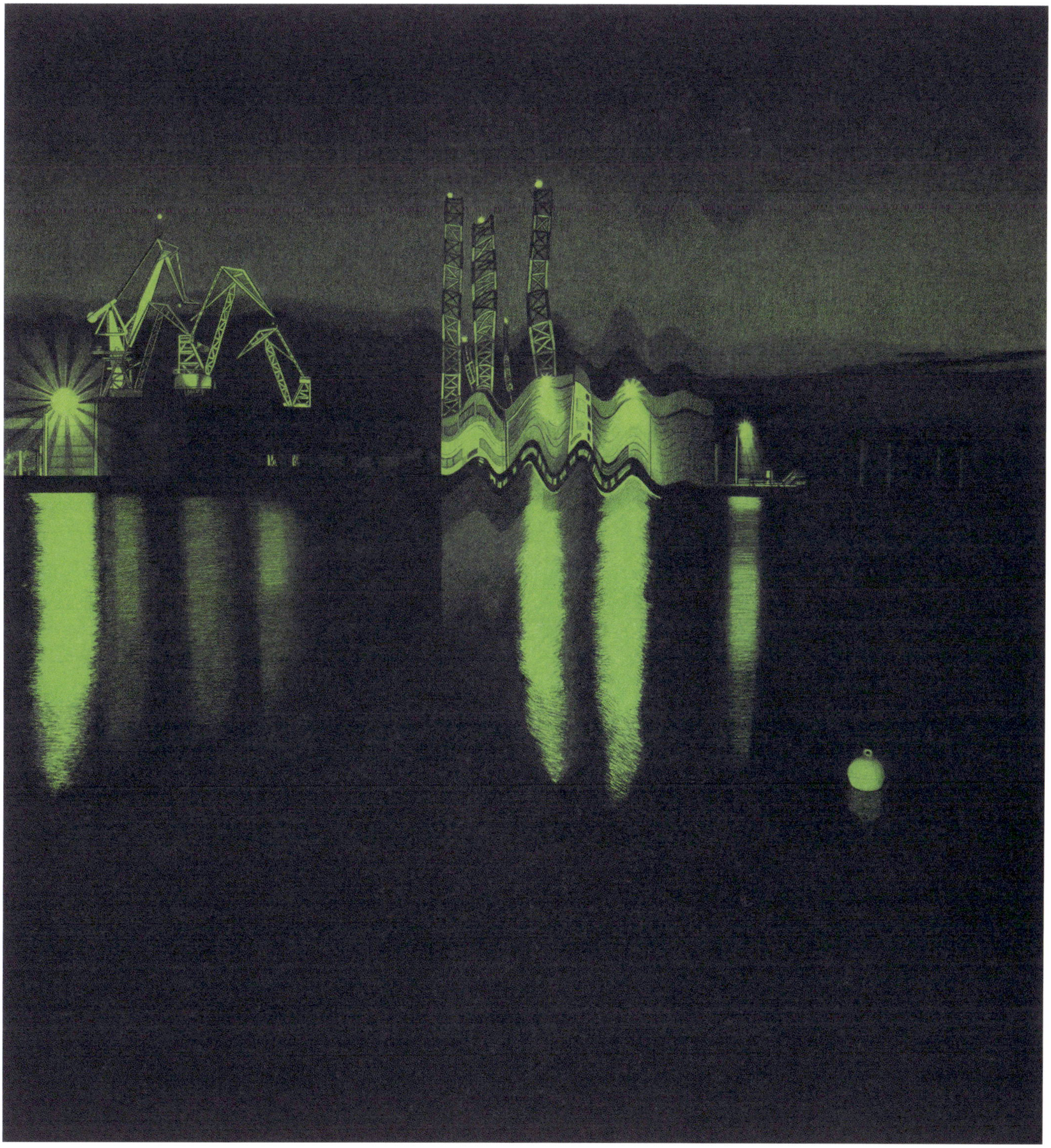

Neither ends nor begins 04, 2021
Charcoal, crayon and pastel on paper
mounted on Alu-Dibond, 114 × 121 cm
Courtesy of the artist and LOOCK Galerie, Berlin

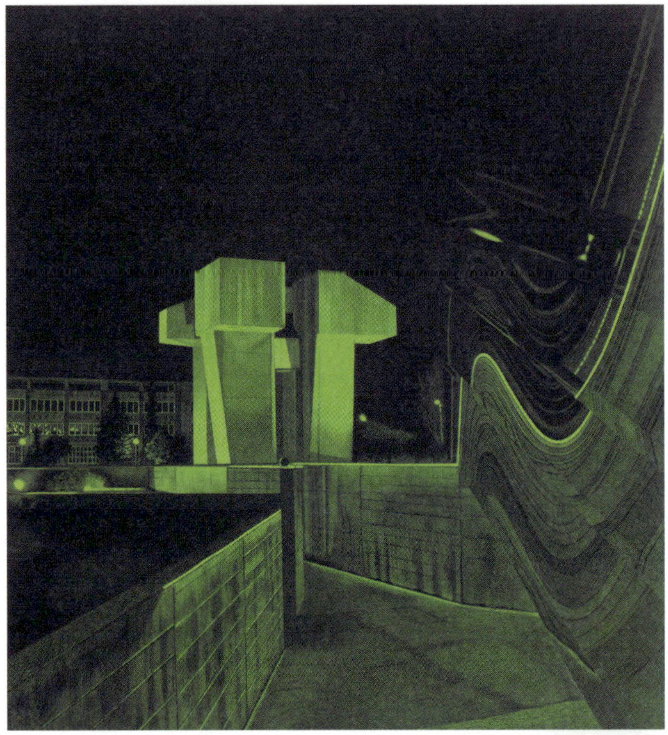

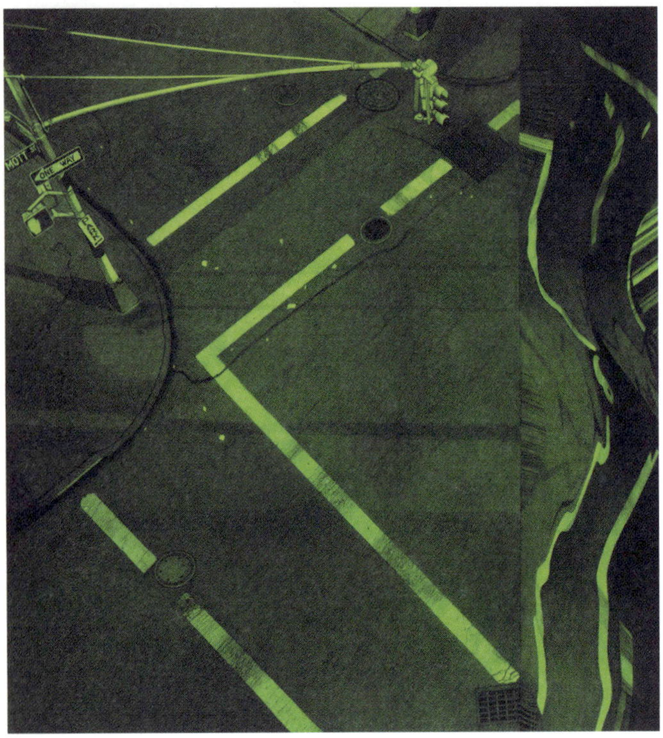

Neither ends nor begins 04, 2021
Charcoal, crayon and pastel on paper mounted on Alu-Dibond, 114 × 121 cm
Courtesy of the artist and LOOCK Galerie, Berlin

Neither ends nor begins 08, 2022
Charcoal, crayon and pastel on paper mounted on Alu-Dibond, 114 × 121 cm
Courtesy of the artist and LOOCK Galerie, Berlin

Neither ends nor begins 11, 2022
Charcoal, crayon and pastel on paper mounted on Alu-Dibond, 114 × 121 cm
Courtesy of the artist and LOOCK Galerie, Berlin

Neither ends nor begins 09, 2022
Charcoal, crayon and pastel on paper mounted on Alu-Dibond, 114 × 121 cm
Courtesy of the artist and LOOCK Galerie, Berlin

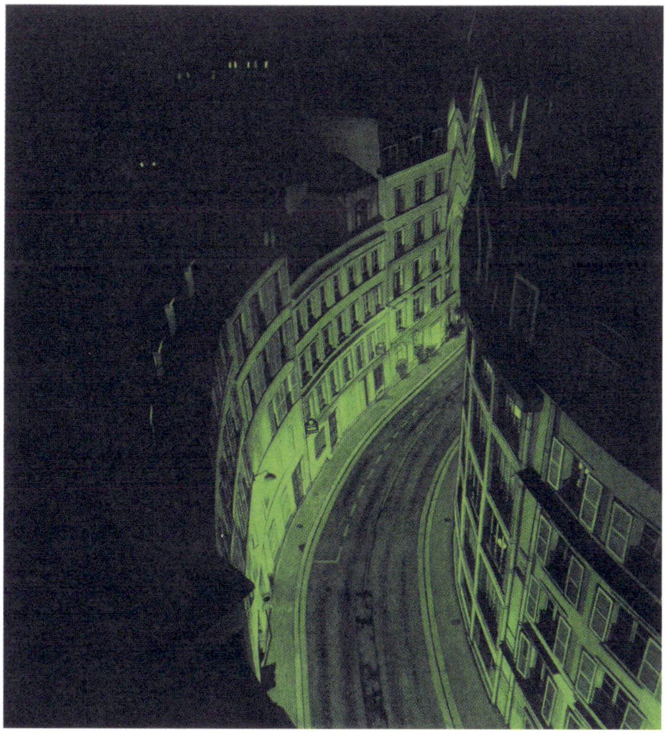

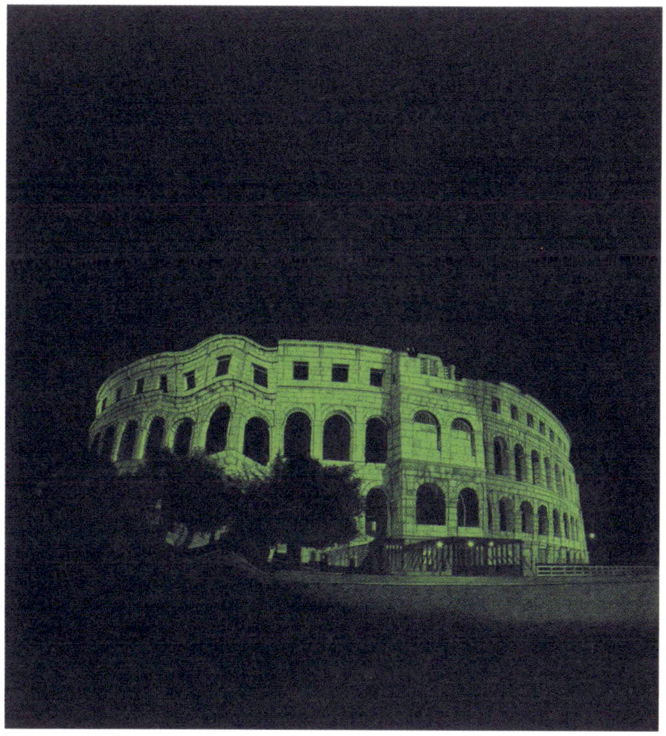

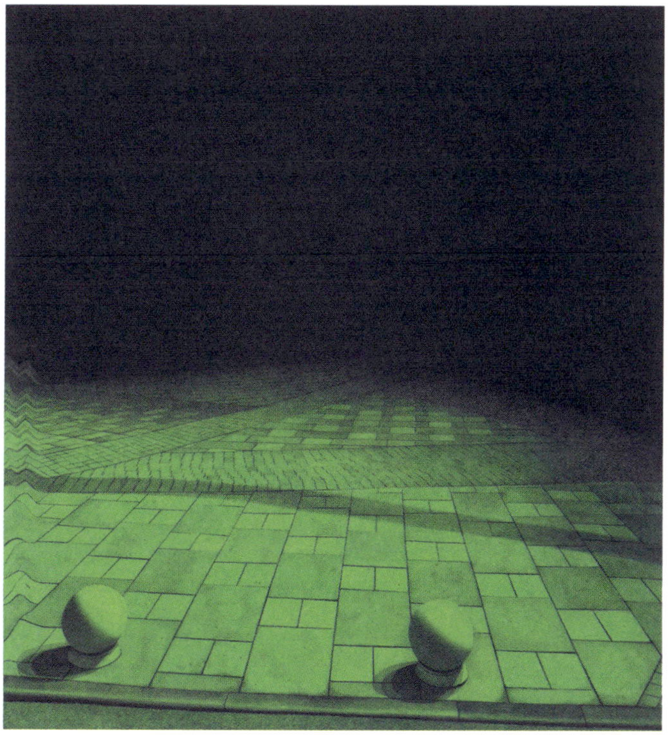

Neither ends nor begins 12, 2023
Charcoal, crayon and pastel on paper mounted on Alu-Dibond, 114 × 121 cm
Courtesy of the artist and LOOCK Galerie, Berlin

Neither ends nor begins 14, 2023
Charcoal, crayon and pastel on paper mounted on Alu-Dibond, 114 × 121 cm
Courtesy of the artist and LOOCK Galerie, Berlin

Neither ends nor begins 13, 2023
Charcoal, crayon and pastel on paper mounted on Alu-Dibond, 114 × 121 cm
Courtesy of the artist and LOOCK Galerie, Berlin

Stefanos Tsivopoulos

History Zero, 2013
Pijacal, Labin

(28)

The film *History Zero* depicts the experiences of three people, with very different conceptions of the value of money. A young immigrant from Africa wanders around in the streets of Athens pushing a supermarket trolley and collecting scrap metal. A foreign artist that visits Athens seeking inspiration for a new artwork in the confusing landscape of the city. And an elderly art collector who suffers from dementia due to Alzheimer's disease and lives all alone in her museum-like house surrounded by works of contemporary art. The film's narrative explores the effect that monetary exchange can have in human relations and the political and social implications. Gregory Sholette aptly writes that Stefanos Tsivopoulos is almost „reinterpreting Marx's famous formula M-C-M (money-commodity-money) as M-M-M (memory-money-memory). The three episodes of *History Zero* do not resolve the artist's inquiry into art and capital, but rather keep it in suspension."

It is worth taking a look at the way Tsivopoulos works, about which the artist says the following in an interview with Katerina Gregos: „Cinema and television often conceal their techniques in favour of privileging the message, whereas in many of my works the process or technique by which television is constructed becomes the content. I am thus mainly concerned with the structure, or language if you prefer, of the moving image and how the language that is so constructed gains credibility. I'd like here to draw attention to what I find fascinating in moving image and image-making in general: the aura of authenticity."

According to Walter Benjamin, aura is a "strange web of time and space, an apparition of a distance, however close it may be". On the other hand, authenticity is the result of checking the true value of an object. Although these concepts may seem quite contradictory, they are far more closely related than one might initially think. When Tsivopoulos speaks of the aura of the authentic, he means both the appreciative moment in relation to the world of images and that our perception of this world of images activates our authenticity. In this case, the aura of authenticity is lived aesthetic experience of desire.

Stefanos Tsivopoulos (*1973, Prague, Czech Republic) is an interdisciplinary artist, film-maker, educator, and organizer living and working between New York, Amsterdam, and Athens. His art practice is driven by a sense of urgency to examine the anthropological dimension of global crises in the economy, immigration, and the environment. He exhibited extensively in art institutions worldwide, including the biennials of Athens, Beijing, Budapest, Limerick, Manifesta, Moscow, Thessaloniki, Venice, Xinjiang, the Riga Quadrennial, and the Documenta 14, Kassel. He represented Greece at the 55th Venice Biennale with *History Zero*, a film in three episodes and an archive. Tsivopoulos teaches contemporary video at The New School in New York and at Piet Zwart Institute in Rotterdam. He's the initiator and co-director of the pedagogical platform Artists for Artists.

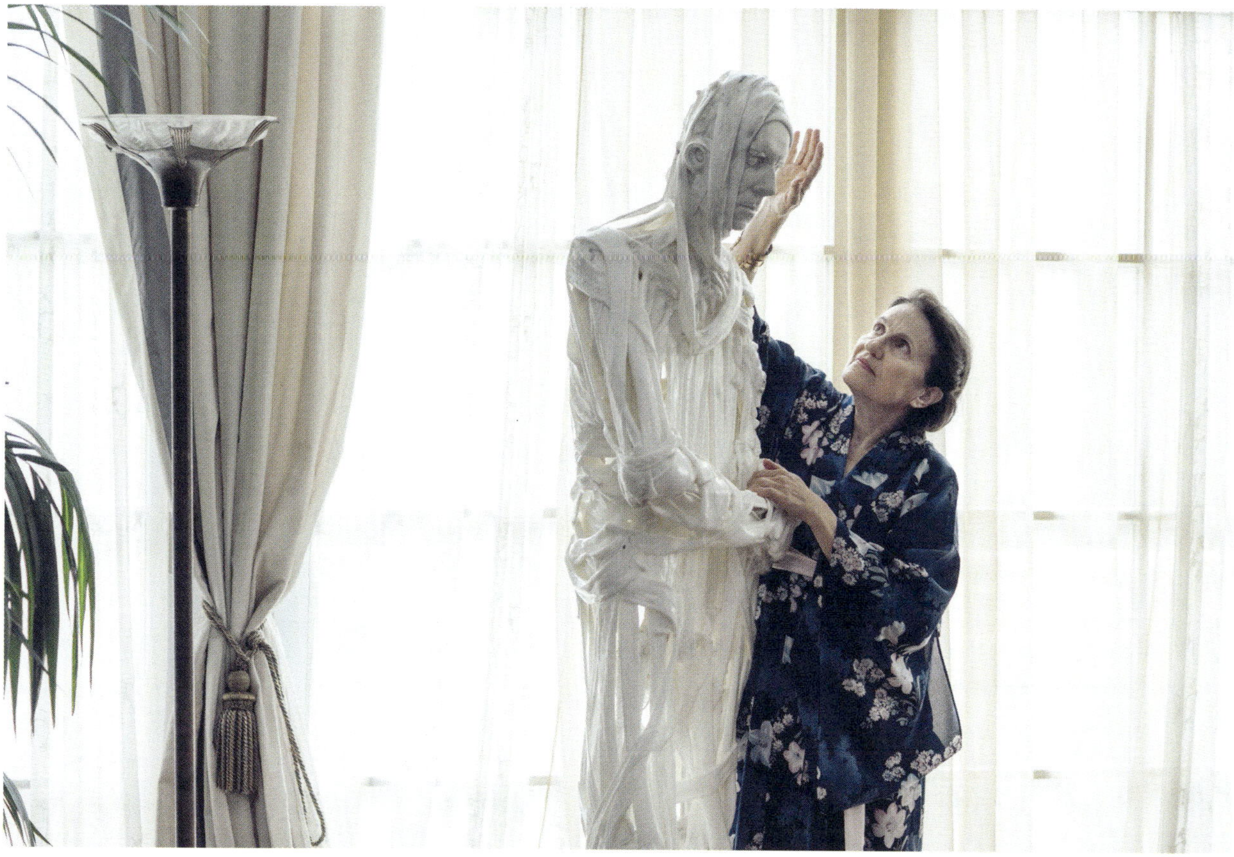

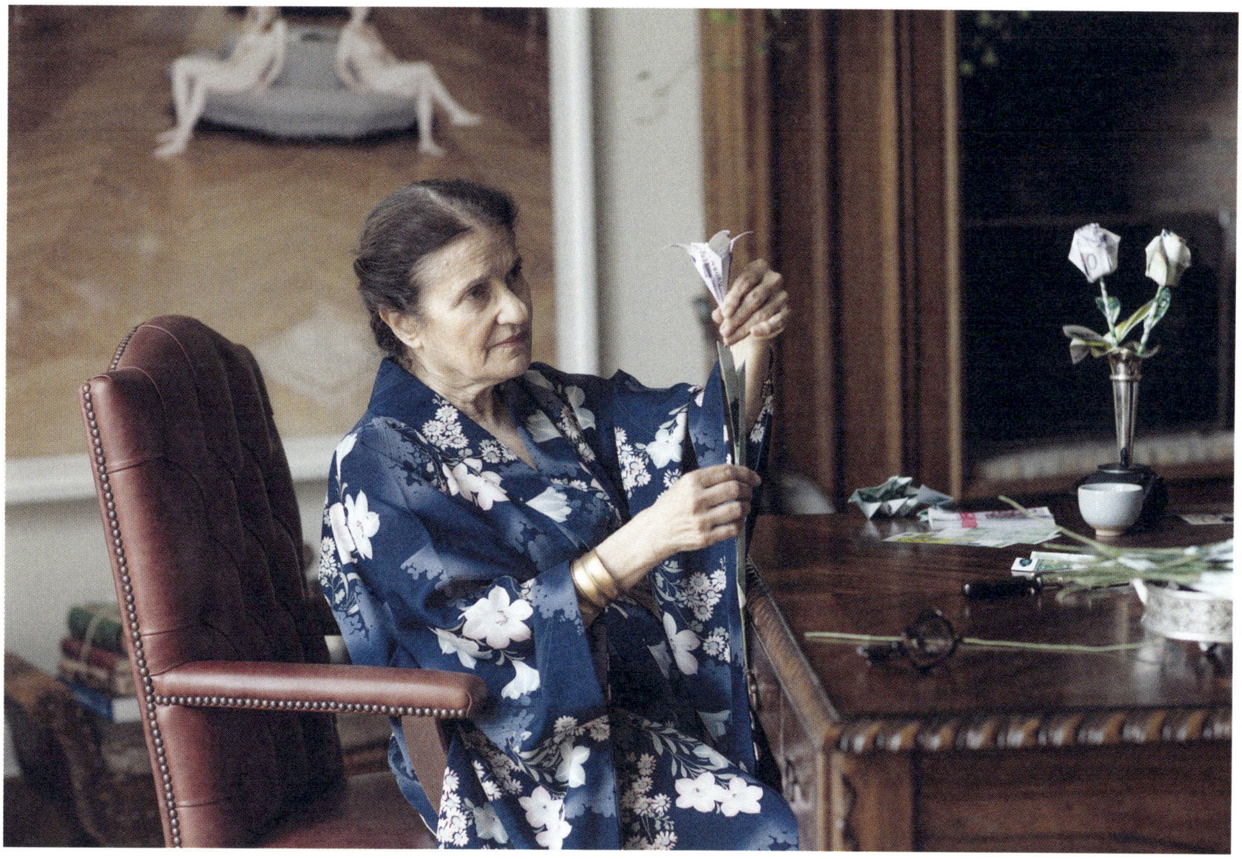

History Zero, 2013
Video stills of a film in three episodes, presented as a three-chanel video installation.
Duration of each episode: 11 min.

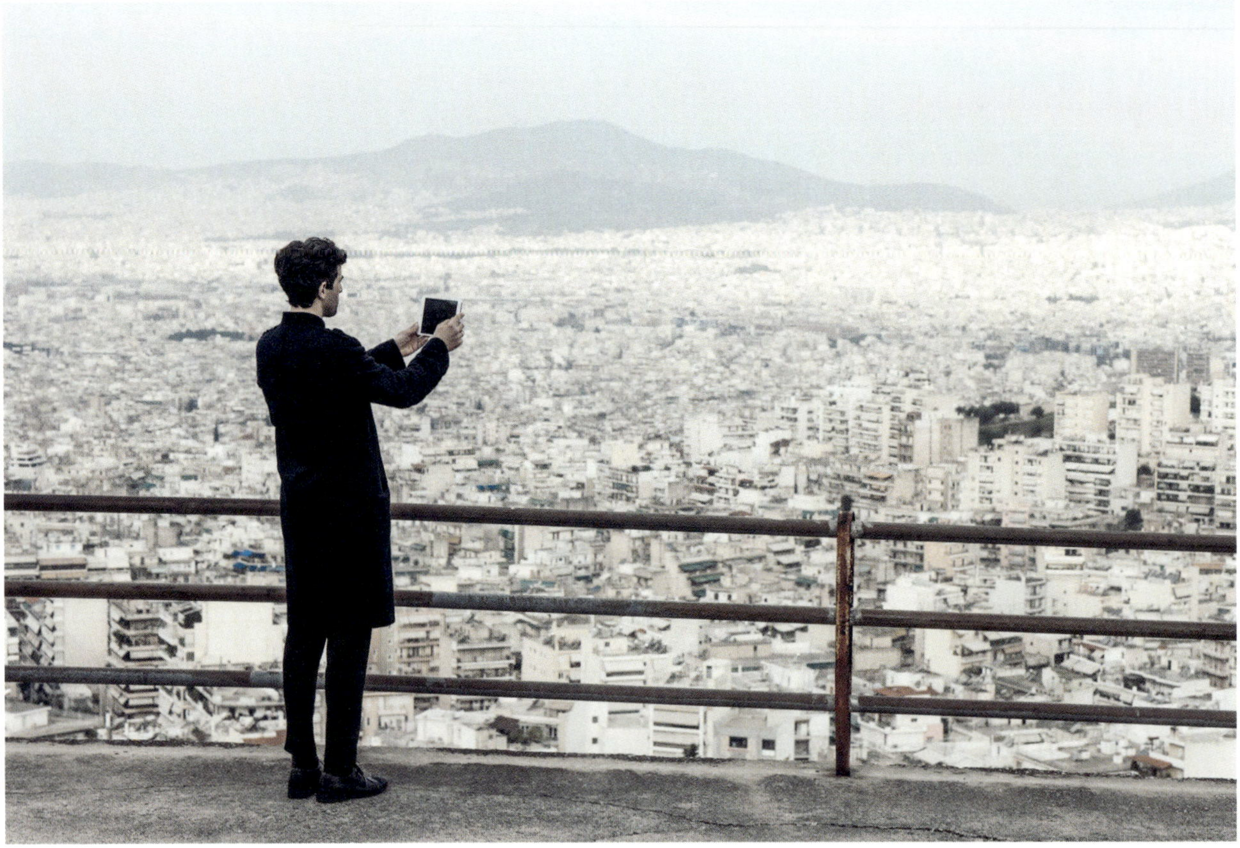

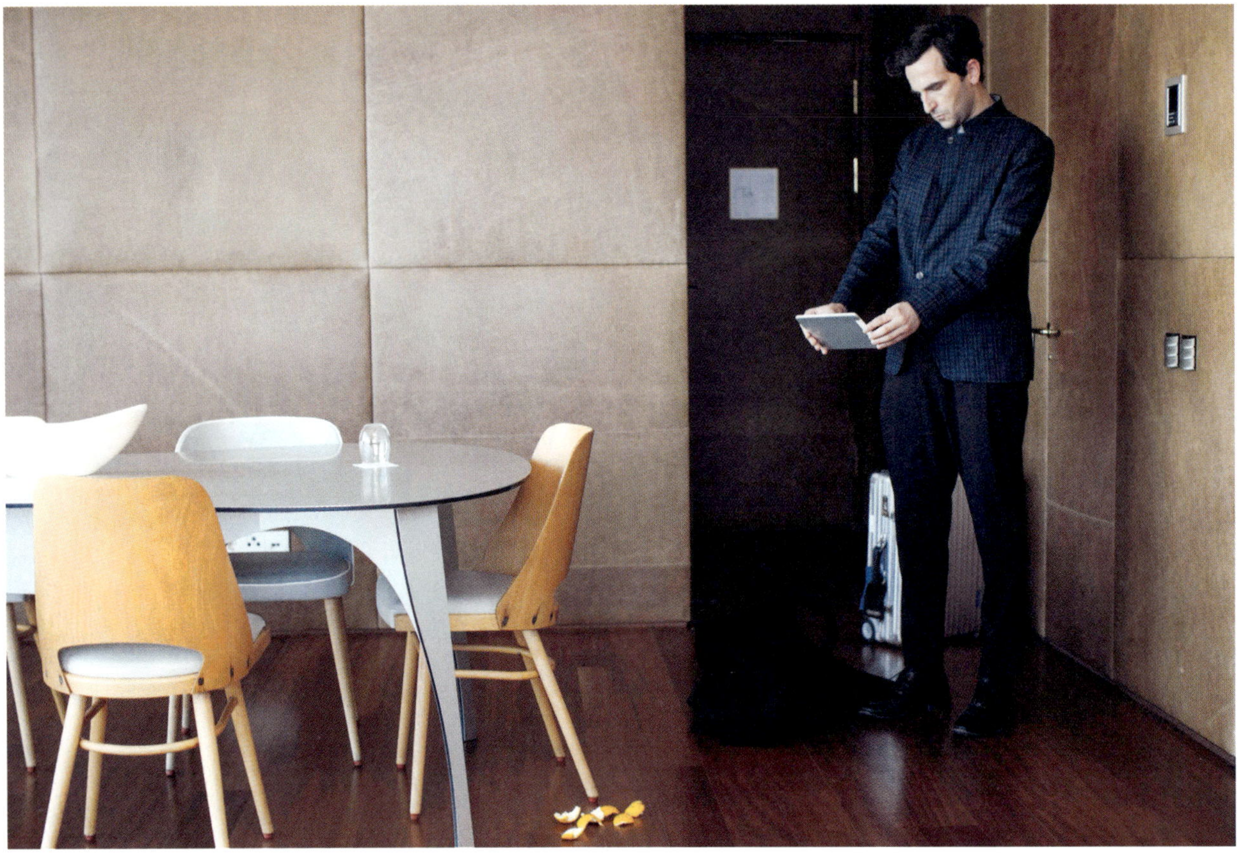

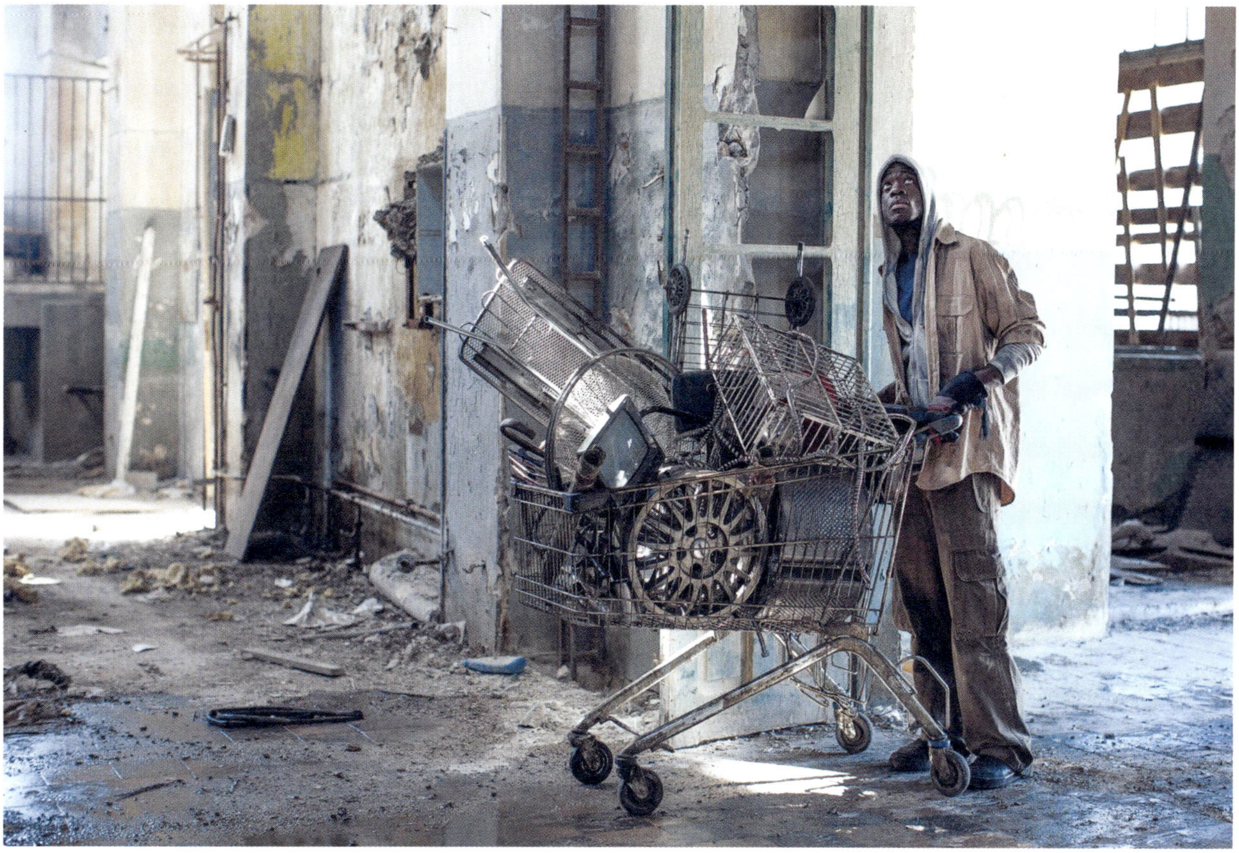

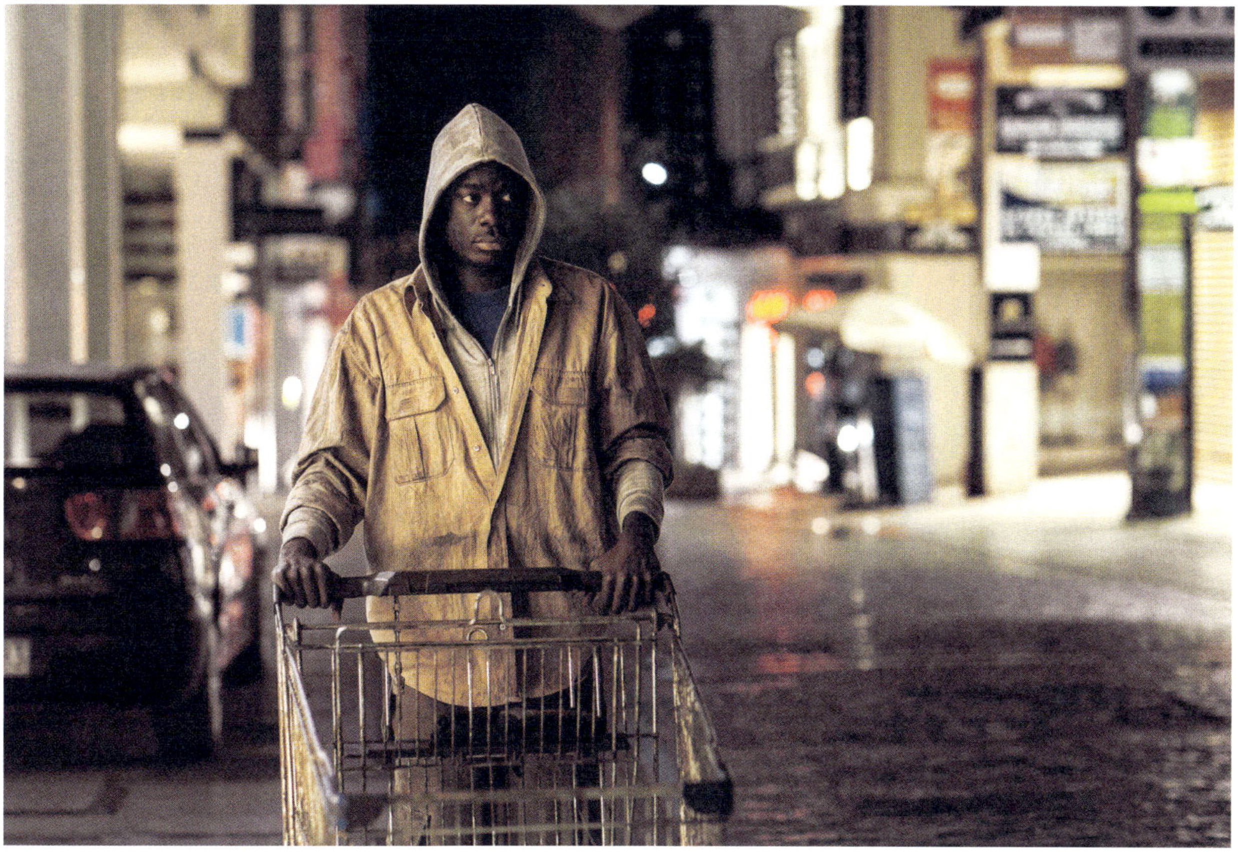

Viktor Zahtila

Sleeping Beauty, 2023 (29)
Pijacal, Labin

The homoerotic view has the freedom to fundamentally understand everything from the perspective of being different. As a result, relationships, circumstances and one's own perception always appear to be changeable. The consequences that result from the awareness of being different can be implemented in the political and social spheres, but also within art. This is the case with Viktor Zahtila in the context of his film work, who, as a gay artist, consciously relies on the homoerotic gaze as a generator of fantasies. Zahtila says: "Every sexual fantasy reflects a personal history. It's a collage of memories, exposures, impressions and exerted pressures that insist on arousing us. Those inspired by love and camaraderie can feel liberating and light; those twisted by repression can feel like a plague."

One can certainly say that an enormous emancipatory potential can be combined with a homoerotic view and gay concerns. Seen in this way, homosexual themes in art not only have a political, but also a progressive function. Achieving this realisation was a rocky road for Viktor Zahtila, as he explains: "Since I was a kid, this world taught me that being gay is reducible to sex – men fucking men. Some weaponize this impoverished concept to stigmatize and persecute us; others think they mean well when they say that we are just like them, human after all, and if they prick us, do we not bleed? (Bleed a little, won't you dear?)"

A homosexual individual first has to find his or her specific perspective, since their upbringing has primarily made them heterosexual. One problem is that the acquired identity has nothing to do with his suddenly discovered identity. That is, it oscillates between two different identities. In this space lies the key to freedom. First of all, though, this is a space for loneliness and frustration. You first have to realise and then learn to be "different from the others" in order to experience it positively. Zahtila comments: "We often internalize and act upon this double image: on the one hand chasing after a pipe dream of the conventional relationship and on the other an elusive feeling of emotional fulfilment and perfect bliss that always feels just around the corner, between the buttocks of somebody that looks for the very same thing." Zahtila describes his attitude as follows: "I'm still there, trying to find my bearings."

Viktor Zahtila (*1984, Labin, Croatia) lives and works in Zagreb. He studied Bachelor of Arts at the Academy of Dramatic Arts in Zagreb (2015–2018) and Master of Arts at The Netherlands Film Academy – The Amsterdam University of the Arts (2019–2021). He works since 2007 as independent filmmaker and since 2010 as media producer for Labin Art Express XXI. Since 2007 he is freelance journalist for various employers. His work as a film director is dedicated to the creation of experimental pornographic video works that show fully fleshed human beings with emotional depth and curiosity. He has been an LGBT activist from his teens.

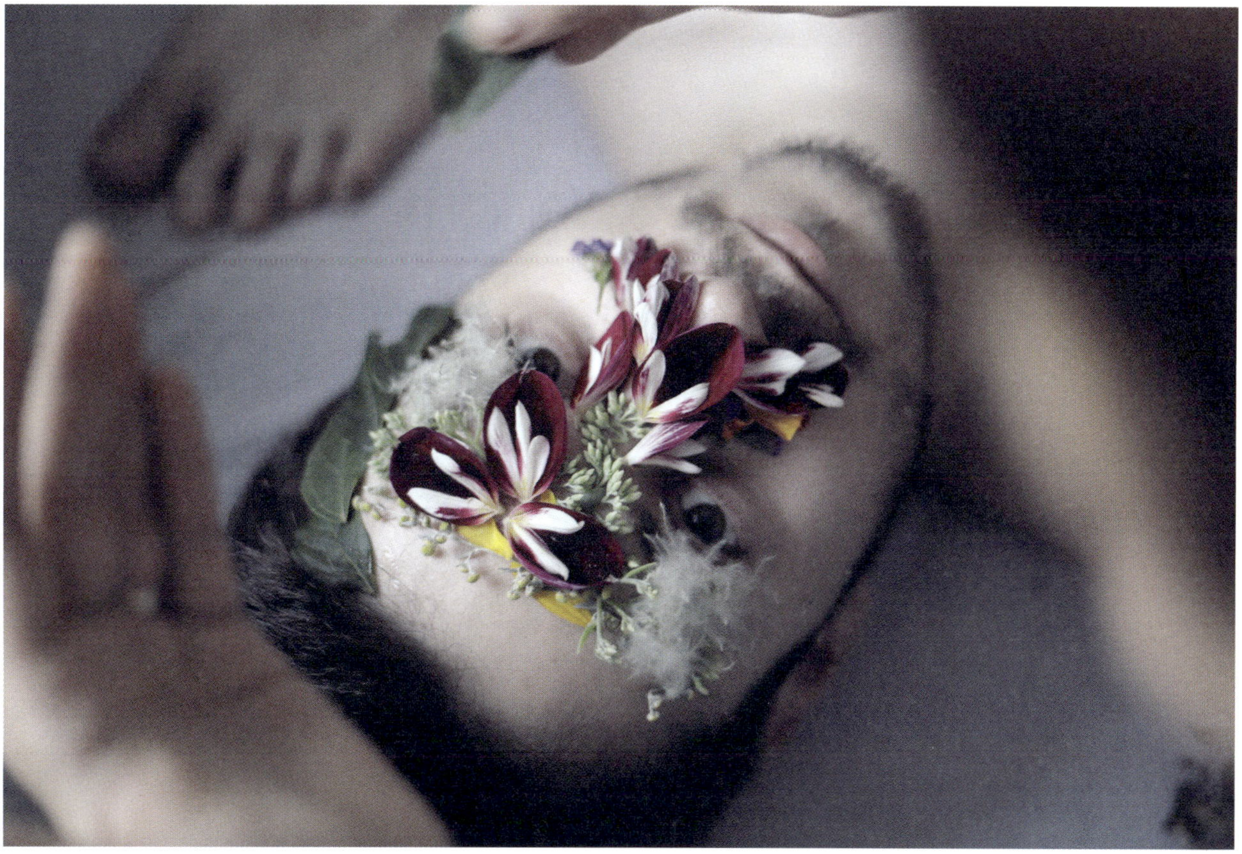

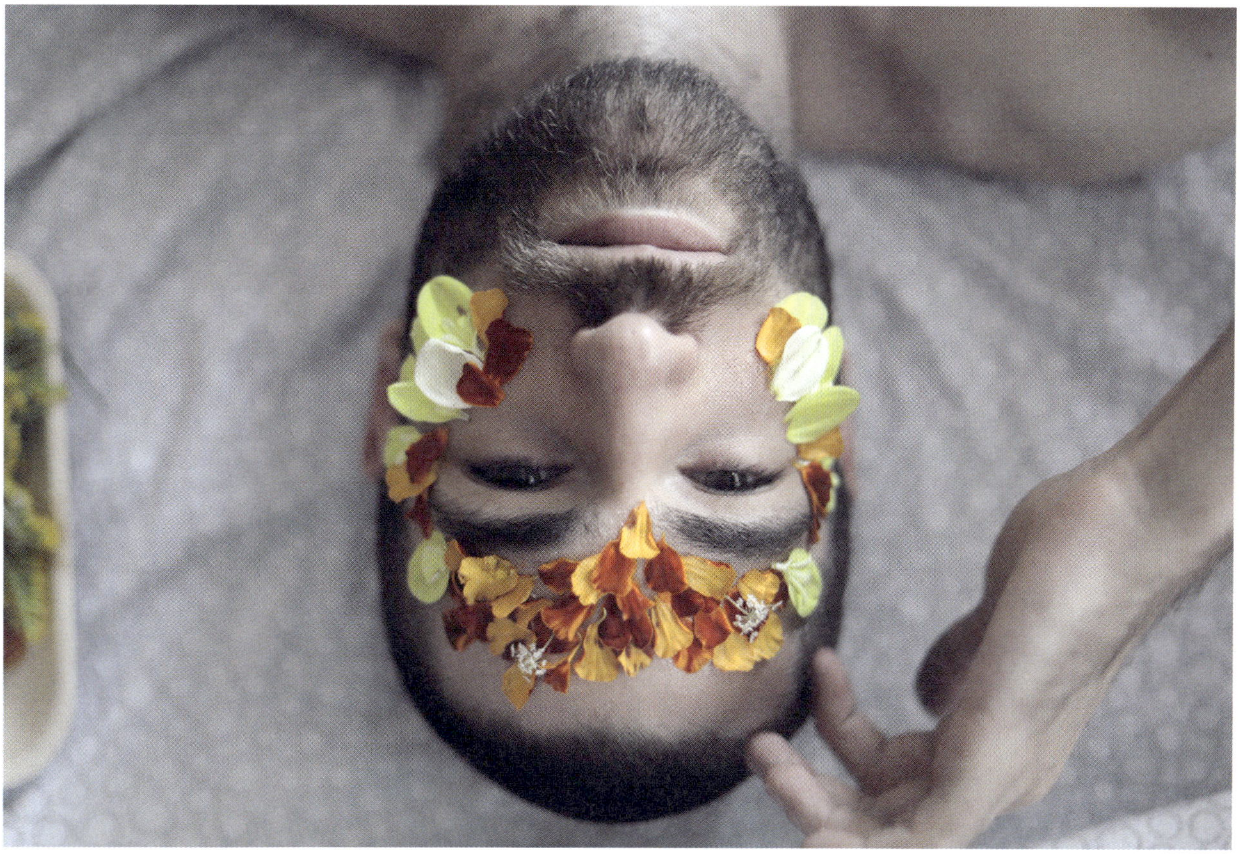

Sleeping Beauty, 2023
Stills of a two-channel audio-visual installation enveloped in foliage

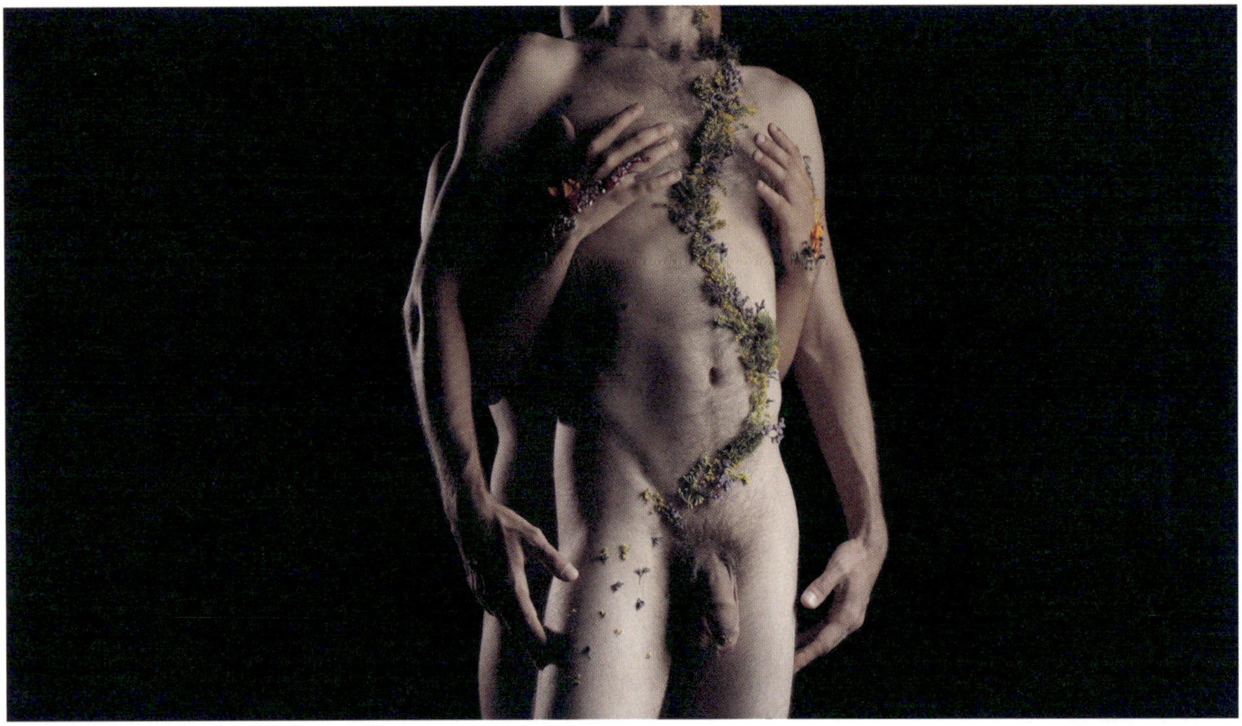

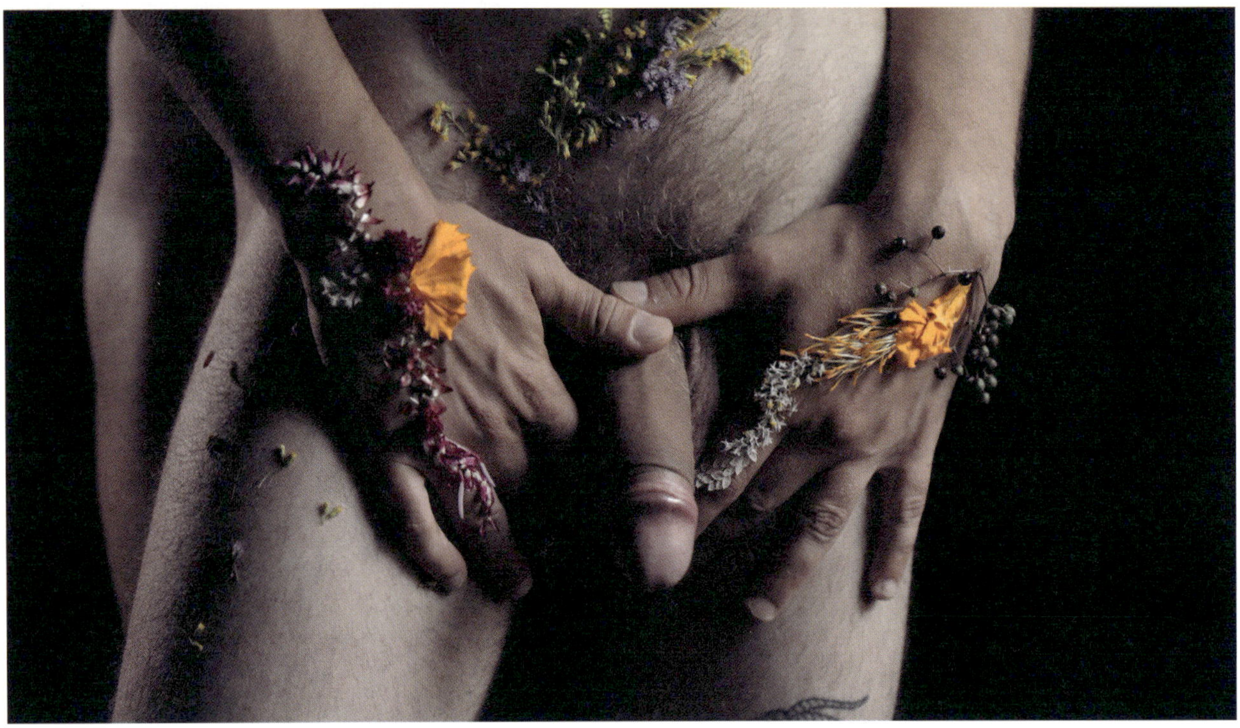

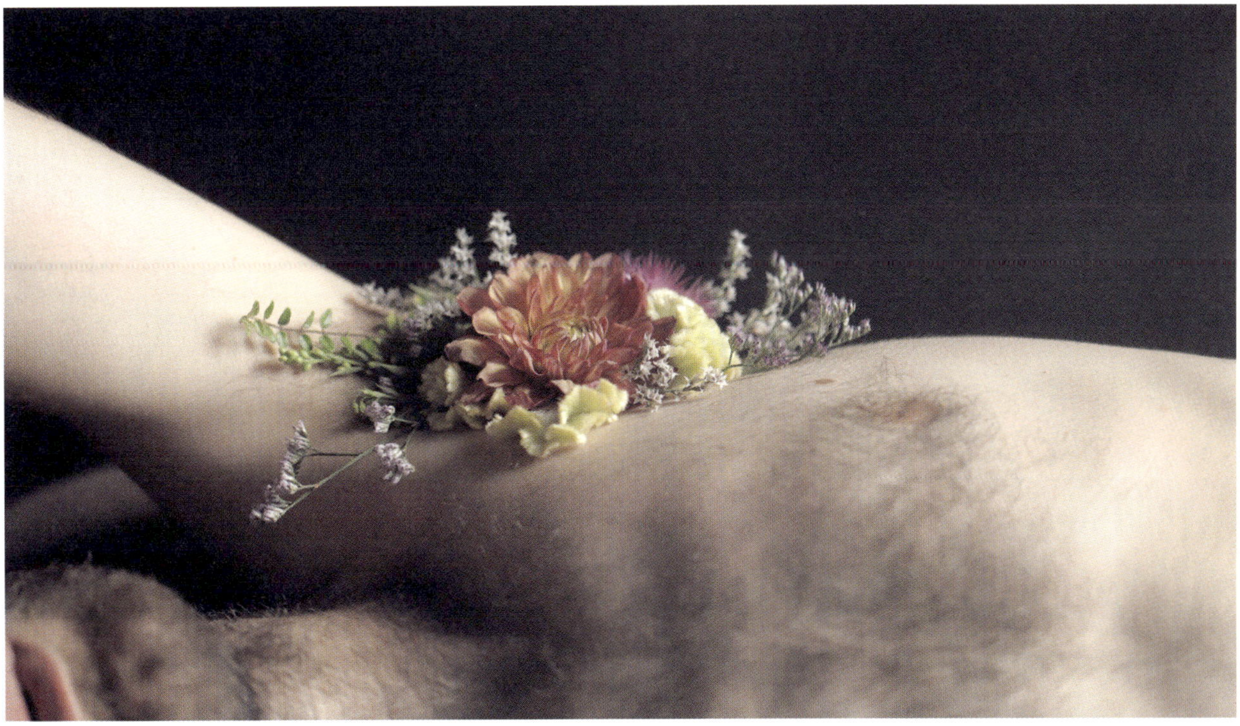

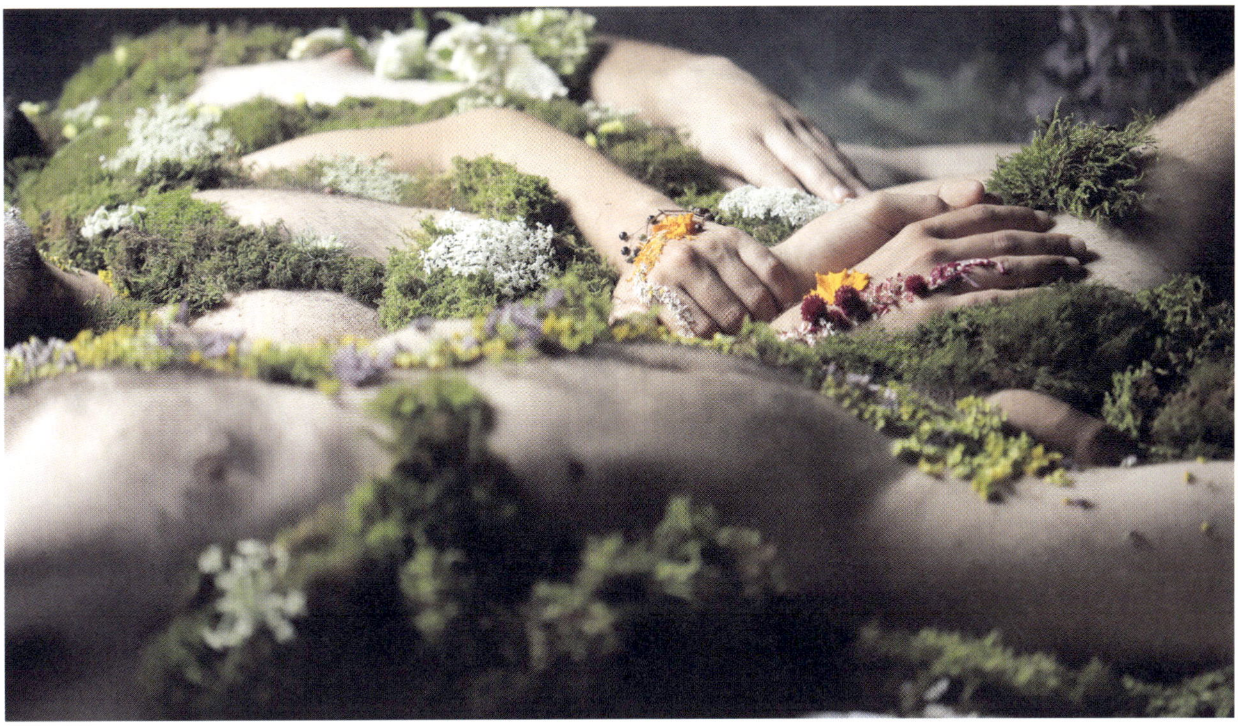

Paolo Bianchi

(*1960, Baden, Switzerland) is a lecturer, curator and art critic. Since the early 1990s he has been realizing art projects as a freelance exhibition maker in a national and international context, such as the upcoming *Villa Karbach* project for Bad Ischl (Austria) as European Capital of Culture in 2024. As an author and guest editor, he writes in the art magazine Kunstforum International in Cologne. Most recently, he published there on topics such as creativity, sense of art, the art of walking and beauty. Since 2004 he has been a lecturer in Curatorial Studies and since 2015 founding director of the Certificate of Advanced Studies course CREATIONSHIP at the Zurcher Hochschule der Künste (ZHdK). He is a new curator for visual arts and performance on the Board of Trustees of the Canton of Aargau (Switzerland).

Marie-Janine Calic

(*1962, Berlin, Germany) is Professor of History of Eastern and Southeastern Europe at the Ludwig Maximilians University in Munich. She has worked as Political Advisor to the Special Coordinator of the Stability Pact for South Eastern Europe in Brussels, as well as at the UNPROFOR headquarters in Zagreb. Her publications include the monographs *Südosteuropa. Welgeschichte einer Region* (Southeast Europe. World History of a Region) (C. H. Beck, Munich 2016), *Tito. Der ewige Partisan* (Tito. The Eternal Partisan) (C. H. Beck, Munich 2020) and *Geschichte Jugoslawiens* (History of Yugoslavia) (C. H. Beck, Munich 2022). She is a frequent interlocutor on current Balkan issues in the media. Her text published in this book was commissioned by the Burgtheater Magazin as part of the premiere of *Three Winters*. With the kind permission of the author and the Burgtheater Wien to reprint.

Christoph Doswald

(*1961) is a Swiss art critic, curator and university lecturer. He studied history, art history and political science and has been curating exhibitions since the 1980s. Doswald has held various teaching positions and guest professorships, e.g. at the Zürcher Hochschule der Künste (ZHdK) and at the Akademie der Künste, Stuttgart. He was chairman of the Public Art Programm of the city of Zurich (2008–2020) and curated a series of exhibitions dealing with urbanistic transformations in the post-industrial society. In 2021 Doswald was named artistic director of ART FLOW, an initiative investigating the changes in the agglomeration of Zurich, alongside the Limmat valley.

Tatjana Gromača

(*1971, Sisak, Croatia) studied comparative literature and philosophy at the University of Zagreb. In 2001 she received a grant from the Berlin Academy of Arts. From 2000 to 2008 she worked as a journalist for the political-satirical weekly Feral Tribune (Split) and for the daily newspaper Novi list (Rijeka). Since 2017 she has been writing literary reviews, essays, travelogues and humanities articles for Croatian radio. She has published five novels, three books of short prosa, one book with selected reportage stories and a book of poetry. A second poems book will be published in May 2023. Tatjana Gromača lives in Pula, in a small creative community, with her husband Radenko Vadanjel, also a writer, and their daughter Marta.

Isabella Flego

(*1937, Arsia/Raša, Croatia) is an award-winning and multifaceted writer and poet. In 1959 she came to Koper in Slovenia (Capodistria in Italian) to begin her teaching career. She later became the principal of the Italian language elementary school Pier Paolo Vergerio il Vecchio. Over the years she has carried out an intense socio-political activity. Flego is highly appreciated as an author of books, essays and research works by literary critics and the public, including her 2017 work *Memorie da sopra l'equatore* (Memories from above the equator), to name but one, which has received numerous awards.

Jules Spinatsch

(*1964, Davos, Switzerland) is a Swiss photographer and artist. He has exhibited at MoMA in New York, the Fondation Cartier in Paris, the Villa Arson in Nice, the Walker Art Center in Minneapolis, the Tate Modern in London, the SFMoMA in San Francisco, the Kunsthaus in Zurich and the Fotomuseum Winterthur, among others. His artistic strategy is driven by an intrinsic interest in the relationship of aesthetic phenomenas and their political, social, economical or social backgrounds. Spinatsch's legendary research on the fringes of global events like the G8, titled *Temporary Discomfort*, was awarded 2005 with the book award of the Rencontres d'Arles.

Supporter

swiss arts council
prohelvetia

mondriaan fund

ifa Institut für Auslandsbeziehungen

Federal Ministry
Republic of Austria
Arts, Culture,
Civil Service and Sport

LAND TIROL

austrijski kulturni forum zag

SAHA
SUPPORTING CONTEMPORARY ART FROM TURKEY

AUTONOME PROVINZ BOZEN SÜDTIROL
PROVINCIA AUTONOMA DI BOLZANO ALTO ADIGE

Project Partners

Mediteranski kiparski simpozij
Mediterranean Sculpture Symosium
PARK

arheološki muzej istre

mmsu

ppmi POVIJESNI I POMORSKI MUZEJ ISTRE
MUSEO STORICO E NAVALE DELL´ISTRIA

PUČKO OTVORENO UČILIŠTE LABIN

galerija VAJNER

Sponsors

KAMEN PAZIN

1.MAJ Labin

formarmo

DEROSSI METALI

HOLCIM

Supporting Partners

Organizer

Labin Art Express XXI (L.A.E. XXI), www.lae.hr

Co-organizer

Lamparna j.d.o.o., www.lamparna.hr

Project Partners

Open Public University (POU), Labin
Mediterranean Sculpture Symposium (MKS), Labin
Archaeological Museum of Istria (AMI), Pula
Historical and Maritime Museum of Istria (PPMI), Pula
Gallery Cvajner, Pula
Museum of Modern & Contemporary Art (MMSU), Rijeka

Supporter

Landscapes of Desire has been generously supported by

Ministry of Culture and Media of Republic of Croatia
Istria County
Istria Tourist Board,Poreč
Primorsko-Goranska County
City of Labin
Labin-Rabac Tourist Board
City of Pula
Tourism Office Pula
City of Rijeka
Municipality of Raša
Pro Helvetia, Zürich
Mondriaan Fund, Amsterdam
IFA – Institut für Auslandsbeziehungen, Stuttgart
SAHA Derneği, Istanbul
Austrian Cultural Forum, Zagreb
Republic of Austria – Federal Ministry for Arts, Culture, the Civil Service and Sport
Land Tirol
Provincia autonoma di Bolzano – Alto Adige

Sponsors

Kamen d.d., Pazin
HOLCIM d.d., Koromačno
1.Maj, Labin
Derossi metali, Labin
FORMARMO, Labin

Additional Support

Restaurant Peteani, Labin
Restaurant Amfiteatar, Pula
Restaurant Kvarner, Labin
Bishopric of Poreč-Pula / Parish office of Raša
WART d.o.o., Vodnjan
Port of Pula Authority
Luka Pula d.o.o. / Port of Pula
Elektra d.o.o., Labin
Herculanea d.o.o. Pula
Towing service Lakovac, Labin
Valamar d.d., Rabac
Public Fire Brigade Labin
Alkomet d.o.o., Labin
Strojar, Labin
Fabrika, Pula

Supporting Galeries

Galleria Continua, San Gimignano / Paris
Dirimart, Istanbul
Galerie EIGEN+ART, Berlin
Grieder Contemporary, Küsnacht (Zurich)
Galerie Martin Janda, Vienna
König Büro, Zurich
Galerie Fabian Lang, Zurich
LOOCK Galerie, Berlin
Lullin+Ferrari, Zurich
Galerie nächst St. Stephan / Rosemarie Schwarzwälder, Vienna
Almine Rech
Galleria Lia Rumma, Milan / Naples
Galleria dello Scudo, Verona

Special thanks

Narodni muzej Labin / Labin Museum, Mini Cantanti choir, Croatian Golf Association, Croatian Forests - Labin Office

Media sponsors

Radio Labin, tportal, Kulturpunkt.hr, istra24,

Organizer

Supporter

Colophon

This book is published on occasion of the 4th Industrial Art Biennial: *Landscapes of Desire*, Pula, Raša, Labin, Rijeka, May 13 – June 30, 2023
www.lae.hr
www.industrialartbiennale.eu

Exhibition

Organizer: Labin Art Express XXI (L.A.E. XXI), Rudarska 1, HR-52220, www.lae.hr
Co-organizer: Lamparna j.d.o.o., Rudarska 1, HR-52220 Labin, www.lamparna.hr

President: Dean Zahtila
Artistic Director: Damir Stojnić
Curators: Paolo Bianchi, Christoph Doswald
Producer: Noel Mirković
Admistration, finances: Davorka Milevoj, Alberta Miletić
Media, public relations: Alexei Monroe & Viktor Zahtila,
Hospitality: Ivona Verbanac
Production and technical team: Kristijan Stojić, Branka Cvjetičanin, Igor Dundara, Nikola Tasić, Goran Brezac, Rusmir Rebronja, Franko Mohorović, Ivor Bađura

Catalogue

Editors: Paolo Bianchi, Christoph Doswald
Editing: Paolo Bianchi, Manuel Bonik, Christoph Doswald
Concept: Karin Holzfeind, Zurich
Design, typesetting: Karin Holzfeind, Zurich
On-site photography: Jules Spinatsch
Text contributions: Paolo Bianchi, Marie-Janine Calic, Christoph Doswald, Isabella Flego, Tatjana Gromača and Nina Obuljen Koržinek
Artists' texts: Paolo Bianchi and Christoph Doswald
Translations: Viktor Zahtila (Tatjana Gromača from Croatian to English), Carrie Brooks (Isabella Flego from Italian to English), Carrie Ann Rabinowitch (artists' texts from German to English)
Editorial, proofreading: Katharina Gewehr
Digital imaging: Pixelstorm
Printing and binding: Tiskara Zelina d.d., Sveti Ivan Zelina, Croatia

Photo credits
Bernd Borchardt, Berlin: 179–181
Mateo Gobo: 41
Werner Feiersinger: Cover and inside, 1–32
Jules Spinatsch: Backcover, 50–81, 87–93, 99–101, 111–123, 136–137, 143–149, 155–157, 163–177
Viktor Zahtila (L.A.E. XXI): 41
All materials: Courtesy of the artists, if not stated otherwise

Published by
VfmK Verlag für moderne Kunst GmbH
Schwedenplatz 2/24
A-1010 Vienna
hello@vfmk.org
www.vfmk.org

ISBN 978-3-99153-019-0

Printed in Croatia

Distribution
Europe: LKG, www.lkg-va.de
UK: Cornerhouse Publications, www.cornerhousepublications.org
USA: D.A.P., www.artbook.com

Bibliographic information published by the Deutsche Nationalbibliothek:
The Deutsche Nationalbibliothek lists this publication in the Deutsche Nationalbibliografie; detailed bibliographic data is available in the Internet at dnb.de.

Acknowledgements

Landscapes of Desire was generously supported by all contributing artists and by many people of our network and beyond. The curators would especially like to thank them for their support, inspiration and contribution to this extraordinary project.

Harry Acland
Borjan Batagelj
Branka Benčić
Fiona Biggierio
Donald Blašković
Roland Bless
Manuel Bonik
Krunoslav Božičević
Dalibor Brnos
Tamara Brussich
Silvija Burić
Sara Ceroni
Yilmaz Dziwior
Anna Ebner
Karin Engler
Canan Erbil
Seamus Farrell
Corrado Ferrari
Baris Gezidlioglu
Kora Girin
Astrid Glavičić
Valter Glavičić
Patrik Glušić
Marko Gljuščić
Damian Grieder
Elliott Griffith
Rasim Halilović
Olga Hammermeister
Leo and Markus Hongler Beltran
Gitti Hug
Melli Ink
Denis Ivošević
Silvia Jaklitsch
Ivan Jakovčić
Danijel Jakovljević
Martin Janda
Sonja Jelača
Aline Juchler
Julia Kapfer
Gracijano Kešac
Renata Kiršić
Ksenia and Marcos Kogan Amaro
Susanne König
Darko Komšo
Vedran Kos
Manuela Kraljević
Aleksandra Krebel
Irena Kregar Šegota
Martin Hugo Kunzi
Luka Labinjan
Fabian Lang
Paul Loderer
Friedrich Loock
Rahel Loretan
Etienne Lullin
Judy Lybcke
Gerald Matt
Medard Meier
Samuel Mizrachi
Catherine Munger
Nina Obuljen Koržinek
Hazer Özil
Levent Özmen
Glorija Paliska
Sandi Paucic
Suzanne Pellaux
Ivan Perko
Denis Peteani
Emina Popović Sterpin
Paola Potena
Beat Raeber
Felix Sandberg
Ivan Šarar
Johannes Schäfer
Stephan Schmidt-Wulffen
Rosemarie Schwarzwälder
Madeleine Schuppli
Nicola von Senger
David Manuel Stoeger
Dorothea Strauss
Zvonko Šaina
Julija Škoro
Sabrina Štemberga Vidak
Patrik Thomas
Vladimir Torbica
Alexis Vaillant
Florijan Veneruzzo
Ivona Verbanac
Jeroen Versteele
Goran Visintin
Mirko Vukšić
Kerstin Wahala
Julia Walter Rosjar
Kaspar Wenger
Belia Winnewisser
Ekrem Yalçindağ
Deniz Zembo
Filip Zoričić